Texas School Law: A Practical Guide

Editors

Kelly Frels
Jeff Horner
Bill Camp
Vianei Lopez Robinson

DISCLAIMER

The National Organization on Legal Problems of Education (NOLPE) is a private, nonadvocacy and nonprofit association of educators and attorneys. The opinions expressed in this publication are those of the authors and do not represent official views of the Organization.

ISBN 1-56534-070-1

Published by

National Organization on Legal Problems of Education
3601 S.W. 29th Street, Suite 223
Topeka, Kansas 66614
(913) 273-3550

About the Editors

Kelly Frels–Mr. Frels is the managing partner of the law firm of Bracewell & Patterson, L.L.P. Mr. Frels works out of the firm's Houston office, which also has offices in Dallas, Austin, Washington, D.C., and London. Mr. Frels is a 1966 graduate of Southwest Texas State University, and a 1970 graduate of the University of Texas Law School. He has been actively involved for over twenty-five (25) years in the representation of school districts and junior colleges, and is a frequent speaker and writer on school law issues. Mr. Frels has served as the Chairman of the National School Boards Association Council of School Attorneys, Chairman of the Texas Council of School Attorneys, and has been President of the National Organization on Legal Problems of Education (NOLPE). He has also served as president of the Houston Bar Association and as a director of the State Bar of Texas.

Jeff Horner–Mr. Horner is a partner in the Houston law firm of Bracewell & Patterson, L.L.P. He is a member of the firm's School Law Section, and actively represents school districts and junior colleges. He has published over twenty-five articles and monographs related to school law. Mr. Horner is a 1980 *summa cum laude* graduate of Vanderbilt University and a 1983 graduate of the University of Virginia School of Law. He has served as Chairman of the Texas Council of School Attorneys and Vice President of NOLPE. He also teaches education law at South Texas College of Law in Houston.

Bill Camp–Dr. Camp is a professor of education at California State University, San Bernardino. He formerly taught education law at North Texas State University in Denton. He was also previously employed as a school principal and assistant superintendent. Dr. Camp is the co-editor of "The Principal's Legal Handbook," a NOLPE publication. He is an active member of NOLPE and other school law organizations.

Vianei Lopez Robinson–Ms. Robinson is presently employed as an employment law attorney with the law firm of Wagstaff, Alvis, Stubbeman, Seamster & Longacre, L.L.P. in Abilene, Texas. She was formerly employed as an attorney in the School Law Section at Bracewell & Patterson, L.L.P. Ms. Robinson is a 1988 graduate of Princeton University and a 1991 graduate of the University of Texas School of Law. She is a frequent speaker regarding employment and school law issues.

About the Authors

Chris Borreca is an associate in the Houston office of Bracewell & Patterson, L.L.P. He is a graduate of Vanderbilt University and the University of Houston Law Center.

Tim Brightman is an associate in the Dallas office of Bracewell & Patterson, L.L.P. He is a graduate of Austin College and Baylor University Law School.

Lisa Brown is an associate in the Houston office of Bracewell & Patterson, L.L.P. She is a graduate of the University of Texas for both undergraduate and law school.

Chris Gilbert is an associate in the Houston office of Bracewell & Patterson, L.L.P. He attended Cornell University and the University of Michigan Law School.

Ray Gregory is an associate in the Houston office of Bracewell & Patterson, L.L.P. He is a graduate of the University of Texas and the University of Houston Law Center.

Tracy Hester is a partner in the Houston office of Bracewell & Patterson, L.L.P., specializing in environmental law. He is a graduate of the University of Texas and Columbia University Law School.

Janet Horton is a partner in the Houston office of Bracewell & Patterson, L.L.P. She is head of the School Law Section. She is a graduate of the University of Texas for both her undergraduate and legal work.

Jennifer Jacobs is a partner in the Houston office of Bracewell & Patterson, L.L.P. She is a graduate of Southern Methodist University and Harvard Law School.

Arturo Michel is a partner in the Houston office of Bracewell & Patterson, L.L.P. He is a graduate of Northwestern University and the University of Michigan Law School.

Gray Muzzy is a partner in the Houston office of Bracewell & Patterson, L.L.P., specializing in real estate law. He is a graduate of Yale University and the University of Texas Law School.

Rick Peebles is a solo practitioner from Baytown, Texas. He regularly represents school districts and junior colleges in his practice.

Jennifer Piskun was formerly an associate in the Houston office of Bracewell & Patterson, L.L.P. She is a graduate of the University of Texas and the University of Houston Law Center. She is now a lawyer in the office of Texas Governor George Bush, focusing on education issues.

Merri Schneider-Vogel is a partner in the Houston office of Bracewell & Patterson, L.L.P. She is a graduate of the State University of New York at Oneonta and the University of South Carolina School of Law.

Cynthia Stroman is an associate in the Houston office of Bracewell & Patterson, L.L.P. She is a graduate of Cornell University and the University of Michigan Law School.

Foreword

This book is intended to provide Texas educators and lawyers with general knowledge concerning various education law issues. This book focuses on Texas law, and also slants toward providing practical, rather than theoretical, guidance. The editors and authors hope that this book provides helpful insights regarding basic Texas school law issues.

However, this book is not intended to provide in-depth information concerning Texas school law. Furthermore, the purchase and use of this book does not establish an attorney/client relationship, and the contents of the book are not intended as legal advice. If a matter involving the application of Texas school law arises, the editors and authors encourage you to consult with a qualified school attorney to assist with your individual situation.

Preface

Conceptually, this book has been in the making for over twenty (20) years. I have always wanted to write a book on Texas school law, but client needs and the demands of the courthouse have always diverted the effort. About four or five years ago, Jeff Horner and I started a concerted effort, along with other members of our law firm, to complete this project. We enlisted the assistance of Dr. Bill Camp and eventually Vianei Lopez Robinson. At long last, the project has come to fruition. Our final completion date was delayed because the Texas Education Code was revised in 1995, but we believe the final product will be enhanced by the inclusion of these changes.

This book is intended to provide Texas educators and lawyers with general knowledge on a variety of education law topics. As the title of the book suggests, we try to give practical information where possible to provide insight into "real life" situations.

I give my personal thanks to the editors and many authors of chapters, most of whom are members of the law firm of Bracewell & Patterson, L.L.P. The book would not have been possible without their contributions. I particularly wish to thank Jeff for his work in arranging for the drafting and editing of the chapters. I also appreciate the contributions of NOLPE for publishing the book and the Texas Association of School Administrators (TASA) for marketing it.

I hope this practical presentation of Texas school law will be of help to you, whether you are a teacher, administrator, or a lawyer.

Kelly Frels
Houston, Texas
July, 1996

Table of Contents

Section 1 - School Boards and Superintendents

1. School Board Members' Authority and Relationship with Staff 3
2. The Texas Open Meetings Act 19
3. Competitive Bidding and Proposal Requirements for Texas School Districts 41
4. Law of Nepotism and Conflicts in Texas 49
5. Religion in the Public Schools 57
6. Environmental Issues Relating to Public Schools and Junior Colleges in Texas 75
7. Copyright Law 85
8. Real Estate Issues Relating to School Districts and Colleges .. 93
9. Elections Law 101

Section 2 - Teachers and Other Staff

1. The First Amendment and School Employees 117
2. Employment Discrimination and Related Claims 137
3. Sexual Harassment of Employees 151
4. The Preemployment Process: Avoiding Impermissible Inquiries 167
5. The Texas Public Information Act 189
6. Employment Practices Regarding the Disabled Employee 199
7. Employment Contracts 217
8. Investigating Employee Wrongdoing 231
9. Documentation for Teacher Improvement or Termination 241
10. Implementing a Meaningful Grievance Process 249

Section 3 - Students

1. Tort Liability and Governmental Immunity 261
2. The First Amendment Rights of Students 271
3. Student Discipline Law 287
4. Application of the Fourth Amendment to Searches and Seizures Conducted by School Officials 299
5. Education of Children with Disabilities 307
6. Attendance, Residency and Absences 325
7. Sexual Abuse or Harassment of Students 331

SECTION 1

School Boards and Superintendents

SCHOOL BOARD MEMBERS' AUTHORITY AND RELATIONSHIP WITH STAFF

By: Kelly Frels

I. Introduction

One of the most common issues that arises in school districts and colleges is where the authority of the board of trustees ends and the responsibility of the superintendent and the administration begins. Although it is understood that the board makes policy and the administration implements it, the line between the two is not clear, and policymaking and policy administration often appear indistinguishable. This chapter was developed to aid boards and administrators in understanding the legal standards applicable to school boards and their relationship with the administrative staff who apply board policies and handle the day-to-day functioning of the school district or college. Some practical suggestions for implementing these relationships are also included.

II. The Authority of Members of a Board of Trustees

A. A Trustee is a Public Officer

A trustee of an independent school district holds a "public office" as does an alderman or city council member. The trustee is a public official even though he or she may not receive compensation for the performance of his or her duties.[1] The duties of municipal officers, such as council members and members of an independent school district board, relate to the exercise of certain governmental functions in the public interest. The legislative authority creating each position comes from the same source, the people, so the public nature of the service is the same.[2]

B. The Power of a Board of Trustees

The power of the board of trustees and the extent of its power is determined by the statute creating it plus what is implied as a necessary incident to the jurisdiction expressly given by the statute.[3] The powers granted to the board of trustees include the power to adopt reasonable rules and regulations as are necessary for the control and management of the schools.[4]

Under most circumstances, the individual members of these governing boards may only exercise their statutory powers when sitting as a body in a formally convened meeting.[5] The purpose of this rule, according to the court decisions, is to ensure that the public receives the benefit of proper deliberation and debate on matters of general concern.

Numerous cases have reaffirmed the courts' commitment to the rule that individual board members are lacking in authority except when participating in an official meeting. For example, in *Buechele v. Woods*,[6] a Texas appellate court observed: "[t]he Board of Trustees being a body corporate, the members of the Board can perform no valid act except as a body at meetings properly convened."[7]

Another example of this rule is discussed in *Davis v. Duncanville ISD*.[8] In this case, the superintendent of schools had made statements at several meetings with community groups that the bonds to be approved in an upcoming election would not be sold unless the school population increased. The same information was later distributed to groups and to residents in the area on a leaflet that included the names of all board members. Several board members assisted in its distribution. The school enrollments did not rise. Nevertheless, the board voted to use some of the bond money to build a swimming pool for the school district. The court held that the school district was not bound by either the representations of the superintendent or the statements contained in the leaflet because they were not formally adopted by the board at a properly called meeting. The court held that, where the legislature has committed a matter to a political subdivision of the state, the subdivision may act only as a body corporate at a properly called meeting.

C. The Delegation to Individual Board Members to Perform Ministerial Acts

One narrow exception to the rule that individual board members lack lawful power to act on behalf of the district exists in situations where a board has formally delegated certain of its powers to an individual board member for a limited time and a specific purpose. It is, of course, necessary that any authority conferred in this manner be a power that the board may lawfully delegate to another. Texas courts have long held that boards may delegate what are called "ministerial acts," but are not permitted to delegate any powers that involve an exercise of discretion. As the court in one early case stated, "[i]t is true that a city may do by agent many things which it is empowered to perform . . . but without express authorization from the legislature, it could not surrender the exercise of the powers so granted into the unrestrained control of any person and thus abandon the discretion which it was expected at all times to employ."[9]

From examining the case law, a general rule can be formulated regarding what a "public" body can delegate to agents. Those powers given to a "public" body by statute, through the legislature, which require the members of the body to exercise discretion and reason, cannot be delegated. It also appears that "public" bodies can delegate the performance of ministerial duties to agents, but they must perform all governmental duties as a governmental body.

III. Actions which must be taken by the Board of Trustees

The powers and duties of the board of trustees must be inserted into the framework of the general rules formulated above. Texas Education Code § 11.151 sets forth the general powers of the board of trustees. Section 11.151 specifies that the board of trustees constitutes a body corporate and, in the name of the independent school district, may acquire and hold real and personal property, sue and be sued, and receive bequests and donations or other moneys or funds coming legally into its hands. The trustees have the exclusive power to govern and oversee the management of the public schools of the district. All powers and duties not specifically delegated by statute to the Texas Education Agency or State Board of Education are reserved for the local boards of trustees. All rights and titles to the school property of the district, whether real or personal, are vested in the trustees and their successors in office. Section 11.151 concludes by specifying that the trustees may adopt such rules and by-laws as they deem proper. The trustees operate the district under these general powers unless granted a specific power or charged with a specific duty by statute. This general law relating to school districts is applicable to junior and community colleges under Tex. Educ. Code § 130.084.

With few exceptions, these statutory provisions specify that the trustees or board of trustees shall and may institute certain policies or take specific courses of action. Some of the most important of these provisions are those dealing with the employment of school personnel, the adoption of a discipline management program, land and building transactions, adoption of the annual budget and supplementary budgets, selection of a depository, the calling of trustee and bond elections, the issuance of bonds, and the award of competitive purchasing contracts, except produce and vehicle fuel, valued at an aggregate of $25,000 or more in a twelve-month period.[10]

One area that continues to be the subject of discussion is the expenditure of funds that are within budget categories approved by the board.

While many boards approve the expenditure of funds as an agenda item at each regular meeting, it does not appear that board action is required on all items. While it is clear that the board must approve all contracts, once those contracts have been executed and a budgeted amount approved by the board, payment from the district is ministerial and may be made by the staff. If an expenditure is not included in a budget, the board must approve a budget amendment before the expenditure can be made. The board may, of course, require that all expenditures be submitted to it for approval. This process may or may not be administratively feasible, depending upon size and other characteristics of the district.

Other statutes specifically provide for the delegation of the trustees' power to employees. As an example, Texas Education Code § 44.002 charges the superintendent with the duty of preparing a budget or causing a budget to be prepared. This section in essence provides for the delegation of the responsibility for preparing the budget to the administrative staff of the district. However, the board must adopt the proposed budget at a meeting.[11] Public funds may not be expended except in accordance with the adopted budget, but under Tex. Educ. Code § 44.006 the board may amend the budget from time to time as needed.

IV. The Role of the Superintendent and the Administration

A. The Superintendent as the Chief Administrative Officer

The superintendent is the chief administrative officer of a school district and is charged with the responsibility of operating the schools on a day-to-day basis within the policies approved by the board. Although most policies set standards for employment and curriculum, they generally recognize that personnel and curriculum matters should be administered on a daily basis under the direction of administrators, teachers, and others in the conduct of their assigned duties.

B. The Accreditation Requirements of the State Board of Education and the Southern Association of Colleges and Schools

The Statewide Standards on Duties of a School Board Member adopted by the State Board of Education in December 1985 provided guidance concerning the role and responsibility of the board and the superintendent:

II. The Board Member shall understand the role and responsibility of the board, the board president and individual board members, and shall contribute to the development of:

a. A statement of educational philosophy expressing the present and future needs of the community and the children therein.
b. Educational goals and objectives reflecting the philosophy of the board.
c. Program activities consistent with the education goals and objectives established by the board.
d. A method by which the needs and values of the community and its diverse elements may be assessed and articulated in order to make appropriate decisions for the school district.
e. An allocation system designed to provide adequate resources to accomplish stated goals and objectives.
f. A systematic and timely review and evaluation of all phases of the programs and operations of the school district including the annual performance report."

III. The Board Member shall understand and respect the role and responsibility of the superintendent, recognizing:
g. The difference between the board's responsibility to set policy and the superintendent's responsibility to administer the school district according to established rules and policies.
h. The responsibility of the superintendent to keep the board informed of applicable laws, rules, and regulations that affect school operations.
i. The responsibility of the superintendent, as chief adviser to the board, to keep the board and the community informed regarding both positive and negative aspects of the school district.
j. The superintendent's responsibility to deal initially with complaints from school district personnel or the community, and the board's responsibility to consider such complaints at public meetings only after failure of an administrative solution.
k. The role of the superintendent as the educational leader of the community and chief executive officer of the school district, responsible for proposing to the board changes appropriate to the enhancement of effective educational programs.
l. The superintendent's responsibility to foster an attitude of unity and harmony within the board."

The Southern Association of Colleges and Schools "Criteria for Accreditation Commission on Colleges" provides a similar standard for governance:

"6.1 Organization and Administration.

The administration of an institution of higher education has the responsibility for bringing together its various resources and allocating them effectively in order to accomplish institutional goals. Although an identical pattern of organization for all member institutions is neither required nor expected, the organizational structure and the administrative processes must be well defined, published and made available to the college community.

The duties of the chief executive officer of the institution, and other administrative officials directly responsible to the chief executive, must be clearly defined and made known to faculty and staff. Administrative officers must possess credentials, experience and/or demonstrated competence appropriate to their areas of responsibility. The effectiveness of administrators must be evaluated periodically.

The organizational pattern of an institution is important to its development and affects the morale of its faculty and staff. Adequate communications are essential for effective implementation and institutional policy."

"6.1.2 Governing Board.

Although the title and function of governing boards vary, there must be a clearly identifiable body which is responsible for policy making. The governing board is the legal body responsible for the institution, which it holds in trust. Except under clearly defined circumstances, board action must result from a decision of the whole–no individual member or committee can take official action for the board unless authorized to do so.

The duties and responsibilities of the governing board must be clearly defined in an official document. This document must also specify: the number of members, length of service, rotation policies, organization and committee structure, and frequency of meetings. There must be appropriate continuity in the board membership, usually provided by staggered terms of adequate length. In addition, the document should include provisions governing the removal of a board member from office. A board member may be dismissed only for cause and by procedures involving due process.

The responsibilities of the governing board include establishing broad institutional policies, securing financial resources to support adequately the institutional goals and selecting the chief executive officer. In addition, the governing board must have in place proper procedures to ensure that the board is adequately informed about the financial condition and stability of the institution. The governing board must not be subject to undue pressure from political, religious or other external bodies. Furthermore, the governing board should protect the administration from similar pressures.

There must be a clear distinction, in writing and in practice, between the policymaking functions of the governing board and the responsibility of the administration and faculty to administer and implement policy. General institutional policies should originate within the board or should be approved by the board upon the recommendation of the administration. Once these have become official policies, the administration should implement them within a broad framework established by the board."

"6.1.4 Official Policies

The institution must publish official documents which contain, but are not limited to, the following information: the duties and responsibilities of administrative officers, the patterns of institutional organization and governance of faculty, statements governing tenure or employment security, statements governing due process, and other institutional policies and procedures that affect the faculty, the administrative staff and other personnel."

C. The Superintendent's Job Description

The superintendent's statutory duties as described in Texas Education Code, Section 11.201 are relatively broad. They include:

1. assuming administrative responsibility and leadership for planning, operation, supervision, and evaluation of educational programs and facilities, and the annual performance appraisal of staff;
2. serving as the district's educational leader and administrative manager;
3. assuming administrative authority and responsibility for the assignment and evaluation of all staff, and making recommendations for the selection, promotion and dismissal of all personnel;
4. managing the district's day-to-day operations;
5. within local policies and applicable state rules and accounting principles causing the district's budget to be prepared;
6. recommending policies to the board and overseeing the implementation of policies;
7. developing administrative guidelines to implement policies;

8. providing leadership for the attainment of student performance based on state indicators; and
9. performing other duties assigned by the board.

Additional and more specific duties of the superintendent may be found in state accreditation standards, local board policies, the job description adopted by the board, and the superintendent's contract.

D. The Superintendent and Policy Formulation

Although the board has the power and responsibility to enact policies, the administration often will recommend policies to the board. Policies are generally recognized as those board actions that establish rights and duties between and among persons in the school district and that are not in the form of contracts. Policy recommendation is a proper function of the administration, and the board is free to accept or reject the recommendation.

E. The Superintendent and Personnel Decisions

Senate Bill 1, enacted by the Texas Legislature in 1995, completely revised the Texas Education Code. One significant area of revision concerns the roles of the board of trustees and the superintendent in making personnel decisions. Section 11.163 states that the superintendent has sole authority to make recommendations to the board for all personnel selections other than the superintendent. The board may accept or reject the superintendent's recommendation, but may not make its own selection. If the board rejects the recommendation, the superintendent will make alternative recommendations until the board accepts a recommendation. Also, Section 11.163 makes clear that the board by policy may delegate authority to the superintendent to determine the terms of employment of all other personnel with the district.

V. The Responsibility of the Board President and the Superintendent When Issues Arise Concerning the Roles of the Superintendent and Members of the Board

Situations inevitably arise in many school districts concerning the proper roles of the superintendent and members of the board. It is perfectly normal that these conflicts arise, but these conflicts need not lead to disruptions that interfere with the educational process. The effective leadership of the board president can be a significant factor in keeping a normal question of roles from negatively influencing the fulfillment of duties by the administration and the board.

When conflicts arise, the most effective corrective action is the universal antidote for relational conflicts: communication. If the board president, or another officer in the absence of an effective president, assumes a leadership role in identifying the problem and in bringing the parties together, this vital communication is possible. Except in a few instances, presidents are elected with the expectation that they will provide leadership for the board. Board presidents must assume this responsibility when role conflicts arise or the superintendent may feel compelled to seek intervention of third parties, such as the Texas Education Agency Accreditation Division.

Often the conflict can be resolved by the president identifying the issues and talking with the board member and superintendent, or if more than one or two board members are involved, it may be desirable for the board and the superintendent to meet in executive session under Tex. Govt. Code § 551.074. A properly noticed executive session can provide a forum for the parties to talk about the issues. The president must have a plan to lead the parties through the discussion to a resolution that includes a course for future dealings. Of course, a discussion of the relationship between the superintendent and the board also must be a part of the superintendent's assessment process. In the absence of a clear understanding of what each party expects of the other, it is not easy to avoid significant role conflicts.

The superintendent can assert similar leadership when conflicts concerning roles surface. It is often helpful for the superintendent to talk with the individual board members who the superintendent perceives have stepped across the line. If the relationship is such that this is not feasible or the discussions are unsuccessful, the superintendent might then talk with the president. Normally the president, or a natural leader on the board, can bring the parties together informally or at a properly called and noticed executive session as described above where the matter can be openly examined.

VI. The Use of Third Parties to Assist the Board and the Superintendent to Recognize Their Proper Roles and to Function Together

Occasionally, leadership is not present to resolve conflicts and bring the board and superintendent together. Also, sometimes the personalities involved or the climate in the district is such that the conflicts cannot realistically be resolved internally. When this occurs, the intervention of a third party is desirable and often necessary to bring all parties together. Unless third party intervention occurs early, the first visit from an independent source might be from the Texas Education Agency Accreditation Division to talk about governance.

Third party involvement in the board-superintendent relationship may take many forms. The most effective third party intervention is injected at a stage before the situation seriously deteriorates. Some effective third party intervenors are retired administrators, government officials, and school board members who have the stature and respect to be accepted as impartial by the superintendent and the board. Sometimes the district's legal counsel or another attorney can be effective in setting forth the appropriate legal and accreditation standards and mediating the disputes. The Texas Association of School Boards is available to present board training sessions, and the Texas Education Agency Accreditation Division will intervene if the relationship becomes a significant governance problem. Third party intervention appears to be the most successful when involvement begins early before the relationship deteriorates and when the intervenor is accepted by the board members and the superintendent as competent and impartial.

VII. Practical Approaches to Resolve Natural Conflicts of Roles

Because the line of authority and responsibility between the board and the administration is so hazy, it is necessary for the board and superintendent to work together to operate within these general standards. Set out below are several practical suggestions on how board members and the administration might work together to balance their roles.

A. Balancing the Board Member's Right of Access to Existing Copies of the School District's Records Under the Public Information Act with the Correct Use of Those Records and the Creation of Documents for Board Members

Board members are certainly entitled to access to all records of the school district to which a member of the public has access. If a board member has an educational need to have access to a student record, the board member may do so under the Family Education Rights and Privacy Act of 1974 (FERPA) and the Texas Public Information Act (PIA), Texas Government Code, Chapter 552. Other records of the school district which are not disclosable to a member of the public under the PIA are probably disclosable to individual board members for the board member's official duties. However, board members in their individual capacities have no greater right to documents than the public at large. Therefore, a board member should carefully examine the purpose for which he or she is requesting a document, because the inappropriate review of documents could have adverse future legal consequences for the individual board member.[12]

When records are accessible by board members, the question then becomes one of how those records may be used. Student records may not be released to those not authorized under FERPA to see them. Likewise, a board member is not free to release other documents not disclosable under the PIA without the approval of the board or consent by the superintendent, who is the statutorily designated custodian of the records. The PIA specifically gives the superintendent the authority to make certain school records disclosable, but the PIA says nothing about the role of the board, which possesses the district's ultimate authority in other situations. Thus, the PIA itself obscures the line between the authority of the superintendent and that of the board.

School board members and employees who are not the custodian of the records should exercise caution when called upon to release documents, particularly those that come within the nondisclosure provisions of Subchapter C of the PIA.[13] When faced with the decision whether to release Subchapter C documents, the superintendent, who is the custodian of the records, should be consulted.

Board members individually cannot legitimately release information provided by the board's attorney under the attorney-client privilege. The board as an entity, rather than individual board members, owns the attorney-client privilege; therefore, it takes board action to waive the privilege. Because it takes an assertion of the claim of the privilege to prevent disclosure in litigation, and because there is no certain penalty that can be imposed on a board member who discloses a privileged communication with the attorney, this standard of behavior is difficult to enforce except through the mutual respect of all board members for the privilege.

Particular care must be taken by board members in disclosing information about a specific employee or student that the board member secures through an executive session under the Texas Open Meetings Act (OMA) or through a document not subject to public disclosure under the PIA. To protect the privacy of employees and officials, most boards restrict complaints against employees as officials to a closed session under the OMA. There is no legal requirement that these complaints be aired in closed session, but if the employee or official who is the subject of the complaint wishes to have the complaint made in public, the employee may require that the portion of the meeting be open to the public. If made public, such confidential information may be an invasion of the employee's personal privacy or may affect the person's reputation in the community. When such disclosure accompanies a negative job action, such as a demotion, nonrenewal, or termination, the constitutionally protected liberty interest may be implicated, thereby entitling the employee to a hearing before the board to clear his or her name.[14]

On occasion, the information a trustee might release could be libelous, and the release would be a publication that would subject the trustee to an individual libel action. Unless the trustee releases libelous material on behalf of the board, the trustee, rather than all board members or the school district would normally be liable. This does not mean, of course, that all board members and the district would not be named as parties in a defamation suit.

Board members individually do not have the authority to request that the superintendent "prepare a report" on a particular subject. To do so is not a request for existing records of the school district; rather, it is a request to prepare new documents, even if the records from which the information is taken already exist. Virtually every superintendent will, nevertheless, prepare the report for the board member because the superintendent must maintain acceptable relations with each board member. Occasionally, these requests from individual board members become so numerous or overwhelming that the process places an undue burden on the administration and regular administrative functioning suffers. Preferably, such requests should only come from the board as a whole.

One approach used in some school districts to accommodate the board members' desire for information that is not reflected in existing records and to limit the time spent by the administration in preparing reports has been for the board to require that any request for the preparation of a report or new documents be submitted in writing to the board or presented to the board verbally at a board meeting. If a majority of the board agrees that the report should be prepared, it can vote to have it done. This process treats all board members alike and takes the superintendent out of the delicate position of telling a board member "no."

B. Balancing the Role of the Board Member as a Responsive Elected Representative of the School Patrons with the Need to Remain Uninvolved in the Daily Management of the School

When receiving community concerns or complaints, especially about a person or an action taken at a school, board members should get the relevant information about the complaint. When the complaint appears serious or complex, an effort should be made to secure a letter stating the concerns. The following steps should be considered in reacting to the complaint.

1. Refer the complaint to the person responsible at the school or the central office where the complaint arose, or refer the person to the superintendent for referral to the appropriate administrator. A question as simple as "Have you talked with the teacher or principal?" may put the person on the right track, the right track being to talk with the person responsible for the action or his or her immediate supervisor.

2. The superintendent or designated employee to whom complaints are referred should have the proper employee contact the concerned patron to address the problem, or the patron should be referred to another employee who has authority to resolve the problem. (This is also the proper role of PTO/PTA officers and parent advisory members at a specific school, who should refer concerns.)

3. When this process is followed, especially a referral to the superintendent, the board should then hold the superintendent responsible for addressing the issue.

4. If the board member becomes involved in the investigation of a complaint against an employee and there is a hearing before the board on that complaint, the board member may not be impartial and might not be able to hear it.

5. Patrons may come back to the board member if the problem is not resolved after referral and appeals to those up the line. The board member should again engage the superintendent or designee to address the issue. If unresolved after these efforts, the patron can take the issue before the entire board through a specific process under board policy or through the hearing of citizens at a board meeting.

6. The referral process should not be cumbersome. The person to whom the patron is referred should either address the issue and attempt to resolve it, or, if not successful, refer the patron to that person's supervisor, or refer the patron to the person within the school district who has the authority to address and resolve the issue. This process is recognized as providing leadership. If the issue is ultimately one of policy, the issue may end up before the board or be addressed through the political process.

7. Board members (and higher echelon administrators) should be cognizant that not all requests or complaints of patrons are meritorious. There are almost always two sides to any complaint. If a complaint is found to be groundless after administrative review, someone, generally an administrator or, in some limited cases, a board member, should have the courage to say so and accept responsibility for the decision. If the decision is one of administration, the superintendent has the ultimate

responsibility, recognizing that the complaint can ultimately be taken to the board through a hearing process. If the decision is one of policy, the board is ultimately responsible. If the policy issue is not addressed to the satisfaction of a significant enough segment of the patrons, the voters have the ultimate control over the composition of the board.

VIII. Resolving Disputes and Interpreting Board Policy

The administration has the responsibility to administer the policies of the board and resolve disputes on a daily basis. If an employee feels a policy has been improperly applied to him or her, the employee may file a grievance with the appropriate administrator under § 617.005 of the Texas Government code. The administrators with whom employees file grievances must be "those in a position of authority in order to air their grievances."[15] In considering a grievance, administrators are often required to interpret board policies. If the employee is not satisfied with the resolution, including the interpretation of board policy, an appeal process is provided which ultimately ends with the board. Likewise, each district's discipline management system provides a route for the resolution of student discipline matters which can also end before the board.

The board has the ultimate authority within the district to decide disputes that arise under its policies. The board not only has the authority to make findings of fact and apply its policies in these disputes, but it may interpret its own policies. Absent a clearly erroneous application or interpretation of its policy, the board's interpretation of the policy must be upheld by a court.[16] Although the board may provide otherwise in its policies, the minimum required under § 617.005 of the Government Code and Article I, § 27 of the Texas Constitution is that the board "stop, look, and listen" to the complaints of the allegedly injured employee.[17] Likewise, the board must "stop, look, and listen" to a citizen's petition, redress, or remonstrance, but it need not negotiate or otherwise respond.[18]

Currently, there are no state rules or statutes applicable to grievances prescribing the type of hearing that a local board must provide an employee grievant. There are, however, statutes generally preserving the types of hearings required under the former Term Contract Nonrenewal Act and the Probationary and Continuing Contract Law.[19]

Hearings before school boards are usually prescribed by policy. Certain student disciplinary hearings, especially expulsions, are established in the discipline management policies, and employee grievances are often the subject of a particular policy. All other hearings or appearances before school boards are normally accomplished through a "hearing of citizens" portion of board meetings for which individuals can sign up to speak for short time periods designated by the board. The board is not required to take any action beyond stopping, looking, and listening, but, if the board wishes to consider some action, the item can be placed on the agenda for a subsequent meeting, or considered if a properly posted agenda item for the current meeting so permits.

ENDNOTES

[1] Kimbrough v. Barnett, 93 Tex. 301, 55 S.W. 120 (1900).
[2] *Kimbrough, supra.*
[3] Mesquite ISD v. Gross, 123 Tex. 49, 67 S.W.2d 242 (1934).
[4] Love v. City of Dallas, 120 Tex. 351, 40 S.W.2d 20 (1931); Bishop v. Houston ISD, 119 Tex. 403, 29 S.W.2d 312 (1930).
[5] City of San Antonio v. French, 80 Tex. 575, 16 S.W. 440 (1891).
[6] 528 S.W.2d 95 (Tex. Civ. App. - Tyler 1975, *no writ*).
[7] *See also* Toyah ISD v. Pecos-Barstow ISD, 446 S.W.2d 337 (Tex. Civ. App.–San Antonio 1971 *no writ*); Grubbs v. White Settlement ISD, 390 F. Supp. 898 (N.D. Tex. 1975).
[8] 701 S.W.2d 16 (Tex. App.–Dallas 1985, *writ dismissed*).
[9] City of Corpus Christi v. Central Wharf and Warehouse Co., 27 S.W. 803, 805 (Tex. Civ. App. 1894). *See* Al Moody v. Texas Water Comm'n, 373 S.W.2d 793 (Tex. Civ. App.–Austin 1964, *writ ref'd n.r.e.*); Fromen v. Goose Creek ISD, 148 S.W.2d 460 (Tex. Civ. App.–Galveston 1941, *writ dism'd*); Horne Zoological Arena Company v. City of Dallas, 45 S.W.2d 714 (Tex. Civ. App.-Waco 1931, *no writ*); Wright v. Jones, 120 S.W. 1139 (Tex. Civ. App. 1909, *no writ*).
[10] Tex. Educ. Code § 44.031.
[11] Tex. Educ. Code § 44.004.
[12] *See* Op. Atty. Gen. No. JM-119 (1983).
[13] Tex. Gov. Code §§ 552.101 *et. seq.*
[14] Bishop v. Wood, 426 U.S. 341, 96 S. Ct. 2074 (1976).
[15] Corpus Christi ISD v. Padilla, 709 S.W.2d 700 (Tex. App.–Corpus Christi 1986, *no writ*).
[16] Board of Educ. of Rogers, Ark. v. McCluskey, 458 U.S. 966, 102 S. Ct. 3469 (1982); Towles v. Midland ISD, No. 027R16-1083 (Comm. Ed., June 1984).
[17] Texas Ass'n of College Educators v. El Paso Community College, 678 S.W.2d 94 (Tex. App.–El Paso 1984, *writ ref'd n.r.e.*).
[18] Texas Ass'n of College Educators, *supra,* at 96-97.
[19] *See* Tex. Educ. Code § 21.001, *et seq.*

THE TEXAS OPEN MEETINGS ACT

By: Merri Schneider-Vogel

I. Introduction

The stated purpose of the Texas Open Meetings Act ("Act") is to open governmental decision-making to the public. The Act is intended to safeguard the public's interest in knowing the workings of its governmental bodies.[1] The Act requires that advance notice be given for each meeting of governmental bodies. Notice ensures that the public will be informed with reasonable specificity of the subject matter of each item to be considered at a meeting of a governmental body, particularly when the subject is one in which the public can reasonably be expected to have a special interest.[2] The Act enables citizens to monitor and be informed of the governmental activities considered by their elected officials. The public is entitled to know which members are present for closed sessions and whether there is a quorum present prior to entering a closed session. The Act intends to keep public business in the open so citizens can know how their representatives vote. This openness also allows citizen input in the decisionmaking process prior to the governmental body taking final action on an issue.[3] This chapter will provide an overview of the Act and provide practical guidance on how to follow the Act.

II. Definitions

A. Generally

Section 551.001 defines several terms used throughout the Act. Specifically, the term "meeting" is defined as any "deliberation" *i.e.*, verbal exchange, between: (1) a quorum of a governmental body, or (2) a quorum of a governmental body and any other person, during which "public business or public policy over which the governmental body has supervision or control is discussed or considered, or during which the governmental body takes formal action." The term does not include the gathering of a quorum of a governmental body at social functions unrelated to the board's public business or at regional, state, or national conventions or workshops, so long as no formal action is taken and any discussion of public business is incidental to these events. Therefore, if a quorum of members is in attendance at a workshop, a member of the board will be able to discuss his or her district's public business as it relates to the topic of the workshop without fear of violating the Act.

The term "deliberation" is defined as a verbal exchange during a meeting between a quorum of a governmental body, or between a quorum of a governmental body and another person, concerning an issue within the jurisdiction of the governmental body or any public business.

School boards are specifically included in the definition of "governmental body" and are subject to the Act. The definition of governmental body does not, however, include groups subordinate to the school board. For example, in *City of Austin v. Evans*[4], the court of appeals held that a grievance committee of a city is not a "governmental body" within the Act; therefore, the committee meetings were not required to be open to the public. If a meeting is composed only of staff (not board members), there is no open meeting requirement.[5]

B. Board Committee Meetings

Although Section 551.121 states that the Act applies to meetings that contain a quorum of the board, the Attorney General believes that the presence of even one board member on a committee otherwise composed of staff members subjects those committee meetings to the Act.[6] Attorney General opinions do not have the force of law, but will be given deference by the courts. Therefore, the most prudent course for school districts and colleges to take is to require all committees with at least one board member to comply with the Open Meetings Act. Compliance with the Act includes the posting of meetings as well as maintaining minutes of the meetings.

Although board committee meetings must be posted in accordance with the Act, the committees may go into closed session for any of the reasons listed under Subsection D, Section 551.071-551.084 of the Act, that apply. For example, if the district's attorney is offering legal advice to a board committee, the committee could enter closed session under Section 551.071. Similarly, if the board has a committee that considers real estate transactions and makes a recommendation to the board on the advisability of purchasing, leasing, or exchanging real property or the value of real property and the discussion would give an advantage to a purchaser or seller, the committee could go into closed session under Section 551.072.

All meetings of the board committees must begin in open session, just like regular board meetings. An announcement that the committee will go into closed session for a purpose allowed by the Act must be made prior to adjournment into executive session. Additionally, if the committee knows that it will adjourn into closed session during the meeting, the topic that will be covered in the closed session must be included on the notice of the committee meeting. Finally, a certified agenda or tape recording of the closed session must be made and maintained.

C. Meetings by Telephone Conference Call

Section 551.121 of the Act provides that special called meetings of governing bodies of institutions of higher education, including junior or community colleges, may be conducted by telephone conference call. This provision applies to special meetings that require immediate action when it is otherwise difficult or impossible to convene a quorum of the board of regents in a location. A community college must comply with certain requirements to utilize the telephone conference call provision of the Act. Specifically, any part of a meeting that is required to be open to the public and that is held by telephone conference call must be available to be heard by the public at the normal meeting time for the board of regents and must be tape recorded. The tape recording must be made available to the public. Additionally, the junior college must post the meeting in the same way it would post any other meeting. For purposes of the meeting, the place of the meeting held by conference call is the normal meeting place of the board of regents. This provision of the Act applies only to institutions of higher education defined by Section 61.003 of the Texas Education Code. This term includes public junior colleges, public technical institutes, public senior colleges or universities, etc. School district boards cannot meet by using telephone conference calls.

III. Notice and Posting Requirements

Section 551.041 requires that written notice of the (1) date, (2) hour, (3) place and (4) subject of each meeting must be given.

A. Posting the Notice

Section 551.043 requires that notice of all meetings be posted in a place readily accessible to the general public at all times for at least seventy-two (72) hours before the scheduled time of the meeting.[7] Section 551.052 provides that a school district must also have a notice posted on a bulletin board located at a place convenient to the public in its central administrative office and must give notice by telephone or telegraph to any news media requesting such notice and agreeing to pay all expenses incurred by the district in providing special notice.

If any of the seventy-two (72) hours of the posting period are to occur during the weekend or on holidays when the administration building is to be locked, the notice must be posted on the building's door also. If the door is glass, the notice can be posted on the inside with each page visible through the glass. All pages of the notice must be visible. If there is no glass in the vicinity of the door, the notice can be affixed to the outside. A copy of the notice should also, of course, be placed on the bulletin board in the administration building in the usual manner. If the posting is on the door and/or glass, it would be advisable to have the area lighted so the notice may be read at all times.

B. Emergency Meetings or Emergency Items

Another frequent question that arises under the Open Meetings Act concerns Section 551.045 of the Act relating to emergency meetings, where there is an emergency or urgent public necessity. This provision permits the meeting notice to be posted only two (2) hours before a meeting is convened, rather than the usual seventy-two (72) hours before the meeting. Section 551.045 limits cases of emergency and urgent public necessity to situations where there are imminent threats to public health and safety or reasonably unforeseeable situations requiring immediate action by the governmental body. These situations must be clearly identified in the notice. However, even this explicit definition of "emergency" and "urgent public necessity" is inadequate for a board to determine with certainty whether a situation falls into these categories. To ensure compliance with the posting provisions, school districts and colleges should first make a specific finding that urgent public necessity exists before proceeding with the meeting.

The courts have found and the Attorney General has opined that an emergency did not exist in the following situations. An emergency did not exist when a school board knew as early as May 9 that action concerning the lease of a football stadium would have to be taken no later than May 31, but refused to act until May 31 when it called an emergency meeting.[8] An emergency did not exist when a city council held an emergency meeting to discuss indemnifying council members in a lawsuit, but an answer in the lawsuit was not required to be filed for over 20 days from the date of the emergency meeting.[9] When a school board stated that the availability of land for purchase made it necessary to hold an emergency meeting, the Attorney General opined that, on those bare facts, an emergency did not exist.[10] However, in Opinion No. JM-985, the Texas Attorney General emphasized that the existence of an emergency necessarily depends on the facts in any given case and, that under the facts presented, it was not clear whether an emergency existed. These comments by the Attorney General emphasize the need to have the board publicly state the facts that require an emergency meeting.

Where a meeting has already been called with appropriate notice, additional subjects may be added to the agenda for such meeting by posting a supplemental notice of the new items that are emergency items.

The supplemental notice is similar to the notice for an emergency meeting in that it must state that consideration of additional subjects of emergency or urgent public necessity is required and why. Many times matters that must be considered at the meeting are inadvertently left off the public meeting posting. These supplementary agenda items (which are emergencies or constitute urgent public necessities) may be considered at a meeting if the emergency notice requirements, as set forth above, are followed. In these emergency situations, notice must also be given by telephone or telegraph to any news media previously requesting such notice and consenting to pay expenses. If supplementary items are not emergency items, they may not be posted if there is less than seventy-two (72) hours before the beginning of the board meeting.

C. Subjects to be Included in the Notice

The requirement of Section 551.041 that the subject to be considered at each meeting be stated in the notice has been the cause of much debate. The Texas Supreme Court held in *Cox Enterprises, Inc. v. Austin Independent School District*,[11] "the advanced notice given under 3(A)(a) [predecessor to Section 551.041] should specifically disclose the subjects to be considered at the upcoming meeting." In *Cox Enterprises*, a standard is provided for determining what notice is required by the Act. To be in substantial compliance with the Act (legally acceptable), notice must provide "a full disclosure of the subject matter of the meetings," executive sessions as well as open sessions. Each item on which the board anticipates discussing or taking action should be listed in the meeting notice. A notice of a meeting to discuss "new business," "old business," "regular business," "other business which may come before the Board," "routine business" and other similar generalities which do not specify a subject *does not comply with the Act*. Instead, the specific subject to be considered should be disclosed in enough detail so a reasonable person could read it and be informed of what subjects will be discussed or voted upon.

When boards intend to take action concerning an employee, whether the action pertains to an individual employee or class of employees, the notice should specifically identify the position of the employee(s), *e.g.*, teachers, principals, noncontractual employees, etc. A 1990 appellate court decision concerning specificity of notice for employment suggests that the most prudent course for districts is to specifically identify all positions or classes of positions upon which action may be discussed or taken.[12]

The standard for posting notice of a specific position is whether "special public interest" exists in a position. According to the courts that have considered this issue, special public interest may exist because of the inherent qualities of the position or if public interest develops in a position, even if that interest is shown by only one person. Even if controversy does not exist concerning a lower level position at the time of posting, a controversy may develop after posting but before action is taken at the meeting. Accordingly, the safest course for a district or college is to specifically post any positions or classes of positions regardless of whether a special public interest exists at the time of the posting. It is not necessary, however, to identify a specific employee by name, such as when an employee is to be proposed for nonrenewal. The notice due under the Act is that owed to the general public, not to an individual employee who may be under consideration.[13]

If error is to be committed in posting notices of impending employee selections and other closed session items, it should be committed in favor of posting the position. If an action taken at a meeting on an insufficiently posted subject is properly challenged in the courts, the action is subject to invalidation by the courts. Although the chances of invalidation are minimal, the possibility of it occurring is a contingency which should be considered in determining whether to give the subject more specific notice.[14]

One court has addressed the problem of the sufficiency of public notice through newspapers. It held that local notoriety or newspaper publicity of proceedings expected in a future meeting of a public body cannot supply the notice required by the Act.[15] An agenda that satisfies the time and content requirements set out in the Act must be posted to constitute adequate notice under the Act. Newspaper publicity, in addition to the posted agenda, is an effective means of providing supplemental notice about a coming meeting. However, it is now clear that a combination of newspaper publicity or other notice with only part of the notice required by the Act will not fulfill the literal language of Sections 551.044 - 551.046, which call for posting "in a place readily accessible to the general public at all times . . ."[16]

In another opinion, the Texas Attorney General opined that notice of a school board meeting to consider an employee's grievance in executive session under 2(g) of the Act (now Section 551.074) should include the name of the grievant.[17] The Attorney General did not state how specific the district had to be concerning the nature of the grievance, but he did advise districts to err on the side of including information. Although the subject matter of a grievance may not have to be posted in all situations, the subject matter of the grievance should definitely be included if the nature of the grievance is of special public interest. This guideline applies to grievances only; it is not necessary to name specific employees being considered for employment actions.

A 1991 court decision clarifies that the purpose of the Act's posting requirement is to enable public access to and to increase public knowledge of government decisions. It does not, however, require a governmental body to provide notice tailored to reach *specific* individuals whose private interests are most likely to be affected by the proposed action. Thus, in *City of San Antonio v. Fourth Court of Appeals*,[18] the court found that the City's notice indicating that the City would be considering a condemnation ordinance, that the land subject to consideration was located in four county blocks in Southwest Bexar County, and that the purpose of the proposed action was to construct the Applewhite Water Supply Project was posted appropriately. The court rejected the challenger's argument that the notice was faulty because it did not inform individual landowners that their *particular* tracts of land might be condemned.

D. Notice Required for Closed Sessions

Notice of all "meetings" of the school board must be given. No authorized closed session can be held unless the board first meets in open session for which notice has been given, and the presiding officer announces that a closed session will be held and specifies the subsection of the Act that is applicable to the executive session.

As noted above, the Texas Supreme Court's standard for determining whether a notice is sufficient applies to executive sessions as well as open sessions. The "full disclosure of the subject matter" standard does not require that the public know exactly what is to be said in closed session, but it does require that the public be given fairly detailed notice of the subject matter of each topic to be considered in closed session. In other words, "as long as a reader [of the notice] is alerted to the topic for consideration, it is not necessary to state all of the consequences which may flow from consideration of the topic."[19]

Posting a meeting notice listing only such general terms as "Personnel," "Litigation," "Consultation," or "Real Estate Matters" fails to give adequate notice of topics to be considered in executive session. Rather, the advance notice should specifically disclose the subjects to be considered in some detail. The governing body must inform the public of its action, even though it may deliberate in private.

IV. Subjects that may be Considered in Closed Sessions

The Act requires that before any closed session, a *quorum* of the governmental body must convene in open meeting for which notice has been properly given. At the convened open session of a quorum of the board, the board president or presiding officer must publicly announce that a closed session will be held and identify the sections of the Act authorizing the holding of a closed session.[20] It does not appear that the presiding officer is required to specify the subject matter to be discussed in executive session as part of his or her announcement during the open meeting. Matters that may be discussed in a session closed to the public are enumerated in Subchapter D of the Act with the most common matters identified in Sections 551.084, 551.071, 551.072, 551.073, 551.074, 551.082, 551.076, 551.083 and 551.075.

A. Section 551.084 - Witness Exclusion

Section 551.084 permits the board to exclude any witness or witnesses from a hearing that is either open or closed during the examination of another witness in the matter being investigated. This is commonly known as "invoking the rule" in a court proceeding.

B. Section 551.071 - Consultation with Attorneys and Litigation

Section 551.071 permits closed consultation between the board and its attorneys in those instances in which the board seeks the attorney's advice with respect to: (1) pending or contemplated litigation and settlement offers and (2) matters where the duty of the attorney to his or her client, the board, pursuant to the Code of Professional Responsibility of the State Bar of Texas, clearly conflicts with the Act.

The attorney-client relationship under the Act was discussed in Attorney General Opinion No. JM-100 (1983). The Texas Attorney General advised that Section 2(e) [predecessor to Section 551.071] requires the communication between the board and its attorney in closed session be related to an opinion on law or legal services or assistance in some legal proceeding. Thus, the board may hold a closed session to seek or receive the advice of its attorney only with regard to matters in which it seeks the attorney's legal advice or with regard to matters which relate to a specific pending or contemplated legal proceeding. If the discussion does not relate to a specific legal proceeding, the closed door discussion with the attorney must be limited to legal matters upon that the attorney owes confidentiality to the board. General discussion of policy, unrelated to legal matters, is not permitted under Section 551.071 merely because an attorney is present. This discussion with the school attorney may be in person or via a speaker telephone, if the attorney is not present at the meeting. Clearly, a board cannot retire into executive session under this authority if the attorney does not participate at all.

Attorney General Opinion No. JM-238 (1984) advises that governmental bodies may admit their agents or representatives to executive session meetings held under Section 551.071 where the third party's interest is aligned with the body's and where his or her presence is necessary to the body's full communication with its attorney. Whether a particular person may be admitted must be decided by a case-by-case analysis of all relevant facts.

C. Section 551.072 - Real Estate

Section 551.072 permits boards to conduct closed sessions when discussing the purchase, exchange, lease, or value of real property. A closed session to discuss the possible sale of surplus property was upheld in *Cox Enterprises*. Unless the board determines that public discussion will have a detrimental effect on its negotiating position, the discussion must be open to the public. When posting a closed session under Section 551.072, districts and colleges should specify the kind of real estate transaction to be discussed. For example, if the board is considering purchasing property to be used as an athletic field, the notice should so state. Boards should avoid merely reciting in the notice all of the possible transactions allowed under the Act. However, as discussed earlier, the Texas Supreme Court has determined that it is not necessary to describe the location of the property in question by block and lot. The general location will suffice.

D. Section 551.073 - Prospective Gifts and Donations

Section 551.073 permits the board to have a closed session to deliberate a negotiated contract for a prospective gift or donation if deliberation in an open meeting would have a detrimental effect on its negotiating position with a third party.

E. Section 551.074 - Personnel

Section 551.074 allows the board to have closed sessions to discuss matters "involving the appointment, employment, evaluation, reassignment, duties, discipline or dismissal of a public officer or employee or to hear complaints or charges against an officer or employee. The board may not conduct a closed session, however, if the officer or employee who is the subject of the deliberation or hearing requests a public hearing. Again, it should be noted that an employee grievance committee not composed of board members is not covered under the Act; therefore, such a meeting may be closed with or without the employee's consent.[21]

Once a teacher requests an open hearing regarding a proposed change in employment status, the entire meeting, including the deliberations of the board, must be held in open session.[22] The teacher, however, *must object* to a closed session for this provision to be binding. In *Bowen v. Calallen Independent School District*,[23] the court held that a school board did not violate the Act when it moved into closed session to consider a teacher's employment status because the teacher did not object to the closed session. It also appears, however, that an employee may withdraw a request for an open hearing as it relates to the board deliberating in closed session. This is normally accomplished by the employee's attorney and the attorney presenting the Administration's case agreeing, and stating on the record, that the board may deliberate in closed session.

Furthermore, a closed session may be held only to discuss the status of *public officers* and *employees*. In Attorney General Opinion No. MW-129 (1980), the Texas Attorney General opined that discussions concerning the employment of independent contractors, such as engineers, lawyers, and consultants, must be held in public because the closed session exception is applicable only to the discussion of public employees or officers.

Questions often arise concerning when boards can enter closed session to consider or hear complaints against employees or board members. The Act addresses hearings to consider complaints in two separate sections. Section 551.074 allows the board to hear a complaint or charge against an officer or employee in closed session. Section 551.082 allows a board to hold a closed hearing and deliberate when considering a complaint brought by one employee against another employee.

Whether a board can recess to closed session over the objection of the grievant will probably depend on whether the content of the grievant's grievance is truly a complaint and charge against another employee. Additionally, it is not the employee complained of who has the right to request the board to go into closed session. Rather, the board has the right to determine whether to go into closed session to hear complaints and charges against another employee. If, however, the employee complained of wants the hearing to be held in open session, the board must heed that request.

Section 551.082 also permits the board to go into closed session to conduct a hearing and deliberate when considering a complaint or charge brought by one employee against another employee and the complaint or charge directly results in a need for a hearing. The board may not, however, conduct the hearing in closed session if the employee against whom the complaint or charge is brought requests in writing that the hearing be conducted in open session.

F. Section 551.082 - School Children; School Employees; Disciplinary Matter or Complaint

Section 551.082 permits the board to conduct closed hearings when considering the discipline of public school children "unless an open hearing is requested in writing by a parent or guardian of the child." Because eighteen-year-olds are entitled to full adult rights, eighteen-year-olds may themselves make the written request for an open hearing.

This exception does not apply to student disciplinary hearings conducted by junior or community colleges. For purposes of this section, junior and community colleges are not public schools, but institutions of higher education under Section 61.003 of the Texas Education Code.

As mentioned previously, Section 551.082 also allows a board to conduct closed hearings and deliberations when considering a complaint or charge brought by one employee against another employee and the complaint or charge directly results in a need for a hearing. The board may not conduct the hearing in closed session, however, if the employee against whom the complaint or charge is brought requests an open hearing in writing.

G. Section 551.076 - Security Personnel or Devices

Section 551.076 specifically provides that the board is not required to deliberate in open session regarding the deployment or specific occasions for implementation of security personnel or devices. Discussions about bomb threats and deployment of security to prevent disruptions at graduation ceremonies fall under this exception.

H. Section 551.083 - Directions for Consultation Under Section 13.901

Section 551.083 allows boards operating under consultation agreements authorized by Section 13.901 of the Texas Education Code to deliberate regarding the standards, guidelines, terms, or conditions they will follow, or instruct their representatives to follow, in consultation with representatives of employee groups. After the closed session, any formal action to be taken as a result must be done upon motion and vote in open session. If the closed discussion only involves strategy or instructions to the consultation representatives, no formal action in open session is necessary or desirable.

I. Section 551.075 - Conferences with Staff to Receive Information

Conferences with employees of the governmental body for the sole purpose of receiving information from the employee(s) or to ask questions of the employee(s) need not be in open session. However, no discussion of public business or district policy affecting public business may take place between or among members of the governmental body in any informal setting or closed session under this exception.

Although Section 551.075 is included in the portion of the Act that authorizes certain subjects to be discussed in executive session, in No. JM-1058 the Texas Attorney General opined that conferences between board members and an employee for the sole purpose of receiving information is not a meeting within the Act subject to any of the requirements of the Act. We suggest, however, that whenever possible, closed meetings with employees for this purpose should be properly noticed. The presiding officer should still announce that the board is going into closed session for this purpose, and minutes should be kept of the meeting if a quorum is present.

Absolutely no discussions between or among board members may occur when the board is in closed session under 551.075. If deliberations between or among board members occur, the meeting is illegal, and board members present at the meeting are subject to potential civil and/or criminal prosecution, unless another exception that allows the board to deliberate in closed session exists and has been properly posted.

V. Certified Agenda or Tape Recording of Closed Sessions

Section 551.103 requires a tape recording or a "certified agenda" of closed sessions. The requirement of a tape recording or certified agenda of closed sessions obviously reflects the Texas Legislature's concern that local boards discuss more in closed sessions than is allowed by the law. This requirement of record keeping strengthens the law and provides members of the public and press with previously unavailable evidence if they believe the Act has been violated in closed session. Further, boards have greater incentive to police themselves because it is a crime (Class C misdemeanor) for any board member to participate in a closed meeting with knowledge that a tape recording is not being made or a certified agenda is not being kept.[24] An individual found guilty of a Class C misdemeanor may be punished by a fine not to exceed $500.00.[25]

A. Private Consultations with Attorneys

The only closed sessions which will not be subject to tape recording or a certified agenda are private consultations between a governmental body and its attorney properly held under Section 551.071 of the Act. These private consultations may, but are not required, to be recorded or certified because most attorney-client communications are recognized as privileged and confidential. Boards must recognize that if a closed session includes a consultation with an attorney as well as other topics, a certified agenda or tape recording must be made covering the other topics.

B. Requirements of a "Certified Agenda"

Section 551.103 requires that an agenda be kept. Further, the presiding officer must certify that the agenda is "a true and correct record of the proceedings." The certified agenda contemplated by the Act is a written list of business or discussion items brought up at a closed meeting that is confirmed by the presiding officer as being true and correct. In other words, the certified agenda must be more detailed than the notice of the closed meeting, but not nearly so detailed as actual minutes of the meeting. Certification is usually accomplished by signing the document before a notary public; however, it appears that a formal statement in the certified agenda signed by the board president attesting that it is a true and correct record will also suffice.

Given this basic definition, Section 551.103(b) states that every certified agenda must include: a statement of the subject matter of each deliberation; a record of any further action taken; and an announcement made by the presiding officer at the beginning and end of the meeting indicating the date and time. The "announcement" by the presiding officer must be both oral at the open session and in writing as part of the certified agenda.

C. Requirements of a Tape Recording

In lieu of fulfilling all the requirements for maintaining a certified agenda, Section 551.103 allows a governmental body to make a tape recording of its closed session proceedings. Section 551.103 requires only that the tape recording of the proceedings include an announcement indicating the proper time and date which is to be made by the presiding officer at the beginning and end of the closed meeting.

D. Preservation and Maintenance of Certified Agenda or TapeRecordings

Section 551.104 provides that the certified agendas or tape recordings of closed sessions be preserved for at least two years after the date of the meeting. If a lawsuit involving a meeting is commenced during the preservation period, the certified agenda or tape must be preserved pending the outcome of the suit. If a lawsuit is pending, it is advised that the certified agenda or tape be kept until the final appeal of the suit has been ruled upon. Any premature disposal of such document prior to a final dissolution of the suit could have severe legal and public relations effects upon the district.

The certified agenda or tape is a confidential record of the school district or college. The Act allows for it to be made available for public inspection and copying only upon court order in an action brought under the Act. In Open Records Decision No. 495 (1988), the Attorney General held that certified agendas or tapes made pursuant to the Act are deemed confidential by law and are not subject to disclosure under the Open Records Act (now the Texas Public Information Act). In fact, the Attorney General found that he lacked authority to review certified agendas or tapes of executive sessions to determine compliance with the Open Meetings Act. Because these records are confidential, they should be kept at the district's headquarters in a secure place that has limited access. A district vault or appropriate file in the superintendent's office should suffice.

E. Court Proceedings

A certified agenda or tape recording must be available for an *in camera* inspection by a court if a lawsuit has been brought involving an alleged violation of the Act.[26] An *in camera* inspection takes place either when the judge reviews the records in the privacy of his or her chambers or when all spectators are excluded from the courtroom. Upon entry of final judgment, the court may admit the certified agenda or tape into evidence in whole or in part. The court has considerable leeway in granting the equitable or legal relief it considers appropriate to remedy any violation of the Act. The decision of the court in framing a remedy is subject only to the limitation that the court not abuse its discretion. Section 551.104(b)(3) specifically provides that the judicial relief given may include an order that the governmental body make available to the public the certified agenda or tape of any part of a meeting that was not authorized to be closed under the Act.

Although a civil court may provide appropriate equitable or legal relief to remedy violations of the Act, the misdemeanor criminal penalties provided for by the Act must still be properly prosecuted in criminal court. Therefore, if individual board members or the board as a whole illegally participate in a meeting in violation of the Act, a separate criminal proceeding must be brought through the district attorney's office before any board member may be found criminally liable.

VI. Wrongful Publication of Closed Session Deliberations

Section 551.146 also provides that an individual (including a school board member), corporation, or partnership will be subject to criminal and civil liability if the individual or entity knowingly makes public, without lawful authority, the certified agenda or tape recording of any meeting or any portion of a meeting which was closed. This wrongful disclosure of the required records of properly closed deliberations is a Class B misdemeanor.[27] Any person who is injured or damaged by the wrongful disclosure of confidential deliberations may seek relief in civil court against any person wrongfully making the deliberations public.[28]

It appears that the party injured or damaged by the wrongful disclosure has standing to bring suit against the violator and may press charges with the district attorney for prosecution of the misdemeanor. The Act provides a defense to prosecution in criminal proceedings and an affirmative defense in any civil action for parties releasing the confidential information. The defense is provided if the person releasing the certified agenda or tape had good reason to believe the release was lawful or that the release was the result of a mistake of fact concerning the nature or content of the certified agenda or tape. Good reason to believe the release was lawful could be based on the advice of legal counsel. The defense that the release was a result of a mistake of fact concerning the nature or content of the certified agenda or tape might apply to a situation where a board member releases the contents of the deliberation because he or she mistakenly believes that the Act was violated in closed session. However, it would always be more appropriate for the board member to disclose the alleged violation to a court sitting *in camera*, instead of making an alleged violation public.

VII. Voting on Matters Considered in Closed Session

After the announcement that the board will go into closed session under one of the specific sections, the board may discuss only those items under the posted sections. While the board may deliberate on certain matters in closed session, no final action, decision, or vote on any matter considered in the closed session may be made except in a meeting which is open to the public and held in compliance with the notice requirements of the Act. A motion may be formulated in the closed session and agreement reached concerning who will make and second the motion, but the motion should not be made or seconded until the board is in open session. Voting by secret ballots may not be used to contravene the Act, and all votes must be taken so the public can see how each board member voted. The vote must actually be taken in open session.[29] Board members may express their opinions on an issue or announce how they expect to vote on the issue in the open meeting while in closed session, but no actual vote may be taken in the closed session. Straw votes or polls of board members in executive session are in violation of the Act if they cause the later vote in open session to be a sham because the actual resolution of the matter was conducted in closed session.[30]

Recent court decisions affirm that many "decisions" arrived at by boards in closed sessions are not "final actions" within the meaning of Section 551.102. Such decisions will not be subject to rescission simply because they were not made in open meeting. It is difficult to ascertain what "decisions" courts may hold do not amount to "final actions, decision, or votes" under Section 551.102; therefore, in cases of doubt the board should save its actual vote or resolution of the matter for open meeting.

If the board does not contemplate reconvening in open session immediately following the closed session and taking final action on the matters discussed, the notice requirements pose no problems. Proper notice of the subject matter discussed at the closed session to be voted upon may be given for a subsequent meeting. A possible problem arises when the board adjourns to a closed session for discussion and wishes to immediately reconvene to take final action on the matters discussed. Section 551.102 requires that final action must be taken after the notice requirements are met. Section 551.041, of course, requires that notice of the "subject" of each meeting be given. There is a risk in taking action following the closed session unless the matter has been individually posted. To avoid this potential problem, specific notices of actions can be posted for consideration in closed session and then board approval.

VIII. Recording and Broadcasting of Meetings

Meetings "may be recorded by any person in attendance by means of a tape recorder, *video camera*, or any other means of oral or visual reproduction."[31] The Act allows governmental bodies to adopt reasonable rules to maintain order at the meeting place. The "reasonable" rules may include a determination of the location of the recording equipment and the manner in which the recording is conducted, but the rules may not have the effect of preventing or unreasonably impairing camera coverage or tape recording. Districts should adopt rules for orderly video and tape recording of board meetings as official board policy so little confusion will exist about how this recording will be conducted at open board meetings.

The courts have held that unless a majority of the governing body consents, closed sessions of meetings may not be recorded. In *Zamora v. Edgewood Independent School District*,[32] the court reasoned that because the Act specifically authorizes the use of tape recorders at public meetings but makes no similar provisions for their use in closed sessions, the Texas Legislature necessarily denied their use in closed sessions. A closed session may be taped only with the approval of the governing body.

IX. Criminal Penalties for Conducting Illegal Closed Meetings

The Act contains criminal penalties for violating its provisions by conducting an illegal closed meeting. The penalties provide for punishment by fine of not less than $100.00 nor more than $500.00 or imprisonment in the county jail for not less than one month nor more than six months or both. Any board member (1) who willfully calls or aids in calling or organizing a special meeting or session that is closed to the public, or (2) who willfully closes or aids in closing a regular meeting or session to the public, or (3) who willfully participates in a regular or special called meeting or session that is closed to the public where a closed meeting is not permitted by the provisions of the Act, shall be guilty of a misdemeanor, and upon conviction, shall be subject to the penalties mentioned above.[33]

Section 551.143 of the Act provides penalties for any member or group of members who knowingly conspires to circumvent the provisions of the Act by meeting in numbers of less than a quorum to deliberate secretly. According to the Texas Penal Code, a person acts knowingly "when he is aware of the nature of his conduct" or "when he is aware that his conduct is reasonably certain to cause the result."[34] Knowingly merely implies that a person is aware the law is being broken.

Section 551.143 provides that any member or group of members who conspire to circumvent the provisions of the Act by meeting in numbers less than a quorum for the purpose of secret deliberations in contravention of the law shall be guilty of a misdemeanor. Upon conviction, such member(s) is subject to a fine of not less than $100.00 nor more than $500.00 or imprisonment in the county jail for not less than one month nor more than six months or both.

X. Unlawful Acts are Statutorily Voidable

Section 551.142 of the Act allows any interested person to seek injunctive or mandamus relief in court to reverse or void actions taken by a governmental body in violation of the Act. An action taken by the board that is in violation of the Act is voidable.[35] If the action is voidable, a further problem arises in that ratification at a properly noticed meeting does not have retroactive effect.[36]

XI. Court Costs and Attorney's Fees

Section 551.142(b) also states that in any court action brought to prevent or reverse violations of the Act, the court may assess costs of litigation and reasonable attorneys' fees incurred by the plaintiff or defendant who "substantially prevails." Three inquiries are relevant to an award of attorney fees: (1) whether the party substantially prevailed in litigation; (2) whether the suit was brought in good faith; and (3) whether the governmental body's conduct had a reasonable basis in law.[37] The court may, not must, award these expenses. A court might, in its discretion, still choose not to award any legal expenses against the losing party.

XII. Recordkeeping for Open Sessions

Section 551.021 specifically requires governmental bodies to "prepare and retain minutes or make a tape recording of each of its open meetings." The official minutes must state the subject matter of each deliberation and indicate each vote, order, decision, or other action taken by the governmental body.

The minutes or tapes prepared under Section 551.021 are public records and shall be made available for public inspection and copying on request to the chief administrative officer of the governmental body (school superintendents or college presidents) or to any other official designated by the chief administrative officer.[38]

Section 551.022 does not address how long the open meeting minutes or tape recordings must be maintained. However, because these materials are deemed to be public records, they fall under the requirements of Section 201.001 of the Local Government Code, the Local Government Records Act. Under this Act, governmental entities are prohibited from destroying any governmental records until a record retention schedule is prepared and filed with the Texas State Library and Archives Commission unless the entity receives prior approval from the Commission. If tape recordings are made in lieu of minutes, you should not destroy or erase these tape recordings. Tape recordings are included in the definition of governmental records under the Local Government Records Act.

XIII. Accessibility to Meetings by Disabled Individuals

School districts should consider including in all notices that are posted pursuant to the Open Meetings Act a statement that the district will take reasonable efforts to make meetings accessible to individuals with disabilities. Title II of the Americans with Disabilities Act ("ADA")[39] became effective on January 26, 1992. Title II prohibits discrimination in services, programs and activities provided by state and local governments, and any of their agencies or instrumentalities. All public schools are covered by Title II. The anti-discrimination provision of Title II provides that no qualified individual with a disability shall, by reason of such disability, be excluded from participation in or be denied the benefits of the services, programs, or activities of a public entity, or be subjected to the discrimination by any such entity. Because school board meetings are activities of a public entity, Title II requires school districts and colleges to ensure that qualified individuals with disabilities are able to participate in public meetings to the same extent that nondisabled individuals may participate.

The regulations implementing Title II require that the public entity make available to applicants, participants, beneficiaries, and other interested persons information regarding the provisions of Title II and its applicability to the services, programs, or activities of the public entity, and make such information available to them in such manner as the entity finds necessary to apprise such persons of the protections against discrimination assured by the Act. Accordingly, unless the district posts a general notice concerning compliance with Title II, the district should include an accessibility statement in each notice of its meetings. The notice should state that the district will make efforts to ensure that its meetings are accessible to qualified individuals with disabilities by furnishing appropriate auxiliary aids and services and making reasonable accommodations. You should also identify the person in the district to whom the qualified disabled person should contact to seek an accommodation or supplementary aid or service that will ensure that the meeting is made accessible for that person. It is reasonable to place the burden on the qualified disabled individual to make a request for an accommodation or supplementary aid or service in advance of the meeting.

XIV. Conclusion

The requirements of the Act can be very complex, particularly when put into practice at scrutinized and often controversial board meetings. This chapter has attempted to provide an overview of the most important aspects of the Act. This overview does not cover all fact situations, and is not a substitute for the advice of the school attorney. If individual review of a situation involving the Act is needed, the author suggests referral of the matter to your school attorney.

ENDNOTES

[1] Cox Enterprises, Inc. v. Austin Indep. Sch. Dist., 679 S.W.2d 86 (Tex. App.–Texarkana 1984), *modified*, 706 S.W.2d 956 (Tex. 1986).
[2] Op. Tex. Att'y. Gen. No. H-1045 (1977).
[3] 706 S.W.2d 956.
[4] 794 S.W.2d 78 (Tex. App.–Austin 1990, *no writ*).
[5] *See* Op. Tex. Atty Gen. No. H-772 (1976).
[6] Op. Tex. Att'y Gen. No. JM-1072 (1989); *see also* Op. Tex. Att'y Gen Nos. JM-340 (1985); H-238 (1974); H-3 (1973); Hitt v. Mabry, 687 S.W.2d 791, 795 (Tex. App.–San Antonio 1985, *no writ*).
[7] Although the Act requires 72-hour notice for meetings, school districts should also be aware of the special posting requirements for budget hearings. Section 44.004(b) of the Texas Education Code requires a 10-day public notice of the meeting at which the budget is adopted. At that meeting, the public must have an opportunity to be heard on the budget proposal.
[8] River Road Neighborhood Ass'n v. South Tex. Sports, 720 S.W.2d 551, 557-58 (Tex. App.–San Antonio 1986, *writ dism'd*).
[9] Op. Tex. Att'y Gen. No. JM-1037 (1989).
[10] Op. Tex. Att'y Gen. JM-985 (1988).
[11] 706 S.W.2d 956.
[12] Point Isabel Indep. Sch. Dist. v. Hinojosa, 797 S.W.2d 176 (Tex. App.–Corpus Christi 1990, *writ denied*).
[13] Stockdale v. Meno, 867 S.W.2d 123 (Tex. App.–Austin 1993, *writ denied*).
[14] *See* Lower Colo. River Authority v. City of San Marcos, 523 S.W.2d 641 (Tex. 1975); Wells v. Hutchinson, 499 F. Supp. 174 (E.D. Tex. 1980).
[15] Coates v. Windham, 613 S.W.2d 572 (Tex. Civ. App.–Austin 1982, *no writ*).
[16] *See* Thornton v. Smith County, 690 S.W.2d 949 (Tex. App.–Tyler 1985), *modified*, 726 S.W.2d 2 (Tex. 1986).
[17] Op. Tex. Att'y Gen. No. JM-1112 (1989).
[18] 820 S.W.2d 762 (Tex. 1991).
[19] Cox Enterprises, Inc., 706 S.W.2d 956 (Tex. 1986).
[20] § 551.101; *Cox Enterprises, Inc.*, 706 S.W.2d 956 (Tex. 1986).
[21] City of Austin v. Evans, 794 S.W.2d 78 (Tex. App.–Austin 1990, *no writ*).
[22] Corpus Christi Classroom Teachers Ass'n v. Corpus Christi Indep. Sch. Dist., 535 S.W.2d 429 (Tex. Civ. App.–Corpus Christi 1976, *no writ*).
[23] 603 S.W.2d 229 (Tex. Civ. App.–Corpus Christi 1980, *writ ref'd n.r.e.*).
[24] *See* § 551.145.
[25] Tex. Penal Code Ann. §12.23.
[26] *See* § 551.104(b).
[27] The penalty which may be assessed upon conviction of a Class B misdemeanor is: (a) a fine not to exceed $2,000.00; (b) confinement in jail for a term not to exceed 180 days; or (c) both such fine and imprisonment.

[28] The party violating the Act shall be liable to the injured party for: (a) actual damages including, but not limited to, lost wages, damages due to defamation of character, or mental or other emotional distress, or other personal injury or damages; (b) costs of court; (c) reasonable attorney's fees; and (d) exemplary or punitive damages in the discretion of the trier of fact (jury).
[29] *See* § 551.102.
[30] *Cox Enterprises, Inc.*, 679 S.W.2d at 89.
[31] *See* § 551.023.
[32] 592 S.W.2d 649 (Tex. Civ. App.–Beaumont 1979, *writ ref'd n.r.e*).
[33] *See* § 551.144.
[34] TEX. PENAL CODE ANN. §6.03.
[35] *See* § 551.141.
[36] *See* City of San Marcos, 523 S.W.2d 641 (Tex. 1975). *See also* City of Bells v. Greater Texoma Util. Auth., 790 S.W.2d 6 (Tex. App.–Dallas 1990, *writ denied*).
[37] Austin Transportation Study Policy Advisory Comm. v. Sierra Club, 843 S.W.2d 683 (Tex. App.–Austin 1992, *writ denied*).
[38] *See* § 551.022.
[39] 42 U.S.C. § 12101 *et seq.*,

COMPETITIVE BIDDING AND PROPOSAL REQUIREMENTS FOR TEXAS SCHOOL DISTRICTS

By: Jeffrey J. Horner

I. Introduction

There are approximately 1,100 school districts in Texas subject to the competitive bidding and proposal laws, which control the ultimate expenditure of millions of dollars of school revenues. These laws relate to the acquisition of nearly all types of personal and real property by school districts and colleges. The interpretation and application of these laws is critical to the school employees who implement them, particularly with the changes included in Senate Bill 1 passed in 1995. This chapter will outline the basic requirements imposed on school districts concerning bidding and proposals.

II. Section 44 of the Texas Education Code– Bidding and Proposals on School District Contracts

The former bid law applicable to school districts and colleges was Section 21.901 of the Texas Education Code. This statute provided that all contracts proposed to be made by a Texas public school board, except for produce or motor fuel, shall be submitted to competitive bidding when the property is valued at $25,000 or more. However, due to the 1995 changes in the Texas Education Code, this section was significantly changed. Under the new Texas Education Code 44.031 ("Section 44.031"), all school district contracts, except contracts for the purchase of produce or vehicle fuel, valued at $25,000 or more in the aggregate for a twelve-month period shall be made in one of the following six methods:

1. Competitive Bidding,
2. Competitive Sealed Proposals,
3. Request for Proposals,
4. Catalogue Purchases,
5. Interlocal Contracts, or
6. Build/Design Contracts.

Unlike the prior law, a school district or college is no longer required to competitively bid these contracts. A district is now free to choose whichever one of the following methods provides the best value to the district. This statute significantly increases the options of schools entering into purchase contracts. Competitive bidding is included as an option, but other options, most notably requests for proposals, are now permitted.

Further, under this section, in determining to whom to award a contract, a district or college may consider various factors, including:

1. The purchase price,
2. The reputation of the vendor,
3. The quality of the vendor's goods or services,
4. The extent to which goods or services meet the district's needs,
5. The vendor's past relationship with the school district,
6. The impact on the ability of the district to comply with laws related to historically underutilized businesses (HUBs),
7. The total long-term cost to the district, and
8. Any other relevant factor that a private business entity would consider in selecting a vendor.

Therefore, a school district or college can look at whatever reasonable factors it deems appropriate to make a determination on which bid or proposal to accept. A myriad of factors can be considered to determine which bid or proposal is appropriate. If a school district can articulate a reasonable basis for making a decision, it is doubtful that the courts will second guess these decisions.

Furthermore, under the statute, to the extent of any conflict, this section prevails over any law relating to the purchasing of goods and services except laws relating to contracting with HUBs.

The notice requirements for bids or proposals remain basically the same as prior law. That is, notice of the time and place when bids or proposals will be received shall be published in the county in which the district's central administrative office is located for at least two (2) weeks before the date established for awarding the contract. If there is no newspaper in the county where the central administrative office is located, the advertising shall be published in the newspaper in the county nearest the county seat of the county in which the district's office is located.

Like the old law, under Section 44.031(h) the new law affords an emergency exception in cases in which resort to the proposal or bidding process would constitute an inappropriate delay. If school equipment is destroyed or severely damaged, and the school board determines that the delay posed by the bidding process would prevent or substantially impair the conduct of classes or other school activities, then a contract for the replacement or repair of the equipment may be made without competitive bidding or proposals.

Further, the statute allows an educational entity to acquire computers and computer-related equipment through the General Services Commission. As in the old law, under Section 44.031(j) a school board may continue to purchase sole source items without resort to the bidding or proposal process. In addition, a contract proposed to be made by a school board for the purchase or lease of one or more school buses must be submitted to competitive bidding when the contract is valued at $20,000 or more. This provision will apply competitive bidding requirements to most school bus purchases.

Like prior law, criminal penalties for violation of the competitive bidding laws exist. Under Section 44.032, component, separate, and sequential purchases are outlawed. This provision refers to the illegal practice of splitting a purchase into several separate purchases so that the value of each component is not sufficient to trigger competitive purchasing requirements. If the component purchases logically should have been made as a single purchase, then the law is violated and criminal sanctions can apply.

Any officer, employee, or agent of the school district commits an offense if the person with criminal negligence makes or authorizes separate, sequential, or component purchases. The offense is considered a Class B misdemeanor and is an offense involving moral turpitude. Furthermore, the final conviction of a person results in that person's removal from office for four (4) years after the final conviction. This provision now applies to school board members as well as school employees. Furthermore, under Section 44.032(f), a court may enjoin the performance of a contract made in violation of the statute. Such action may be brought by a county attorney, a district attorney, or a citizen of the county in which the school district is located. If this person prevails in the action, he or she is entitled to the recovery of reasonable attorneys' fees.

The statute requires a simplified procedure for purchases of personal property valued between $10,000 and $25,000. Under Section 44.033, for each twelve-month period a school district shall publish a notice in two successive issues in a newspaper of general circulation, specifying categories of personal property to be purchased under this section. Through this publication, the school district must solicit names, addresses, and telephone numbers of vendors interested in supplying such categories to the district. It must then create a list consisting of all responding vendors or any additional vendors the district elects to include. Before the district makes a purchase from a particular category, it must obtain written or telephone price quotations from at least three (3) vendors on the list, unless the list is shorter than three (3). Telephone quotes should be reduced to writing. The purchase shall be made from the lowest responsible bidder in each category.

The new law also contains a section regarding notification of the criminal history of a contractor. Under Section 44.034, a person or business entering into a contract with a school district must give advance notice to the district if the person operating the business has been convicted of a felony. The notice must include a general description of conduct resulting in the conviction. A school district retains the right to terminate a contract if the district determines after the fact that the relevant person was convicted of a felony and appropriate notice was not given.

Finally, this statute allows a special proposal procedure for the acquisition of energy conservation measures by school districts. Under Section 44.901, a school board may enter into a contract to acquire energy conservation measures, including contracts for insulation, storm or multi-glazed windows or doors, automatic energy control systems, heating, ventilating/air conditioning system modifications or replacements, energy recovery systems, and lighting fixtures. Before entering into such a contract, a school board shall require the filing of a performance bond by the contractor. Such a contract, which can be a lease/purchase agreement, shall not exceed ten (10) years in duration. Furthermore, the contract must be obtained under competitive proposal procedures. The requests for proposals must solicit quotations and specify the relative importance of guaranteed savings, price, financial performance and stability, technical ability, experience, and other relevant factors.

III. Applicability of Section 271.021 et seq. of the Texas Local Government Code

Section 271.021 *et. seq.* of the Texas Local Government Code is commonly known as the "Public Property Finance Act" ("Act"). Under Section 271.024 of the Act, if a governmental entity is required by statute to award a contract for the repair, renovation, or construction of buildings on the basis of competitive bids, bidding on the contract must be accomplished in the manner provided in the Act. Specifically, the contract must be awarded to the lowest responsible bidder, but the contract may not be awarded to a bidder who is not the lowest bidder unless before the award, each lower bidder is given the opportunity to appear before the school district's governing body or its designee to present evidence concerning the bidder's responsibility.

The passage of Section 44 of the new Texas Education Code has raised the applicability of the Act to question. One line of thought is that because Section 44 of the Education Code no longer requires school districts to competitively bid purchase contracts, then the Act no longer applies to school districts. Under this theory, a school district may secure construction services through competitive bidding, requests for proposals, and/or the other methods outlined in Section 44.031(a).

This question was answered by the Texas Attorney General in a recent opinion.[1] In this opinion, General Morales opined that when a school board determines that competitive bidding on a construction project will provide the best value to a school, Section 44 requires the school to competitively bid the contract. In that circumstance, the school must comply with the procedures outlined in Section 271 of the Act. In essence, if a district competitively bids a project, the hearing procedures of Section 271 are applicable. Further, the Attorney General opined that Chapter 44 applies to junior and community colleges as well as school districts.

IV. Section 272.001, et seq. of the Texas LocalGovernment Code-Bidding on the Exchange or Sale of Real Property

Section 272.001, *et seq.* of the Texas Local Government Code relates to notice of sale or exchange of property by a school district. With some exceptions, before property owned by a school district may be sold or exchanged for other land, notice to the general public of the offer of land for sale or exchange must be published in a newspaper of general circulation. The notice must include a description of the property, and a procedure by which sealed bids to purchase the property or offers to exchange the land may be submitted.

These notice and bidding requirements do not apply to plats of land or real property interests owned by a political subdivision as described below. However, the property not subject to bidding may not be conveyed, sold, or exchanged for less than fair market value. Fair market value is determined by an appraisal obtained by the political subdivision which owns the property; the appraisal is conclusive of fair market value. The notice and bidding requirements do not apply to the following real property interests:

1. narrow strips of land;
2. streets or alleys, owned in fee or used by easement;
3. an easement for which one or more abutting property owners own the underlying fee simple;
4. streets, rights-of-way, or easements that the school district chooses to exchange for other land to be used for the same purposes;

5. land that the school district wants to have developed by contract with an independent foundation;

6. a real property interest conveyed to a governmental entity that has the power of eminent domain; or

7. a municipality's land that is located in a reinvestment zone designated as provided by law.

V. Professional Services

Another issue that arises in the bidding area is the services that constitute "professional services" under § 44.301(f) which need not be submitted for bids or proposals. In one opinion, the Texas Attorney General opined that the services of a construction management consultant were "personal services" under Texas Local Government Code § 271.001, which governs bidding by counties.[2] The Attorney General specifically left open the issue of whether the services should be classified as "professional services." It seems likely that construction management services would fall within the exception to the bidding/proposal law under § 44.301, because these services involve extensive engineering skills.

More clearly, the employment of architects, attorneys, fiscal agents, and other professionals is not subject to competitive bidding under § 44.301(f). Indeed, the Professional Services Procurement Act (Tex. Govt. Code § 2254.001 *et. seq.*) forbids school districts and other governmental entities from procuring the services of accountants, architects, physicians, optometrists, land surveyors, and engineers through competitive bidding. Rather, the selection of these professionals must be made on the basis of qualifications, demonstrated competence, and the reasonableness of their prices.

One area of recent scrutiny is whether the purchase of insurance is subject to competitive bidding. Prior to the passage of the new Education Code, the Attorney General opined that insurance was not a "professional service" and was thus subject to the bidding laws.[3] Under the new law, presumably the Attorney General still would not consider insurance to be a "professional service"; however, insurance can now be acquired not only through competitive bidding, but also requests for proposals and the other methods outlined in § 44.301(a).

VI. Conclusion

There are few court cases dealing specifically with the interpretation of bidding and proposal laws affecting public school districts. Indeed, with the recent passage of Section 44 of the Texas Education Code, this area has changed drastically. Probably the best piece of advice for a school district or college to follow is if there is any doubt whether a particular transaction should be submitted to the competitive bidding or proposal process, err on the side of bidding the transaction or putting the transaction out for proposals. The need to follow these procedures is underscored by the adoption of civil and criminal penalties for violation of these laws. Once a particular transaction has been submitted to the competitive bidding or proposal process, a school district has a wide range of discretion on which bids or proposals to accept. While school districts generally award a contract to the lowest bidder or proposer, the district is free to accept whatever bid or proposal is deemed to best serve the interests of the district, so long as a legitimate, articulable basis exists for the decision and all appropriate procedures are followed in reaching that decision.

ENDNOTES

[1] *See* Op. Att'y Gen. No. DM-387 (1996).
[2] *See* Op. Att'y Gen. No. JM-940 (1988).
[3] *See* Op. Att'y Gen. No. DM-347 (1995).

LAW OF NEPOTISM AND CONFLICTS OF INTEREST IN TEXAS

By: J. Timothy Brightman

I. Development of the Law of Conflicts of Interest

Prior to 1983, Texas courts took a dim view of local governmental entities entering into business or contractual relationships with private business in which a local public official maintained an interest. The courts were adamant in maintaining that even the appearance of a conflict of interest could undermine the public's confidence in the faithful and impartial administration of local government. The result of this court-created, or common law, doctrine was to void virtually all actions taken by a governing body of a local governmental entity if a board member had a financial interest in any action taken.

In 1983, the Texas Legislature passed Article 988b of the Texas Revised Civil Statutes to overrule the more rigid aspects of the common law doctrine. The intent of the Legislature was to allow the board to clear its conflicts by having the affected member sign and file an affidavit stating the nature of his interests in the business or company doing business before the board. The affected board member would then abstain from any further participation or voting in the matter. However, the Texas Attorney General issued numerous opinions that stated that the conflict of interest statute merely supplemented the common law and did not preempt it.

Consequently, in 1989, the Legislature amended Article 988b to repeal all common law conflict of interest doctrines as applied to local public officials. The conflict of interest statute was then transferred to Chapter 171 of the Local Government Code. Although Chapter 171 repeals prior law, board members should still be aware of their common law fiduciary duty as a member of a board.

A. Chapter 171 of the Local Government Code

Chapter 171 of the Local Government Code applies to all local public officials. This definition includes all members of boards of trustees of colleges and independent school districts. It does not apply to school employees, such as teachers or administrators. The law also encompasses the relatives of public officials who are within the first degree of consanguinity or affinity.

Under Chapter 171, a board member should be concerned whenever an item before the board will have a special economic effect on a business entity or real property in which that board member (or first degree relation) has a substantial interest. A special economic effect is generally one that benefits the business entity in a separate and distinct manner from the public at large.

An individual has a substantial interest in a business entity if:

1. The person owns 10% or more of the voting stock or shares of the business entity or owns either 10% or more or $5,000 or more of the fair market value of the business entity; or
2. Funds received by the person from the business entity exceed 10% of the person's gross income for the previous year.

A person is considered to have a substantial interest in real property if the interest is an equitable or legal ownership with a fair market value of $2,500 or more.

If a board member has a substantial interest in the action before the board and it is reasonably foreseeable that the action will have a special economic effect that is distinguishable from that to the public, the board member must file an affidavit stating the nature and extent of his interest and abstain from further participation or voting on the matter. The affidavit may be filed on an agenda item basis, or the affidavit related to a specific substantial interest may be filed in advance of any related item ever appearing on the agenda.

The affidavit must be filed with the official recordkeeper of the school district prior to the board considering the item. When the agenda item is presented, the board member should announce his interest, that he has an affidavit on file, and that he will abstain from voting. The board member may not contribute to the debate on the agenda item and should not take action which gives the appearance of influencing the outcome.[1]

If a board member files an affidavit stating the nature and extent of his interest on a budget item, the board as a whole must take specific action. In such an instance, the budget item on which the board member has a substantial interest must be voted on separately. The affected board member may not vote on that separate item; however, he may vote on the final budget if the board member has complied with the filing of the affidavit, abstained from participation on the separately considered matter, and the matter on which the board member is concerned has been resolved by the rest of the board.

Knowing violations of the provisions of Chapter 171 will subject the board member to criminal prosecution for a Class A misdemeanor. A Class A misdemeanor is punishable by a $2,000 fine, one year in prison, or both.

B. Depositories for School Districts

In selecting a depository for the school district, an additional conflict may arise for individual members of the board of trustees who are associated with a bank's board of directors. Similar to Chapter 171 of the Local Government Code, § 45.204 of the Texas Education Code permits a board to select a depository bank, even if a board member holds a position with the bank, so long as that board member abstains from voting on the depository contract to that bank.

C. Two Offices of Emolument

Article 16, Section 40 of the Texas Constitution prohibits an individual from holding two offices of emolument. Although a member of the board of trustees is an officeholder, such a position is not considered an office of emolument because board members are not paid a salary. Therefore, a school board member can be employed in a paying position by the state government and can continue his service as an unpaid board member. For example, a state legislator holds an office of emolument by the fact that he receives a salary for holding a legislative office. Reimbursement of expenses does not constitute an emolument, and can be fully recovered by public officials.

D. Incompatibility of Offices

Another conflict-of-interest issue is the common law doctrine of incompatibility of offices. This doctrine applies when an individual attempts to hold two offices that require conflicting loyalties. The doctrine is not just a prohibition on specific action items before the school board, but is a general prohibition against holding the two potentially incompatible offices. Typically, employment with a governmental entity does not constitute an office. The one exception to this rule is when an individual would be considered to be employing himself or herself. For example, an employee of the school district could not serve as a board member for that district, because he would be considered to be employing himself. In contrast, a board member may be employed by a neighboring school district as a teacher, and the holding of these two positions would not be incompatible.

E. Official Oppression

Board members should also be wary of the criminal laws relating to official oppression. Official oppression occurs when a public servant, acting under the authority of his office, intentionally denies or impedes another in the exercise or enjoyment of any right, privilege, power, or immunity, knowing his conduct is unlawful.[2] For example, a police chief was found guilty of official oppression by harassing a female subordinate. He used his office as a vehicle to engage in the harassment and, therefore, was guilty of using his office to impede another from the exercise of a right (employment). A violation of the conflict of interest laws, under certain circumstances, constitutes official oppression.

F. Bribery

The penal provision relating to bribery is violated when an individual intentionally or knowingly offers, confers, or agrees to confer on another, or solicits, accepts, or agrees to accept from another:

1) any benefit as consideration of the recipient's decision, opinion, recommendation, vote, or other exercise of discretion as a public servant, party official, or voter;
2) any benefit as consideration for the recipient's decision, vote, recommendation, or other exercise of official discretion in judicial or administrative proceedings; or
3) any benefit as consideration for a violation of duty imposed by law on a public servant or party official.

A benefit is considered to be anything reasonably regarded as pecuniary gain or pecuniary advantage, including benefit to another person in whose welfare the beneficiary has a direct and substantial interest. It is important to remember that the benefit need not necessarily go directly to the board member, but may go to an individual in whom the board member has a direct interest.[3]

The following are a list of pecuniary benefits which are not considered gifts for the purposes of the bribery statute:

1) Fees prescribed by law;
2) Gifts or benefits on account of kinship or a personal, professional, or business relationship independent of the office; and
3) Food, lodging, transportation, or entertainment accepted as a guest and, if required by law to report those items, they were reported.[4]

II. The Laws on Nepotism

Texas law on nepotism is designed to prohibit government officials from showing favoritism to their relatives. The principal provisions regarding nepotism are found in Chapter 573 of the Texas Government Code. The prohibition applicable to public officials, such as officers of a school district, provides:

A public official may not appoint, confirm the appointment of, or vote for the appointment or confirmation of the appointment of an individual to a position that is to be directly or indirectly compensated from public funds or fees of office if:

> (1) the individual is related to the public official within a degree described by Section 573.002[5]; or
> (2) the public official holds the appointment or confirmation authority as a member of a state or local board, the legislature, or court within a degree described by Section 573.002.[6]

A. Who?

The definition of a public official under the statute explicitly applies to "an officer of . . . school district." Officers of a school district are the members of the school board. This section does not apply to the superintendent or other employees. The superintendent is considered to be an employee of the district and not an officer.[7]

B. What Is Prohibited?

Members of the board may not appoint, confirm the appointment, or vote to appoint or confirm the appointment of an individual to a position that will be compensated, either directly or indirectly, from public funds, if the individual is related to the board member within the second degree of affinity or consanguinity. A board member is also prohibited from taking action on the salary, fees, or compensation of an individual who is related within the second degree of affinity or third degree of consanguinity when the salary, fees, or compensation are to be paid in whole or in part, either directly or indirectly, from public funds.

Section 573.041(2) applies to a board member that has the appointment authority and the individual in question is related to another board member within the second degree of affinity or the third degree of consanguinity. Such a situation is unlikely to arise in a school district.

C. Exceptions for School Districts

Relatives of a board member are not prohibited from retaining their previous employment with a school district under the following conditions:

(1) If the member of the board was appointed, the relative must have been continuously employed for at least thirty (30) days prior to the appointment of the board member;
(2) If the member of the board was elected in an election other than a general election, the relative must have been continu-

ously employed for the six (6) months . ior to the member being elected; or

(3) If the board member was elected in a general election, the relative must have been continuously employed for at least one (1) year prior to the election of the board member.

The board member is still prohibited from participating in the deliberation or voting on the appointment, reappointment, employment, confirmation, reemployment, change in status, compensation, or dismissal of the relative, unless the action to be taken regards a bona fide class or category of employees.[8]

D. Consanguinity and Affinity

Consanguinity is typically considered to be a blood relationship, while affinity is considered to be a relationship by marriage. Two persons are related to each other by consanguinity if one person is a descendent of the other person or they share a common ancestor.[9] Affinity relationships are those brought about by marriage. In other words, two persons are related by affinity if they are married to each other or, the relationship is brought about by marriage.

E. Calculating Degrees of Relationship

The method of computing degrees of a relationship was changed by the Legislature in 1991, and further amended and codified in 1993. Degrees of a relationship are currently calculated by first identifying the common ancestor between the individual in question and the board member; unless, the individuals are direct descendents of each other.[10] The degrees are calculated by counting the number of generations between the individual in question and the nearest common ancestor, and then counting the number of generations between that ancestor and the board member. For example, if the individual in question is the first cousin of the board member, the nearest common ancestor is the individual's grandparent. There are two generations between the individual in question and the grandparent (the nearest common ancestor). There are also two generations between that common ancestor and the board member. The total number of generations are then added together, in this case the individual in question and the board member are related by the fourth degree of consanguinity. Relationships by affinity are calculated the same as the degree of underlying relationship by consanguinity. For example, if A and B are related to each other by the second degree of consanguinity, A's spouse is related to B by the second degree of affinity.

III. Conclusion

The conflict of interest and nepotism statutes in Texas exist to prevent board members from exercising influence in their offices which may result in favoritism or an economic windfall to the board member. School officials in Texas should be careful to avoid situations which violate those statutes or create even the appearance of impropriety. Interpretation of these statutes, particularly in computing the appropriate degrees of consanguinity or affinity, can be confusing. The author suggests contacting your local school attorney if an interpretation of these statutes is needed.

ENDNOTES

[1] If a majority of the remainder of the board have filed similar affidavits of special interest, the affected board members need not abstain from further participation.
[2] Tex. Penal Code § 39.02.
[3] Tex. Penal Code § 36.02.
[4] Tex. Penal Code § 36.10.
[5] Tex. Govt. Code § 573.041. The prohibited degrees of a relationship are described further in the section discussing "What is Prohibited" and "Consanguinity and Affinity."
[6] *Id.* This subsection will seldom, if ever, be applicable to school districts; however, it is detailed more thoroughly in the section discussing "What is Prohibited."
[7] Pena v. Rio Grande City Consol. Indep. Sch. Dist., 616 S.W.2d 658 (Tex. Civ. App.–Eastland 1981, *no writ*).
[8] Tex. Govt. Code § 573.062.
[9] Tex. Govt. Code § 573.022.
[10] If the individuals are direct descendents of each other, the number of generations separating the two constitutes the degree of relationship. *See* Tex. Govt. Code § 573.023.

RELIGION IN THE PUBLIC SCHOOLS

By: Lisa A. Brown and
Christopher B. Gilbert

I. Introduction

The constitutional propriety of religious displays on government property, such as a Nativity scene, have reached the highest court in two fractured and contentious decisions which leave district courts, if not local school board officials, in a Serbonian Bog.[1]

Religion and its role in the public schools continues to be a volatile issue. Students and their parents are becoming more willing to challenge practices that have gone unquestioned for decades, and several large–and well-funded–special interest groups stand willing to back their lawsuits. Deciding how to approach such an emotionally-charged and value-laden issue can be difficult for school officials. This chapter will attempt to provide an outline of the current case law interpreting the First Amendment. The chapter will focus on cases throughout the country, not just in Texas.

II. An Overview of the First Amendment

The First Amendment of the United States Constitution states that "Congress shall make no law respecting an establishment of religion, or prohibiting the free exercise thereof . . . ." Although it refers only to Congress, the First Amendment has been found to apply to local and state governments,[2] including school boards.[3] The First Amendment contains two separate religious clauses: the Establishment Clause and the Free Exercise Clause.

The Establishment Clause requires that a governmental entity refrain from any activity which may tend to "establish" or promote any specific religion or religion in general. The Establishment Clause has also been interpreted to forbid practices or acts that are hostile toward religion. Courts look very closely at practices in schools alleged to violate the Establishment Clause. Because of compulsory attendance laws, school children present a captive audience vulnerable to influence by authority figures. The U.S. Supreme Court has repeatedly cautioned that young school children are especially impressionable in matters relating to religion.[4]

The test that courts have employed for the past twenty (20) years in deciding whether a specific act, policy, or practice violates the Establishment Clause was set forth by the Supreme Court in *Lemon v. Kurtzman*.[5] According to the so-called *Lemon* test, an activity of a governmental entity will pass constitutional muster if it complies with the following three-prong test:

(1) there is a legitimate, secular, non-religious purpose for the activity;
(2) the primary effect of the activity neither advances nor hinders religious belief or practice; and
(3) the activity does not foster excessive entanglement between the governmental entity and religious concerns.

If an activity meets these three requirements, it is deemed constitutional and permissible. If it fails any one of them, it is unconstitutional.

Recent U.S. Supreme Court decisions have cast serious doubt, however, on the continued viability and application of the *Lemon* test. In *Lee v. Weisman*,[6] the Supreme Court refused to use the *Lemon* test to decide the constitutionality of prayer at graduation. In the past six (6) years, five (5) of the current sitting Justices have either explicitly or implicitly called for the repeal of *Lemon*.[7] In one of the latest Supreme Court cases to interpret the Establishment Clause, both parties explicitly asked the Court to rule on whether *Lemon* was still a valid test; the Court, however, ignored the request, mentioning *Lemon* twice only in passing.[8] The most recent Supreme Court case does not even mention *Lemon*, instead focusing on the neutrality of the government action.[9] Whether the courts will continue to use the *Lemon* test in deciding cases involving the Establishment Clause in the future is unclear. Until the Court explicitly overrules it, however, it is still valid law.

The second prong of the First Amendment is the Free Exercise Clause, which generally prohibits the government from burdening an individual's exercise of his or her religious choice. The test for whether a specific government practice violates the Free Exercise Clause is two-fold: whether the government has placed a substantial burden on the observation of a central religious belief or practice and, if so, whether a compelling governmental interest justifies the burden.[10] Among other things, the Free Exercise Clause guarantees parents the right to control their child's religious upbringing and education.[11] It does not, however, require schools to tailor the curriculum to satisfy everyone's religious sensibilities; to do so would result in "[n]othing but educational confusion and a discrediting of the public school system . . . ."[12] This highlights the inherent tension between the two religion clauses of the First Amendment; were a school to attempt to please a certain religious faith, it would in all likelihood violate the Establishment Clause by promoting that religious faith.[13]

III. Religion in Curriculum and the Bible in the Classroom

One question continuously faced by school administrators is the extent to which religion or values commonly associated with religion may be taught as part of a school's curriculum. Disputes occasionally arise over the role of the Bible in the education of children. The Bible obviously may not be used as a tool for endorsing or promoting religion; such a use would violate the *Lemon* test. However, the courts have made it clear that the Bible does have a place in the public schools. The Bible, as well as other religious texts, may be used in the public schools as part of a secular course of education, such as in a history class or a class on comparative religions.[14] The Bible may also be shelved in a school library, provided that Christianity (or any other religious sect) is not favored by the library over other religions and provided the Bible's inclusion in the library does not show a preference for religious works in general.[15]

Ultimately, the role of the Bible in the public schools is a limited one. The Supreme Court has made it clear that the use of the Bible must truly be secular; mandatory Bible readings at the beginning of a school day are unconstitutional. This is true even if school officials do not comment about the verses, and even if students are given permission to leave the room during the reading. Where the Bible may be used as part of a secular course of education, classes teaching the Bible by itself are unconstitutional.[16] Teachers may not begin the day with extemporaneous Bible readings, prayers, or telling stories with a biblical basis.[17] Courts will assume that such activity is religious unless the school can demonstrate a secular purpose. Some teachers have argued that they have a right to teach about religion; however, prohibiting such acts does not violate the teacher's free exercise rights.[18] The Tenth Circuit Court of Appeals has gone as far as prohibiting a teacher from reading the Bible silently to himself during a free reading period in his class; the court felt that as an authority figure, such acts by the teacher would tend to endorse Christianity.[19]

Curriculum choices made by a school may also run afoul of the Free Exercise Clause. The Free Exercise Clause is concerned with coercion, not exposure. The courts have consistently noted that mere exposure to ideas that offend a person, on religious or other grounds, does not violate that person's right to religious freedom.[20] Some students have complained that a school has coerced them by forcing them to read certain books that conflict in some way with that student's religious beliefs. Requiring students to read or use such books does not violate the student's free exercise rights under the First Amendment.[21] The coercion involved in requiring students to read a book is not the type of coercion that violates the Free Exercise Clause. Being required to read a book is not the same as being required to profess or deny a belief in what one is reading. In addition, requiring that certain textbooks be used does not require students to engage in practices contrary to their religious beliefs, nor does it require students to refrain from engaging in practices required by their faith.

Several courts recently have dealt with claims by students and parents that certain textbooks promote certain religions. Many of these cases revolve around the subject of "secular humanism." Although there are many different definitions of "secular humanism," it is generally defined as a system of belief that denies the existence of the transcendent or the supernatural, and concentrates on the physical and knowable world.[22] In *Smith v. Board of School Commissioners of Mobile County*, the Eleventh Circuit Court of Appeals decided that the textbooks used by Alabama did not violate the Establishment Clause by promoting "secular humanism," largely on the basis that it was highly unlikely that a reasonable observer would think that the use of the textbooks was meant to promote any sort of religion.[23] The court noted that even if the textbooks tended to coincide with a "secular humanism" point of view, a government practice is not unconstitutional just because it happens to coincide or harmonize with a particular religion. The fact that the history books used by the state did not mention religion's role in our nation's history may have been a poor choice educationally, but this did not make them unconstitutional. Similarly, the Ninth Circuit decided in *Grove v. Mead School District* that the use of the book *The Learning Tree* did not violate the First Amendment by establishing the religion of "secular humanism," where the primary effect of the book was found to be secular.[24] Lastly, Bible classes may not be taught as an attempt to balance the perceived "secular humanism" in books used in other classes. Even if textbooks did advance the religion of "secular humanism," this did not justify the establishment of a second religion (Christianity) in the schools.[25]

Recently, claims have been made that certain textbooks advance not secular humanism, but the more esoteric religions of Satanism, Neo-Paganism, Witchcraft and Wicca. Generally, the books in question have contained stories with a Halloween-type theme, often containing witches, goblins, magic, and the like. In two recent decisions, both the Seventh and Ninth Circuits examined the same national series of textbooks, which are used in elementary schools and which contain such stories. Both courts found that the presence of witches and related figures in the books did not violate the Establishment Clause.[26]

IV. Religious Symbols in the Public Schools

Whether a religious symbol, such as a cross or a nativity scene, may be displayed in the public schools is a question that will turn largely on the facts of the specific situation. The fact-intensive nature of such cases is illustrated by *Lynch v. Donnelly*[27] and *County of Allegheny v. American Civil Liberties Union*,[28] two U. S. Supreme Court decisions that dealt with the propriety of religious displays at courthouses during the Christmas season. In *Lynch*, the Court found that a display that included a nativity scene, a Santa Claus house, a Christmas tree, and a banner that read "SEASONS GREETINGS," all in close proximity to each other, did not violate the Constitution. But in *County of Allegheny*, the Court found that a nativity scene, standing by itself inside a courthouse, violated the Establishment Clause, while a menorah, standing outside the courthouse next to a Christmas tree and a sign saluting liberty, did not. Such a narrow focus on the specific facts of each case has done little to provide guidance for dealing with displays in the future.[29] A third, more recent decision of the Court held that the government was required to allow a private display of the Latin cross in a public forum, but this case focused on the private nature of the display and the traditionally neutral history of the forum–a marked difference from the governmentally - sponsored displays in *Lynch* and *County of Allegheny*.[30] In addition, schools should take great care in applying even the limited guidance provided by *Lynch* and *County of Allegheny*; both cases dealt with adults in adult settings, and the courts have made it clear that different standards will be applied to children in school settings.[31]

The Supreme Court has decided one case that dealt specifically with religious symbols in a school setting. In *Stone v. Graham*, the Court held that a school may not require that the Ten Commandments be posted in every classroom.[32] The Court found that the Ten Commandments are preeminently religious in nature, and a legislative declaration that they are the basis for Western legal codes could not change that fact. The fact that posting the Ten Commandments might be seen as only a "minor encroachment" is no defense to a violation of the Establishment Clause. In addition, lower courts have made it clear that schools should take great care in establishing any sort of religious display that is intended to be permanent. Permanent religious displays in the public schools have generally been found to violate the Establishment Clause, because the courts feel that they have no independent secular purpose. For example, it was unconstitutional to hang a permanently-fixed portrait of Jesus Christ outside a principal's office.[33] A permanent mural of the crucifixion painted on the wall outside a school auditorium was likewise found to be unconstitutional.[34]

However, the courts will analyze the content and context of the alleged religious display to determine whether a reasonable observer would feel that the "principal or primary effect" of the display is to "advance or inhibit religion." One court has found that the use of the "Blue Devil" as a school mascot did not violate the Establishment Clause by advancing Satanism, where the mascot had an undeniable secular purpose ("to provide a menacing type of figure for sporting events"), and no reasonable observer could think that the school was trying to advocate Satanism.[35]

Recently, schools have been under much pressure to expand upon their traditional curriculum to include more culturally and ethnically diverse subjects. However, because of the more active role of religion in some other cultures, teaching about that culture can come close to teaching about that culture's specific religion. In *Clever v. Cherry Hill Township Board of Education*, a federal court in New Jersey approved a school policy that allowed displays of "the cultural, ethnic, and religious customs and traditions of others during the appropriate season", holding that it did not violate the Establishment Clause.[36] The Court found that because the displays were limited in time to the appropriate season and were part of a program of learning about other cultures and societies, they served a permissible secular purpose.

V. Prayer in School

Individual students may engage in quiet, private prayer, as long as the prayer is not disruptive, does not violate neutrally-applied classroom rules (i.e. a student cannot decide to engage in silent prayer just as the teacher calls on that student), and does not violate the rights of other students to be left alone. Constitutional difficulties arise when the prayer becomes vocal, when it becomes a group prayer, or when the school somehow sponsors (or is seen as sponsoring) the prayer. Student or adult-led prayer at school during the school day has generally been found by the courts to be an "inherently religious" activity,[37] and therefore not constitutionally permissible. In most situations, prayer is not allowed in school because it violates the first prong of the *Lemon* test: i.e. it has no secular purpose.[38] A few courts have found that using prayer to "solemnify" an event is a permissible secular purpose,[39] but later courts have noted that this rationale for prayer only makes sense when the school is seeking to solemnify a singular and somewhat unique event, such as a high school graduation ceremony. Events that take place daily or even weekly, such as sporting events, do not require the same "solemnization" as once-a-year events. Therefore, prayer at such events would not be appropriate.[40]

The fact that student or adult-led prayer may be voluntary, or may be both nonsectarian and nonproselytizing, does not protect it from violating the Establishment Clause.[41] As was discussed above, when a teacher gives extemporaneous Bible readings, delivers prayers, tells stories with a biblical basis, or reads the Bible silently to him or herself in class, a violation of the Establishment Clause may also occur. However, while prayer that is part of the school's program is generally forbidden, schools must take great care in dealing with prayer by students that just happens to take place on school grounds. While such situations could include the student who audibly says grace before lunch, it more commonly occurs when a group of students request permission to meet on school grounds for the purpose of prayer. These situations are generally covered by the Equal Access Act and are discussed below.

The courts have dealt with prayer at several different "extracurricular" events. Much of the recent litigation surrounding prayer has dealt with prayer at graduation ceremonies. In 1992, the U.S. Supreme Court decided *Lee v. Weisman*, which held that prayer at graduation is unconstitutional as a violation of the Establishment Clause.[42] The prayer at question in *Lee* was delivered by a rabbi, who was chosen by the school principal. Although the prayer was required to be nondenominational, the Court focused on the coercive effect of such prayer on the students attending the ceremony. The Court also rejected the argument that the graduation prayer was only an attempt to accommodate the desires of those students who wanted the prayer:

> What to most believers may seem nothing more than a reasonable request that the nonbeliever respect their religious practices, in a school context may appear to the nonbeliever or dissenter to be an attempt to employ the machinery of the State to enforce a religious orthodoxy.[43]

Because some students were being forced to participate in a religious practice against their will, the graduation prayer violated the Establishment Clause.

At least in the Fifth Circuit, there exists one exception to the ban on graduation prayers set forth by the Supreme Court in *Lee*. In *Jones v. Clear Creek Independent School District*,[44] which was decided shortly after *Lee*,[45] the Fifth Circuit Court of Appeals, which has jurisdiction over Texas, found constitutional a school policy that allowed student-initiated, student-led, and student-controlled graduation prayer. The court held that the prayer must be nonsectarian and nonproselytizing. The plaintiffs in *Jones* asked the Supreme Court to overturn the Fifth Circuit's decision on the basis of the *Lee* decision, but the Supreme Court declined to hear the case. For the time being, any school district that wishes to have prayer at graduation should consult an attorney before establishing a graduation prayer policy and should adhere as closely as possible to the exact policy found constitutional in *Jones*. The Fifth Circuit recently ruled in *Ingebretsen v. Jackson Public School District* that the state of Mississippi's attempt to extend the "student initiated, student led" rationale of *Jones* to other school activities, such as sporting events, was unconstitutional.[46] The Court found that prayers at middle school graduations were not permitted under the Establishment Clause. School districts located outside the boundaries of the Fifth Circuit should be especially cautious in following *Jones*, as at least two courts have explicitly disagreed with the *Jones* decision.[47]

The fact that a school event is "extracurricular" and takes place after the normal school day does not mean that prayer at the event becomes permissible. In *Jager v. Douglas County School District*, the Eleventh Circuit found that prayers at football games, delivered over the loudspeaker system prior to the game, violated the Establishment Clause.[48] This was true even though the district had established an "equal access" plan, whereby all school clubs or organizations could designate members to give the football prayers, and any student, parent, or staff member could submit their names as candidates. The student government would then randomly select the invocation speakers, which could not include ministers. The school also explicitly stated that it would not monitor the content of the invocations. The fact that football invocations were a long-standing tradition in the district did not make them constitutional. In addition to football, the Fifth Circuit found in *Doe v. Duncanville Independent School District* that group prayers by a basketball team prior to games violated the Establishment Clause where the prayers were led by the coach.[49] Finally, a federal court in Houston held that the fact that a prayer took the form of a school song, which was sung at sporting events and pep rallies, did not save the prayer from violating the Establishment Clause.[50]

Several states have recently passed statutes that either authorize or require moments of silence at the beginning of every school day. The new Texas Education Code states that "[a] school district may provide for a period of silence at the beginning of the first class of each school day during which a student may reflect or meditate."[51] The Georgia Moment of Quiet Reflection in Schools Act requires each school to start the day with a period of silence up to sixty (60) seconds.[52] The leading case on moment of silence statutes is *Wallace v. Jaffree*,[53] in which the U.S. Supreme Court struck down an Alabama statute mandating a moment of silence "for meditation or voluntary prayer." The Court focused on the purpose for the statute, which it felt was undoubtedly to return prayer to the public schools, and held that this showed an intent on the part of the legislature to endorse religion. Therefore, the statute violated the Establishment Clause.

What is important about the *Wallace* decision is that it did not simply hold that all moment of silence statutes are unconstitutional; it focused on the specific facts and circumstances surrounding Alabama's statute. A district court in Georgia has recently upheld the constitutionality of the Georgia Moment of Quiet Reflection in Schools Act. In *Brown v. Gwinnett County School District*,[54] the court also focused on the legislative purpose of the statute, but, unlike in *Wallace*, the Georgia statute had a very well-documented secular purpose; it was passed as one of three bills designed to curb school violence, and the sponsor of the bill testified at length that he felt that students needed a moment of silence in this hectic world to stop and think about the day and center themselves for what lay ahead. He had come up with the idea for the bill after reading about a school where the students gathered for a moment of quiet reflection after a series of killings. The Act also contained a provision stating that it was not intended to serve as a religious service or exercise. The court, impressed with this purpose and safeguard, ruled that the mere fact that some of the legislators undoubtedly voted for it as a "pro-prayer" statute, and that it would allow students to silently pray, did not render the statute unconstitutional.

What this will mean for the Texas statute is uncertain. Texas does not have Alabama's history of state-mandated prayer in school, but the Texas statute also does not have the well-documented legislative purpose and explicit disavowal of the Georgia statute. In fact, the Texas statute was passed as part of a monumental redrafting of the entire Education Code, so in some sense the legislators were not voting directly for or against the moment of silence provision. Only time will tell whether Texas's statute follows the path of Georgia or that of Alabama.

VI. Use of Public Facilities by Religious Groups

Schools often receive requests from religious groups who wish to use the school's facilities for purposes that might be deemed religious. These requests vary, from student groups who wish to hold Bible study meetings after school, to requests from outside churches to use a school auditorium for weekly religious services. The general rule is that public schools are not traditional public forums, and a school may exercise the right to refuse access to all persons during noninstructional hours.[55] A school, however, may also choose to allow access by community groups or students. Once organizations are allowed access during non-instructional hours, the school has opened its previously non-public forum and must treat all similarly-situated individuals in a similar manner. If the school allows a student group to meet on school property, it becomes subject to the Equal Access Act, which states:

> It shall be unlawful for any public secondary school which receives federal financial assistance and which has a limited open forum to deny equal access or a fair opportunity to, or discriminate against, any students who wish to conduct a meeting within that limited open forum on the basis of the religious, political, philosophical, or other content of the speech at such meetings.[56]

A limited open forum is created whenever a school grants "an offering to or opportunity for one or more noncurriculum related student groups to meet on school premises during noninstructional time."[57] The Supreme Court held in *Board of Education of Westside Community Schools v. Mergens* that even where a school allows only one noncurriculum related student group to use its premises, the Equal Access Act is triggered and the school may not deny access to other groups based on the content of their speech.[58] At least one court has held that lunchtime should be considered "noninstructional time," and that if a school permits student groups to meet during lunch, it must allow all such groups–including religious groups–to also meet during lunch.[59]

There are limitations on the actions of student groups under the Equal Access Act. Such meetings may not be school sponsored, and school personnel may not be present in any capacity other than a "nonparticipatory" one.[60] For example, in *Sease v. School District of Philadelphia*,[61] a school gospel choir had requested the use of school property for rehearsals. The school refused, based largely on the fact that the choir was led by the school secretary. The court found that the school had not violated the Equal Access Act, because the participation of the secretary eliminated the group from the protection of the Act. In *Doe v. Duncanville Independent School District*,[62] the Fifth Circuit ruled that it does not violate the free exercise, free association, or free speech rights of school employees when the school district prevents them from participating in student prayers. In an earlier phase of the *Doe* litigation, the Fifth Circuit ruled that the Equal Access Act only applies to "noncurricular" groups, and that therefore a basketball team that prayed before each game was not protected by the Act because it was an extracurricular group, rather than a noncurricular one.[63]

Where a school has allowed nonstudent groups to use its facilities, use by other groups is generally regulated by the First Amendment of the United States Constitution. The leading case in this area is *Lamb's Chapel v. Center Moriches School District*.[64] In *Lamb's Chapel,* a church asked a school if it could show a film series that dealt with raising children from a "Christian perspective." The school denied the request, claiming that if it permitted the church to use its facilities, it would violate the Establishment Clause. The Supreme Court found that the denial violated the Free Speech Clause of the First Amendment by discriminating between groups on the basis of their speech. For example, where one group could use the school to show a film series on raising children from a legal or financial point of view, a different group could not show the religious point of view. The Court found that allowing the church to show its film would not violate the Establishment Clause. Under the circumstances surrounding the showing of the films, the court concluded there would be no chance that the community would think the school district was promoting religion in general or any specific creed by permitting the showing of the film.

The lesson that courts appear to have learned from *Lamb's Chapel* is that religious speech is not, by itself, a specific category of speech that may be excluded. Rather, the religious perspective is a separate and permissible viewpoint on a wide variety of secular subjects. In *Good News/Good Sports Club v. School District of the City of Ladue*,[65] a school district passed a policy that limited use of its facilities from 3-6 p.m. to the district's athletic groups and to all scouting groups. The policy was in reaction to complaints from citizens concerning the Club, which had met at the school since 1986 and which promoted religious, though nondenominational, moral development of students. The Boy Scouts were permitted to continue meeting from 3-6 p.m. because of the district's "long-standing tradition of cooperation with scout programs."[66] Following the rationale of *Lamb's Chapel*, the court compared the Scouts–which promoted a secular moral development of students–and the Club, which promoted religious moral development. Because the policy allowed one perspective but not the other, it constituted unconstitutional viewpoint discrimination and therefore violated the First Amendment.

In *Shumway v. Albany County School District No. One Board of Education*, a district court followed the holding in *Lamb's Chapel* and ruled that when a school has an open door policy that allows many groups to use its facilities, denying a group of students the right to hold a private religious baccalaureate in the school gym prior to graduation would violate the First Amendment.[67] In some ways, this case appears to conflict with decisions like *Lee v. Weisman*,[68] which denied the right to pray at graduations. The key distinction, however, is the past use of school property permitted by the district. In *Lee*, the court found that graduation ceremonies were not traditional open forums of the sort that would permit students to speak on any topic they liked. *Shumway*, however, dealt with a broader range of school property, which had been available for general use by the public in the past. The plaintiff students argued, and the court agreed, that once the school building had been opened for indiscriminate use by the general public, the school could not exclude groups based on the group's purpose or speech, as long as the use of the building by the group did not interfere with the school's educational program.

The Supreme Court has extended the neutrality rationale of both *Mergens* and *Lamb's Chapel* to student group funding. In *Rosenberger v. Rector & Visitors of the University of Virginia*,[69] the court ruled that a university's refusal to fund a Christian-oriented student newspaper was unconstitutional viewpoint discrimination, where the university funded all other student publications. The university argued that it had to deny funding to avoid violating the Establishment Clause. As it did in *Mergens* and *Lamb's Chapel*, the court emphasized that the Christian-oriented newspaper was only one player in a neutral game: "More than once have we rejected the position that the Establishment Clause even justifies, much less requires, a refusal to extend free speech rights to religious speakers who participate in broad-reaching government programs neutral in design."[70] The court rejected the university's concern that it would be seen as endorsing the newspaper's religious orientation as "not a plausible fear."[71]

VII. The Distribution of Religious Literature

Another issue increasingly facing schools is when they may allow, or must prohibit, the distribution of religious material on school grounds during school hours. The distribution of written material is considered speech protected by the First Amendment.[72] Generally, schools have argued that this right is balanced by the school's need to prevent a violation of the Establishment Clause. In *Hedges v. Wauconda Community Unit School District No. 118*, the court held that a school district may not forbid the distribution of religious material on school grounds on the basis that persons might perceive the school to be endorsing the material and, hence, religion.[73] The court did hold, however, that the school could establish reasonable time, place, and manner restrictions on the distribution of the literature. In general, the current position of the courts is that students at the secondary level are mature enough to understand that a school does not support or endorse speech merely because it allows it on a nondiscriminatory basis.[74] Because the courts have recently been treating the distribution of religious material on school campuses as more of a free speech issue than a religion issue, this topic is covered in greater detail in the chapter on the First Amendment rights of students.

VIII. The Religious Freedom Restoration Act

The Religious Freedom Restoration Act (Act) was signed into law on November 16, 1993. The stated purpose of the Act was to reverse the United States Supreme Court's decision in *Employment Division, Department of Human Resources v. Smith,*[75] which held that generally-applicable statutes that burden an individual's exercise of his or her religion do not violate the First Amendment. Under the new legislation, a governmental entity may impose a substantial burden upon a person's free exercise of religion only if the government establishes that it has a compelling governmental interest and that it has adopted the least restrictive means to further that interest. The Act further states that it shall not be "construed to affect, interpret, or in any way address that portion of the First Amendment prohibiting laws respecting the establishment of religion" (referred to in this section as the "Establishment Clause").

The effect of the Act on school districts remains uncertain. The *Smith* decision had been somewhat of a surprise and a departure from previous case law. Few cases were decided that relied explicitly on the decision in *Smith*, so in some ways the Act merely returns First Amendment analysis to what it had been prior to 1990. One of the few courts to have interpreted the Act so far held that a school district's policy of not allowing knives on school property violated the religious rights of three Khalsa Sikh children, whose faith requires them to carry a kirpan, or knife, at all times. In *Cheema v. Thompson,*[76] the Ninth Circuit upheld the district court's injunction requiring the school district to allow the children to attend school with their kirpans pending the trial on the merits. The Court found that the no-knife policy imposed a substantial burden on the tenets of the students' religion, and that while student safety was undoubtedly a compelling governmental interest, the school district had failed to show that it had adopted the least restrictive means possible to ensure safety. Further interpretation will have to wait until the courts have a chance to decide exactly how the Act has changed the interpretation of the First Amendment. One thing does seem likely, though: the Act will increase the tension that exists at the heart of the First Amendment between the Establishment Clause and the Free Exercise Clause.

ENDNOTES

[1] Clever v. Cherry Hill Township Bd. of Educ., 838 F. Supp. 929, 936 (D.N.J. 1993) (quoting John Milton, *Paradise Lost*, Bk. II, lines 591-94).

[2] Cantwell v. Connecticut, 310 U.S. 296, 60 S. Ct. 900 (1940).

[3] Wiley v. Franklin, 468 F. Supp. 133 (E.D. Tenn. 1979).

[4] *See, e.g.*, Edwards v. Aguillard, 482 U.S. 578, 583-84, 107 S. Ct. 2573, 2577 (1987).
[5] Lemon v. Kurtzman, 403 U.S. 602, 91 S. Ct. 2105 (1971).
[6] Lee v. Weisman, 112 S. Ct. 2649 (1992).
[7] *See* Lamb's Chapel v. Center Moriches Union Free Sch. Dist., 113 S. Ct. 2141 (1993) (J. Scalia, *concurring*). Justice Scalia's view of the *Lemon* test bears repeating: "Like some ghoul in a late night horror movie that repeatedly sits up in its grave and shuffles abroad, after being repeatedly killed and buried, *Lemon* stalks our Establishment Clause jurisprudence once again, frightening the little children and the school attorneys of Center Moriches Union Free Sch. Dist." *Id.* at 2149-50. *See also* Board of Educ. of the Kiryas Joel Sch. Dist. v. Grumet, 114 S. Ct. 2481, 2500 (1994) (O'Connor, J., *concurring*) ("As the Court's opinion today shows, the slide away from *Lemon*'s unitary approach is well under way. A return to *Lemon*, even if possible, would likely be futile . . . .").
[8] *See Grumet*, 114 S. Ct. at 2481.
[9] Rosenberger v. Rector & Visitors of the Univ. of Va., 115 S. Ct. 2510 (1995).
[10] Hernandez v. Commissioner, 490 U.S. 680, 699, 109 S. Ct. 2136, 2148 (1989); Wisconsin v. Yoder, 406 U.S. 205, 215, 92 S. Ct. 1526, 1533 (1972).
[11] *Yoder*, 406 U.S. at 230-31, 92 S. Ct. at 1540-41.
[12] McCollum v. Board of Educ., 333 U.S. 203, 235, 68 S. Ct. 461, 477 (1948) (Jackson, J., *concurring*).
[13] *See, e.g.*, Epperson v. Arkansas, 393 U.S. 97, 106, 89 S. Ct. 266, 271 (1968).
[14] School Dist. of Abington v. Schempp, 374 U.S. 203, 83 S. Ct. 1560 (1963).
[15] Roberts v. Madigan, 702 F. Supp. 1505, 1513 (D. Colo. 1989), *aff'd*, 921 F.2d 1047 (10th Cir. 1990).
[16] Doe v. Human, 725 F. Supp. 1503 (W.D. Ark. 1989).
[17] Breen v. Runkel, 614 F. Supp. 355 (W.D. Mich. 1985); Fink v. Board of Educ., 442 A.2d 837 (Pa. Commw. Ct. 1982).
[18] *Id.*
[19] Roberts v. Madigan, 921 F.2d 1047, 1055-56 (10th Cir. 1990).
[20] Brown v. Hot, Sexy and Safer Productions, Inc., 68 F.3d 525, 538-39 (1st Cir. 1995); Mozert v. Hawkins County Bd. of Educ., 827 F.2d 1058, 1068 (6th Cir. 1987) (quoting Bethel Sch. Dist. No. 403 v. Fraser, 478 U.S. 675, 683-84, 106 S. Ct. 3159, 3164 (1986)).
[21] *Id.* at 1066.
[22] *See* Smith v. Board of Sch. Comm'rs of Mobile County, 655 F. Supp. 939, 980-983 (S.D. Ala. 1987). Although the district court's decision was overturned by the Eleventh Circuit, it contains a lengthy and fairly useful discussion of secular humanism.
[23] Smith v. Board of Sch. Comm'rs of Mobile County, 827 F.2d 684 (11th Cir. 1987).
[24] Grove v. Mead Sch. Dist., 753 F.2d 1528 (9th Cir. 1985).
[25] Doe v. Human, 725 F. Supp. 1503 (W.D. Ark. 1989).
[26] Brown v. Woodland Joint Unified Sch. Dist., 27 F.3d 1373 (9th Cir. 1994); Fleischfresser v. Directors of Sch. Dist. 200, 15 F.3d 680 (7th Cir. 1994).
[27] Lynch v. Donnelly, 465 U.S. 668, 104 S. Ct. 1355 (1984).
[28] County of Allegheny v. American Civil Liberties Union, 492 U.S. 573, 109 S. Ct. 3086 (1989).
[29] This highly fact-specific inquiry has been dubbed "the Three Plastic Animals" test by the Fifth Circuit. *See* Jones v. Clear Creek Indep. Sch. Dist., 977 F.2d 963, 965 n.4 (5th Cir. 1992).
[30] Capitol Square Review & Advisory Bd. v. Pinette, 115 S. Ct. 2440 (1995). *Pinette* is remarkable less for the result in the case and more for the routes the various Justices used to get there, showing a fractured view of the Establishment Clause all too common since the demise of *Lemon*.
[31] Edwards v. Aguillard, 482 U.S. 578, 583-84, 107 S. Ct. 2573, 2577 (1987); Lee v. Weisman, 112 S. Ct. 2649, 2658 (1992); School Dist. v. Ball, 473 U.S. 373, 390, 105 S. Ct. 3216, 3226 (1985).
[32] Stone v. Graham, 449 U.S. 39, 101 S. Ct. 192 (1980).
[33] Washegesic v. Bloomingdale Pub. Sch., 813 F. Supp. 559 (W.D. Mich. 1993), *aff'd*, 33 F.3d 679 (1994).

[34] Joki v. Board of Educ. of Schuylerville Cent. Sch. Dist., 745 F. Supp. 823 (N.D.N.Y. 1990).
[35] Kunselman v. Western Reserve Local Sch. Dist., 70 F.3d 931 (6th Cir. 1995). The fact that the Plaintiffs were personally offended by the mascot was insufficient under the reasonable observer test. It also didn't hurt that the school had adopted its mascot to copy Duke University, which in turn had copied an elite corps of WWII French alpine soldiers. The court couldn't believe that either Duke or the French had meant to advance Satanism, either.
[36] Clever v. Cherry Hill Township Bd. of Educ., 838 F. Supp. 929 (D.N.J. 1993).
[37] Engel v. Vitale, 370 U.S. 421, 424-25, 82 S. Ct. 1261, 1264 (1963).
[38] *Id.*
[39] *See, e.g., Jones*, 977 F.2d at 966-67.
[40] *See* Ingebretsen v. Jackson Pub. Sch. Dist., 1996 WL 205 (5th Cir. 1996).
[41] *Engel*, 370 U.S. at 430, 82 S. Ct. at 1266-67 ("Neither the fact that the prayer may be nondenominationally neutral nor the fact that its observance on the part of the students is voluntary can serve to free it from the limitations of the Establishment Clause."); Jaffree v. Wallace, 705 F.2d 1526, *aff'd*, 472 U.S. 38, 105 S. Ct. 2479 (1985).
[42] Lee v. Weisman, 112 S. Ct. 2649 (1992).
[43] *Id.* at 2658.
[44] *Jones, supra.*
[45] *Jones* was actually pending before the Supreme Court at the time that it decided *Lee*. The Supreme Court vacated the original Fifth Circuit opinion in *Jones* and remanded it for a second decision in light of the *Lee* decision.
[46] 1996 WL 205 (5th Cir. 1996).
[47] Harris v. Joint Sch. Dist. No. 241, 41 F.3d 447 (9th Cir. 1994), *vacated*, 115 S. Ct. 2604 (1995); Gearon v. Loudoun County Sch. Bd., 844 F. Supp. 1097 (E.D. Vir. 1993). Because the United States Supreme Court vacated *Harris* and remanded it without reaching the merits of the case, it is unlikely the Court will resolve the dispute between the Circuits over student-initiated prayer in the near future.
[48] Jager v. Douglas County Sch. Dist., 862 F.2d 824 (11th Cir. 1989).
[49] Doe v. Duncanville Indep. Sch. Dist., 994 F.2d 160 (5th Cir. 1993).
[50] Doe v. Aldine Indep. Sch. Dist., 563 F. Supp. 883 (S.D. Tex. 1982).
[51] Tex. Educ. Code § 25.082(b).
[52] O.C.G.A. § 20-2-1050 (Supp. 1995).
[53] 472 U.S. 30, 105 S. Ct. 2479 (1985).
[54] 895 F. Supp. 1564 (N.D. Ga. 1995).
[55] *Lamb's Chapel*, 113 S. Ct. at 2146.
[56] 20 U.S.C. § 4071.
[57] 20 U.S.C. § 4071(b).
[58] Board of Educ. of Westside Community Sch. v. Mergens, 496 U.S. 226, 110 S. Ct. 2356 (1990).
[59] Ceniceros v. Board of Trustees, 66 F.3d 1535, 1537-38 (9th Cir. 1995).
[60] 20 U.S.C. § 4071(c)(3).
[61] Sease v. Sch. Dist. of Phila., 811 F. Supp. 183 (E.D. Pa. 1993).
[62] Doe v. Duncanville Indep. Sch. Dist., 70 F.3d 402, 406 (5th Cir. 1995).
[63] Doe v. Duncanville Indep. Sch. Dist., 994 F.2d 160 (5th Cir. 1993).
[64] *Lamb's Chapel, supra.*
[65] Good News/Good Sports Club v. School Dist. of the City of Ladue, 28 F.3d 1501 (8th Cir. 1944).
[66] *Id.* at 1503.
[67] Shumway v. Albany County Sch. Dist. No. One Bd. of Educ., 826 F. Supp. 1320 (D. Wyo. 1993).
[68] Lee v. Weisman, *supra.*
[69] 115 S. Ct. 2510 (1995).
[70] *Id.* at 2522.
[71] *Id.* at 2523.
[72] United States v. Grace, 461 U.S. 171, 176, 103 S. Ct. 1702, 1706 (1983).
[73] Hedges v. Wauconda Community Unit Sch. Dist. No. 118, 9 F.3d 1295 (7th Cir. 1993).

[73] Hedges v. Wauconda Community Unit Sch. Dist. No. 118, 9 F.3d 1295 (7th Cir. 1993).
[74] *See, e.g.,* Mergens, 496 U.S. at 250, 110 S. Ct. at 2372; Slotterback v. Interboro Sch. Dist., 766 F. Supp. 280, 295 (E.D. Pa. 1991).
[75] Employment Division, Dep't of Human Resources v. Smith, 494 U.S. 872, 110 S. Ct. 1595 (1990).
[76] 67 F.3d 883 (9th Cir. 1995).

ENVIRONMENTAL ISSUES RELATING TO PUBLIC SCHOOLS AND JUNIOR COLLEGES IN TEXAS

By: Tracy D. Hester and Cynthia A.M. Stroman

I. Introduction

Environmental regulations designed to protect public health and the environment now impact not only industry, but virtually every aspect of society: our worksites, our homes, and our schools. The regulations apply in the context of all environmental media–air, water and land–and generally contain comprehensive requirements that are supported by a rigorous enforcement scheme. In many instances, schools, school officials and school employees are subject to federal, state, and/or local environmental laws, regulations and ordinances.

Schools and school officials have felt the effects of environmental laws and regulations in many contexts. Employees and students have made claims of exposure to hazardous materials. Removal of asbestos has resulted in temporary or permanent closure of some school buildings. The release of toxic materials from nearby landfills or industrial sites has required evacuations or school closings. Governmental agencies have also subjected schools to enforcement actions for cleanup of hazardous substances or leaks from petroleum storage tanks. Consequently, school officials cannot afford being uninformed of environmental regulations.

This chapter provides a broad overview of many of the federal and corresponding Texas environmental laws and regulations applicable to academic institutions. It is not exhaustive, but it should provide a helpful reference point for academic institutions.

II. Discussion

A. Air Emissions

1. Clean Air Act

The Clean Air Act ("CAA") regulates the nation's air quality and limits the emission of specific harmful substances into the air. The CAA regulates many aspects of school operations. For example, school power plants, laboratory chemicals, or solvents may emit volatile organic compounds or substances considered to be hazardous air pollutants, both of which are regulated under the CAA. The following discussion addresses the CAA's requirements concerning air quality in the context of ambient air emissions from stationary and mobile sources, and employee trip reduction programs.

(a) Ambient Air Emissions from Stationary Sources.

Federally mandated ambient air quality standards are designed to ensure the quality of the air to which the general public is exposed. The CAA focuses on limiting emissions of air pollutants from mobile sources (buses and cars) and from stationary sources (heaters, heating plants, furnaces, boilers andother combustion units, and solid waste incineration units). The regulations require operators of stationary sources to obtain a permit before construction or modification of regulated sources, to install pollution control equipment, and to meet specified emissions standards and monitoring requirements.[1] In Texas, any source that may emit air contaminants must obtain a permit from the Texas Natural Resources Conservation Commission ("TNRCC") unless the source appears on the list of exempted facilities or was constructed prior to, and remained unmodified since, September 1, 1971.[2]

Air emissions or certain hazardous air pollutants–e.g., paints, solvents, or cleaners–are regulated under the federal CAA as well as under the parallel Texas Clean Air Act.[3] Air emissions from adjacent facilities may also be of concern to schools, particularly schools attended by students who may be very sensitive to environmental effects, such as very young children or pregnant students. Atmospheric conditions, topography, and other factors influence the movement of pollutants in the ambient air and could result in potentially hazardous conditions in receptor properties downwind. Schools operating in the vicinity of industrial areas should be aware that air quality may be adversely impacted in their area as a result of accidental releases of air pollutants, or otherwise. In certain circumstances, contingency plans should reflect such special conditions and close coordination with industry may be appropriate.

(b) Ambient Air Emissions from Mobile Sources

Under Texas law, any school district operating more than fifty (50) vehicles used for transporting school children must operate thirty percent (30%) of those vehicles on alternative fuels (clean fuels) by September 1, 1994, and more than fifty percent (50%) on alternative fuels by September 1, 1996.[4] Alternative fuel is defined by the TNRCC in 30 T.A.C. 114.11 to mean compressed natural gas, liquefied petroleum gas, methanol or methanol/gasoline blends, ethanol or ethanol/gasoline blends or electricity. As a direct result of this regulation, county and local school districts may not purchase or lease any motor vehicle used for transporting school children unless that vehicle can be fueled by alternative fuels.[5]

(c) Employee Trip Reduction Programs

Many states, including Texas, have established programs that require employers to reduce work-related vehicle trips and miles traveled by employees. In Houston and other severe ozone non-attainment areas, the original program required employers of 100 or more people to increase the average passenger occupancy per vehicle by at least twenty-five percent (25%). The original program also instructed affected employers to register with the TNRCC by September 1, 1993; submit an approvable Employer Trip Reduction Plan ("ETR Plan") beginning in May 1994 through November 1994, depending on the number of employees; and achieve compliance with the ETR Plan no later than two years after the initial submittal deadline.[6]

In April 1995, however, Governor Bush signed legislation that suspended the ETR Plan for one-hundred and eighty (180) days and allowed for 45-day extensions of the suspension at the Governor's discretion. In December 1995, Congress amended the federal CAA to make the ETR Plan optional. Consequently, TNRCC has proposed the repeal of the ETR Plan regulations.

2. Indoor Air Quality

Occupational safety and health authorities traditionally have taken the lead on regulating indoor air quality. As CAA regulations are reviewed and improved, however, there is additional focus on indoor air quality as an environmental concern for any building occupant, whether in the context of employment or otherwise. In light of the current focus on indoor air, academic institutions should make the quality of indoor air a primary concern.

Perhaps the most common example of an indoor air concern is asbestos. For many years, building materials used for insulation, fireproofing, flooring, or other purposes contained asbestos. The hazardous air pollutant standards address asbestos emissions from building renovation and demolition operations.[7] The Asbestos Hazard Emergency Response Act ("AHERA") establishes a comprehensive regulatory framework for schools to identify and abate asbestos hazards in school buildings.[8] These regulations are designed to prevent or minimize the release of asbestos from building materials into the school's indoor air. EPA's prior policy on asbestos in schools was to manage such asbestos in-place. This policy required schools to survey for friable asbestos and generally to enclose or encapsulate such asbestos.

In 1994 and 1995, however, OSHA promulgated new asbestos regulations that impose additional burdens on employers such as schools. The new policy requires employers to perform initial monitoring of all employees who are or who may reasonably be expected to be exposed to asbestos above the permissible exposure limit. Additionally, all surfacing material, thermal system insulation, and asphalt and vinyl flooring material installed in 1980 or earlier must be treated as asbestos-containing material ("ACM") until the employer demonstrates otherwise. Consequently, a school must perform a full asbestos survey to identify the presence, location and quantity of any ACM, and inform employees of this information. The new policy also imposes labeling and record keeping requirements.

Asbestos is the best known, but not the only, indoor pollutant. As Congress and environmental agencies focus on indoor air quality, other common indoor air pollutants are being identified and addressed. They include volatile organic compounds, metals, carbon dioxide, carbon monoxide, microorganisms, aeroallergens, adhesives, solvents, and formaldehyde. Such indoor air contaminants may result in serious health risks to faculty and students, including nausea, dizziness, and skin rashes.

Environmental regulations in many cases do not yet directly regulate these pollutants in the indoor context, but various incidents of "sick-building" syndrome have called attention to the issue and caused school officials to become involved in assessment and remediation activities. Schools should closely monitor such conditions since regulatory requirements and toxic tort liability may result. Academic institutions may also want to assess the adequacy of their indoor air management practices, such as ventilation systems, to minimize potential toxic tort liability.

B. Water Discharges

Water quality regulations relating to surface water, storm water, groundwater, and drinking water also permeate the school environment as discussed below.

1. Surface Water

As in the air programs, the flagship of the surface water quality regulatory framework is a permit system. The Clean Water Act ("CWA") establishes comprehensive permitting requirements under the National Pollutant Discharge Elimination System, which apply to direct dischargers of pollutants to rivers, streams, or other surface water bodies.[9] Such permits establish limitations on the volume and nature of pollutants that may be discharged by the regulated facility, and may require the discharging facility to install equipment to treat the water before discharge.

Many school facilities are indirect dischargers of domestic sewage and other school wastewaters into a publicly-owned treatment works ("POTW") operated by a city or other local municipality or entity. In those situations, a permit like the one described above may not be required, but the school's discharge generally must be approved by the POTW and must meet certain pretreatment standards, including pH levels, flammability, metal content, biochemical oxygen demand content, etc. Such pretreatment standards are generally established by agreement with the POTW or by self-implementing regulations and are directly enforceable against the discharger without the need for a permit.[10] Schools with construction projects that exceed five (5) acres must also obtain a storm water discharge permit.[11] If the school wishes to be covered by the General Permit for Storm Water Discharges from Construction Sites, it should file a notice of intent at least two (2) days prior to initiation of construction activities.[12]

2. Storm Water

The CWA also regulates discharges of storm water, including snow melt runoff, surface runoff, and other drainage, to rivers, streams or other surface bodies. Storm water discharges are regulated if they are "associated with industrial activity" or associated with construction operations in excess of five (5) acres. As a general rule, schools are not subject to the storm water regulations because, based on the Standard Industrial Code for academic institutions, they do not meet the "associated with industrial activity" requirement. Academic institutions, however, are subject to storm water regulations for construction activities that disturb five or more acres of land.[13] Schools with construction projects which exceed five (5) acres must obtain a storm water discharge permit.[14] If the school wishes to be covered by the general permit for storm water discharges from construction sites, it should file a notice of intent at least two (2) days prior to initiation of construction activities.[15]

3. Groundwater

Environmental regulations affecting groundwater may also significantly impact schools. The use of groundwater, for example, may be subject to permit requirements that apply to the installation of operation of water withdrawal wells. These requirements may affect the location or depth of the wells and may limit the amount of water that can be drawn from the wells and its designated use. Conversely, the injection of fluids into the ground where they may reach groundwater also may be subject to the injection well permit requirements or other regulatory limitations.

4. Drinking Water

The Safe Drinking Water Act ("SDWA") regulates drinking water systems and establishes national standards for levels of contaminants in drinking water and for the protection of certain aquifers.[16] Although academic institutions often receive drinking water from municipal or private water systems, some schools operate their own systems. Schools operating their own systems may need to meet certain water quality standards and requirements, including testing, reporting, record keeping and notice to the public of failure to meet standards.

Whether the water entering the school is from on-site or off-site, concerns regarding its lead content are often raised. Sources of lead in drinking water may include lead pipes, solder, flux, fixtures, or other lead-containing parts in the plumbing or drinking water system, such as lead-lined tanks in water coolers. The SDWA prohibits the use of such substances in drinking water systems by requiring lead-free materials.[17]

C. Land Disposal

1. Hazardous Wastes

The Resource Conservation and Recovery Act ("RCRA") and its Texas counterpart govern the generation, handling, and disposal of solid and hazardous wastes on land.[18] Such regulations apply to generators of solid or hazardous wastes, and to owners or operators of treatment, storage or disposal facilities. Generators are required to determine whether the waste is hazardous when generated and thus regulated, and to proceed in accordance with strict shipping and record keeping requirements designed to ensure that the waste is delivered to a properly permitted disposal facility. Owners and operators of hazardous waste treatment, storage, or disposal facilities are subject to separate comprehensive requirements.

Most academic institutions produce some volume of hazardous waste and are regulated as generators. For example, chemical use in laboratories will result in the need for disposal of excess chemicals, mixtures, reaction products, acids, etc. The developing solutions used by photography shops contain silver compounds and are, therefore, hazardous waste. Additionally, paints, solvents, oils from capacitors, or transformers containing PCBs are routinely used in schools and may be considered hazardous waste when discarded.

Schools generating reportable quantities of hazardous substances on a monthly basis may be regulated as generators. The classification of a school as a generator or a storage facility will depend upon the volume of waste generated and the on-site duration of the storage. Schools that generate less than 100kg/month of hazardous waste (approximately 1/2 of a 55 gallon drum) are generally exempt from RCRA's generator regulations as a "conditionally exempt small quantity generator." Schools generating between 100kg and 1000 kg/month meet the "small quantity generator" standard and, although not exempt from RCRA, are subject to less stringent RCRA generator requirements.

Most schools may benefit from an exemption from classification as a storage facility if hazardous wastes are stored on the generator's site for fewer than ninety (90) days. Long-term storage, or on site treatment or disposal of hazardous wastes normally would require a permit and compliance with rigorous standards.

2. Underground Storage Tanks

The solid waste regulatory program also focuses on releases of petroleum or other substances from underground storage tanks ("USTs"). The regulations generally require school districts that own or operate USTs which contain petroleum or other designated substances to comply with the TNRCC and U.S. Environment Protection Agency regulations on USTs.[19] Such regulations include: (1) registering new and existing tanks; (2) complying with the construction requirements for new and existing tanks; (3) installing leak detection and monitoring equipment; (4) complying with financial responsibility requirements in the form of self insurance, guarantee, insurance coverage, surety bond, letter of credit, or trust fund; (5) inspecting and/or monitoring tanks to ensure that they are not leaking; (6) taking corrective action in the event any such problems are detected; and (7) disposing of contaminated soil in accordance with the regulations. Problems that have gone undetected for years may give rise to costly remediation obligations.

In June 1990, EPA suspended the deadline for compliance by local governments until EPA proposed additional methods for local governments to comply with the financial responsibility requirements, such as a bond rating test for local governments and standards for local government financial guarantees.[20]

EPA promulgated new rules in 1994, and the compliance deadline for local government entities was February 18, 1994. Schools owning or operating USTs must demonstrate financial responsibility in the per-occurrence amount of $500,000 and in the annual aggregate amount of $1 million.[21] The regulations provide several mechanisms by which an owner or operator may provide this financial assurance.[22]

D. Other Toxic Substances

Present environmental regulations also focus on the use and handling of specific toxic materials. Toxic substances subject to regulation include lead paint; poisons and chemicals, such as those found in science laboratories; janitorial and other cleaning supplies; pesticides; rodenticides; and lawn care products and applications.

Academic institutions should ensure that use of registered pesticides, including disinfectants, is conducted in a manner which is consistent with the pesticide's labeling. In addition, many schools are licensed to handle low-level radioactive wastes for use in physics laboratories or medical facilities. Such radioactive wastes are subject to comprehensive and stringent regulation under the Nuclear Regulatory Commission Act.

E. Environmental Liability from Real Estate Transactions

1. Environmental Laws or Regulations that Create Liabilities

Environmental laws or regulations that create liabilities or restrict land use may substantially impact a school district's real estate transactions. For example, the Comprehensive Environmental Response, Compensation and Liability Act ("CERCLA") creates liability for present and past owners and operators of property contaminated with hazardous wastes or pollutants or contaminants.[23] The Resource Conservation and Recovery Act ("RCRA") and the Texas Solid Waste Disposal Act regulate USTs and confer liability on present and past owners and operators of property contaminated with petroleum and certain other substances released from USTs. The Toxic Substances Control Act ("TSCA") creates liability for owners and operators for on-site conditions, including polychlorinated biphenyls ("PCBs"), radon, lead and asbestos.[24] Finally, the Asbestos Hazard Emergency Response Act ("AHERA") requires inspection for asbestos containing materials and implementation of response actions for dangerous asbestos conditions.[25]

2. Environmental Laws and Regulations that Restrict Land Use

On the other hand, other environmental programs restrict land use. The Endangered Species Act restricts development in certain critical habitats of endangered species, and restricts development that would harm an endangered species. The Federal Water Pollution Control Act, Section 404, also restricts development in areas designated as wetlands, limits the draining or filling of wetlands, and requires permits before construction commences. Finally, the National Historic Preservation Act restricts development of historical properties.

3. Minimization of Environmental Liability

Purchasers of real estate may identify, quantify, and allocate environmental risk prior to purchase. Purchasers can quantify and minimize environmental liability by performing a due diligence review of prior land use, off-site disposal practices, remediation needs, and prior compliance practices. Purchasers may also allocate environmental risks through warranties and indemnifications.

In Texas, the voluntary cleanup program also provides sellers and purchasers with a mechanism for insulating the purchaser against liability for past contamination of a property. The program requires cleanup of the site after entering into an agreement with the TNRCC concerning the cleanup. On completion of the cleanup, TNRCC issues a certificate of completion which releases future owners and lenders from liability to the state for the contamination that was the subject of the cleanup. EPA has also agreed to refrain from enforcement action against sites that have obtained a certificate of completion.

F. Enforcement and Liability

Existing environmental laws and regulations contain ample means to ensure compliance. Enforcement provisions include civil and administrative penalties, criminal sanctions, injunctive relief, and monetary liability for the cost of correcting damage to the environment. Penalties are assessed on a daily basis and aggregate rapidly.

The environmental statutes also typically contain citizen suit provisions that allow citizens to bring actions in court for penalties to be assessed against the violator. As a general rule, citizens tend to be less tolerant of violations than government prosecutors. School officials would not want the government pursuing an enforcement action, but even less desirable would be the wrath of a parent pursuing a citizen suit.

A parallel scheme generally allows affected parties that spent funds in remediating the site to collect a percentage of those costs from responsible parties. Under the Superfund, for example, any person who incurs costs in responding to the release of a hazardous substance may file suit to recover these funds from current and past owners and operators of the facility, and from transporters or other parties that may have contributed to the contamination. Schools may be subjected to liability under CERCLA either because of problems that occur at sites that schools acquire, at sites that schools owned or operated in the past, or at third party sites to which the school shipped some of its waste materials.

Last, schools and school officials should also consider the possibility of liability for lawsuits arising out of alleged exposure to hazardous substances. These "toxic tort" lawsuits usually include common law claims of negligence and nuisance. While Texas colleges and school districts are protected from liability by governmental immunity, defense costs can be significant. Actual cases have included claims by employees and students. Sources of contaminants in these cases have been chemicals used on school property, renovations or construction, and substances arising from underground contamination.

III. Conclusion

Federal, state, and local environmental laws, regulations and ordinances govern many school operations. Activities at a school facility, like at many commercial or light-industrial facilities, may involve the emission of pollutants to the air, the discharge of pollutants to water, or the use of land in a manner that constitutes disposal of certain materials. Likewise, as with many commercial entities, schools are often involved in real property transfers that may give rise to liability. Furthermore, lead, radon, radioactive materials, pesticides, or fertilizers may also be sources of liability for academic institutions.

Schools should recognize that environmental regulations are comprehensive and require strict compliance. Schools and school officials should familiarize themselves with these requirements, and strive for full compliance with all federal, state and local environmental laws, regulations, and ordinances.

ENDNOTES

[1] 42 U.S.C. §§ 7401-7671.
[2] 30 T.A.C. § 116.110.
[3] *See generally,* Control of Air Pollution from Volatile Organic Compounds, 30 T.A.C. §§ 115, *et seq.*
[4] 1 T.A.C. §§113.23, 125.65.
[5] 1 T.A.C. § 113.23.
[6] 30 Tex. Admin. Code § 1145.21.
[7] 40 C.F.R. Part 61, Subpart M.
[8] 15 U.S.C. §§ 2641-2656.
[9] 33 U.S.C. § 1342.
[10] 33 U.S.C. § 1317.
[11] 40 C.F.R. § 122.26(b)(14)(x).
[12] 40 C.F.R. § 122.28.
[13] 33 U.S.C. §1342(p).
[14] 40 C.F.R.. § 122.26(b)(14)(x).
[15] 40 C.F.R. § 122.28.
[16] 42 U.S.C. §§ 300f-300j-26.
[17] 42 U.S.C. §§ 300j-21 to 3001-24.
[18] 42 U.S.C. §§ 6901-6992k.
[19] 30 T.A.C. Chapter 334.
[20] 55 Fed. Reg. 24692 (June 18, 1990).
[21] 40 C.F.R. § 280.93; 30 T.A.C. § 334.93.
[22] 40 C.F.R. §§ 280.95-280.107; 30 T.A.C. § 334.94.
[23] 42 U.S.C. §§ 9601-9675.
[24] 15 U.S.C. §§ 2601-2672.
[25] 15 U.S.C. §§ 2641-2656.

COPYRIGHT LAW

By: Lisa A. Brown

I. Introduction

A long-standing myth in the public schools is that educators may duplicate copyrighted materials without permission so long as their purpose is non-profit and educational. In fact, the copyright statute does not contain any special exemptions for educators. This chapter will provide an overview of the copyright laws and will suggest practical tips for ensuring compliance with the law.

Contained primarily in the United States Code and called the "Copyright Remedies Clarification Act of 1990" (Act), the law of copyright[1] gives authors and owners of original materials the exclusive right to use or duplicate those materials. A copyright is a form of "intellectual property" designed to encourage creative expression by ensuring that those who produce particular works may benefit from them, financially and otherwise.[2] Copyrights are given for materials such as literary works; magazines; music, both printed and performed; dramatic works, both printed and performed; graphic and sculptural works; motion pictures, including television programs; and computer software.[3] Copyright laws affect numerous aspects of school operation, including teaching, researching, publishing teaching materials or manuscripts, printing the school newspaper or yearbook, and duplicating television programs or computer software.

The law of copyright protects copyright owners by providing criminal and civil penalties against individuals who infringe copyrights.[4] The law describes the copyright owner's rights and articulates the limited situations in which another individual legally may "infringe" those rights. The law does not protect ideas, concepts, or systems.[5]

II. Rights of a Copyright Holder

A copyright holder has the exclusive right to reproduce the work, to prepare derivative works, to distribute copies for sale or lease, and to perform or display the work in public. An individual owns a copyright when he reduces his or her work into some tangible form.[6] The individual need not register the copyright unless the work was created prior to 1978 or if the copyright is being infringed. Registration is a prerequisite to filing an infringement lawsuit.[7]

III. Employee-Created Works

When an employee of a school district or college creates a work, the school district is considered the author for copyright purposes. Section 201(b) of the Act–the "Works Made for Hire" doctrine–states that the employer is the author "unless the parties have expressly agreed otherwise in a written instrument signed by them." A work made for hire is something produced within the scope of the employee's employment and includes instructional materials and workbooks. As the copyright holder, the district may change or distribute the work in any manner it chooses. A school district may adopt a policy providing that the district is the sole owner; that the district and the employee will jointly own the property; or that the district merely has a right of first refusal.

IV. Fair Use of Copyrighted Materials

In limited circumstances, an individual lawfully may infringe a copyright under the doctrine of "fair use." The doctrine is an exemption from liability. An individual may make "fair use" of copyrighted materials "for purposes such as criticism, comment, news reporting, teaching (including multiple copies for classroom use), scholarship or research." In determining what constitutes fair use, courts consider the following factors:

1. the purpose and character of the use, including whether such use is of a commercial nature or is for nonprofit educational purposes;
2. the nature of the copyrighted work;
3. the amount and substantiality of the portion used in relation to the copyrighted work as a whole; and
4. the effect of the use upon the potential market for or value of the copyrighted work.

The factors are not exclusive but merely illustrative.[8] The doctrine of fair use is an equitable rule of reason, and each case must be decided on its own facts. Consider the case of a teacher who makes 20 copies of an algebra workbook to avoid having to pay $20 per workbook. Contrast that scenario with a teacher who makes 20 copies of an out-of-print booklet. In the first case, the publisher has lost $400; in the second case, the publisher arguably has lost no income because the product is no longer for sale. Similarly, consider the teacher who duplicates half of a poetry book. Compare that situation to a teacher who distributes a single poem from two books. The first teacher should have ordered enough books for her entire class if she knew she would be relying so heavily on the book.

The Supreme Court has stated that the user should ask himself: "Would the reasonable copyright owner have consented to the use?" The fair use doctrine applies to published and unpublished works.[9] Therefore, documents such as unpublished letters or a yet-to-be published manuscript are subject to the doctrine.

As stated in the introduction, despite the unique and pervasive needs of educators, there is no special "fair use" rule or privilege for school districts or colleges. Rather than adopt a specific statutory exemption, the House Committee on the Judiciary endorsed a private agreement between the representatives of the publishing industry and the education community. The agreement contained guidelines for photocopying that appear in the legislative history in the codified statute. These guidelines state the minimum, not the maximum, standards for educational fair use as to books, periodicals, and music. The guidelines state that there may be instances where photocopying that does not fall within the guidelines is nonetheless fair use. Although these guidelines are not "law," courts often consult the guidelines when deciding cases.[10]

The classroom guidelines focus on three general factors: brevity (*i.e.*, quantity); spontaneity (*i.e.*, not enough time to seek permission); and cumulative effect. In essence, a teacher may copy only a small portion of a given work, must have a non-profit purpose, and must not have the intent to use the materials semester after semester.[11]

Instructors should be discouraged from collecting stories and articles and creating photocopied anthologies. The practice of making homemade anthologies or course packets has come under fire in the courts. In one case[12], several book publishers filed suit against Kinko's, a photocopy center that routinely had copied entire chapters from books without the publishers' permission. The court held that this photocopying was not fair use of these materials, despite the fact that professors had submitted their copy requests to Kinko's. The court found that Kinko's primary purpose was to make money. Kinko's did not show that its operation would be disabled if required to seek prior permission from publishers. The Kinko's case shows that any person or organization that routinely photocopies large amounts of the same materials, semester after semester, risks begin sued by the copyright owner. One of its key lessons is that permission should be requested whenever it is feasible to do so.

V. Television Broadcasts & Videotapes

Guidelines for videotaping were promulgated in 1981. The videotape guidelines for off-the-air recording establish specific timelines for maintaining and destroying recordings. The guidelines state that a recording may be retained for forty-five (45) days and may be shown no more than twice during the first ten (10) days of retention. Programs may not be recorded on a regular basis. Although a limited number of copies may be produced for legitimate teaching needs, teachers may not alter the tape recording or combine it with other recordings.

Some commentators have criticized the guidelines as overly restrictive and cumbersome.[13] This area of the law remains a difficult one. The Supreme Court examined this issue in *Sony Corp. v. Universal City Studios*,[14] in which the court held that consumers may lawfully use their videocassette recorders to record a television program for later viewing. The court emphasized that home recording was a non-profit, non-commercial fair use.

Although beneficial to consumers, the rationale in *Sony* does not shield educators from liability for unlawfully recording television programs. For example, in *Encyclopedia Britannica Corp. v. Brooks*,[15] copyright owners brought suit against an educational services board alleging copyright infringement for use of videotaped television programs. The board maintained a library of programs. By using the library, schools could avoid having to rent or purchase tapes of the programs. The court agreed with the publishers that the educational services board's practice of making videotapes was not a "fair use."

Although the *Brooks* court found infringement, it declined to use the videotape guidelines to reach its decision. Instead, the court considered the four factors of fair use enumerated above and carefully scrutinized the final factor regarding the marketability or value of the copyrighted work.

The guidelines do not apply to situations in which schools actually rent or purchase tapes. In those instances, the school is not making a copy; therefore, the market for the product is not adversely affected. However, when an instructor rents or purchases a tape, he or she should not duplicate the tape.

Although the 1981 videotape guidelines have been criticized and may be revised in the future, until new guidelines are drafted, school districts and colleges should consider the four "fair use" factors and the videotaping guidelines in assessing whether a particular act of videotaping is a "fair use." As with the photocopy guidelines, not all permissible uses are expressly addressed by the video guidelines. In the event of an infringement complaint, it will be helpful for the district to show that it made a good faith effort not to exceed fair use.

VI. Computer Software

Use of copyrighted computer software is addressed in Section 117 of the Act. Section 117 states, in part, that it is not an infringement for the owner of a computer program to copy or authorize the copy of a computer program provided:

1. the copy was created as an essential step in utilizing the program and is used in no other manner; or
2. the copy is for "archival purposes," and all copies made for this purpose are destroyed if the holder of these copies ceases to own the computer program.

The first exception recognizes that, to use a program, one must load the program on a diskette into the disk drive of a computer, which then copies the program into its memory. The second exception is the "back-up" exception. It refers to those backup copies made by the owner in case the original computer program is damaged or destroyed because of mechanical or electronic failure.[16] The accompanying manuals and written documentation for the computer software usually are covered by a separate copyright, and thus are subject to the copyright provisions and guidelines for printed materials. In view of these limited exceptions, a district should not allow students to use the district's equipment to duplicate copyrighted software. If an instructor needs numerous individual copies of a program, the district should purchase each separately. Copyright notices should be placed wherever computers are used.

VII. Works in the Public Domain

Not all works are copyrighted. Some materials are in the "public domain" and may be copied, displayed or performed without risking copyright liability. For example, most government documents are in the public domain. Other materials in the public domain are those on which the copyright has expired or on which no copyright was ever secured. For example, because William Shakespeare's plays are in the public domain, a theater group may perform "The Taming of the Shrew," without permission and for profit. "Public domain" materials include those published prior to January 1, 1978 without a copyright notice, which were not registered within five (5) years of that date.

VIII. Musical and Dramatic Performance

Does a school district have to pay a licensing fee when records are played at a school dance or when the drama club performs *Death of a*

Salesman? The copyright laws exempt certain non-profit performances in which no fee is paid to the performers and no fee is charged, unless the receipts are used for charitable or educational purposes.[17] If a school activity exceeds these requirements, the school district should pay the appropriate licensing fees.

IX. Practical Tips

First, when individuals need more than "fair use," they should be encouraged to seek permission of the copyright owner. The letter to the copyright holder should describe the purpose of the requested use and the extent of the requested use. The letter should state that the copyright holder will receive a credit line or acknowledgment in the reproduced material. The copyright holder has several options: full permission, permission with restrictions, permission for a fee, and no permission. Although some publishers will be uncooperative, many publishers are receptive to the needs of the educational community.

Each school should place notices regarding copyright law on copying machines and near computers. Section 108 of the Act states that neither a library nor its employees are liable for misuse of copy machines located in the library, so long as each machine displays a copyright law notice. Accordingly, districts should place a brief statement concerning copyright infringement directly on all copying machines or in any area where copying is done. The notice should state that individuals using the copy machines will remain liable for misuse. If the district maintains photocopy centers where teachers may submit orders, warnings should also be placed in those areas as well. The library or copy center should reserve the right to refuse to accept a copying order that, in its judgment, would violate the copyright laws.

The notices should be printed in bold type (at least 18 point) and should be displayed prominently. Copy center order forms also should contain a notice. A sample warning for self-serve machines is as follows:

> **NOTICE**
>
> AN INDIVIDUAL USING THIS MACHINE MAY MAKE A PHOTOCOPY OF A COPYRIGHTED DOCUMENT FOR THE LIMITED PURPOSE OF PRIVATE STUDY, SCHOLARSHIP, OR RESEARCH. USE OF THIS MACHINE TO PHOTOCOPY COPYRIGHTED MATERIALS IN EXCESS OF "FAIR USE" IS EXPRESSLY PROHIBITED. INDIVIDUALS WHO INFRINGE A COPYRIGHT OR EXCEED "FAIR USE" ARE SUBJECT TO CIVIL AND CRIMINAL

PENALTIES UNDER THE COPYRIGHT LAWS OF THE UNITED STATES.

A sample warning for photocopy centers is, as follows:

NOTICE

THE COPYRIGHT LAWS OF THE UNITED STATES GOVERN THE MAKING OF PHOTOCOPIES OF COPYRIGHTED MATERIALS. UNDER CERTAIN CONDITIONS SPECIFIED IN THE LAW, THIS LIBRARY MAY FURNISH A PHOTOCOPY OR OTHER REPRODUCTION. ONE CONDITION IS THAT THE COPY BE USED ONLY FOR PRIVATE STUDY, SCHOLARSHIP OR RESEARCH. IF A USER MAKES A REQUEST FOR, OR LATER USES, A PHOTOCOPY OR REPRODUCTION FOR PURPOSES IN EXCESS OF "FAIR USE," THAT USER MAY BE LIABLE FOR COPYRIGHT INFRINGEMENT. THIS INSTITUTION RESERVES THE RIGHT TO REFUSE TO ACCEPT A COPYING ORDER IF, IN ITS JUDGMENT, FULFILLMENT OF THAT ORDER WOULD VIOLATE COPYRIGHT LAWS.

Also, make copies of the school's copyright policy, along with copies of the photocopying and video guidelines, available to all faculty and staff. Publish the policies and guidelines in existing library or curriculum guides.

X. Conclusion

To protect themselves from liability, school districts and colleges should take steps to educate their faculty and staff about copyright laws. Many school personnel feel that they may reproduce copyrighted material at will for teaching purposes. This is a dangerous misconception that can conceivably lead to liability for copyright infringement. School personnel should be instructed to consider the "fair use" doctrine before reproducing materials and to consider alternatives when the elements of "fair use" do not apply.

ENDNOTES

[1] 17 U.S.C. § 101, *et seq.*

[2] *See* Basic Books Inc. v. Kinko's Graphics Corp., 758 F. Supp. 1522, 1529-30 (S.D.N.Y. 1991).

[3] 17 U.S.C. §§ 101, 102(a).
[4] *See* Copyright Remedy Clarification Act of 1990, Pub. L. No. 101-553, (amending 17 U.S.C. §§ 101-914 (1988)); *see generally* Burgoyne, "The Copyright Remedy Clarification Act of 1990: State educational institutions now face significant monetary exposure for copyright infringement," 18 J. College & Univ. L. 367 (1992).
[5] 17 U.S.C. § 102(b).
[6] 17 U.S.C. § 102.
[7] 17 U.S.C. §§ 304(a), 405(a), 411.
[8] Harper & Row Publishers v. Nation Enters., 471 U.S. 539, 105 S. Ct. 2218, 2230 (1985).
[9] Salinger v. Random House, 811 F.2d 90 (2d Cir. 1987), *opinion supplemented*, 818 F.2d 252, *cert. denied*, 484 U.S. 890 (1987).
[10] Marcus v. Rowley, 695 F.2d 1171 (9th Cir. 1983).
[11] Smith, *Classroom Use of Copyrighted Materials*, 43 Ed. Law Rptr. 1 (1988).
[12] Basic Books Inc. v. Kinko's Graphics Corp., 758 F. Supp. 1522 (S.D.N.Y. 1991).
[13] *See, e.g.*, Dratler, "To Copy or Not to Copy: The Educator's Dilemma," J. Law & Educ. *1* (Winter 1990).
[14] 464 U.S. 417, 104 S. Ct. 774 (1984).
[15] 558 F. Supp. 1247 (W.D.N.Y 1983).
[16] Micro-Sparc Inc. v. Amtype Corp., 592 F. Supp. 33, 35 (D. Mass. 1984).
[17] 17 U.S.C. §§ 304(a), 405(a)(2), 411.

REAL ESTATE ISSUES RELATING TO SCHOOL DISTRICTS AND COLLEGES

By: Gray H. Muzzy and Jeffrey J. Horner

I. Introduction

School districts and colleges are confronted with numerous different real estate issue–sales, purchases, donations, and other types of conveyances. This chapter will outline the major legal issues relating to real estate.

II. Sale of Property

Before entering into a contract for the sale of school property, an educational entity's governing board must authorize the sale through a formal motion, and designate the property to be surplus or desirable of sale. This step is required by Texas Education Code § 11.154 which reads, in relevant part: "The board of trustees of any independent school district may, by resolution, authorize the sale of any property, other than minerals, held in trust for free school purposes."[1]

In most cases, the sale of school property must be made through a bid procedure discussed later in this chapter.[2] For the following types of property, however, bidding is not required:

(1) narrow strips of land, or land that because of its shape or small area cannot be used independently under its current zoning or under applicable subdivision or other development control ordinances;
(2) streets or alleys, owned in fee or used by easement;
(3) land or a real property interest originally acquired for streets, rights-of-way, or easements that the political subdivision chooses to exchange for other land to be used for streets, rights-of-way, or easements, including transactions partly for cash;
(4) land that the political subdivision wants to have developed by contract with an independent foundation;
(5) a real property interest conveyed to a governmental entity that has the power of eminent domain; or
(6) a municipality's land that is located in a reinvestment zone designated as provided by law, and that the municipality desires to have developed under a project plan adopted by the municipality for the zone.[3]

To satisfy the requirements of § 272.001 of the Texas Local Government Code, the types of property enumerated above need only be sold for a sum of not less than the fair market value of the land or interest sold. The fair market value is conclusively determined by an appraisal obtained by the educational entity that owns the land or interest.[4] Furthermore, if the sale is to one or more abutting property owners who own the underlying fee simple, the sale may be for less than the fair market value.[5] This is a very limited qualification, but would apply in instances where an educational agency is disposing of rights-of-way or easements to the owners of the underlying fee simple.

The Texas Local Government Code also provides other very limited exemptions to the bidding requirement. For example, a school district may sell land to an entity for development of low or moderate income housing on terms "so as to effectuate and maintain the public purpose", including receiving less than fair market value in appropriate situations.[6]

The sale of most real estate, however, will require compliance with the public notice and bidding procedure established by § 272.001(a) of the Texas Local Government Code. This procedure mandates that notice of the proposed offer of sale be given to the general public by publication in a newspaper of general circulation in the county in which the property is located or, if there is no such newspaper, in an adjoining county. Publication must take place on two separate dates, set forth a description of the land, including its location, and the procedure by which sealed bids to purchase the land may be submitted.[7] No sale may occur until after the fourteenth (14th) day after the date of the second publication.[8]

There are no requirements as to what the bid package must contain. It is recommended, however, that the package contain the form of purchase agreement which the school is willing to sign, with the purchase price left open for each bidder to complete, and an instruction letter to the bidder. In addition to provisions generally found in contracts for sale of property, the form of purchase agreement should contain any special terms and conditions required by the school, including the reversionary restrictions against use or operation of the property for a segregated school more fully discussed below, and any other use restrictions the school may wish to impose on the property.

Most sales will be for cash. An installment sale may be permitted; however, compliance with these statutes is difficult or, at best, time consuming.[9] The bid instructions should instruct the bidder to complete the purchase price in the form of purchase agreement, sign and date the purchase agreement, and should specify a date certain by which the bid must be received by the school. In addition, the bid instructions should specify that the school can reject any and all bids and should specify a date by which all bidders will be notified as to whether their bid is accepted.

Once the terms and conditions of the purchase agreement are satisfied, the property will be conveyed by deed. It is recommended that the deed be without warranty or with special warranty of title only. The deed must recite the resolution of the school board authorizing the sale and, for elementary and secondary schools, *must* contain the reversionary restrictions against use or operation of a segregated school required by the order of Judge William Wayne Justice in *United States of America v. State of Texas, et al*, in Civil Action No. 5281. That is, the party to which the property is being sold must agree not to use the property for the purposes of a segregated school, or the property will revert back to the school district. Alternative language to this reversionary clause is available upon prior approval by the Texas Education Agency. Failure to include this language in the closing documents could render the real estate transaction void.

III. Purchase of Real Property

The method of purchasing real property for school districts and colleges does not differ from those used in private transactions, in those cases where the purchase is financed.[10] No bidding requirements exist for school districts and colleges relating to the purchase of property. Rather, property may be purchased for the best negotiated price. Preclosing steps include securing:

(1) an executed purchase agreement;
(2) a commitment for an owner's policy of title insurance issued by a qualified title company;
(3) a survey of the property (usually at the seller's cost);
(4) an environmental audit to detect possible environmental hazards and to comply with requirements of the Texas National Resources Conservation Commission;
(5) satisfactory evidence that the property has adequate access and all necessary utilities will be available for the use of the property at acceptable rates, including necessary storm water drainage; and
(6) an engineer's report, if buildings or other structures are included in the property.

Section 271.004 allows school districts and colleges to purchase real property through financing, if certain criteria are met. Specifically, if such a contract is proposed, notice of the contract should be published not less than sixty (60) days prior to execution of the contract in a newspaper of general circulation. If within this period, a written petition of at least five percent (5%) of the registered voters is received, approval of the contract is subject to public referendum.

At the closing, the school district should receive:

(1) a warranty deed conveying property to the district in fee simple title, subject only to the exceptions to title disclosed by the survey and title commitment and approved by the school district;
(2) evidence of authority from the seller to sell the property;
(3) an owner's policy of title insurance insuring title to the property (generally at seller's expense); and
(4) A FIRPTA affidavit signed by the seller certifying the seller's tax identification number and that the seller is not a foreign entity.

The closing will be very similar to closings for private transactions.

Prior to the closing of a real estate purchase, it is important that a school district perform the research or due diligence necessary to ensure the property to be acquired is satisfactory for the school's intended use. This would include the following:

(1) Title and Survey: Prior to closing. the school district should secure a survey of the property to be acquired as well as a commitment for title insurance covering the property. Approval of both should be a condition precedent to the school district's obligation to close the transaction. The survey will provide the school district with a physical drawing of the property, and all encumbrances locatable on the ground, including any encroachments, improvements, easements, or building set back lines. The title commitment will identify the owner of the property (which should be identical to your seller), and all encumbrances or restrictions filed of record such as use restrictions, easements, outstanding mineral interests, leases and mortgages or other liens against the property. The title commitment also constitutes the binding obligation of the issuer, following satisfaction of the requirements set forth therein, to ensure the school district's fee simple title in the property following closing, subject only to those matters set forth in the title commitment. The title commitment and survey should be reviewed carefully to ensure that there is nothing disclosed that would prevent or prohibit the school district from using the property for its intended purpose.

(2) Environmental Audit: By acquiring land, a school district is also exposing itself to the cost of remediating any environmental contamination of the land, notwithstanding that the school district may not have caused the contamination. In addition, should the property contain more than one (1) acre and is to be developed, the Texas Health and Safety Code requires testing samplings to be taken of the property to confirm that the property is not located on a municipal landfill.[11] Consequently, as a condition to closing, a school district should also require that it has secured and approved an environmental audit of the property to be bought. The audit is generally done at the buyer's expense and should include a detailed study of past uses of the property, including a study of existing aerial photos from prior years, to determine if there have been any past uses which might suggest a contamination problem. Also, a review of the records of the Texas Railroad Commission to determine if there has been any oil and gas development activity on the property, a review of the records of the Environmental Protection Agency, the Texas Natural Resources Conservation Commission, and any local agency charged with responsibility for environmental conditions is advisable. In addition, the audit should include a physical inspection of the property to determine if there is any stressed vegetation or other visible signs that might suggest contamination, as well as subsurface testing sufficient to satisfy the requirements of Texas Health and Safety Code § 361.538. If there are indications of potential contamination, additional physical testing of the soil and groundwater may also be required to determine the existence of contamination.

(3) Wetlands: A determination should be made as to wheth- any portion of the property would be considered wetlands by the Environmental Protection Agency or U.S. Corps of Engineers guidelines. This may be included as part of the environmental audit.

(4) Access and Utilities: A determination should be made as to whether the property has adequate access for the contemplated use, including curb cuts and median cuts to enable the orderly flow of school buses or other traffic. Additionally, it should be determined whether the site has adequate utility service for its intended use, including the

physical location of pipelines and electrical service. If the school site is located within a private utility district, special attention should be given to securing commitment letters for water and wastewater capacity and the rates at which that capacity will be provided. Also, be attentive to special charges such as stand-by fees which may be extraordinarily high for school districts. Because school districts are not tax-paying entities, private utility districts will often make up the loss in tax revenues by charging increased fees for school-owned land.

(5) Storm Water Detention: A determination should be made as to whether any storm water detention requirements may be imposed upon the school as a condition to the construction of any improvements on the land.

(6) Engineering: If the school is buying improved property, an engineering study of the improvements should be conducted to determine their integrity and establish that all necessary permits have been acquired.

To provide adequate time to complete its due diligence, the school district should require a due diligence period in its purchase agreement. Sixty (60) to one-hundred and twenty (120) days following execution of the purchase agreement is not uncommon. During this time, the school district would have access to the property to conduct its inspections and would be entitled to terminate the purchase agreement for any reason prior to the end of the due diligence period. Most purchases will be made from cash already available for that purpose. As described above, however, the purchase may be financed.[12] There is no customary form of real property purchase agreement, although many concepts are consistent throughout. It is recommended that a purchaser secure the advice of an attorney as to any purchase agreement.

IV. Conclusion

In most respects, school district real estate transactions do not vary from those in the private sector, particularly regarding the purchase of real property. With regard to the sale of real property, however, certain statutes, such as those outlined in this article, are unique to school districts and should be followed. In particular, all bidding requirements regarding the sale of school property should be observed where required.

ENDNOTES

[1] Tex. Educ. Code § 11.154(a). The sale of mineral interests by a school district is governed by Tex. Educ. Code § 11.153.
[2] Tex. Loc. Govt. Code § 272.001, *et. seq.*
[3] Tex. Loc. Govt. Code § 272.001(b).
[4] *Id.*
[5] *Id.*
[6] *Id.* at § 272.001(g).
[7] Tex. Loc. Govt. Code § 272.001.
[8] *Id.*
[9] *See* Tex. Educ. Code § 20.922.
[10] Tex. Local Govt. Code § 271.004.
[11] *See* Tex. Health and Safety Code § 361.538.
[12] Tex. Loc. Govt. Code § 271.004.

ELECTION LAW

By: Arturo G. Michel

I. Introduction

The ability of and the procedure by which Texas school districts and junior colleges conduct elections is governed primarily by statute. The most common types of elections are elections of officers, e.g., members of the board of trustees. The Texas Education Code also permits elections for annexations, detachments, consolidations, abolition of districts, establishment of single-member districts, and the issuance of bonds. Without specific statutory authority to hold an election, the Texas Attorney General has opined that a government entity cannot conduct or participate in conducting an election even if it is simply a non-binding referendum to test public opinion.[1] Texas elections are also affected by certain constitutional provisions, both federal and state. Additionally, a federal statute, the Voting Rights Act of 1965, and the federal regulations interpreting it, apply to all changes concerning elections which are the result of the board's discretion, regardless of how minor they may appear. This chapter will outline general Texas election law.

II. Trustee Elections

All the above laws affect the scheme by which a district's trustees are elected. Trustees may be elected under single-member district or at-large schemes or a combination of the two (2). Additionally, for school districts but not junior colleges, the 1995 legislative changes to the Education Code in Senate Bill 1 also permit cumulative voting for at-large elections.[2] The majority of districts elect their trustees under an at-large method. Most districts that have adopted a singlemember district plan have done so in response to a challenge by racial and/or ethnic minority voters under the Voting Rights Act. Due to recent court decisions, it has become harder for plaintiffs to prevail in these challenges.

For school districts, the Texas Education Code permits single-member district plans in which not fewer than seventy percent (70%) of the trustees are elected from single-member districts. Therefore, for a district with a seven member board, the district could have all single-member districts, or five single-member districts and two at-large positions, or as a final alternative, six single-member districts and one at-large position. For most junior colleges, the Education Code requires only that a majority of the trustees be elected from single-member districts.[3]

Regardless of the number of single-member districts, these districts must cover the entire territory of the school district. All territory in a particular single-member district must be contiguous. The Education Code further requires that all single-member districts must have an equal total population within a ten percent deviation. This requirement is necessitated by the constitutional one personone vote requirement.

A board may voluntarily adopt a single-member district plan. A school district board may also be required to adopt a single-member district plan if approved by a majority vote in an election. A referendum election is required if at least fifteen (15) percent or 15,000 of the registered voters of the district, whichever is less, sign and present a valid petition requesting the referendum to the board. The general junior college statute does not provide the referendum option.

Under the general school district statute, at the first election at which a single-member district plan may be implemented, the board must hold elections for all trustee positions unless a five singlemember district and two at-large plan ("5-2 plan") is adopted. Under a 5-2 plan, board members are allowed to serve at-large for the remainder of their terms, and the at-large and single-member district positions are phased in as the terms under the old plan expire. However, the order of implementing the positions under the new plan is determined by lot. A consequence of this random implementation is that board members who wish to continue on the board by running for election under the new plan will very likely not have the position for which they wish to run coincide with the expiration of their terms. The general junior college statute permits a phase-in upon implementation in all situations.[4] The board is required to revise single-member district boundaries after the publication of each federal decennial census when the data indicates a deviation greater than ten percent (10%) between the population of the most populous district and least populous district.

III. Voting Rights Act

Districts with significant populations of racial and ethnic minorities may be sued under the Voting Rights Act of 1965 (Act) in a challenge to an at-large scheme of electing trustees. Plaintiffs often request from the court as a remedy that the district be required to change its election scheme to a single-member district plan. The success of plaintiffs in prevailing under the Act depends primarily on their ability to meet a three-part test, although court opinions emphasize that the analysis is very fact intensive and will include review of potential discrimination in all areas of the district, e.g., employment, bidding, contracting, and all socioeconomic factors affecting the district. The three-part test is:

(1) the minority group is sufficiently large and geographically compact to constitute a voting age majority in at least one (1) single-member district, e.g., sufficiently large and compact to form a "safe" district;

(2) the minority group is politically cohesive; and

(3) the white majority votes sufficiently as a block to enable it–in the absence of special circumstances, such as the minority candidate running unopposed–usually to defeat the minority group's preferred candidate.

The plaintiffs have the burden of proof and will usually prevail if they establish the above three factors. However, plaintiffs will lose unless they establish all three factors.

The above elements are means for the court to test whether the district's voters have historically voted along racial lines, and whether, given this racially polarized voting, a single-member district scheme would allow minority voters an equal opportunity to elect candidates of their choice in at least one single-member district. Therefore, the first element of having the minority group constitute a voting age majority in at least one single-member district is to determine whether a single-member district system would allow the relevant minority group's vote to prevail if a singlemember district plan is adopted. For this purpose, a basic inquiry by the court is whether a singlemember district can be drawn in which the relevant minority voting age population is at least 50% of the total voting age population. Whether distinct minority groups, e.g., blacks and Hispanics, can be considered a single minority group for Act purposes will depend on whether they historically have voted as a group and the extent to which they vote as a group.

The remaining elements in a suit under the Act determine whether people vote along racial lines to the detriment of the relevant minority community. The second element of a politically cohesive minority group seeks to determine whether the relevant group votes in significant numbers for the same candidates, which is usually shown by statistically analyzed election results, although anecdotal evidence is permitted. The final element of block voting is the ultimate test to determine whether racially polarized voting is adverse to the discernable minority group's voting interests. However, the Act does not provide a guarantee of minority electoral success or a guarantee of minority trustees. The statute's goal is to provide an equal opportunity for all voters when historical patterns show that voters vote along racial lines.

Plaintiffs may also sue under the Fourteenth and Fifteenth Amendments to the United States Constitution and comparable Texas constitutional provisions. However, these constitutional provisions require plaintiffs to prove a factor that is not necessary under the Act. Namely, plaintiffs must prove an intent to discriminate under these constitutional provisions. The absence of having to prove intentional discrimination is what makes an Act claim the preferred cause of action for plaintiffs.

All single-member district plans, whether developed as a result of a lawsuit, threat of a lawsuit, or by an independent desire of the board, must be approved by the United States Department of Justice or by a federal court in Washington, D.C. before they may be implemented. Review by the Justice Department is the most common means of obtaining preclearance of the plan. The regulations concerning Justice Department review and the demographic and statistical analysis in developing plans, including the difficult decisions in adopting the plan, and the involvement of various segments of the district community, make the implementation of a single-member district plan a lengthy process taking several months or longer.

IV. Cumulative Voting

As previously stated, the majority of districts hold their elections for trustees under an at-large scheme by position. Consequently, in each election, all qualified voters in the district have an opportunity to vote for each trustee position. The 1995 legislation to the Education Code has added a variation to at-large voting known as cumulative voting.[5] In a cumulative voting plan, positions are unnumbered. Therefore, the ballot lists all candidates without reference to any particular position. Each voter has the opportunity to cast the number of votes that is equal to the number of positions to be filled at the election. These votes may be cast in any combination among the various candidates. Therefore, if there are three (3) trustee positions and several candidates have applied for those positions, the voter may cast all three (3) of his or her votes for a single candidate. Alternatively, the voter may cast one (1) vote each for three (3) different candidates, or he or she may cast two (2) votes for one (1) candidate and one (1) vote for another candidate. The voter may also choose to simply cast one (1) vote without using his or her remaining two (2) votes.

The philosophy underlying cumulative voting is that it allows a particular segment of voters to marshall their votes to a particular candidate in sufficient numbers to prevail in an election, when this would not have been possible under an at-large voting scheme by position. It is viewed as an alternative to single-member districts. Cumulative voting schemes are closely scrutinized by the Justice Department under the Act to determine whether these schemes provide equal voting opportunities for minority voters relative to alternatives, such as single-member district plans.

V. Election Dates

Regardless of the type of election scheme used, regular elections for trustees are held on one of the uniform election dates required by law. These uniform election dates are the third Saturday in January, the first Saturday in May, the second Saturday in August, and the first Tuesday after the first Monday in November.[6] The first Saturday in May is the most common uniform election date for districts followed by the third Saturday in January. School district trustees serve three-or-four year terms.[7] Elections for trustees for three-year terms are held annually and are staggered, so that the terms of one-third of the trustees, or as near to one-third as possible, expire each year.[8] Elections for trustees with four-year terms are staggered so that the terms of one-half of the trustees, or as near to one-half as possible, expire every two years.[9] The 1995 changes to the Education Code standardized trustee terms to the three or four year options by requiring districts which had two- or six-year terms to make the transition to a three- or four-year term.[10] Junior colleges are governed by separate statutes, which provide for six-year terms.[11]

A significant change arising from the 1995 legislation is the elimination of runoff elections for most school districts. There is no longer any authority for runoff elections under the statute providing for at-large elections by position.[12] Only certain school districts governed by special statutes retain the ability to hold runoff elections.[13] Consequently, for most school districts, voters will elect their trustees by plurality, rather than majority vote. However, in contrast, the statutes governing junior college elections require a majority vote and thus require runoff elections.[14]

VI. Trustee Qualifications

There are several qualifications to be a school trustee. One of the primary requirements is valid residency. Trustees are required to reside within the boundaries of the district.[15] Specifically, a trustee must reside within the district's boundaries for six (6) months immediately preceding his or her election or appointment, and must further reside continuously in the state for twelve (12) months preceding the appointment or election.[16] A trustee elected from a single-member district must reside in that single-member district for the six (6) months immediately preceding the date of the appointment or election.[17]

Residence means domicile, i.e., one's home and fixed place of habitation to which he or she intends to return after any temporary absence.[18] Residence is determined in accordance with the common law as modified by the Texas Election Code. It is not lost by leaving home to go to another place for temporary purposes only when the person does not intend to make it his or her home. Rather, residence is the place where one lives with an intent to live there and return after any absence. Therefore, the elements to establish residency are volition, intention, and action.[19] Courts have found that the determination of residency is dependent upon particular circumstances and largely dependent on the present intention of the person.[20] A person is presumed to reside where he lives.[21] While a person's declarations concerning residency are admissible and relevant in a court proceeding, the actual facts are controlling over such declarations.[22]

The authority placed in districts to conduct elections imposes several duties on trustees and election officials. One duty is the requirement that the board order the election. The secretary of the board, as the authority with whom an application for a place on the ballot is filed, has the duty to review the application.[23] He or she determines whether the application meets the requirements as to form, content, and procedure. In this review, the board secretary may only rely on the assertions of the candidate in the application and existing public records.[24] The board secretary's review of applications occurs during the filing period. The deadline for filing is 5:00 p.m. of the 45th day before the day of the election, and the application may not be filed earlier than the 30th day before this deadline.[25]

VII. Election Notices and Voting Procedures

Districts are also required to publicize elections. Not later than the 21st day before election day, a copy of the election notice must be posted at a public place in each election precinct.[26] Additionally, the district must publish the election notice once in a newspaper not sooner than the 30th day or later than the 10th day before election day.[27] The district must additionally post notice of the election on a bulletin board at a place convenient to the public in the central administrative office of the district not later than the 21st day before election day.[28] An election notice must state: (1) the nature and date of the election; (2) the location of each polling place, (3) the hours that the polls will be open; and (4) any other information required by law, e.g., the location of the main early voting polling place, the regular dates and hours that early voting will be conducted, and the early voting clerk's official mailing address.[29]

The Election Code places several duties on the board concerning early voting. The board designates the location of the main early voting polling place, which must be in the territory covered by the election.[30] The board also has the discretion to order early voting at the main location on one or more Saturdays.[31] If fifteen (15) registered voters request early voting on one or more Saturday or Sundays, then the board must order early voting on at least one Saturday (if a Saturday was requested) and at least one Sunday (if a Sunday was requested). The board is also permitted to establish temporary branch polling places for early voting.[32]

Another duty of the board's secretary is to prepare the official ballot for the election.[33] To prepare the ballot, the board secretary determines the order of names on the ballot by drawing lots.[34] The board secretary must post in his or her office the notice of the date, hour, and place of the drawing. The notice remains posted continuously for seventy-two (72) hours immediately preceding the time of the drawing and the place of the drawing, except for a runoff election, when twenty-four (24) hours suffices. Additionally, the board's secretary must send written notice of the date, hour, and place of the drawing by mail to each candidate at the address listed on his or her application, not later than the fourth day before the date of the drawing.

The board's secretary is also the authority with whom a request to withdraw from the ballot must be filed.[35] To be valid, a withdrawal request must be timely filed, in writing, signed and acknowledged by the candidate.[36] The withdrawal deadline is generally thirty-six (36) days before the election.[37] When the filing deadline is closer to the election, e.g., when there is a special election, withdrawal may occur up until the second day before the beginning of early voting by personal appearance, i.e., 22 days before the election.[38]

The 1995 changes to the Election Code has added provisions permitting school districts to cancel elections when a candidate is unopposed. As of the time of the publication of this book, the Elections Division of the Texas Secretary of State's office has taken the position that this new legislation permits a cancellation of an election only when all elections for all positions on the ballot are unopposed and there is no proposition appearing on the ballot. Although this interpretation is questionable and a court may reach the opposite result, districts should follow the Secretary of State's interpretation until a court or the Attorney General's office rules otherwise. This ability to cancel elections does not exist for junior colleges under the 1995 legislation, because it applies only when there is a write-in candidate deadline prior to election, which prevents additional write-in candidates emerging on election day.[39] Junior colleges do not have such a deadline.

The process for canceling an election begins with the board's secretary certifying in writing that a candidate is unopposed when only one candidate's name is to be placed on the ballot for that office, and no candidate's name is placed on the list of write-in candidates[40] The board secretary is to deliver this certification to the board as soon as possible after the filing deadline for a write-in candidacy.[41] On receipt of the certification, the board may declare each unopposed candidate elected to the office and the election is not held.[42] On election day, a copy of the order or ordinance declaring the election of each unopposed candidate must be posted at each polling place.[43]

Determination of valid write-in candidacies is another duty of the board secretary. A declaration of a write-in candidacy must be filed with the board secretary and requires the applicant to satisfy all the Election Code requirements for a place on the ballot.[44] The deadline for filing a declaration of a write-in candidacy is generally 5:00 p.m. of the 30th day before the date of the election.[45] This deadline is extended to 5:00 p.m. of the 27th day before the date of the election for an office in which a candidate whose name is to appear on the ballot dies or is declared ineligible after the 33rd day before the date before the election.[46] It appears that the Texas legislature attempted to change the thirty (30) day deadline to a forty-five (45) day deadline to conform to the regular filing deadline, but it did so by amending the Education Code version repealed by Senate Bill 1. Principles of statutory construction require that the thirty (30) day deadline under Senate Bill 1 prevail because of a specific conflicts provision in Senate Bill 1. A challenge to a declaration of a write-in candidacy may not be made after the 15th day before election day.[47]

VIII. Criminal Penalties and Other Prohibitions

District and election officials must also be aware of prohibitions concerning elections. An officer or employee of a political subdivision may not spend or authorize spending of public funds for political advertising.[48] Such conduct is a crime (Class A misdemeanor). However, this prohibition is inapplicable to a communication that factually describes the purposes of a measure if the communication does not advocate the passage or defeat of a measure.[49]

Electioneering for or against a candidate, measure, or political parties is prohibited within one hundred (100) feet of an outside door through which a voter may enter a building in which a polling place is located during the time period when the polls are open.[50] There is a comparable provision that applies to early voting.[51] The district's regulation of activity beyond the one hundred (100) foot limit is a freedom of expression issue under the First Amendment of the United States Constitution and comparable Texas constitutional provision. District grounds may be a limited public forum depending on the degree to which the district allows political speech on these grounds. Districts may prohibit political speech altogether on district grounds for district elections during the times when the polls are open. This may be the simplest course of action for a district, because to allow any political expression would mean that the district cannot selectively prohibit speech beyond the one hundred (100) foot range based on the viewpoint of the speaker.

IX. Recounts and Election Contests

District and election officials also have duties with regard to challenges to the outcome of an election. The two most common forms of challenges are a recount and an election contest, the latter being a particular type of lawsuit filed to challenge an election. A recount is an administrative process that may be instituted only by a candidate.[52] This type of challenge is limited to counting errors.[53] For a recount request to be valid, it must be in writing, identify the office, state the grounds for the recount, identify the election precincts and method of voting in each precinct, be signed, and contain several other pieces of information concerning the requestor and opposing candidates or agents.[54] A prerequisite to obtaining a recount requires that the difference in votes necessary to change the outcome with regard to the requestor is less than ten (10) percent.[55] This requirement is inapplicable if the total number of votes received by all candidates for the office is less than 1,000 as shown by the election returns or if an electronic voting system is used.[56]

A recount petition must also be timely and properly submitted. It must be submitted to the board president by 5:00 p.m. of the fifth day after election or 5:00 p.m. of the second day after completion of the canvass.[57] The recount coordinator must review the petition for compliance with the requirements within forty-eight (48) hours after receipt.[58] Prompt notification of a defect is required. Improper form of a petition is a defect, as is the lack of the proper amount of deposit. An amendment to correct a defect must be submitted no later than the petition deadline or 2:00 p.m. of the second day after notice of the defect is received.[59] Only one amendment is permitted.[60] A recount must be held not later than the seventh day after approval of the petition.[61] The canvass of the election is not delayed by a recount.[62] There are special time lines for an expedited recount when there is a runoff.[63]

An election contest may be filed by any candidate in the state district court in the county where the election occurred.[64] The scope of the inquiry in this type of suit is not simply whether fraud, illegal conduct, or mistakes occurred, but whether the activities complained of resulted in a change of the outcome.[65] An election contest must be brought within thirty (30) days of the official results, or ten (10) days if there is a run-off.[66] The contestee assumes and remains in office until there is a final judgment ordering a new election or declaring the contestant elected.[67]

A successful candidate or an appointee to a board position does not succeed to office until he or she has taken the oath of office. There are two oaths that must be taken. One is a statement which must be filed with the Secretary of State disavowing bribery.[68] The Secretary of State's office provides a form for this oath which must be signed by the officer and notarized.[69] The second oath is the oath of office which is filed with the district. There are wide variety of officials who may administer the oath of office, including a notary public.[70] Neither oath requires a formal ceremony or a board meeting. The administration of the oath of office may be done privately, but this event often occurs at a board meeting for ceremonial purposes.

X. Resignations and Vacancies

Trustees who resign, choose not to run, or who are defeated in election continue to hold office and perform the duties of a trustee until their successors are duly qualified.[71] This requirement is commonly known as the holdover doctrine. Its purpose is to prevent vacancies and the cessation of the functions of government.[72] These obligations of office continue even when an officer resigns and his or her resignation is accepted.[73]

Several issues arise when a board member resigns. A trustee's resignation must be in writing, signed, and delivered to the board president, board secretary, or a clerk to the board.[74] A vacancy through resignation occurs on the date the resignation is accepted by the board or on the eighth day after receipt of the resignation by one of these individuals, whichever occurs earlier.[75] The board president, board secretary, or clerk may not refuse to accept the resignation.[76]

The trustee's resignation may be a resignation to take effect in the future, even if it is beyond the eighth day after receipt by the appropriate authority. The Elections Division of the Texas Secretary of State's office has interpreted the statutory requirement concerning the effective date of a resignation to mean effective with regard to beginning the process to fill the vacancy. Thus, a board may call a special election to fill a vacancy as of the eighth day after receipt by the appropriate authority or earlier if the board has voted to accept the resignation - even though the trustee continues to serve beyond these dates in accordance with the letter of resignation.

A vacancy on the board of trustees of an independent school district or a junior college may be filled by appointment, with the appointee to serve until the next trustee election.[77] As an alternative, the board may order a special election to fill the vacancy for the remaining term.[78] However, this option of filling a vacancy by election is not available to most junior colleges.[79]

If more than one year remains in the term of the position vacated for a school district board, the vacancy must be filled not later than the 180th day after the occurrence of the vacancy.[80] There is no comparable provision for junior colleges, although there is a statute requiring junior college boards to be governed in the establishment, management, and control of the junior college by the general law in these areas applying to independent school districts insofar as the general law is applicable.[81] It is questionable whether this provision places a timeline on junior colleges to fill vacancies in office.

The board must order a special election to fill a vacancy as soon as practicable after the vacancy occurs.[82] Generally, the special election to fill a vacancy must be held on the first authorized uniform election date occurring on or after the 30th day after the date the election is ordered.[83] The special election must be ordered at least twenty-five (25) days prior to the election.[84] The filing deadline for a special election will vary, according to how far in advance of the election the board adopts its election order.[85]

XI. Conclusion

The election laws are extremely technical, and should be followed to the letter to ensure compliance, particularly in the areas of trustee resignations and vacancies. If specific questions arise regarding the election laws, the author suggests contacting your school attorney for guidance.

ENDNOTES

[1] Tex. Att'y Gen. LO-94-091 (1994); Op. Tex. Att'y Gen. No. H-425 (1974).
[2] Tex. Educ. Code § 11.054.
[3] Tex. Educ. Code § 130.0822(a).
[4] Tex. Educ. Code § 130.0822(g).
[5] Tex. Educ. Code § 11.054.
[6] Tex. Elec. Code § 41.001.
[7] Tex. Educ. Code § 11.059.
[8] *Id.*
[9] *Id.*
[10] *Id.*
[11] Tex. Educ. Code §§ 130.082(e), 130.0821(c), 130.0822(c), 130.083(d), 130.088(m).
[12] Tex. Educ. Code § 11.057; Tex. Elec. Code § 2.001; Tex. Att'y Gen. LO-95-087 (1995).

[13] *E.g.*, Tex. Educ. Code § 11.062; Tex. Att'y Gen. LO-95-087 (1995).
[14] Tex. Educ. Code §§ 130.082(g), 130.0821(f), 130.0822(c), 130.083(f), 130.088(l).
[15] Tex. Const. Art. 16, § 14.
[16] Tex. Elec. Code § 141.001.
[17] *Id.;* Brown v. Patterson, 609 S.W.2d 287 (Tex. Civ. App.–Dallas 1980, *no writ*); Op. Tex. Att'y Gen. No. JM-909 (1988).
[18] Tex. Elec. Code § 1.015.
[19] Culberson v. Palm, 451 S.W.2d 927 (Tex. Civ. App.–Houston [14th Dist.] 1970, *no writ*).
[20] Guerra v. Pená, 406 S.W.2d 769 (Tex. Civ. App.–San Antonio 1966, *no writ)*; Mills v. Bartlett, 377 S.W.2d 636 (Tex. 1964).
[21] McBeth v. Streib, 96 S.W.2d 992 (Tex. Civ. App.–San Antonio 19__, *no writ*).
[22] Stratton v. Hall, 90 S.W.2d 865 (Tex. Civ. App.–El Paso 1936, *writ dism'd*); McBride v. Cantue, 143 S.W.2d 126 (Tex. Civ. App.–San Antonio 1940, *no writ*); McWhorter v. Reynolds, 156 S.W.2d 312 (Tex. Civ. App.–Eastland 1942, *no writ*).
[23] Tex. Elec. Code §§ 144.004, 141.032.
[24] McClelland v. Sharp, 430 S.W.2d 518 (Tex. Civ. App.–Houston 1968, *writ ref'd n.r.e.*); Hayes v. Harris Co. Democratic Exec. Comm., 563 S.W.2d 884 (Tex. Civ. App.–Houston 1978, *no writ*).
[25] Tex. Educ. Code § 11.055(a).
[26] Tex. Elec. Code § 4.003(a)(2).
[27] Tex. Elec. Code § 4.003(a)(1).
[28] Tex. Elec. Code § 4.003(b).
[29] Tex. Elec. Code §§ 4.003(b), 85.004, 95.007(a), 83.010.
[30] Tex. Elec. Code § 85.002(d).
[31] Tex. Elec. Code § 85.006.
[32] Tex. Elec. Code § 85.062(a)(2).
[33] Tex. Elec. Code § 52.004(4).
[34] Tex. Elec. Code § 52.094.
[35] Tex. Elec. Code §§ 145.093, 145.053, 144.004.
[36] Tex. Elec. Code § 145.001.
[37] Tex. Elec. Code § 145.092.
[38] *Id.*
[39] Tex. Elec. Code §§ 2.051, 146.001
[40] Tex. Elec. Code § 2.052.
[41] Tex. Elec. Code § 2.052(b).
[42] Tex. Elec. Code § 2.053.
[43] *Id.*
[44] Tex. Educ. Code § 11.056; Tex. Elec. Code §§ 141.031, 146.023.
[45] Tex. Educ. Code § 11.056.
[46] *Id.*
[47] Tex. Elec. Code § 146.027.
[48] Tex. Elec. Code § 255.003.
[49] *Id.*
[50] Tex. Elec. Code § 61.003.
[51] Tex. Elec. Code § 85.036.
[52] Tex. Elec. Code § 212.001.
[53] *Id.*
[54] Tex. Elec. Code § 211.001.
[55] Tex. Elec. Code § 212.022.
[56] Tex. Elec. Code §§ 212.022, 212.0241.
[57] Tex. Elec. Code §§ 212.026, 212.028, 212.0245.
[58] Tex. Elec. Code § 212.029.
[59] Tex. Elec. Code § 212.030.
[60] *Id.*
[61] Tex. Elec. Code § 212.031.

[62] Tex. Elec. Code § 212.033.
[63] Tex. Elec. Code § 212.081-212.088.
[64] Tex. Elec. Code §§ 232.002, 221.002, 232.006.
[65] Tex. Elec. Code § 221.003.
[66] Tex. Elec. Code § 232.008.
[67] Tex. Elec. Code § 221.051.
[68] Tex. Const., Art. 16, § 1.
[69] 1 Tex. Admin. Code §§ 73.43, 73.44(b).
[70] Tex. Gov. Code §§ 602.002, 602.006; Tex. Local Gov. Code § 22.042(d).
[71] Tex. Const., Art. 16, § 17.
[72] Plains Common Consol. Sch. Dist. No. 1 v. Hayhurst, 120 S.W.2d 322.
[73] *Id.*
[74] Tex. Elec. Code § 201.001.
[75] Tex. Elec. Code § 201.023.
[76] Tex. Elec. Code § 201.001.
[77] Tex. Educ. Code § 11.060, 130.082(d), 130.088.
[78] *Id.*
[79] Tex. Educ. Code §§ 130.0822(I), 130,083(d).
[80] *Id.*
[81] Tex. Educ. Code § 130.084.
[82] Tex. Elec. Code § 201.051.
[83] Tex. Elec. Code § 201.052.
[84] Tex. Elec. Code § 201.054.
[85] Tex. Elec. Code § 201.054.

SECTION 2

Teachers and Other Staff

THE FIRST AMENDMENT AND SCHOOL EMPLOYEES

By: Lisa Brown and
Merri Schneider-Vogel

I. Introduction

The First Amendment guarantees that, under most circumstances, even the most junior public employee can openly criticize his employer without fearing for his job.[1] When it comes to freedom of speech, both the tenured teacher and the at-will bus driver stand on equal ground. As recent court cases demonstrate, however, this right of free speech is not limitless. During the last few years, the federal courts have had the opportunity to consider a variety of First Amendment retaliation claims and to refine the scope of the free speech rights of public employees. Nonetheless, some issues remain unresolved, and the specter of lawsuits persists. In the years ahead, school officials and board members will need to keep abreast of major judicial developments and to carefully evaluate the First Amendment issues that often arise in school management decisions.

The problem, of course, is that school officials often are uncertain about the legal standards and the effect of those standards on their management decisions. Although many commentators have analyzed this issue from a legal or academic point of view, few have examined the practical aspects of applying the First Amendment on a day-to-day basis. This chapter is designed to suggest management techniques to aid public officials in balancing the needs of the school against the constitutional rights of the school's employees.

II. First Amendment Standards in School Employment

A. Legal Standards

Generally speaking, the First Amendment prohibits a public entity, such as a school district or public college, from restricting the speech rights of any citizen based upon the content or subject matter of the citizen's speech.[2] This general rule, however, does not apply with equal force when the citizen also happens to be an *employee* of the public entity. Special rules govern the rights of public employees. These rules balance the employee's rights against the needs of the institution.

Courts focus on several issues when determining whether an employee's rights have been violated:

1. Type of Violation

Was the violation of constitutional magnitude? Was the employee fired, transferred, or merely given an assignment he or she did not like? Some "violations" are considered too trivial to merit constitutional protection.[3]

2. Type of Speech

Did the speech address a matter of public concern, such as the school's racial policies,[4] or did the speech address a matter of private concern, such as the employee's desire for higher pay?[5] The U.S. Constitution is not violated when an employer disciplines an individual whose speech concerned only personal matters.

3. Effect on the Employer

Did the speech disrupt the workplace or impair morale?[6] The Supreme Court has held an employee's speech rights must be balanced against the employer's interest in maintaining an efficient operation.

4. Motivation for Employment Decision

Was the teacher disciplined or terminated because he or she spoke out on matters of public concern? Or would the employee have been disciplined regardless of the speech activities?[7] Courts have held that employers may not be held liable unless the free speech was a substantial factor behind the employment decision. The remainder of this section will analyze the factors and show how they have been applied in real cases.

A trio of United States Supreme Court cases[8] establishes the framework for analyzing First Amendment retaliation claims of public employees. The seminal case is *Pickering v. Board of Education,*[9] in which the United States Supreme Court first introduced the concept of balancing a public employee's free speech rights against a school's interest in maintaining an efficient operation. *Pickering* held that several factors are relevant in balancing the free speech rights of the individual against the interests of the government: (1) whether the speech interfered with employee performance and operation; (2) whether it created disharmony among co-workers; (3) whether it undercut an immediate supervisor's discipline over an employee; and (4) whether it destroyed the relationship of loyalty and trust required of confidential employees. The Court also articulated the concept of "protected" and "unprotected" speech:

for an employee's speech to be protected, it must pertain to a *matter of public, as opposed to personal, concern.*

The Supreme Court offered additional guidance in *Mt. Healthy City School District Board of Education v. Doyle.*[10] In *Mt. Healthy*, the Court announced a three-part test to determine whether a public employee has been deprived of his or her First Amendment rights. The first prong of the test is whether the employee's speech is *protected speech.* If the court determines that the employee engaged in a protected speech activity, then the jury must decide whether that protected conduct was a substantial or motivating factor in the school official's decision to take adverse action against the employee, and whether the adverse action would have taken place anyway, regardless of the protected conduct.

The *Mt. Healthy* test was designed in part to prevent teachers and other public employees from shielding their inadequacies under the guise of First Amendment activity. The test, however, protects those public employees who are performing satisfactorily and who have chosen to speak out on matters of public concern. When an employee with a good record speaks out on a public matter that a school or college finds embarrassing, the school or college may not discipline the employee as a result of that protected conduct.

In 1983, the U.S. Supreme Court further refined the concept of "public" and "personal" speech. In *Connick v. Myers*,[11] an assistant district attorney who was denied a reassignment distributed a questionnaire in the form of an interoffice memorandum. She asked questions about employee morale, transfer procedures, the need for a grievance committee, and pressure to contribute to political campaigns. In finding that the memorandum was not speech protected by the First Amendment, the Supreme Court emphasized that speech-related activity is not constitutionally protected unless it pertains to a matter of "public" as opposed to "private" concern. The Court determined that the memorandum in *Connick* related primarily to the assistant district attorney's personal grievances and, thus, did not constitute protected speech.

The Court explained that determining whether speech concerns a "public" issue requires an examination of the *content, form*, and *context* of the speech. If the speech is found to concern a private or personal matter, the issue of free speech is concluded in favor of the defendant school official; however, if the court finds that the speech was on a matter of public concern, a court must then apply the *Pickering* and *Mt. Healthy* tests. If a court finds that an employee's speech did involve a matter of public concern, then the jury must determine whether the protected speech was a substantial or motivating factor in the school or college's decision to take adverse action against the employee. If the jury answers the motivating factor question in the affirmative, the jury then must determine, "but for" the speech, would the employee's status have been altered? If this question is answered "yes," the defendant school official should prevail; however, should it be answered "no," the employee should prevail.

B. Application of the Legal Standards

How does a supervisor know when an employee is speaking out as a citizen on a matter of "public concern," rather than as an employee on a matter of "personal" concern? Numerous factors have influenced the courts: whether the speech addressed an issue being debated in the community,[12] whether the speech involved testimony before a governmental body,[13] whether the speech addressed public safety issues,[14] whether the speech addressed concerns about race or gender discrimination,[15] whether the speech concerned abuse of office or criminal activity,[16] and whether the speech concerned the performance of a politician.[17]

Although not a decisive factor, one consideration is whether the employee will *personally benefit* from the speech. For example, in *Thompson v. City of Starkville*,[18] the court of appeals found in favor of a police officer who complained about other officers' misconduct. The court stated that he "stood to gain little personally through his grievance." In *Stewart v. Baldwin County Bd. of Education*,[19] the court found in favor of a group of employees who had walked out on the superintendent while he was delivering a speech urging increased taxes. In *Stever v. Independent School District*,[20] a school nurse complained about other employees' failure to follow immunization laws. In contrast, where an employee complained about his own salary[21] or his own demotion[22] or publicly defended his own severe grading policy,[23] the courts held that the complaints were unprotected, personal speech. A good illustration of the difference between employee speech and citizen speech is found in *Dodds v. Childers*,[24] in which an instructor complained about the hiring of the board's president's sister-in-law in her department. Although unlawful nepotism generally is a matter of public concern, the evidence in *Dodds* showed that the plaintiff had spoken out because she was jealous that someone else was given the job she had coveted. By and large, employee grievances have been held not to constitute matters of public concern.[25] One notable area of debate concerns complaints about sexual harassment. Courts disagree whether complaints about sexual harassment are considered speech protected by the First Amendment.[26]

In some situations, an employee might engage in speech on matters of private concern that incidentally touch on a matter of public concern–what *Connick* calls a matter of limited public concern. In *Connick*, the limited public concern question concerned the pressure to contribute to campaigns. The essential thrust of her speech, however, was personal. For this reason, the entire speech activity was not protected. Even when speech concerns some protected content, under *Pickering*, a school or college may take adverse action against the employee if the employee's speech negatively impacts the workplace.[27] When an employee's speech hinders or threatens to hinder the efficiency of the office or agency for which she works, termination or other action is lawful.[28]

In *Berg v. Hunter*, for example, the court determined that the employee's repeated "antagonistic and threatening communications" and his "clear assault" on a superior's authority "could serve only to undermine" the superior's ability to maintain discipline and harmony.[29] Actual disruption or a substantial likelihood of disruption is required to remove the protected status of speech on matters that are of public concern.[30] In *Jeffries v. Harleston*,[31] the court upheld the removal of a department chair who had made derogatory off-campus remarks about a religious minority. The college had determined that there was a reasonable expectation that the speech would harm the College. In *Nieto v. San Perlita Independent School District*,[32] the school district terminated its maintenance supervisor after he appeared before the school board and complained about the basketball coach's use of profanity and physical abuse of students. Although the maintenance supervisor spoke on a matter of public concern, there was sufficient evidence showing that his conduct was disruptive. While "investigating" the coach, he had pulled students out of class to interview them and he had eavesdropped on teachers' conversations. There was evidence that he was at odds with many employees and that he refused to do work requested of him. Accordingly, the court ruled in favor of the school officials. The lesson to be learned from these cases is that the closer the employee's speech touches on matters of public concern, "the greater must be the employer's showing that the speech is likely to be disruptive."[33]

III. The Usual First Amendment Case

The usual First Amendment case involves a not-so-perfect employee who has not been evaluated or whose performance has been found acceptable by his or her supervisor over some period of time. This situation often arises in schools in which the principal or department chair exerts little or no leadership. The supervisor may have orally told the employee about some performance problem, or the employee may have been the recipient of parental or student complaints about performance. The supervisor, however, might not have memorialized the problems by preparing a memorandum or by noting the deficiency in an evaluation document. Subsequently, the employee participates in some speech-related activity, such as a making or speech to the school board, joining a union, or writing a letter to the editor. The speech-related activities then cause the supervisor, board member, or an administrator to scrutinize the employee's behavior. If the employee's behavior is antagonistic to the school officials' position, the focus invariably turns to whether this employee is a good employee, *i.e.*, whether the employee has performed satisfactorily. The officials discover that the employee is performing poorly, and a series of events, including documentation of inadequate performance, then occurs. Termination or other negative job action follows. Parental complaints about the teacher from the past are resurrected and investigated. After the termination, the employee files a lawsuit alleging that his or her protected speech (or associational activity) was a substantial or motivating factor in the school board's decision to terminate.

While an employee's First Amendment activity may reflect his or her true feelings about the subject at hand, often employees may become involved in activities to shield themselves from negative job action. Regardless of the reasons for the speech activities, school officials are then faced with the time and expense of defending a lawsuit. Experience suggests that many employees sue primarily because they believe they have been treated unfairly. Others sue because of the perception that school officials have somehow deprived the individual of his or her personal dignity. The First Amendment issue often is raised by an employee on the chance that a jury might focus on the speech-related activity and miss the real reason the employee has been terminated.

IV. Special Situations

A. Classroom Speech and Other School-Sponsored Speech

Some retaliation lawsuits are filed by faculty members who were disciplined or nonrenewed over statements made during class time. Courts have held that employers may control classroom speech if the restriction is supported by legitimate pedagogical concerns.[34] As a general matter, classrooms are not a public forum for personal speech.[35] Interestingly, in cases involving classroom speech, several courts have abandoned the *Pickering-Connick* test in favor of a test known as the *Kuhlmeier* test.[36] The case of *Hazelwood School District v. Kuhlmeier*[37] concerned the right of a school district to regulate the content of the high school newspaper. The U.S. Supreme Court held that a school district may regulate speech that students, parents, or members of the public might reasonably perceive to bear the "imprimatur" of the school.[38] Where school-sponsored speech is concerned, regulation of style and content is permissible if the regulation is reasonably related to legitimate pedagogical concerns. Some courts have discarded the *Pickering-Connick* test in favor of the analysis of *Kuhlmeier* because *Pickering-Connick* ignores the "significant interests of the state as educator."[39] In many instances, because of its emphasis on legitimate pedagogical interests, the *Kuhlmeier* test will be easier for school districts to satisfy than the *Pickering-Connick* test. As of the date this chapter was written, the U.S. Supreme Court has not ruled on the standard to be applied to classroom speech.

Some retaliation lawsuits have been filed by employees who have the responsibility of serving as the official spokesperson for their schools or colleges, e.g., a human resources director who might have to talk to the media about a pending sexual harassment investigation. If an employee makes unauthorized statements in his or her official capacity, the employer may discipline the spokesperson, depending on the circumstances. In *Kotwica v. City of Tucson*,[40] the employee complained about a suspension that she received after making comments to the local media. She had been expressly directed not to talk about certain policy developments. In rejecting her retaliation claim, the court observed that the plaintiff had been interviewed "not because of her stature but because she represented the department . . ." The court held that the government had a legitimate stake in the accurate announcement of its own policy and that the employee misappropriated the interview for her own purposes.

While there is a difference between speech a school must tolerate and speech a school must promote, employers must proceed cautiously when considering discipline against an official spokesperson–for even official spokespersons have First Amendment rights. In evaluating this type of retaliation claim, courts often look at the employee's written job description, written instructions given to the employee, or board policy to determine whether the employee/spokesperson deviated from official duties and whether the employee/spokesperson had notice of what was expected of him or her.

B. Discipline of Employees Who are in a Confidential Relationship with Their Superior

May a school superintendent or college president terminate his personal secretary for publicly criticizing the handling of a recent public controversy? May a school board terminate a superintendent who made public statements contrary to the board's wishes? The courts have recognized that public employers have a right to expect loyalty from employees who occupy confidential positions. For example, in *Kinsey v.*

Salado Independent School District,[41] a superintendent actively opposed certain candidates for the school board. When those candidates won, the board forced the superintendent out of office. Although the superintendent's speech involved a matter of public concern, the board had an essential need for a close and positive working relationship with the superintendent. The court concluded that the superintendent's activities were sufficiently disruptive of the relationship. Similarly, in *Soderstrum v. Town of Grand Isle*,[42] the court held that a new police chief lawfully could fire his secretary, who worked for the chief's predecessor and who was related to the predecessor. The secretary claimed that she was fired solely because of her political associations. The court held that the secretary occupied a confidential position and that the new chief was entitled to complete trust and personal cooperation from his own secretary.

C. Hearsay Allegations and the First Amendment

In some instances, a supervisor will learn from hearsay reports that an employee has engaged in certain speech activities. For example, a college dean might learn from a student about statements made by a faculty member during class. In *Waters v. Churchill*,[43] the U.S. Supreme Court discussed the ability of an employer to discipline or terminate the employee which it believes to have engaged in unprotected speech. Justice O'Connor, on behalf of a four-justice plurality, recognized that the government, as an employer, has a significant interest in achieving its goals quickly and efficiently. She wrote that it would be unreasonable to require the employer, before disciplining an employee, to conduct an investigation as if courtroom rules of evidence and procedure applied. In a separate opinion, Justice Souter observed that "a public employer who reasonably believes a third party report that an employee engaged in unconstitutionally-protected speech may punish the employee in reliance upon that speech, even if it turns out that the employee's actual remarks were constitutionally protected. To avoid liability, the public employer must reasonably investigate the third party report and actually believe the report." Before taking adverse action against an employee, the school should undertake a reasonable investigation of the hearsay allegations. The school should document its investigation and its efforts to determine the content of the employee's speech.

V. Preventing the First Amendment Case

Because the common reasons employees file lawsuits, including First Amendment actions, often can be influenced by school officials, the management objective becomes one of avoiding the circumstances that encourage the filing of lawsuits.

A. The Role of the Immediate Supervisor–Leadership

In avoiding lawsuits, one must focus on the primary cause of many First Amendment suits: the relationship of the employee and his or her direct supervisor. The supervisor is expected to exert leadership and directly communicate with his or her subordinates and identify any issues of concern or need. The supervisor is expected to be a leader and resolve the concerns or needs of the employees when it is within his or her level of responsibility and to refer questions that are outside the supervisor's authority to a superior. When the immediate supervisor fails to provide leadership and perform these responsibilities, a First Amendment problem may develop. The employees may feel as if the supervisor is ignoring their concerns; they may attempt to express their concerns elsewhere. Supervisors should be instructed about their responsibility to address and resolve problems and to communicate with those under their supervision. Supervisors who fail to do so should be assessed accordingly at evaluation time.

B. Recognition of the Employee's Rights Under the First Amendment

School officials must recognize that employees have First Amendment rights and may speak out on issues of public concern. These free speech rights extend to statements made in private conversations as well as those made in public settings. Although balancing the school's interests and the employee's rights is difficult for courts, it is even more difficult for supervisors who are in the midst of a controversy. Supervisors must attempt to remove themselves from the controversy and remain as objective as possible. The supervisor should seek the assistance of others, including administrative superiors and legal counsel. Applying the legal standards to a set of real facts is the first critical step in the prevention of a First Amendment suit, and it is a step that should not be taken lightly.

C. Effective Evaluation and Documentation

The use of an effective and carefully crafted documentation system is an essential component of preventing a First Amendment case. School officials should systematically evaluate and document employee performance and should inform employees about existing problems. Documentation of employee performance over a period of years not only allows the employee to improve in weak areas, it serves as tangible evidence in the event of a lawsuit. Courts and juries are suspicious of evaluations and reprimands that occur only after the employee engages in a protected activity. A practical and useful system of documentation is found in the NOLPE monograph, *A Documentation System for Teacher Improvement or Termination*.[44] A skeletal outline of that system is included here.

Effective documentation requires communication. A cardinal rule of documentation is to confer with the employee first and follow up with a written memorandum to summarize the conference. If the issue is important enough to generate an individual memorandum, it is important enough to have a personal conference with the employee involved. In preparing any memorandum, the supervisor should rely on the facts and should avoid conclusion. Inflammatory words such as "stupid," "ridiculous," "unbelievable," "dumb," and "insubordination" should be avoided. Educational jargon should not be used extensively, because laypersons on a school board or jury may eventually be asked to understand the language. The communication should be personalized by using the first person, yet it should be direct and to the point. Memoranda are judged not by their length, but by their quality. No communication should be written and sent when the supervisor is upset or angry; however, the writing must be sent soon after the incident or conference to secure the desired effect.

It is advisable to have the employee sign a copy of the memorandum to acknowledge receipt. If the employee refuses, simply have another person sign a statement that the employee was given a copy on a certain date but refused to acknowledge receipt. Each memorandum should recite the date of the conference, the topics discussed, the items agreed upon, and any directions given. The concluding paragraph should offer the opportunity for the employee to submit any disagreement with the contents in writing or to have a further conference to discuss any differences.

D. Using the Grievance or Complaint Process for Resolving First Amendment Claims

If, after using the management strategies outlined above, an employee complains about retaliation for the exercise of First Amendment rights, a process should be available for the prompt resolution of the claim. The claim should not languish unnoticed or unresolved. An unresolved First Amendment claim often may snowball and attract other employees within its sweep. Many school districts define "grievance" to include allegations of First Amendment violations and other discriminatory acts. The formal grievance process then becomes the procedure available to resolve such claims. The availability of this dispute resolution process is helpful to the employee because it provides an avenue to seek redress, to complain, and to ventilate. Likewise, the process provides the administrator with a process that the employee must follow.

While the courts expect school districts and their administrators to obey established constitutional standards, the courts generally will defer to the decisions of school districts where a conscious effort has been made to adhere to constitutional standards. Such adherence to standards can be demonstrated partially by a school district's willingness to provide a process within the school to resolve claims prior to litigation. Once a process is provided, however, school officials must be ready and willing to hear and consider an employee's First Amendment allegations. If the hearings show that an employee's First Amendment rights have been violated, school officials must respond by providing an appropriate remedy for the violation. Remedies may include the restoration of lost benefits, a cessation of the inappropriate action, and a commitment not to undertake the action in the future. Often a memorandum to the offending supervisor containing a directive on future behavior is necessary to set a legal future course of action. The evaluation of these claims depends upon the facts of each case, and the district's legal counsel should be consulted in the evaluation of the First Amendment claim and its resolution, if a violation is found.

VI. Potential First Amendment Pitfalls

Administrators are continually faced with management decisions and potential pitfalls. These potential problems include the requirement to use the chain of command, the challenge of the civilly disobedient employee, and the challenge presented when an administrator must gain control of an out-of-control school department, school, or school district.

A. The Chain of Command

Many school officials are sensitive to the management concept that employees must follow the chain of command when seeking a resolution to a school problem. The chain of command remains a fertile litigation area. While some courts may hold that requiring adherence to the chain of command is a valid restriction on time, place and manner of speech,[45] other courts may find that chain of command requirements are invalid when the employee's speech is on a public issue as opposed to a private matter.[46] Speech concerning the reporting of criminal violations is high in the hierarchy of protected speech, and the federal government and many states have enacted "whistleblowing" statutes to provide additional protection. The classic worst case scenario is the school district official who states: "I fired him because he went to a school board member about a problem when I told him not to talk with any school board members."

To minimize these concerns, one must take a balanced approach. The first step is for the supervisor to recognize that an employee generally has the right to speak out on all issues of public concern, and the supervisor should assume that this right includes the employee's right to speak to school board members about these matters without following the chain of command. The second step involves the supervisor communicating this understanding to the employee while advising the employee that there is an internal process available to resolve issues. The employee should further be advised that the supervisor cannot resolve problems that are not brought to the supervisor and that the supervisor is available and willing to deal with an issue brought to his or her attention or refer it to the next person up the chain. It is often necessary for the immediate supervisor to present his or her views about the employee's concern to the next level supervisor. A third step is for the supervisor to put steps one and two in a memorandum to the employee after discussing the resolution of the matter.

For this system to work effectively, the board of trustees must assume its proper role as a policy-making body, rather than as the administrator of those policies. When a board member is approached by an employee about a problem, the board member should receive the information and refer the employee back to the appropriate member of the administration. In some districts, the superintendent might be designated as the referral person; in others, board members may send the employee directly to the person with authority to resolve the problem. Obviously, if the employee has not attempted to have the matter resolved by his or her immediate supervisor and the supervisor has the authority to resolve it, the supervisor would be the appropriate starting point.

When issues are raised outside the chain of command or internal administrative process by an employee, the immediate supervisor should be directed to conduct and prepare a report on the issues and recommend what steps, if any, should be taken to resolve any problems. The immediate supervisor should be expected to resolve any issue within his or her level of responsibility.

The concerns or needs of most employees can be met through this type of communication and an occasional memorandum. Sometimes, an employee may attempt to set up a supervisor by casually making statements that the employee really wants the supervisor to ignore so the employee can later claim that his or her complaints were disregarded. If this appears to be occurring, the supervisor should either take the initiative to deal with the issue or ask the employee to put his or her concerns in writing. The supervisor should prepare a memorandum to document the request and any action taken.

B. Employee Civil Disobedience

A situation closely akin to the chain of command problem involves an employee who does not like what is happening at the district and who may be at political odds with the administration or the board of trustees. This can occur with all levels of employees: administration, faculty, and classified. Virtually everyone recognizes that employees have the right to disagree with policy matters and take appropriate steps to try to change the policy or philosophy of the board or administration. The problem occurs either when the disagreement is reflected in the employee's performance or when the employee perceives that the supervisor is retaliating against him or her because of the policy or political posture. Just as surely as retaliation for the exercise of protected rights has no place in a school system, civil disobedience is unacceptable, especially when it impairs an employee's effectiveness or hampers the achievement of educational goals. Balancing the rights of the employee with the needs of the school in this setting is especially difficult.

The supervisor should continue to assess the job related aspects of such an employee's behavior and avoid stating: "It's because of your views that you are not doing your job right." Instead, the supervisor should conference with the employee and acknowledge to the employee that he or she has a right to disagree on policy or political matters, and voice his or her opinion about those issues. The supervisor should then advise the employee that he or she does not have to like the policy or philosophy, nor does he or she have to like the person with whom he or she is dealing, but the employee is hired to perform a job and he or she will be expected to do it. An employee must perform according to the job description and directives of his or her superiors, so long as the instructions are not directed to an illegal activity. Disagreement with why things are as they are does not justify performing job tasks in an unacceptable manner.

C. Cleaning up an Out-of-Control School or School District

A fertile ground for the germination of a First Amendment case is an out-of-control school or department. Generally, an out-of-control school or department is a product of inadequate or poor leadership. Gaining control of the out-of-control situation is a real challenge to even the best of administrators. The same situation is faced by a new superintendent who comes into a school district where the previous superintendent lost control. When a leadership vacuum has been created by a weak administrator, someone invariably steps forward to fill the leadership space. In schools this vacuum is often filled by an assistant principal, teacher, or secretary, while the void in the superintendency position is usually filled by a board member or an upper level administrator.

An out-of-control school or department usually attracts the attention of the public and the board who become disenchanted and irritated with the state of affairs. When a new administrator is employed to lead the school, department or district, there is a tendency to tell that person to "clean the mess up," even if it means firing people. The new administrator is usually directed to dive into the task. This offers the perfect opportunity for the creation of the First Amendment case. If the new administrator moves too quickly without getting a feel for the strength of the staff and their alliances, he or she may make irretrievable moves that will lead to his or her failure. These moves may cause the employees to take political stands or seek outside intervention to head off the changes with which they do not agree. Threatened employees often join unions, appear before public bodies, and otherwise engage in protected speech activities. If these employees then suffer adverse job actions, the First Amendment case is born. These employees may furthermore enjoy the support of a large contingent of the staff, in which case the district and its administration will probably have difficulty in marshalling witnesses to present facts and support its position.

An administrator who is sent into a school to "clean it up" should carefully examine the circumstances before taking strong action. Under no circumstances should the administrator issue initial threats if his or her views are not accepted by the staff. If the staff members who can form the basis of a strong faculty feel threatened, they will support the weak ones who will be subjected to strict scrutiny and possibly face adverse job actions. Instead, the new administrator should determine who the strong staff members are and attempt to have them become participants in a program of change. After the strong staff members accept the changes, the weaker ones normally fall in line, and if they do not, the stronger ones generally feel the weaker ones were given a fair opportunity. A lawsuit filed by the weaker employees will probably not be supported by the stronger and more effective employees. The less support an employee receives from his or her peers for a lawsuit, the less is the chance that it will be filed or fully prosecuted.

VII. Evaluation and Executing Adverse Employment Decisions

Another critical state in preventing a First Amendment case occurs when the supervisor must determine whether to recommend an adverse employment action, such as termination, for an employee who has been or will claim to have been engaged in a free speech activity. When such an employee is considered for termination, a supervisor should be ready to confront the issue directly and articulate the reasons in support of termination.

A. Conference With the Employee Before Recommending Termination

Before a final recommendation concerning an employee's termination or nonrenewal is made to the superintendent, and ultimately to the board of trustees, the supervisor and the supervisor's superior should hold a conference with the employee. The employee should be told of any inadequacies or problems and should be given an opportunity to explain his or her version of the facts. This conference can help clarify misunderstandings concerning the basic reasons for the proposed termination.

The employee should be given the opportunity, and actually should be encouraged, to discuss any speech-related issues and any feelings the employee may have that he or she is being discriminated against based upon race, sex, religion, ethnicity, age or disability. If any of these issues are raised, they should be fully discussed. This will give the immediate supervisor and the supervisor's superior an opportunity to consider any additional facts or viewpoints an employee may present, examine the situation more closely, and determine whether termination is the proper alternative.[47]

If, after the conference with the employee, the immediate supervisor and the supervisor's superior determine that a recommendation for termination should be made, it should be prepared. When the recommendation is made, the supervisor should also submit an appropriate notification letter of proposed termination, listing the reasons supporting the proposed termination for review by the district's legal counsel. The supervisor should also prepare a letter for review by the district's legal counsel containing a list of the witnesses together with a description of the statements of those who would testify on behalf of the administration at a hearing. The documents which support the reasons for the termination should also be presented for review at this time. After these items have been reviewed by the district's legal counsel, a conference of the immediate supervisor, the supervisor's superior, and the attorney to review the file is often very helpful. Any First Amendment allegations and other discrimination issues involved in the possible termination should be discussed with the attorney at this time, if they have not been previously reviewed. If the attorney does not ask whether these issues are present, the administrators should volunteer the information. The attorney will then be in a position to evaluate the proposed termination with knowledge of any First Amendment or discrimination claims.

B. Hearing of the First Amendment Issues Before the Board or Hearing Officer

By the time a termination reaches the board of trustees or a hearing officer, the First Amendment status is generally in one of three categories. The school officials are: (1) aware of the specific First Amendment claims by having dealt with them through the grievance process or in the conferences preceding the decision to recommend termination; (2) aware only of vague, unsubstantiated claims made by the employee; or (3) not aware of any real or potential claim. If a claim exists, it is essential that the issue be confronted and resolved at the hearing on the proposed termination.

If the employee's First Amendment allegations are broadly stated and not supported by specific facts, the district's legal counsel or school officials should consider writing the employee's representative that the board or hearing officer intends to fully and completely deal with these allegations and request that he or she supply the administration with a full statement of the facts which support the claim. This accomplishes a dual objective of stating on the record the board's intent to apply constitutional standards, and it attempts to discover the facts in advance of the hearing so the administration can reconsider its position on the termination recommendation or be prepared to rebut the evidence at the hearing. The employee's representative is not required to provide the information about First Amendment allegations, but a failure to do so can be cause for the postponement of a hearing, and a future judge or jury can certainly consider the employee's action unreasonable.

Not infrequently the employee's attorney will attempt to raise First Amendment allegations for the first time when the lawsuit is filed. As a hedge against this possibility and to force the issue to be heard before the board, many school district attorneys will ask the employee at the termination hearing whether he feels, or is in any way claiming, that the employee has been discriminated against based on race, sex, national origin, age or disability, or whether the employee feels the termination is in any way related to First Amendment activities such as speech, association with others or union or political activity. If the employee answers "yes" to any of these questions, the facts surrounding the issue can be pursued and resolved by the board.

When the board considers a First Amendment claim, it should rely upon the advice of counsel to determine whether the speech activity is protected. If there is any doubt, the board should assume that it is protected for purposes of applying the substantial or motivating factor test of *Mt. Healthy*. If the board finds that the First Amendment activity was not a motivating or substantial factor in the proposal to terminate, the inquiry is concluded. If, however, the board determines that the First Amendment activity was a substantial or motivating factor, the board then can determine whether there are lawful reasons for which the person could be terminated. However, once the motivation question is answered "yes," a board should be very cautious about proceeding with the termination because a detached judge or jury who considers the case later may find lawful cause lacking. A "yes" answer to the motivation question generally signals the time to consider alternatives to termination.

Should the employee refuse to answer questions concerning First Amendment or discrimination claims on his or her own, or at the instruction of an attorney, the school attorney can ask the employee's attorney to stipulate that none of these illegal matters are at issue in this case. Even if the attorney refuses, it makes raising the discrimination claims and First Amendment allegations in a lawsuit more difficult. The employee and his or her attorney will certainly be vulnerable to accusations of "laying behind the log," being unfair, and not providing the school board an opportunity to apply the constitutional standards. Courts have been known to remand such cases to the school district for further hearings on the First Amendment issue. When boards have heard the First Amendment claims and have dealt with them, courts tend to give considerable deference to their decisions, and courts have been known to grant summary judgments for school districts when allegations and the facts before the courts are the same as those raised before the boards. At the very least, the board's willingness to consider the issues up front will establish an atmosphere of reasonableness which should have a positive impact on the future course of the litigation.

VIII. Conclusion

The application of the First Amendment in the public employment setting will continue to be a challenge to school officials and attorneys. Although the standards for analyzing the First Amendment claim are subject to further development, school officials can take certain actions to help prevent the First Amendment case from occurring or to place the school and its officials in a better position to prevail, should a case be filed.

A critical step is to establish an environment in the school where employees perceive they are treated fairly. This is founded in leadership, good management practices, and effective communication. An effective evaluation and documentation system is essential to achieve this result. Employees should not be placed in positions where they are forced to lose their personal dignity or where they feel they have been treated unfairly.

The immediate supervisor must assume a leadership role in responding to employee needs and resolving problems. The First Amendment rights of employees should be recognized and respected, but those rights should not be used by an employee to avoid the performance of assigned duties. While internal procedures should be in place to resolve problems, supervisors should recognize that employees can generally discuss public issues with board members. Any First Amendment allegation should be resolved promptly within the school district structure, and boards of trustees and hearing officers should not shy away from dealing with First Amendment claims. When a school district or college deals with these issues in a straightforward manner, it gains better control of its destiny. School employees are less anxious to file suits when they perceive that they and their fellow employees have been treated fairly, and courts are reluctant to overrule or second-guess the decisions of governmental bodies when their resolution process appears fair and reasonable.

ENDNOTES

[1] Porter v. Califano, 592 F.2d 770,779 (5th Cir. 1979).

[2] Police Dep't of City of Chicago v. Mosley, 408 U.S. 921, 92 S. Ct. 2286, 2290 (1972); Lamb's Chapel v. Center Moriches Union Free Sch. Dist., 113 S. Ct. 2141 (1993).

[3] Pierce v. Texas Dep't of Criminal Justice, 37 F.3d 1146 (5th Cir. 1994), *cert. denied*, 115 S. Ct. 1957 (1995); Dorsett v. Board of Trustees, 940 F.2d 121 (5th Cir. 1991).

[4] Givhan v. Western Line Consol. Sch. Dist., 439 U.S. 410 (1979); Tompkins v. Vickers, 26 F.3d 603 (5th Cir. 1994).

[5] Ayoub v. Texas A&M Univ., 927 F.2d 834 (5th Cir. 1991), *cert. denied*, 502 U.S. 817 (1991).

[6] Jeffries v. Harleston, 52 F.3d 9 (2d Cir. 1995), *cert. denied*, 116 S. Ct. 173 (1995); Nieto v. San Perlita Indep. Sch. Dist., 894 F.2d 174 (5th Cir. 1990).

[7] *See, e.g.*, Wagner v. Wheeler, 13 F.3d 86 (4th Cir. 1993) (although employee did report violations of environmental regulations to state authorities, employee was terminated for infractions of work rules and insubordination).

[8] Pickering v. Board of Educ., 391 U.S. 563, 88 S. Ct. 1731 (1968); Mt. Healthy City Bd. of Educ. v. Doyle, 429 U.S. 274, 97 S. Ct. 568 (1977); Connick v. Myers, 461 U.S. 138, 103 S. Ct. 1684 (1983).

[9] 391 U.S. 563 (1968).

[10] 429 U.S. 274 (1977).

[11] 461 U.S. 138 (1983).

[12] *See, e.g.*, Stewart v. Baldwin County Bd. of Educ., 908 F.2d 1499 (11th Cir. 1990) (employee walked out on superintendent's speech concerning tax referendum); Moore v. City of Kilgore, 877 F.2d 364, 370 (5th Cir.), *cert. denied*, 100 S. Ct. 562 (1989) (in interview with media following a deadly fire, a firefighter criticized fire department understaffing). Whether a matter is being publicly debated is relevant but is not absolutely decisive. The Supreme Court has held that even a private conservation on a matter of public concern merits First Amendment protection. *See* Givhan v. Western Line Consol. Sch. Dist., 439 U.S. 410 (1979).

[13] *See, e.g.,* Johnston v. Harris County Flood Control Dist., 869 F.2d 1565, 1578 (5th Cir. 1989), *cert. denied*, 493 U.S. 1019, 100 S. Ct. 718 (1990).
[14] *See, e.g.,* Price v. Brittain, 874 F.2d 252, 258 (5th Cir. 1989).
[15] *See, e.g.,* Givhan v. Western Line Consol. Sch. Dist., 439 U.S. 410 (1979).
[16] *See, e.g.*, Voigt v. Savell, 70 F.3d 1552 (9th Cir. 1995); Scott v. Flowers, 910 F.2d 201, 203-04 (5th Cir. 1990).
[17] *See, e.g.,* Rankin v. McPherson, 483 U.S. 378, 107 S. Ct. 2891 (1987) (county clerical employee could not be terminated for criticizing presidential policies and stating that she hoped President would be assassinated).
[18] 901 F.2d 456 (5th Cir. 1990).
[19] 908 F.2d 1499 (11th Cir. 1990).
[20] 943 F.2d 845 (8th Cir. 1991).
[21] Ayoub v. Texas A&M Univ., 927 F.2d 834 (5th Cir. 1991), *cert. denied*, 502 U.S. 817, 112 S.Ct. 72 (1991).
[22] Hullman v. Board of Trustees, 950 F.2d 665 (10th Cir. 1991).
[23] Hesse v. Board of Educ., 848 F.2d 748 (7th Cir. 1988), *cert. denied*, 489 U.S. 1015 (1989).
[24] 933 F.2d 271 (5th Cir. 1991).
[25] *See generally* Connick, 461 U.S. 138 (employee transfers, need for employee grievance committee, confidence in supervisors); Cliff v. Board of Sch. Comm'r, 42 F.3d 403, 409 (7th Cir. 1994) (although teacher's concerns about student discipline were of interest to the public, "her expression was addressed only to the personal impact" of those issues on herself); Renfroe v. Kirkpatrick, 722 F.2d 714 (11th Cir.), *cert. denied*, 469 U.S. 823 (1984) (employee grievances which in themselves do not relate to matters of public concern).
[26] Davis v. Ector County, Tex., 40 F.3d 777 (5th Cir. 1994) (protected speech); Poulsen v. City of N. Tonqwanda, 811 F.Supp. 884,894 (W.D.N.Y. 1993) (protected speech); Saulpaugh v. Monroe Community Hospital, 4 F.3d 134, 143 (2d Cir. 1993) (not protected speech in the absence of evidence of system-wide discrimination); Woodward v. City of Worland, 977 F.2d 1392 (10th Cir. 1992), *cert. denied*, 113 S. Ct. 3038 (1993) (complaints about sexual harassment not protected speech).
[27] Berg v. Hunter, 854 F.2d 238, 243 (7th Cir. 1988), *cert. denied*, 489 U.S. 1053 (1989).
[28] *Id.* at 243 (citing *Connick*, 461 U.S. at 152).
[29] *Id.* at 244.
[30] *Jeffries*, 52 F.3d at 13 (citing Waters v. Churchill); Voigt v. Savell, 70 F.3d 1552, 1560-61 (9th Cir. 1995) (affidavits by coworkers concerning plaintiff's disparaging comments showed plaintiff's speech was disruptive and undermined office harmony).
[31] 52 F.3d 9 (2d Cir. 1995), *cert. denied*, 116 SCt. 173 (1995).
[32] 894 F.2d 174 (5th Cir. 1990).
[33] *Jeffries*, 52 F.3d at 13.
[34] *See, e.g.,* Miles v. Denver Pub. Schs., 944 F.2d 773 (10th Cir. 1991) (teacher was disciplined for commenting during class time about the rumored sexual antics of two students); Ward v. Hickey, 996 F.2d 448 (1st Cir. 1993) (teacher's contract was not renewed following her classroom speech about abortion of Down's syndrome fetuses); Silano v. Sag Habour, 42 F.3d 719 (2d Cir. 1994), *cert. denied*, 115 S. Ct. 2612 (1995) (guest speaker was barred from returning to campus after using film clips containing naked adults); Cohen v. San Bernadino Valley College, 883 F. Supp. 1407 (C.D. Cal.1995) (professor's use of profanity and sexual vulgarities were not protected speech; college's interests outweighed teacher's interests).
[35] *See, e.g.,* Miles, 944 F.2d at 775; Kirkland v. Northside Indep. Sch. Dist., 890 F.2d 794, 796 (5th Cir. 1989), *cert. denied*, 496 U.S. 926 (1990) (teacher could not substitute his own reading list for the school's).
[36] *See, e.g., Miles*, 944 F.2d at 775; *Ward*, 996 F.2d at 452-53; *Bishop*, 926 F.2d at 1071; *but see* Scallet v. Rosenblum, 911 F. Supp. 999 (W.D. Va. 1996) (*Pickering* test applied to professor's in-class speech).
[37] 484 U.S. 260 (1988).
[38] *Id.* at 271.
[39] *Miles*, 944 F.2d at 777.
[40] 801 F.2d 1182, 1184 (9th Cir. 1986).

[41] 950 F.2d 988 (5th Cir. 1992), *cert. denied*, 112 S. Ct. 2275 (1992); *compare Rankin*, 107 S. Ct. at 2900 ("where, as here, anemployee serves no confidential, policymaking, or public contact role, the danger to the agency's successful functioning from that employee's private speech is minimal.").
[42] 925 F.2d 135 (5th Cir.1991).
[43] 114 S.Ct. 1878 (1994).
[44] *See generally* K. Frels and J. Horton, A DOCUMENTATION SYSTEM FOR TEACHER IMPROVEMENT OR TERMINATION (NOLPE Monograph Rev. Ed. 1995).
[45] *E.g.*, Boyd v. Secretary of the Navy, 709 F.2d 684 (11th Cir. 1983), *cert. denied*, 464 U.S. 1043 (1984).
[46] Anderson v. Central Point Sch. Dist., 746 F.2d 505 (9th Cir. 1984); Knapp v. Whitaker, 577 F. Supp. 1265 (C.D. Ill. 1983), *aff'd*, 757 F.2d 829 (7th Cir. 1985), *cert. denied*, 106 S. Ct. 36 (1985).
[47] *See* Frels & Horton at 10-11.

EMPLOYMENT DISCRIMINATION AND RELATED CLAIMS

By: Vianei Lopez Robinson

I. Introduction

As public employers, school districts are subject to a great deal of scrutiny concerning their employment decisions. A significant portion of the lawsuits brought against public school districts involve employment discrimination and related claims arising from the working environment. In many instances, these lawsuits are largely unexpected and suspect. Most school districts conscientiously adhere to their policies against discrimination in the workplace, and they make employment decisions based on legitimate, nondiscriminatory criteria. Unfortunately, these efforts are not always enough to prevent employment discrimination lawsuits.

When school districts became involved in employment-related litigation, more often than not there is no good outcome available. There are better and worse outcomes, of course, but increasingly the time, expense, and negative publicity involved in defending against a lawsuit make any victory at best a Pyhrric one. As employment-related litigation has grown increasingly common, school districts have continued to search for strategies that will help shield them from employment law claims. This chapter describes various statutory claims that may arise in an employment discrimination lawsuit, and provides suggestions that may help a school district develop strategies to minimize exposure to these claims.

II. Selected Statutory Provisions

The panoply of claims that can be raised in the employment law context continues to grow. When analyzing employee management practices, it is helpful to keep in mind the claims that an aggrieved employee would most likely raise against a school district employer. The following is a nonexhaustive list of statutory claims that are commonly raised in employment law cases.

A. Title VII of the Civil Rights Act of 1964 ("Title VII")[1]

Title VII prohibits employment discrimination on the basis of an employee's race, color, national origin, religion, or sex. Title VII also prohibits discrimination based on pregnancy, and prohibits sexual harassment or other workplace harassment based on a protected characteristic. Title VII covers employers with fifteen (15) or more employees. To maintain an action under Title VII, an aggrieved employee must first file a charge with the Equal Employment Opportunity Commission ("EEOC") or a comparable state or local agency.

B. Texas Labor Code (Texas Commission on Human Rights Act)[2]

The Texas Labor Code contains provisions that are the state law equivalent of Title VII in Texas. It provides for the maintenance of the Texas Commission on Human Rights ("TCHR") which, along with the EEOC, handles charges of discrimination within the State of Texas. The Labor Code prohibits employment discrimination based on race, color, national origin, religion and sex (like Title VII), as well as based on age and disability (like the federal Age Discrimination in Employment Act and Americans with Disabilities Act). The Labor Code's nondiscrimination provisions apply to employers with more than fifteen (15) employees. The Labor Code also contains provisions prohibiting discrimination for filing a worker's compensation claim,[3] for filing an unemployment compensation claim[4] or for complying with a valid subpoena.[5]

C. Age Discrimination in Employment Act of 1967 ("ADEA")[6]

The ADEA prohibits employment discrimination against employees on the basis of their age. The class of employees protected by the ADEA are employees over the age of forty (40), and the ADEA applies to employers with twenty (20) or more employees. Like Title VII, the ADEA requires that before filing a lawsuit, an employee alleging age discrimination must file a timely charge with the EEOC or a state or local agency, such as the TCHR.

D. Employee Retirement Income Security Act of 1974 ("ERISA")[7]

ERISA is an extensive statute affecting employee benefit plans, and it is the source of COBRA health insurance obligations and numerous other regulations. ERISA also has a nondiscrimination provision, which prohibits discharge or other adverse action against employees that is designed to interfere with attainment of vested retirement benefits or benefits to which the employees may become entitled under a benefit plan.

E. Americans with Disabilities Act of 1990 ("ADA")[8]

The ADA prohibits employment discrimination against individuals with a disability who are otherwise qualified for a given job position. A disability is defined as a physical or mental impairment that substantially limits a major life activity. An individual with a disability is considered otherwise qualified if he or she can perform the essential functions of the job, with or without reasonable accommodation provided by the employer. The ADA applies to employers with fifteen (15) or more employees. Because of the ADA's extensive effect upon school districts, its provisions are discussed at length in a separate chapter.

F. Rehabilitation Act of 1973[9]

The Rehabilitation Act prohibits discrimination against individuals with disabilities by employers receiving federal financial assistance, such as school districts, federal agencies, grant recipients and federal contractors. The Rehabilitation Act, which applies primarily to public entities, was the predecessor to the ADA, which affects both private and public entities and is broader in scope.

G. Family and Medical Leave Act of 1993 ("FMLA")[10]

The FMLA became effective on August 5, 1993. It requires employers to grant twelve (12) weeks of unpaid leave and restoration of the same or equivalent job to an employee for: 1) birth or adoption of a child, or 2) care of oneself or a child, spouse, or parent suffering from a serious health condition. To be eligible for FMLA leave, an employee must have been employed for at least twelve (12) months, and must have worked at least 1,250 hours during the twelve (12) months prior to the leave. Employees at work locations with less than fifty (50) employees are not eligible for leave unless the employer has fifty (50) or more employees employed within seventy-five (75) miles of the work site. Twelve weeks of FMLA leave may be taken once every twelve (12) months; employers may adopt a policy defining the applicable twelve (12) month period.

H. National Labor Relations Act ("NLRA") and Texas Right to Work Laws[11]

The NLRA and the Texas Right to Work laws prohibit employment discrimination based on an employee's membership or non-membership in a union, participation in union activities, or for filing or testifying regarding an unfair labor practice charge. Employers may not take any employment action to retaliate against employees for union activities, or to discourage employees from union membership.

I. Reconstruction Era Civil Rights Act[12]

Passed in the 1860s and 1870s, the Reconstruction Era Civil Rights Act is still commonly used today. The provisions of 42 U.S.C. § 1981 prohibit discrimination on the basis of race in the making and enforcement of contracts, which includes the terms and conditions of employment contracts. 42 U.S.C. § 1983 is used to establish claims against persons, including school districts and school officials, acting "under color of law" to deprive someone of protected constitutional or federal statutory rights. The provisions of 42 U.S.C. § 1985 offer a separate cause of action against a conspiracy to deprive someone of civil rights, and 42 U.S.C. § 1988 allows the recovery of attorney's fees by a prevailing party.

J. Jury Service and Political Activity

Under both federal and Texas law, employers are prohibited from taking adverse action against an employee based on the employee's service on a jury.[13] Texas law also prohibits employers from denying their employees an opportunity to vote on election day and from taking adverse action based on an employee's absence for the purpose of voting,[14] from coercing employees to vote a particular way,[15] and from knowingly prohibiting an employee's attendance at a political convention.[16]

K. Military Service

Both federal and Texas law protect an employee's right to reemployment after being called to active duty military service. [17]The federal law is broader in scope, prohibiting employers from discriminating against an employee in hiring, reemployment, retention, promotion, or other benefits on the basis of the employee's military obligations.

L. Occupational Safety and Health Act of 1970 ("OSHA") and other safety-related statutes

OSHA and its regulations govern workplace safety standards, and OSHA prohibits retaliation against an employee for filing a complaint or testifying as to violations of established occupational health and safety standards.[18] Federal law contains similar provisions prohibiting retaliation against an employee who reports violations or testifies under the Clean Air Act[19] or the Water Pollution Control Act.[20] Texas law also contains protections for employees who report safety hazards, such as protection against retaliation for reporting an illegal use of hazardous chemicals.[21]

M. Fair Labor Standards Act ("FLSA")[22]

The FLSA establishes the national minimum wage and standards for overtime pay which apply to nonexempt employees. Exempt employees include bona fide executive, administrative or professional employees, and learners or apprentices. Employers are prohibited under the FLSA from retaliating against an employee for filing a grievance concerning alleged overtime or minimum wage violations.

N. Equal Pay Act[23]

The Equal Pay Act prohibits discrimination in compensation on the basis of an employee's gender. Equal work must be rewarded with equal pay unless pay differential is based on a bona fide system based on seniority, merit, productivity, quality or another factor not related to gender.

O. Whistleblower Act[24]

The Texas Whistleblower Act applies to only to public employers, including public school districts. The Act prohibits retaliation against an employee for making a good-faith report of illegal workplace conduct to an appropriate law enforcement authority.[25]

P. Title VI of the Civil Rights Act of 1964 ("Title VI") and Title IX of the Education Act Amendments of 1972 ("Title IX")[26]

Title VI and Title IX both apply to educational programs receiving federal financial assistance, such as public school districts. Title VI prohibits discrimination on the basis of race, and Title IX prohibits discrimination on the basis of gender. Employees of qualifying educational programs and participants in such programs may both maintain claims under Title VI and Title IX.

The above list of potential claims, which is not an exhaustive list, demonstrates why school administrators often regard employment law as something akin to a pit full of rattlesnakes. With so many slippery legal concepts coiled around the employment relationship, it is not surprising that unexpected claims frequently arise. Good intentions and common sense, although always helpful, are not enough to shield a school district from inevitable legal claims. School districts, can, however, take steps to significantly minimize their exposure to employment discrimination lawsuits. School districts should ascertain that their employment practices are consistent, fair, and well-documented, and should always be prepared to explain the rationale for each employment decision. Some specific suggestions for implementing this type of risk management are listed below.

III. Specific Considerations Regarding Hiring

There are several legal risks that are particularly relevant to the hiring process. School districts should have a centralized and consistent hiring process, and should review the process periodically to see if it is accomplishing the district's objectives. Ideally, the hiring process should effectively identify and recruit qualified and motivated employees, and should be structured to prevent discrimination and related claims.

A. Applications for Employment

Employment applications should be reviewed periodically to ascertain that they do not ask about any protected information that is not critical to the relevant job. If the job selection process does not require information about sensitive issues such as age, marital status, disabilities, and the like, questions about those issues should be deleted. It is also a good idea to have applications contain a statement that the district is an equal-opportunity employer.

To the extent possible, applications should seek information that is directly relevant to the job that is being sought. Irrelevant information may seem harmless at the time, but it puts the district on notice of facts that may later be used to imply a discriminatory motive behind an employment action.

Particularly in light of recent decisions concerning later-acquired evidence, it is important to have a statement on applications confirming that any falsification or misrepresentation of information on the application is grounds for disciplinary action, including termination. A statement on the application for non-contract employees can also be used to have the applicant acknowledge that any employment relationship will be terminable at-will, and will not be governed by an employment contract. Acknowledgments on employment applications can also be used to obtain an employee's permission to perform a credit check consistent with the dictates of the Fair Credit Reporting Act.[27]

B. Advertising, Recruiting and Interviewing

Any advertising for job applicants should contain a statement that the district is an equal opportunity employer. Advertising should not be placed in a manner that can be shown to exclude persons of a particular protected class. Likewise, recruiting of applicants should be done in a broad-based manner so that recruiting practices cannot be challenged for exclusion of people on the basis of race, age, sex, or another protected characteristic.

Interviewing practices have been significantly restricted due to the influence of various employment laws. Small talk that might disclose marital status, family obligations, disabling conditions, or age now creates a risk of discrimination claims. Discussion of particular job conditions, assignments, or perks can form the basis of breach of contract claims. Due to these risks, the safest option is to restrict the interview to topics directly relevant to the job at issue. To accomplish this goal, some school districts are restricting interviewers to a script of pre-approved interview questions. Alternatively, some districts allow only a limited number of trained individuals to conduct job interviews.

C. Checking Qualifications and Background

School districts are increasingly exposed to claims based on the wrongful acts of school employees. This phenomenon has made it more important for school districts to check the qualifications and background of job applicants.

When seeking background information on an applicant, the district should first ascertain that the information sought is relevant to the job. Uncovering irrelevant information in a background check presents the same risks as seeking irrelevant information on an application or in an interview. Before initiating any kind of background check, the district should decide what information is being sought, and why it is relevant to the job.

Some information is available only upon written consent of the applicant. The applicant can consent to disclosure of credit information and to disclosure of public school transcripts. Higher education transcripts can be requested from the applicant, and in some cases receipt of a degree can be confirmed from the institution itself. Given the surprising incidence of resume fraud, school districts should probably confirm the credentials shown on an applicant's resume, particularly if a specific credential is required for the job.

Because of the safety-sensitive nature of working with or around school children, public school districts have been given the ability to obtain a job applicant's criminal records. School districts must remember, however, that the mere existence of a criminal record is not sufficient cause to refuse to consider a prospective applicant. The EEOC has stated that an employer must take several factors into consideration before determining whether an applicant with a criminal record is qualified for the position sought. These factors include: 1) the nature, gravity and number of the applicant's criminal acts; 2) the length of time since the conviction; 3) the applicant's work record with other employers since the conviction; and 4) the nature of the job sought or held. The EEOC's guidance is intended to prevent consideration of conviction records from disparately impacting a protected class, such as racial minorities. Based on this guidance, a district should be sure that if a criminal record is used as the basis for rejecting an applicant, there is some rational connection between the nature of the criminal record and fitness for the job position in question.

To protect themselves, school districts should document their attempts to check the background of an applicant, and should retain reference letters and similar documentation that demonstrate the applicant's fitness for the job. Any criminal history information should likewise be retained, but must be kept strictly confidential.

School districts should also be careful to periodically evaluate employment criteria and job descriptions to ascertain that job criteria do not lend themselves to a claim of discrimination. Under the ADA, a disabled applicant is otherwise qualified for the job if he or she can perform the essential functions of the job, with or without reasonable accommodation. Because of this standard, it is critical for job descriptions to accurately list the essential functions of a job position. Job criteria may not screen out people of a particular protected class unless the criteria are consistent with business necessity. For example, height or weight requirements that might tend to eliminate women will violate Title VII unless they are absolutely necessary for the job position in question.

Job descriptions and employment criteria are likely to be heavily scrutinized if challenged on the basis of alleged discrimination. School districts should be prepared to defend these items by showing that they accurately reflect the true requirements of the job in question. In general, job descriptions and employment criteria should be drafted carefully, and should be subject to periodic review by school administrators and the district's legal counsel.

D. Hiring Employees

The school district should have a consistent process for notifying applicants that they have or have not been hired. Rejection letters alone do not present much of a liability risk unless the district is careless enough to include a legally impermissible reason for rejection. It is best if rejection letters do not state any particular reason for the applicant's rejection. The district should, however, retain information about applicants in its internal files so that if a rejection is challenged, the legitimate, nondiscriminatory reasons for rejection can be provided.

In contrast to rejection letters, offer letters are a significant source of claims. Representations in offer letters regarding an annual salary or "permanent" employment can give rise to binding contractual obligations.

School districts and their legal counsel should carefully review the language in their offer letters and delete any language creating unintended contractual claims.

Many school districts choose to have new employees sign a statement acknowledging that they received a copy of the district's policies or employee handbook. This type of acknowledgment is a good idea, because it helps limit subsequent claims based on an alleged lack of awareness of the district's policies.

IV. Specific Considerations Regarding Termination

People depend upon their jobs not only for their livelihood, but also for their sense of purpose, self-esteem, and other important factors. Being terminated is always a traumatic event, even more so if the termination is unexpected or perceived to be unjust. It is not surprising that terminated employees often feel they have been grievously wronged, and that many seek legal redress in hope of gaining some recompense. As school districts know, every terminated employee represents a possible lawsuit. School districts should not be afraid to terminate an employee if such action is appropriate, but they should be aware that the termination needs to be handled with sensitivity and with an awareness of the legal claims that may ensue.

Because of the possibility of legal claims, school districts are sometimes reluctant to terminate employees even if their performance is inadequate or if they are guilty of policy violations or other misconduct. It is detrimental to retain employees whose performance or conduct is below par, and districts should not lower their performance standards or fail to enforce policies in an attempt to avoid claims. Making "exceptions" and failing to react to an employee's performance problems or policy violations can backfire later when the district finally decides to take action. School administrators should react to performance problems and other misconduct in a timely manner, and should take appropriate action to either allow the employee an opportunity to improve, or to terminate the employee based on serious or repeated misconduct.

A. Provide Adequate Notice and Documentation

School administrators sometimes fail to give employees adequate notice of poor performance or violations of policy. An employee cannot be expected to improve if he or she has not been notified of any deficiency. Ideally, the district's policies on poor performance and/or misconduct should put a deficient employee on notice of the problem, and should provide consistent documentation of the problem. If a problem is not severe enough to warrant immediate termination, then the employee should be provided with a reasonable opportunity to improve. A fairly applied evaluation policy can help provide this opportunity.

Policies should further require that any notice to an employee of a deficiency will be documented in writing, and that the employee or a witness will sign the notice as proof that a warning was given. Documentation can help support the district's position if an employee terminated for legitimate reasons later raises claims of discrimination or retaliation. The district may also choose to provide a progressive discipline policy, which may include a range of sanctions for particular types of misconduct. This type of policy helps administrators respond to misconduct in a consistent manner, which again provides protection against claims of discrimination or other improper motivation. Courts tend to respect an employer's policies as long as they are facially legitimate and applied consistently; for example, neutral absence control policies have been upheld even when they impact an otherwise protected employee.

B. Review Reasons for Termination

School districts should avoid snap decisions regarding the termination of an employee, and should consider having a centralized authority review all recommendations for termination. Immediate supervisors should be given authority to suspend employees if necessary, but should not be given authority to terminate.

Decisions to terminate an employee should be scrutinized as if they are already the subject of a legal challenge. The district should try to anticipate potential legal claims, and should evaluate whether the documentation and underlying circumstances can overcome a legal challenge. If the termination decision cannot be reasonably justified in front of a jury, then it should probably be reconsidered. The district's administrators and legal counsel should feel comfortable in articulating the reasons justifying the termination, and should feel that the articulated reasons can be adequately supported with written documentation.

The termination should also be reviewed in light of how similar situations were dealt with in the past. Inconsistency or failure to enforce policies can undermine otherwise valid reasons for termination. If the district feels that any aspect of the termination implicates a particular legal issue, the school district's attorney should review the proposed action and the employee's personnel file before any action is taken.

C. Sensitivity Issues

Once the district has decided to terminate an employee, it is necessary to determine how the employee will be notified. A good option is to have the employee meet privately with two supervisors who will notify the employee and explain the decision. Having a second supervisor in the meeting provides a corroborating witness in case the employee raises claims based on the discussions at the meeting.

The supervisors should be calm, civil, and prepared to articulate the reasons for the termination. They should also be prepared to notify the employee of the terms of his or her departure, and the extent of benefits (COBRA, retirement, etc.) that may extend beyond termination. The district should also decide ahead of time whether the supervisors may offer the employee the option of resigning rather than being fired. This option can sometimes ease the transition for the employee and reduce the chances of a legal challenge, even though the employee is still entitled to raise claims based on a constructive discharge theory.

A significant number of legal claims arise from conduct occurring on the day of termination. Humiliating displays, such as having the employee removed from district property by security guards or police, should be avoided when possible. The district and its administration should be sensitive to the employee's situation, regardless of how badly the relationship between the administration and employee may have deteriorated. Again, imagining how the situation might appear to a jury may be instructive.

D. Post-termination Considerations

If the district has an internal grievance policy, terminated employees should be permitted to use the grievance policy to protest their termination. The grievance process will allow the district and its counsel to review the circumstances of the termination and reconsider the decision if appropriate. The grievance process will also identify issues that will likely be raised in any subsequent lawsuit.

To avoid further legal claims, the school district should probably have a policy limiting the information released in relation to job references. The safest alternative is to have all requests for references handled by a single person or department, and to limit the response to neutral information, e.g., dates of employment, job title and last salary. If more information is to be given, it should be strictly factual. Statements of opinion, particularly negative ones, are unnecessarily risky.

Finally, the district should be cautious in replacing the employee, particularly if the replacement is outside the former employee's protected class, or otherwise casts doubt on the reason the former employee was terminated.

V. General Suggestions on Employee Management

Although the law requires that an employee bringing an employment discrimination lawsuit must prove his or her case by a preponderance of the evidence, school districts should nonetheless be prepared to actively defend their employment actions. To be well prepared to present a defense, a school district should consider the following principles in dealing with employees:

A. Maintain Thorough Documentation

It is crucial that any poor job performance or other employment-related problems be documented in writing. Without written documentation, it is very difficult to justify an employment decision if it is challenged, particularly if the challenge occurs many years after the fact. Administrators and supervisors at every level should consistently document the performance of the employees. Many supervisors tend to avoid the unpleasant task of documenting poor performance or misconduct by subordinates. Supervisors must understand the importance of this documentation, and must resist the temptation to minimize or dismiss problems that should be memorialized in writing.

B. Follow Policies and Procedures

Defense of employment decisions is much easier when a school district consistently follows its internal policies and procedures. Employment policies provide guidance for supervisors, and help make the district's response to various employment issues consistent and fair. Most school districts have policies that reflect the requirements of the various statutes listed above, and that provide a fair and neutral mechanism for the airing of employee grievances. School districts should ascertain that their policies reflect the latest developments in employment law, and that they effectively provide employees with due process, protection from discrimination and retaliation, and notice of conduct that can lead to discipline or termination.

C. Train Supervisors and Administrators

Any employee who has supervisory authority over other district employees should have a basic understanding of the issues discussed in this chapter. Supervisory employees should be trained to implement district policies and procedures, and should be required to attend periodic in-service training sessions that emphasize supervisory duties. In particular, supervisory employees need to be made aware of the need for careful and consistent documentation, and close adherence to district procedures relating to employees. Supervisory employees should also be instructed to treat subordinate employees with sensitivity and respect, and to protect confidentiality as much as possible when investigating allegations of misconduct or recommending adverse employment actions.

D. Consider the Employee's Position

Many lawsuits can be traced to personality conflicts or to situations where an employee felt that he or she was treated unfairly or with disrespect. If adverse employment action is necessary, ascertain that the employee was warned of the problem and, if appropriate, was given an opportunity to improve. Be sure that the employee was given adequate notice of the proposed adverse action and an opportunity to tell his or her side of the story. Ideally, school district policies should provide the employee with procedures that will help air grievances and prevent later disputes concerning fairness, due process, or discrimination. An employee who feels that he or she has been treated fairly and openly is less likely to subsequently file a lawsuit against the school district.

VI. Conclusion

In these times of increasing employment litigation, public school districts and colleges should strive to develop strategies that help limit liability exposure and effectively resolve workplace disputes. Although districts and colleges cannot avoid all employment-related claims, those who implement a strategic plan to minimize claims can reap significant benefits by avoiding costly legal battles and by limiting the value of those claims that are eventually raised. Schools and their legal counsel should work together to make employment practices fair, consistent, and responsive to new developments in the law. Because employment discrimination lawsuits are easier to prevent than to resolve, school districts and colleges should focus on prevention of these difficult claims.

ENDNOTES

[1] 42 U.S.C. § 2008 *et. seq.*, as amended.
[2] Tex. Labor Code 21.001 *et seq.*, formerly Tex. Rev. Civ. Stat. Ann. art. 5221k, § 5.01.
[3] Tex. Labor Code § 451.001 *et seq.*
[4] Tex. Labor Code § 201.001 *et seq.*
[5] Tex. Labor Code § 52.051.
[6] 29 U.S.C. § 621-634, *as amended.*
[7] 29 U.S.C. § 1001-1461.
[8] 42 U.S.C. § 12101-12213.
[9] 29 U.S.C. § 701 *et seq.*
[10] 29 U.S.C. § 2601 *et seq.*

[11] 29 U.S.C. § 151-169, *as amended*; Tex. Labor Code § 100.052, formerly Tex. Rev. Civ. Stat. Ann. art. 5207a, § 2.
[12] 42 U.S.C. §§ 1981-1988.
[13] Tex. Rev. Civ. Prac. & Rem. Code Ann. § 1221.001(a); 28 U.S.C. § 1875 (a).
[14] Tex. Elec. Code § 276.004.
[15] Tex. Elec. Code § 276.001(a)(2).
[16] Tex. Elec. Code § 161.007.
[17] 38 U.S.C. § 4301 *et seq.*; Tex. Gov't. Code § 431.006.
[18] 29 U.S.C. §§ 651-678.
[19] 42 U.S.C. § 7622.
[20] 33 U.S.C. § 1367.
[21] Hazard Communication Act, Tex. Health & Safety Code § 502.017. *Also see* Tex. Agric. Code § 125.001 *et seq.* (relating to agricultural workers).
[22] 29 U.S.C. §201 *et seq.*
[23] 29 U.S.C. § 206(d) *et seq.*
[24] Tex. Government Code § 554.002, formerly Tex. Rev. Civ. Stat. Ann. art. 6252 - 16a.
[25] Winters v. Houston Chronicle Publishing Co., 795 S.W.2d 723 (Tex. 1990).
[26] 42 U.S.C. 2000(d) ("Title VI"); 20 U.S.C. § 1681 ("Title IX").
[27] 15 U.S.C. §§ 1681-1681t.

SEXUAL HARASSMENT OF EMPLOYEES

By: Vianei Lopez Robinson

I. Introduction

Litigation concerning sexual harassment in the workplace continues to increase. As employers, public school districts are often the target of sexual harassment charges. Under federal law, public school districts are subject to the same liability for sexual harassment as private employers, except that they are usually shielded from liability for punitive damages. However, school districts suffer increased exposure to liability in other ways. A gender discrimination plaintiff suing a school district has access to various causes of action that traditionally are not available against private employers. Sexual harassment claims brought under Title IX of the Education Act Amendments of 1972 and under 42 U.S.C. § 1983 represent a developing area of liability. The primary body of law concerning sexual harassment, arising under Title VII of the Civil Rights Act of 1964 (Title VII)[1] and its state law equivalent, the Texas Commission on Human Rights Act (TCHRA)[2], is evolving rapidly. This chapter provides a brief overview of sexual harassment law, including specific claims affecting school districts, and offers suggestions concerning the investigation of harassment allegations in the workplace.

II. Sexual Harassment Theories

Under Title VII, it is an unlawful employment practice for an employer "to fail or refuse to hire or to discharge any individual, or otherwise to discriminate against any individual with respect to the terms, conditions, or privileges of employment, because of such individual's race, color, religion, sex or national origin."[3] It is from the above provision against sex discrimination that courts have found a federal prohibition against sexual harassment in the workplace.

Title VII originally provided only equitable remedies to a prevailing plaintiff, but the passage of the Civil Rights Act of 1991 greatly expanded the relief available under Title VII. The Civil Rights Act of 1991 amended Title VII to provide plaintiffs with the right to a jury trial, and the right to recover compensatory and punitive damages with an upper limit of $50,000 to $300,000, depending upon the size of the employer. The 1991 Civil Rights Act exempts from punitive damages "a government, government agency, or political subdivision."[4] Despite this protection, however, there is no doubt that the increased availability of compensatory damages and access to jury trials has raised the stakes in sexual harassment cases involving school districts.

The courts have recognized two types of sexual harassment: quid pro quo and hostile environment, and have developed a different framework for each type. These types of sexual harassment were first recognized by the Supreme Court in the landmark case of *Meritor Savings Bank v. Vinson.*[5]

A. Quid Pro Quo

Quid pro quo sexual harassment occurs when submission to or rejection of sexual conduct by an individual is used as a basis for employment decisions affecting the individual. In other words, quid pro quo sexual harassment occurs when submission to unwelcome sexual advances or conduct is linked to a tangible job benefit or condition of the affected employee.

The Fifth Circuit has designated five elements which a plaintiff must prove to prevail in a quid pro quo sexual harassment case. The elements are, as follows:

1. The employee belongs to a protected group;
2. The employee was subject to unwelcome sexual harassment;
3. The harassment complained of was based upon sex;
4. The employee's submission to the unwelcome sexual harassment was an express or implied condition for receiving job benefits or avoiding a tangible job detriment; and
5. The existence of respondeat superior liability.[6]

With respect to the final element of respondeat superior liability, courts have held that employers are strictly liable for quid pro quo type sexual harassment by supervisory personnel. The Supreme Court stated the rationale for this strict liability in *Meritor*: "Where a supervisor exercises the authority actually delegated to him by his employer, by making or threatening to make decisions affecting the employment status of his subordinates, such actions are properly imputed to the employer, his delegation of authority empowered the supervisor to undertake them."[7]

A federal appeals court stated that under the quid pro quo theory: "Courts have universally held employers liable for the actions of the supervisor because the supervisor is deemed to act on behalf of the employer when making decisions that affect the economic status of the employee. From the perspective of the employee, the supervisor and the employer merge into a single entity."[8]

B. Hostile Environment

Although many cases continue to be brought under the quid pro quo theory, the majority of cases involve the hostile environment theory, which is broader in scope because it does not require a direct link between tangible job benefits and unwelcome sexual advances or other conduct. The hostile environment theory is invoked when harassing conduct, which can comprise discriminatory remarks, innuendoes, physical acts, or other job conditions, unreasonably interferes with an individual's work performance or creates an intimidating, hostile or offensive work environment. The hostile environment theory is not intended to address isolated instances of misconduct or minor indiscretions; to be actionable, the sexual harassment must be sufficiently pervasive as to alter the conditions of employment and create an abusive work environment.

The Fifth Circuit has articulated the following five factors for proof of a hostile environment claim:

1. The employee belongs to a protected class;
2. The employee was subjected to unwelcome sexual harassment;
3. The harassment was based upon sex;
4. The harassment affected a term, condition or privilege of employment; and
5. That the employer either knew or should have known of the harassment and failed to take prompt remedial action.[9]

Although there is a wide range of conduct that can form the basis of a hostile environment claim, the Fifth Circuit Court of Appeals, which includes Texas, has demonstrated that it is not willing to extend the purview of Title VII to conduct that it considers to be *de minimis*. In *DeAngelis v. El Paso Municipal Police Officers Association*,[10] the court considered a situation in which the first female police sergeant in the El Paso police department was the target of repeated sexist satire in the local police association's newsletter. The jury awarded the plaintiff a verdict of $60,000, and the defendant appealed. The Fifth Circuit reversed and rendered judgment in favor of the defendant, writing "The principal issue in this case is whether a jury verdict for the plaintiff in a Title VII sexual harassment case may be supported only by evidence of a few written jibes . . ." In reversing the district court's judgment and dismissing the plaintiff's claim, she concluded: "Title VII cannot remedy every tasteless joke or groundless rumor that confronts women in the workplace."[11] The opinion also noted the difficult legal conundrum that arose when the First Amendment free expression rights of government employees (i.e., in publishing a newsletter) came into apparent conflict with Title VII.

Most cases demonstrate that the primary difference between the quid pro quo theory and the hostile environment theory is the standard for employer liability. Under the hostile environment theory, a plaintiff must demonstrate that the employer either knew or should have known of the harassment and failed to take prompt remedial action. As described further below, prompt remedial action has served to shield employers from liability in several cases.

In a recent case involving a university, the Fifth Circuit addressed whether a plaintiff can base a Title VII claim for sex discrimination or sexual harassment on another employee's sexual relationship with a supervisor. In *Ellert v. University of Texas at Dallas*,[12] a secretary alleged that she was terminated because she became aware of a sexual relationship between her supervisor and another employee, and that the supervisor subsequently harassed and ultimately terminated her. The Fifth Circuit upheld summary judgment in favor of the employer, holding that even if the secretary was terminated because of her knowledge of the relationship, that would not show discrimination based on the secretary's gender. Other courts have agreed that adverse action based on a supervisor's relationship with a third party are not actionable under Title VII.

The majority of reported sexual harassment cases involve a male harasser and a female victim. It is well established, however, that a male victim of a female harasser is equally entitled to legal protection under Title VII. There is some controversy, however, regarding liability for sexual harassment where the alleged harasser and the alleged victim are of the same gender.

In *Garcia v. Elf Atochem North America*,[13] the Fifth Circuit analyzed a sexual harassment case brought by a male employee against a male supervisor, and held that Title VII did not apply to a claim between individuals of the same gender. The court stated that even if the alleged harassment has sexual overtones, Title VII was not intended to address same-sex harassment.

Several federal courts in other jurisdictions have refused to follow the Fifth Circuit's *Garcia* decision, and have found that Title VII provides recourse to a victim of sexual harassment even if the harasser is the same sex as the victim. The EEOC apparently supports the position that Title VII can be used to combat same-sex harassment. The jurisprudence on same-sex sexual harassment will continue to evolve, but for the time being, such cases are unlikely to succeed in Texas due to the Fifth Circuit precedent created in *Garcia*.

III. Guidance From the Supreme Court: The Harris Case

In 1993 the U.S. Supreme Court decided *Harris v. Forklift Systems, Inc.*[14] The *Harris* case involved an alleged hostile environment in which the plaintiff and other female employees were subjected to lewd and discriminatory comments and actions. The harasser was the president of the defendant company, so the *Harris* opinion did not involve questions of employer liability for subordinate employees.

The Supreme Court considered the case to resolve a conflict among the circuits concerning whether the demonstration of psychological injury to the plaintiff is a prerequisite for recovery under a hostile environment theory. In an opinion written by Justice O'Connor, the Supreme Court struck down any requirement that a plaintiff in a hostile environment case be required to show psychological injury.

The Supreme Court reaffirmed the standard articulated in *Meritor*, and stated that when the workplace is permeated with discriminatory intimidation, ridicule, and insult that is sufficiently severe or pervasive to alter the conditions of the victim's employment and create an abusive working environment, Title VII is violated. The Court stated that the above standard "takes a middle path between making actionable any conduct that is merely offensive and requiring the conduct to cause a tangible psychological injury."[15] In dicta, the Court explained that conduct is not actionable unless it meets an objective and subjective test: i.e., that both a reasonable person and the plaintiff would find the conduct in question to create an abusive work environment. However, the Court was careful to note that "Title VII comes into play before the harassing conduct leads to a nervous breakdown."[16]

The *Harris* court admitted that its test was not "a mathematically precise test," and proceeded to list the various factors which can be considered in determining whether an environment is hostile or abusive. These factors "include the frequency of the discriminatory conduct; its severity; whether it is physically threatening or humiliating, or a mere offensive utterance; and whether it unreasonably interferes with an employee's work performance."[17] The presence of psychological injury to the plaintiff is relevant, but is not required.

In a concurring opinion, Justice Scalia complained that the majority's opinion provides little guidance, and "lets virtually unguided juries decide whether sex-related conduct engaged in (or permitted by) an employer is egregious enough to warrant an award of damages." Scalia admitted, however, that he knew of no alternative to the majority's opinion, which he characterized as faithful to the "inherently vague statutory language" of Title VII.

Justice Ginsburg also wrote a concurring opinion stressing that decline in a plaintiff's work performance is not a required element to demonstrate a hostile environment, and stating that the critical issue in hostile environment claims "is whether members of one sex are exposed to disadvantageous terms or conditions of employment to which members of the other sex are not exposed."[18]

IV. Prompt Remedial Action can Prevent Liability

As noted above, the final element of proving a hostile environment sexual harassment claim is that the employer knew or should have known of the harassing conduct, and failed to take prompt remedial action. It follows, therefore, that prompt remedial action when an employer receives notice of alleged harassing conduct can limit employer liability.

The Fifth Circuit has consistently upheld the theory that prompt remedial action by the employer can preclude liability. For example, in *Dornhecker v. Malibu Grand Prix Corp.*,[19] a sexual harassment complaint was made and within two (2) days the alleged victim was informed that she would no longer have to work with the alleged harasser. The Fifth Circuit found that the employer's prompt action in this case barred liability. Several cases have followed in this same vein. In *Carmon v. Lubrizol Corp.*,[20] the Fifth Circuit found that an employer could not be held liable for alleged sexual harassment when the employer promptly and thoroughly investigated the plaintiff's two separate reports of harassment, issued a reprimand after the first report, and issued a memorandum regarding workplace behavior and held various meetings following the second report. The Fifth Circuit stated the following: "Lubrizol twice did what a company ought to do when faced with allegations that an employee has been subject to sexual harassment, engendering a hostile work environment: it took the allegations seriously, it conducted prompt and thorough investigations, and it immediately implemented remedial and disciplinary measures based on the results of such investigations. Holding a company such as Lubrizol liable after it has taken such action would produce truly perverse incentives benefiting no one, least of all actual or potential victims of sexual harassment."[21]

In *Gearhart v. Eye Care Centers of America*,[22] the court granted summary judgment to the employer based on the employer's proper handling of a sexual harassment complaint, which included a prompt investigation resulting in the alleged harasser's resignation. The employer also allowed the alleged victim a transfer to another workplace and a paid leave of absence when she complained of stress. The victim eventually resigned, claiming that the continuing effects of the harassment prevented her from continuing to work, but the court refused to allow recovery on this basis. The court stated that Title VII is not a strict liability statute, and because the plaintiff failed to show a failure by the employer to react properly to her complaint, the employer was entitled to judgment as a matter of law.

Another case emphasizing the importance of prompt remedial action is *Sims v. Brown & Root Indus. Svcs., Inc.*[23] The plaintiff in *Sims* was allegedly harassed by her supervisor, and when she rejected his advances, he retaliated by reducing her hourly rate of pay from $10 per hour to $8 per hour. After a month of working at the reduced rate of pay, the plaintiff reported the sexual harassment to the company, and an investigation was immediately launched. Approximately two (2) weeks later, the investigation was concluded, the harasser was terminated, and the plaintiff was given back pay. The plaintiff resigned shortly thereafter, however, stating she felt "awkward" in the workplace. When the plaintiff sued the employer, the district court dismissed the suit on summary judgment based on the employer's prompt remedial action, which stopped the harassment and restored the plaintiff's lost pay.

Failure to take prompt remedial action, particularly when sexual harassment is of a repetitive nature, can have a high cost. This point was made very clear in *Weeks v. Baker & McKenzie*,[24] where the jury rendered a verdict of $6.9 million in a sexual harassment case. The award was later reduced to approximately $3.5 million. *Weeks* is interesting because the individual plaintiff did not suffer egregious harm, and was employed by Baker & McKenzie, a major law firm, for only a short period of time. The jury's large award was apparently motivated by the fact that the harasser, a firm partner, had victimized several subordinate employees in the past. The firm's failure to take meaningful remedial action in response to repeated reports of harassment paved the way for the large damage award. *Weeks* amply demonstrates the risk inherent in ignoring reports of sexual harassment in the workplace.

V. Other Sources of Liability

Although Title VII is the primary cause of action raised in sexual harassment cases, there are various other causes of action which an alleged victim of sexual harassment can raise against a public school district or individual supervisors. Several alternative causes of action are listed below:

A. Texas Labor Code

Chapter 21 of the Texas Labor Code, known as the Texas Commission on Human Rights Act (TCHRA), is the Texas state law equivalent to Title VII. The stated purpose of the TCHRA is to provide for the execution of the policies of Title VII, and amendments passed by the Texas Legislature brought the remedies available under the TCHRA in line with those added to Title VII by the Civil Rights Act of 1991. Therefore, under the TCHRA, a claimant has the right to a jury trial and the possibility of recovering compensatory and punitive damages, in addition to equitable relief. As under Title VII, punitive damages may not be assessed against a governmental entity, such as a public school district, under the TCHRA.

The TCHRA prohibits discrimination by an employer against an individual in any manner in connection with compensation or terms, conditions, or privileges of employment, or by an action that limits, segregates, or classifies employees or applicants in a way that is adverse to them.[25] This broad prohibition against discrimination encompasses the sex discrimination and sexual harassment prohibitions that have developed out of Title VII.

The cases discussed above with respect to Title VII also apply to cases brought under the TCHRA. When Texas case law fails to address a question raised under the TCHRA, the courts will look to federal case law under Title VII.

B. Title IX of the Education Act Amendments of 1972

Title IX of the Education Act Amendments of 1972 provides: "No person . . . shall, on the basis of sex,. . . be subjected to discrimination under any education program or activity receiving Federal financial assistance."[26] Title IX gained substantial attention due to the U.S. Supreme Court's decision in *Franklin v. Gwinnett Cty. Public Schools.*[27] The *Franklin* case was not an employment case, but involved sexual harassment of a high school student by an instructor. The *Franklin* case is notable because it held that violations of Title IX could result in an award of compensatory damages. The continuing expansion of Title IX claims in the school context is demonstrated by the recent case of *Rowinsky v. Bryan ISD*,[28] where Title IX claims were raised in response to the alleged sexual harassment of two eighth grade girls by male peers. However, the Fifth Circuit held that the school district was not responsible for the alleged hostile environment caused by the male students, because the plaintiffs did not show that the school district responded to the girls' complaints in a sexually discriminatory manner.

In the employment context, Title IX is currently proving to be a poor vehicle for plaintiffs' claims in the Fifth Circuit. In conflict with precedents in other circuits, the Fifth Circuit recently struck down the use of Title IX as a means of raising employment claims that could have been raised through Title VII. In *Lakoski v. James*,[29] the court stated: "Given this compelling evidence that Title IX prohibits the same employment practices proscribed by Title VII, we hold that individuals seeking money damages for employment discrimination on the basis of sex in federally funded educational institutions may not assert Title IX either directly or derivatively through § 1983." In support of this holding, the court argued that Congress did not intend that Title IX "provide a bypass to Title VII's administrative procedures."[30] As this chapter goes to press, the plaintiffs in *Lakoski* are seeking a petition for writ of certiorari to the U.S. Supreme Court in an effort to regain the right to use Title IX as a remedy in employment law cases. Until the Supreme Court addresses this issue, however, the Fifth Circuit's rejection of Title IX in employment law matters will limit the use of Title IX in sexual harassment cases affecting school employees in Texas.

C. State Law Tort Claims

Sexual harassment cases are often brought along with state law tort claims, such as assault, battery, defamation, or intentional infliction of emotional distress. In some cases, tort liability may attach to an individual wrongdoer, but not to the employer as a whole. For example, in *Valdez v. Church's Fried Chicken, Inc.*,[31] the court found that the employer could not be held liable for the sexual assault of one employee by another employee. The court found that the wrongdoer was acting outside the course and scope of his employment, and had not been authorized by the employer to use force against the victim. In this context, respondeat superior liability could not apply to the employer.

Tort claims arise frequently against private employers, but generally are not applicable to public school districts. Public school districts and junior colleges are immune from state law tort claims in almost all circumstances under Texas common law.[32] Even when governmental immunity shields the district, however, an individual employee accused of sexual harassment may still be exposed to state law tort claims, particularly if it is shown that the employee was acting outside of the course and scope of his or her employment.

D. 42 U.S.C. § 1983

In conjunction with claims under the United States Constitution, sexual harassment claims can be brought against governmental entities and government employees (i.e., those acting "under color of state law") through the remedial provisions of 42 U.S.C. § 1983 (Section 1983). However, it is more difficult to prevail against a government employer under Section 1983 than under Title VII. The reason for this is that respondeat superior liability does not apply to claims brought under Section 1983. Rather, liability attaches to a governmental entity under Section 1983 only when there is a demonstration of a custom or policy of illegal conduct. To prevail under Section 1983, a sexual harassment plaintiff would have to demonstrate a custom or policy of deliberate indifference by the governmental employer to the plaintiff's right to be free of sexual harassment under the Equal Protection Clause. As under Title VII, punitive damages are not available against a governmental entity under Section 1983. Individual government employees may be held liable under Section 1983, as described below.

VI. Liability of Individuals

As noted above, an individual government employee accused of sexual harassment may be exposed to liability under various theories. Individual employees are not exposed to liability under Title VII or the TCHRA; these statutes apply to employers only. An individual accused of sexual harassment may, however, be liable under state tort law for assault, battery, intentional infliction of emotional distress, and the like. As individuals acting under color of state law, government employees can also be sued under Section 1983, and may be held liable for a "constitutional tort" against a victim of sexual harassment. Liability under Section 1983 will normally attach only in egregious cases.

Government employees acting within the course and scope of their employment are generally entitled to qualified immunity for their discretionary actions. Texas common law also provides qualified official immunity to public officials exercising discretionary functions. If a government employee commits sexual harassment, however, such conduct generally will not fall within the protections of qualified immunity. Although punitive damages are not available from a governmental entity, individual defendants can be liable for punitive damages under state law or under Section 1983.

Government employees in Texas are also subject to criminal liability for acts of sexual harassment. Texas Penal Code § 39.03 provides the following: "A public servant acting under color of his office or employment commits an offense if he: . . . intentionally subjects another to sexual harassment." The section goes on to define sexual harassment as "unwelcome sexual advances, requests for sexual favors, or other verbal or physical conduct of a sexual nature, submission to which is made a term or condition of a person's exercise or enjoyment of any right, privilege, power, or immunity, either explicitly or implicitly." An offense under § 39.03 is a class A misdemeanor. School district employees should be made aware of the possible criminal consequences of sexual harassment. It may be advisable to reference this provision in school district policy manuals.

VII. Strategies to Minimize Sexual Harassment Liability

There is no strategy that can altogether prevent sexual harassment claims, but a good preventive plan can substantially decrease the chances of a school district ultimately being held liable. At a minimum, all school districts should have a policy that prohibits sexual harassment, provides a means for employees to report harassing conduct, and provides a system for investigating claims and taking prompt remedial action.

The first component of prevention is a strong sexual harassment policy. Under Title IX and its regulations, adoption of a sexual harassment policy and designation of a contact person to receive and handle complaints is mandatory for educational programs receiving federal financial assistance.[33] This requirement generally includes all public school districts.

School districts should ascertain that the policy is effectively disseminated to their employees. The policy should appear in any policy manuals and employee handbooks, and might also be posted if appropriate. A policy that is not publicized or followed can backfire. The policy need not be complicated, and should not be full of legalese or other language that is difficult to understand. The policy should, however, define sexual harassment in general terms and explain that sexual harassment is strictly prohibited and is cause for discipline, up to and including termination. The policy should also specify procedures for filing a complaint of sexual harassment, encourage aggrieved employees to come forward, and strictly prohibit any form of retaliation against the complainant. The procedures should not require that an aggrieved employee always report the complaint to his or her direct supervisor, because in some cases that individual may be the alleged harasser. These same guidelines apply to general employee grievance policies, which should be widely disseminated and should provide an effective system for the airing of employee complaints.

With respect to retaliation, any employee making a complaint of sexual harassment should be advised that he or she is protected from retaliation, and be encouraged to report immediately if any retaliation is perceived to occur. Both Title VII and the TCHRA prohibit retaliation against an employee complaining of discrimination or harassment. The school district should take steps to ascertain that victims of sexual harassment are not stigmatized or retaliated against for coming forward. Ideally, the school district should periodically follow up with any employee who has made an allegation of sexual harassment to determine whether the employee has any complaints about perceived retaliation. Retaliation can take many forms, including derogatory comments, threats, loss of advancement opportunities, inappropriate job assignments, and the like. If a school district does not take steps to investigate and document whether an employee complaining of sexual harassment has ongoing complaints of retaliation, the school district may be confronted with unexpected claims in an EEOC charge or lawsuit.

School districts may choose to have their sexual harassment policies specify that all reports of potential harassment will be investigated. Under current case law, it appears that the school district or college has a duty to investigate all allegations of sexual harassment that come to its attention. The knowledge of administrators, board members, and perhaps even teachers and other personnel may be imputed to the district or college, under certain circumstances, so it is important that all employees know to report allegations of sexual harassment to upper level administration.

From a practical standpoint, the school district minimizes its risks by taking all allegations seriously, and by applying a consistent investigation procedure in all cases. For this reason, even if a complainant specifically asks that no investigation be done, or even if an allegation appears to be little more than a rumor, the safer alternative is for the school district to investigate and take appropriate remedial action, if necessary. School districts also have a duty to investigate potential sexual harassment that comes to their attention without any formal complaint. If harassment is pervasive enough that school district authorities should have known about it, this constructive knowledge is enough to support liability, even if the harassment was never formally reported.

When allegations of sexual harassment come to the school district's attention, an investigation should be conducted as soon as possible. To ensure fairness and consistency, standard procedures should be used to guide the investigation. The investigation should be conducted in as confidential a manner as possible, and employees interviewed should be cautioned to keep the matter confidential. Documents and notes generated in the investigation should be retained in a separate file, and access to the file should be limited. Only formal employment actions such as written reprimands, transfers, demotion, or termination should be reflected in personnel files.

There have been increasing numbers of claims alleging that an employer failed to use its investigation procedure in good faith. School districts must be sure that the investigation is a meaningful attempt to find out the facts of the matter, even if the alleged harasser is a high-level administrator or board member, or if it is otherwise difficult to believe that the alleged conduct took place. An school district that simply goes through the motions of investigating, but does not really take the allegations seriously, is not protected from later liability. For example, in *Cuesta v. TDCJ*,[34] the court stated: "It is not enough, however, for an employer to pay lip service to a sexual harassment policy by setting a grievance procedure that is ineffective or which the employees regard as an empty promise."

A sexual harassment investigation must be meaningful and thorough to provide redress for the aggrieved employee and provide protection for the school district. The district's investigator should be careful to take into account the totality of the circumstances regarding a complaint of sexual harassment. The investigator should take into account all allegations made by the aggrieved employee and corroborating witnesses, and should follow up on all relevant information discovered during the investigation. It is also important for the investigator to take into account whether the alleged harasser has been the subject of similar complaints in the past. Ignoring a history of past complaints is a mistake, as shown by the verdict in the *Weeks* case.

There is some debate concerning who is the most appropriate investigator for a school district or college to use in these sensitive situations. The investigator should be someone who has nothing to do with the circumstances of the sexual harassment complaint, and whom the involved parties feel is impartial. School districts may have upper-level administrators conduct the investigation, or they may ask an outside party, such as outside legal counsel, to undertake the investigation. Having an attorney conduct the investigation may protect the results of the investigation from disclosure under the attorney-client privilege, although this protection from disclosure is not absolute.[35] It can also make the attorney a fact witness, and thus ineligible to represent the district in later litigation. The selection of an appropriate investigator should be carefully considered, and will vary depending upon the facts of each situation.

When analyzing information obtained during an investigation, school districts and colleges should remember that there is no requirement that allegations of sexual harassment be corroborated to be found valid. In some cases there will be no witnesses available to support either the alleged victim or the alleged harasser, and the district will be forced to make a determination based only on an assessment of credibility. If the school district or college feels that the alleged victim is telling the truth, the district may decide, even without corroborative evidence, that sexual harassment occurred. This is consistent with the EEOC's policy guidance on sexual harassment, which permits a finding of harassment based solely on the credibility of the victim's allegations. The EEOC policy guidance states that "if the investigation exhausts all possibilities for obtaining corroborative evidence, but finds none, the Commission may make a cause finding based solely on a reasoned decision to credit the charging party's testimony."[36]

When an investigation is completed, the school district or college should be prepared to take prompt action. If the investigation demonstrates misconduct by the alleged harasser, the school district should take action to discipline the offending employee, and in cases of serious or repeated misconduct, may terminate the employee. Such remedial action should be implemented as quickly as possible after the conclusion of the investigation. In some cases, however, the results of an investigation will be unclear. Nevertheless, the district should seek to take some sort of remedial action if it appears that harassment or improper workplace conduct likely occurred. If the investigation's findings are truly inconclusive, then the district or college may wish to seek a solution where the involved parties are separated through a reassignment of one or both parties. If no wrongdoing was found by either party, however, then the school district should not demote or otherwise penalize either party.

The district or college should ascertain that someone in a position of authority will follow up periodically with any employee who has complained of sexual harassment. Follow-up is particularly important in cases where the alleged victim and the alleged harasser both remain in the same workplace. It is in the district's best interest to find out early if a problem is continuing, or if a past complainant raises allegations of retaliation or continued harassment.

It is important for school districts and colleges to follow due process procedures when an alleged harasser is to be investigated, disciplined, or terminated. Alleged harassers who feel that they have been treated unfairly may be as likely to file a lawsuit as their alleged victims. To help avoid claims by an accused harasser, school districts should treat these individuals with sensitivity and with careful attention to due process procedures. The alleged harasser should always be given notice of the allegations against him or her, and be given a meaningful opportunity to respond. The investigation should be handled discreetly, and information about the investigation should not be disseminated unnecessarily or claims of defamation or denial of liberty interests may ensue.

VIII. Conclusion

Public school districts and colleges need to be prepared for claims of sexual harassment in the workplace. An understanding of current legal standards and theories of liability can help them prepare for any claims that may eventually arise. Advance preparation should include adoption and periodic review of official policy on sexual harassment. The school district or college should also have a standardized investigation procedure so that allegations of sexual harassment or other workplace misconduct can be investigated in a consistent, sensitive and thorough manner. School districts and colleges who are well prepared to handle complaints of sexual harassment can limit the disruption caused by these difficult claims, and can reduce their exposure in any subsequent litigation.

ENDNOTES

[1] 42 U.S.C. § 2000e *et seq.*
[2] Tex. Labor Code §§ 21.001 *et seq.*
[3] 42 U.S.C. § 2000e *et seq.*
[4] 42 U.S.C. § 1981a(b)(1).
[5] 477 U.S. 57, 106 S. Ct. 2399 (1986).
[6] Jones v. Flagship International, 793 F.2d 714, 721 (5th Cir. 1986), *cert. denied*, 479 U.S. 1065 (1987).
[7] *Id.*, 477 U.S. at 70.
[8] Karibian v. Columbia Univ., 14 F.3d 773.
[9] Nash v. Electrospace Sys., Inc., 9 F.3d 401,403 (5th Cir. 1993).
[10] 51 F.3d 591 (5th Cir. 1995).
[11] 51 F.3d at 597.
[12] 52 F.3d 543 (5th Cir. 1995).
[13] 28 F.3d 446 (5th Cir. 1994).
[14] 114 S. Ct. 367 (1993).
[15] 114 S. Ct. 367, 371.
[16] *Id.*
[17] *Id.*
[18] Cited in Kopp v. Samaritan Health Sys., 13 F.3d 264 (8th Cir. 1993).
[19] 828 F.2d 307 (5th Cir. 1987).
[20] 17 F.3d 791 (5th Cir. 1994).
[21] *Id.*
[22] 888 F. Supp. 814 (S.D. Tex. 1995).
[23] 889 F. Supp. 920 (W.D. La. 1995).
[24] 66 F.E.P. Cases 581, 1994 WL 759219 (Cal.Sup., Nov. 28, 1994).
[25] Tex. Labor Code § 21.051.
[26] 20 U.S.C. § 1681.
[27] 112 S. Ct. 1028 (1992).
[28] 1996 WL 153985 (5th Cir., April 2, 1996).
[29] 66 F.3d 751 (5th Cir. 1995).
[30] *Id.*
[31] 683 F. Supp. 596 (W.D. Tex. 1988).
[32] For exceptions to the immunity defense, *see* Tex. Civ. Prac. & Rem. Code § 101.051 (also known as the Texas Tort Claims Act).
[33] 20 U.S.C. § 1681; 34 C.F.R. Part 106 *et seq.*
[34] 805 F. Supp. 451 (W.D. Tex. 1991).
[35] *See* Harding v. Dana Transport, 914 F. Supp. 1084 (D.N.J. 1996).
[36] *See* EEOC Policy Guidance on Sexual Harassment, 1990.

THE PREEMPLOYMENT PROCESS: AVOIDING IMPERMISSIBLE INQUIRIES

By: Janet Little Horton

I. Introduction

The purpose of preemployment activities in a public school district is to obtain the person best qualified and suited for a particular teaching or administrative position. The same is true for the nonprofessional staff who support the school operation. The purpose of an application form and an interview is to obtain as much permissible information as possible which is related to the job for which the applicant is applying. A precise, well-balanced application form will give a personal history, qualifications for the job, and job-related references which can be used to make more in-depth inquiries concerning the applicant in the interview process and in background and reference checks. A school district must avoid making an applicant feel as though the applicant has had his or her privacy invaded by questions which do not relate to the available job. A job application form or an interview which contains many intrusive inquiries can lead to charges of discrimination in hiring.

The courts generally presume that any information requested in an application form or solicited in an interview is a factor upon which the school district will rely in selecting persons to hire. The key question to ask when examining an application form or reviewing the interview process for impermissible inquiries is whether the inquiry is job-related. Is the information really needed to judge an applicant's competence or qualifications for the job in question? To avoid charges of discrimination and bias in hiring, it is important that all inquiries are job-related and that the criteria upon which the school district relies in screening applicants are universally and consistently applied to all persons seeking the position. This chapter will examine the pre-employment process and suggest ways to avoid impermissible inquiries.

II. Inquiries Which Should be Avoided

In determining what inquiries are permissible on a job application form or in an interview, it is best to look first at various types of information which have been found by courts to be impermissible, or which are prohibited by federal law. These impermissible inquiries can be separated into five general categories:

1. Questions concerning marital status and the family situation;
2. Questions regarding personal history which are not job related;

3. Questions concerning associational activities;
4. Questions regarding irrelevant educational and work history data; and
5. Questions which inquire into the existence, nature or severity of a disability.

A. Questions Concerning Marital Status and the Family Situation

Courts have been quick to find that preemployment inquiries about marital status, pregnancy, future childbearing plans, number and age of children, and availability of babysitters may result in discrimination against female applicants.[1] These questions have no bearing on a person's capabilities or competence for performing a particular job. If challenged in a lawsuit, a court may well find that a decision based on a job application containing such questions has been based on sex stereotyping. These questions become job-related and permissible to inquire into only if the person is hired and these factors begin to interfere with job performance.

B. Questions Regarding Personal History Which are Not Job Related

Many sweeping questions concerning an applicant's personal history are often included in application forms because employers tend to think they get a better overall view of a person by the answers given to these questions. However, it is important to keep that key question in mind when examining a job application form: Is the inquiry job-related? If the inquiry is not job-related but is in an application form, the school district is generally presumed to rely on it and, consequently, is open to charges of discrimination and bias in hiring if the applicant believes that an employment decision has been based on something other than the applicant's qualifications for the job.

Questions concerning the applicant's age and sex, for example, are impermissible because it is a violation of federal law to discriminate in hiring on the basis of age or sex, unless an employer can prove these factors are bona fide occupational qualifications.[2] A seemingly harmless question regarding date of birth is not advisable because it elicits information concerning the applicant's age, about which it would be impermissible to inquire outright.[3] A school district may legitimately be concerned with whether an applicant is an adult according to state law. This information can be solicited by inquiring as follows: "Are you above the age of 18?"

Some employment applications have inquiries concerning United States military service. Such inquiries are not related to job qualifications for a teacher, administrator, or nonprofessional staff. Courts have found that inquiries as to rank and type of discharge may have an adverse impact on minorities.[4] Information relevant to job qualifications may encompass special training in the military. However, it is more appropriate to seek this information under a category dealing with educational data or previous experience or training relevant to the position for which the person is applying.

Specific inquiries concerning school activities, hobbies, future employment plans, periodicals regularly read, and other various types of personal questions are generally not related to job qualifications, and should be deleted from application forms and the interview process. Although such questions provide a greater variety of information concerning the applicant, they will not reveal anything concerning the applicant's competency and capabilities for a job as a teacher, administrator, or member of the non-professional staff. It is permissible to ask a general question whether any outside activity will interfere with job performance. Inquiries concerning outside business activities may be relevant to job qualifications because outside business activities could affect job performance. However, these inquiries are relevant only if the school district has a written policy concerning outside job activities or if state law makes the question relevant. If such a policy or state law does not exist, these inquiries may become relevant only after the applicant is hired if outside business activities interfere with the performance of the job.

Similarly, questions concerning personal transportation, personal habits such as smoking and drinking, and other private characteristics such as financial status are totally unrelated to qualifications for a job as teacher, administrator, or member of the non-professional staff. These types of personal inquiries are intrusive of the applicant's privacy and produce no information useful in making employment decisions. These types of questions could very easily lead an applicant to believe that an employment decision was made on something other than the person's qualifications for the job.

One exception to deleting all potentially intrusive inqurities is the question: "Are you willing to take a complete physical examination if conditionally offered a position?" Title I of the Americans with Disabilities Act (ADA) prohibits preemployment inquiries of any type which inquire into the existence, nature, or severity of a disability.[5] The ADA and its implementing regulations[6] allow an employer to require a medical examination of a job applicant who has been offered a job conditioned upon the results of the physical examination, if all persons conditionally offered the job must take a physical examination. An employer may not request all applicants to take a physical examination, but may only require the examination of someone who has met all other job qualifications and has been conditionally offered employment.[7] The ADA and its effect on the preemployment process is discussed below.

A second exception to the rule prohibiting intrusive inquiries concerns prior criminal convictions. Inquiring into convictions rather than merely arrests, however, is permissible because convictions have been found by some courts and federal agencies to be job-related. A school district should review the nature of the offense, the date of the offense, and the relationship between it and the position for which the applicant is applying. For example, conviction for theft or embezzlement might appropriately be considered if the applicant is applying for a bookkeeping position or similar job at a school district in which he or she will handle money. An appropriate inquiry along this line is: "Have you ever been convicted of a felony or any crime involving moral turpitude? If yes, please explain."

It is advisable to define moral turpitude so that the applicant will have a clear understanding of the types of crimes about which the school district is inquiring. Some examples of crimes involving moral turpitude are theft or attempted theft, fraud, and indecency with a minor. The inquiry above is broader than merely asking if the applicant has been convicted of a felony. In Texas, a crime involving moral turpitude may be a misdemeanor and not a felony.

Under no circumstances should an applicant be precluded from completing an application form solely because of a prior conviction. If such an inquiry is included, a school district would be well advised to follow the inquiry with a statement such as: "Conviction of a crime is not an automatic bar to employment. The District will consider the nature of the offense, the date of the offense, and the relationship between the offense and the position for which the applicant is applying."

C. Questions Concerning Associational Activities

The United States Constitution grants persons the right to associate with whom they please. Inquiries regarding membership in organizations are usually not related to job qualifications; additionally, such inquiries may lead a rejected applicant to think that rejection was based on the applicant's affiliation with a particular group instead of his or her qualifications for the job. Inquiries about positions of leadership or responsibility in work or community activities may elicit impermissible information regarding group membership. The name and character of an organization in which an applicant participates may reveal the race, religion, or the national origin of its members, inquiries which are also not permitted under interpretations of federal law.

Similarly, a request for information concerning foreign languages spoken by a person may also be an indirect way of inquiring into the applicant's race or national origin. If information concerning foreign language capability is actually related to the job for which the applicant is applying (such as a bilingual teacher), this information is best elicited in sections regarding educational data or previous work history relevant to the job which is available.

Questions concerning religious affiliation and the frequency of attendance at church are always risky. Such questions may lead an applicant to believe that he or she was rejected because of association with a certain religious sect, or because he or she is not affiliated with a particular religion. Clearly, school districts may not make employment decisions based on a person's race, religion, organizational membership or national origin. All such questions should be deleted from a school district's application form.

D. Questions Regarding Irrelevant Educational and Work History Data

For professional personnel such as teachers and administrators, extensive questions regarding educational background and work history are usually job-related. School districts sometimes face charges of discrimination and bias in hiring because extensive inquiries regarding educational background and work history are asked of applicants applying for non-professional positions, such as members of the clerical staff, grounds and building maintenance, and transportation. A school district should limit such questions of those applying for non-professional positions to educational requirements and work-related information which are actually related to the job for which the applicant is applying. A school district should avoid requiring a level of achievement in formal education or special work experience that is not actually necessary for the successful performance of the job. In the past, courts have found that artificially high education requirements, for example, are discriminatory against minorities.[8]

It is permissible to inquire into educational and work history, of course, but a school district should be careful to use this information only as it relates to the specific job for which the person applies. School districts would be wise to consider separate application forms for those applying for non-professional positions so the second application form can be tailored to elicit only educational background and work history information which are relevant to non-professional staff positions.

E. Questions Which Inquire Into the Existence, Nature or Severity of a Disability The Americans with Disability Act

The ADA is a statute which profoundly affects the preemployment process. Title I, the employment section of the ADA, and its implementing regulations[9] are modeled on Section 504 of the Rehabilitation Act[10] and the interpretation of that law and its implementing regulations over the past years.[11] The ADA applies to private and public employers and covers employers with fifteen (15) or more employees. A discussion of the basic tenets of the ADA is useful in understanding its impact on the preemployment process.

1. Individuals Covered by the ADA

The ADA requires a covered employer to make reasonable accommodation for the known physical or mental limitations of a qualified applicant with a disability, unless the accommodation would cause an undue hardship on the operation of its business. A person with a disability is defined as an individual who (1) has a physical or mental impairment that substantially limits one or more major life activities; (2) has a record of such an impairment; or (3) is regarded as having such an impairment.[12] A physical impairment is defined as any physiological disorder, or condition, or cosmetic disfigurement or anatomical loss affecting one or more of the bodily systems such as neurological, musculoskeletal, special sense organs, respiratory (including speech organs), cardiovascular, reproductive, digestive, genitourinary, hemic and lymphatic, skin and endocrine systems. A mental impairment is defined as any mental or psychological disorder, such as mental retardation, organic brain syndrome, emotional or mental illness, and specific learning disabilities.[13]

A major life activity includes such things as walking, speaking, breathing, performing manual tasks, seeing, hearing, learning, caring for one's self, and working. These are the daily activities of life which an average person performs in a normal fashion.[14]

The term "substantially limits" means that an individual is unable to perform or is significantly limited in the ability to perform an activity compared to an average person in the general population. [15]One must consider the nature and severity of the disability, how long it will last or is expected to last, and its permanent or long-term impact or expected impact. Therefore, a temporary medical condition, such as colds, flu, broken bones, pregnancy, etc., would not be considered physical or mental impairments under the ADA so long as recovery from these ailments is normal. If, however, a temporary illness ultimately results in a long-term or permanent impairment, the person may become covered by the ADA if that impairment substantially limits one or more major life activities.

The ADA not only protects individuals with a physical or mental impairment that substantially limits one or more major life activities, it also protects individuals with a record of a substantially limiting condition. If an applicant for employment has a history of a substantially limiting condition, or has been misclassified or misdiagnosed in the past as having a disability, then the applicant may be protected by the ADA if the prospective employer treats the applicant as if he or she were substantially limited in performing a major life activity based on such a record.[16] If an applicant is rejected from further consideration because such information comes to a prospective employer, or if the applicant is rejected after a post-offer medical exam turns up such a record but the applicant is currently able to perform the essential functions of the job in question, then such a rejection may be a violation of the ADA.

A person may also be covered by the ADA if the applicant is regarded as having a substantially limiting condition. This situation may occur in three different instances. First, the applicant may have an impairment which is not substantially limiting of any major life activities, but the applicant is treated by the prospective employer as being limited in a major life activity. For example, if a post-offer medical examination indicates that the applicant has high blood pressure that is controlled with medication, and the prospective employer rejects the person from employment and withdraws the conditional offer, a violation of the ADA may have occurred. Second, the applicant may have an impairment that is substantially limiting only because of the attitudes of others toward the condition. For example, a violation of the ADA would occur if a prospective employer's only basis for rejecting an otherwise qualified applicant is a disfiguring facial scar. Finally, an applicant may have no impairment at all, but may be regarded by a prospective employer as having a substantially limiting condition. For example, if a false rumor reaches a prospective employer that an applicant is HIV positive, and the applicant is otherwise qualified for the job but is rejected on this basis, it is likely that a violation of the ADA will occur.[17]

In the past, individuals with certain disabilities have been totally excluded from consideration in certain types of positions. These blanket exclusions have usually been established because employers believe them necessary for health and safety reasons or because they had fears concerning higher medical insurance or worker's compensation costs, or higher rates of absenteeism. Such blanket exclusions will not survive scrutiny under the ADA. For example, a blanket exclusion from a specific job of all persons with epilepsy, diabetes or a heart condition would be improper under the ADA. Instead, the ADA requires an objective assessment of a particular individual's current ability to perform the job in question safely and effectively.

The ADA protects only the applicant who is a qualified individual with a disability. This is a two-part determination. First, the prospective employer must determine whether the individual meets the necessary prerequisites for the job such as education, work experience, training, skills, licenses, certificates, or other job-related requirements. If the individual meets these prerequisites, the next inquiry is whether the individual can perform the essential functions of the job in question with or without a reasonable accommodation.[18]

2. Excluded Conditions Under the ADA

Certain persons are excluded from coverage by the ADA. Excluded are persons who are currently illegally using drugs, including persons who use prescription drugs illegally, as well as those who use illegal drugs.[19] People who have successfully completed a rehabilitation program and no longer currently illegally use drugs, or those in the process of completing a rehabilitation program, are protected from discrimination on this basis by the ADA.[20] The state of being addicted is a protected disability under the ADA. However, the applicant for employment who is addicted to drugs or alcohol can be required to follow the same workplace rules regarding a ban on drugs and alcohol.[21]

There are numerous other conditions that are specifically excluded from coverage by the ADA. They include the following:

a. transvestism, transsexualism, pedophilia, exhibitionism, voyeurism, gender identity disorders not resulting from physical impairments, or other sexual behavior disorders;
b. Compulsive gambling, kleptomania, or pyromania;
c. Psychoactive substance use disorders resulting from current illegal drug use; or
d. Homosexuality and bisexuality.[22]

3. Application to Essential Job Functions

The ADA generally provides that no covered employer shall discriminate against a qualified individual with a disability because of the disability in regard to job application procedures, the hiring, advancement or discharge of employees, employee compensation, job training, or other terms, conditions, and privileges of employment. All aspects of the preemployment process and the employment relationship are covered by the ADA.[23]

The ADA does not prohibit the employer from establishing job-related qualification standards. If a qualification standard or selection criteria screens out, or tends to screen out, an individual with a disability on the basis of the disability, the selection criteria must be job-related and consistent with business necessity, and performance of the criteria cannot be accomplished by reasonable accommodation.[24] "Job-related" means that the criteria is a legitimate measure or qualification for a specific job. Job-related criteria can apply to essential functions and marginal functions of a particular position. If a criteria excludes an individual with a disability because of the disability, and does not relate to an essential function of the job, then the criteria is not consistent with business necessity and the applicant cannot be rejected solely on this basis.

For example, if a job description for the superintendent's secretary states that the secretary must be able to take shorthand, but for years the superintendent's secretary has not taken shorthand but has transcribed tapes dictated by the superintendent, then the taking of shorthand, while it may be a job-related function, is a marginal, non-essential function of the job and is not a business necessity. If an applicant is rejected for an inability to take shorthand, and the inability to take shorthand is related to a disability in the applicant, then the ADA has been violated because the applicant has been rejected on the basis of qualifications or standards that are related only to marginal job functions and are not consistent with business necessity.

If an employment decision is challenged, it is extremely helpful for the employer to have a written job description. The job description should describe all the duties of the job, but it should also identify the functions of the job which are essential. An essential job function is defined as a fundamental job duty of the employment position which the applicant with the disability desires to hold. The definition does not include marginal functions of a position. An essential job function is one which is actually done as part of the job and, if someone else did the activity, it would fundamentally alter the job.[25]

A job function may be essential for several reasons. For example, the position itself may exist to perform the function. If a person is hired as a proofreader, accurate proofreading is an essential function of that job. A function may be essential because there are only a limited number of other employees to perform the function, or among whom the function can be distributed. For example, in a small office, a file clerk may also need to answer the telephone because all employees do a variety of tasks and there is no receptionist. Answering the telephone would be an essential function of the position. However, in a very large office where a receptionist is present to answer the telephone, it may not be an essential function of the file clerk's job to also answer the telephone. Finally, a person with special expertise or ability may be hired to perform a highly specialized function. If a person is hired to translate documents into Braille, then reading and knowledge of Braille would be an essential function of the position.[26]

Many factors will be considered in determining whether a job function is an essential or a marginal one. One factor to be examined is the employer's judgment regarding whether the function is essential. The work experience of people who perform the job may also be evidence of its essential functions. Another factor is a written job description prepared before advertising or interviewing for a job which identifies the essential functions. The employer should focus on the purpose of the function and the result to be achieved, rather than on the manner of performance of the job. A disabled person may be able to achieve the same purpose and result by performing the job function in a way which is different than it has ever been performed before. Job descriptions prepared after an alleged discriminatory act will not be considered evidence of the essential functions of the job.[27]

The amount of time spent by an employee performing a function is also a factor to be considered. In some cases a function, although performed infrequently, is essential because there will be serious consequences if it is not performed. The terms of a collective bargaining agreement may also define the essential functions of a job.[28]

Once the essential functions of a job are identified, they can be used to set selection criteria and standards. Applicants can be asked to describe or demonstrate how they would perform the essential job functions with or without accommodation. This information can also be sent to doctors for use in post-offer medical examinations. In any challenge, the employer will have the burden of proof in a lawsuit to show that a function is an essential function of the job.

If the disabled applicant meets all employment criteria and can perform the essential functions of the job without accommodation, the individual is a qualified individual with a disability. Failure to hire the disabled applicant may lead to a charge of discrimination under the ADA. If one or more essential functions of the job cannot be performed, then reasonable accommodation of the applicant must be considered.

4. Reasonable Accommodation Under the ADA

Another area prospective employers must be knowledgeable about in the preemployment process is the reasonable accommodation required by the ADA. If a disabled applicant who meets all employment criteria cannot perform an essential job function, then the employer must consider whether a reasonable accommodation can be made by which the disabled applicant can perform the essential job function. The employer may become aware of the need for an accommodation after a post-offer medical examination, or the disabled applicant may inform the employer in the preemployment process that an accommodation is necessary.

A reasonable accommodation is any modification or adjustment to a job, an employment practice, or the work environment that makes it possible for an individual with a disability to enjoy an equal employment opportunity. Generally, the individual with a disability is obliged to request a reasonable accommodation. It is not the prospective employer's job to guess at whether an accommodation is needed and, if so, what type. The disabled applicant may refuse an accommodation, but he or she may than be disqualified from the particular job in question if it can only be performed with that particular accommodation. An individual with a disability should be given the option of paying all or a portion of the cost of an accommodation if its cost would impose an undue hardship on the prospective employer.[29]

A reasonable accommodation is required in three instances. First, reasonable accommodation is required to ensure equal opportunity in the application process. The employment office or interview site may need to be made accessible to a disabled applicant so that he or she may have an equal opportunity to be considered for a job. Job information itself must be made accessible to disabled applicants, such as telephone numbers to be used by the hearing impaired, forms printed in large type, or recorded job application information for blind applicants. Prospective employers may have to assist those who are mentally challenged or learning disabled with completing job application forms. Second, reasonable accommodation is required to enable a qualified individual with a disability to perform the essential functions of a job. Modifications or adjustments to the work environment or the way in which a job is performed may be required. Finally, a disabled employee is entitled to reasonable accommodation to enjoy equal benefits and privileges of employment.[30]

There are certain basic principles which govern reasonable accommodation. A reasonable accommodation must be effective, although it does not have to ensure equal results or provide exactly the same benefits or privileges. The prospective employer must reasonably accommodate the disabled applicant only to reduce barriers to employment, not to fulfill some other reason. A reasonable accommodation is just that–reasonable. It does not have to be the best accommodation available or the accommodation preferred by the applicant, so long as it is effective. Any personal equipment or devices used by the disabled person on and off the job are not required to be provided by the employer, unless the equipment is required to meet job-related needs. An employer can always make modifications beyond those which would be considered "reasonable" under the ADA.[31]

Whether a reasonable accommodation is effective must be determined on a case-by-case basis. A reasonable accommodation that may be effective for one disabled person may not be effective for another. Each person is unique, and therefore the effect of the reasonable accommodation must be examined in light of each disabled individual's unique needs. A reasonable accommodation must take into account the specific abilities and functional limitations of the particular applicant with a disability. It must also consider the specific functional requirements of the particular job for which the disabled applicant is applying. The accommodation must be reasonable and must enable the specific individual in question to do the job function.[32]

The prospective employer is responsible for notifying applicants of its obligation to provide reasonable accommodation to qualified individuals with a disability. This can be done through EEOC posters, application forms, vacancy notices, personnel manuals, oral communication, etc. It is important for prospective employers to remember that the term "reasonable accommodation" is not a magic phrase. The disabled applicant must only request some adjustment or change in the preemployment process or the work environment to trigger a consideration of reasonable accommodation. If the need for an accommodation is not obvious, or the employer does not believe it is needed, the prospective employer may request documentation from a doctor or other appropriate source to support the request.[33]

If an accommodation is needed, the prospective employer, in consultation with the disabled applicant, should identify potential accommodations and determine how effective each would be in overcoming barriers to performance of essential job functions. The prospective employer may also seek technical assistance from an outside source. There should be a dialogue between the prospective employer and the disabled applicant to determine what accommodation would be effective.[34]

If there are several means of reasonable accommodation, the prospective employer should consider the individual's preference. However, the employer is free to choose among effective accommodations and may choose the one less expensive or easier to provide than the one the individual prefers. The individual may want to provide his or her own accommodation. If so, and as an employee, the disabled person later becomes unwilling or unable to provide the accommodation any longer, then the employer may have a duty to provide such reasonable accommodation at this later date.[35]

There are numerous examples of reasonable accommodation. Reasonable accommodation may include making facilities and job sites accessible and usable by the handicapped individual.[36] Job restructuring or modification may be a reasonable accommodation in some cases. However, the employer is not required to reallocate essential job functions to another employee.[37] A modified work schedule, such as flexibility in work hours or work week, or a part-time work week, may be a reasonable accommodation if it does not cause undue hardship. The employer is not required to provide additional paid leave as an accommodation.[38]

Reassignment to a vacant position may be a reasonable accommodation for a disabled employee when an accommodation is not present in the employee's present job or when an accommodation would cause undue hardship. Reassignment applies only to employees. A job applicant does not have to be considered for different positions if he or she cannot perform the essential functions of the job for which the applicant has applied.[39]

Reasonable accommodation may also include the purchase of equipment or the modification of existing equipment. Tests, examinations, and training programs may need to be modified in their administration to provide equal employment opportunities to individuals with disabilities. A vision impaired employee might be entitled to the provision of a reader as a reasonable accommodation. Likewise, a deaf employee might be reasonably accommodated by the provision of an interpreter on an as needed basis.[40]

5. Undue Hardship and Threat to Health or Safety

If a disabled applicant cannot perform an essential job function but is otherwise qualified to hold the position, and an accommodation is identified by which the disabled applicant would be able to perform essential job functions, the next step for a prospective employer is to determine whether the accommodation is reasonable or not. In other words, does the accommodation create an undue hardship on the prospective employer? This determination is made on a case-by-case basis by looking at the individual resources and operation of the prospective employer.

An undue hardship is any action which is unduly costly, extensive, substantial, disruptive, or that would fundamentally alter the nature or operation of the business.[41] Numerous factors are considered when determining whether an accommodation creates an undue hardship. These include the nature and net cost of the accommodation to the prospective employer, the financial resources of the employer to deal with the accommodation, the number of employees, and the effect of the accommodation on the expenses and resources of a facility. The impact of the accommodation on the operation of the facility of the employer should be considered, including the impact on the ability of other employees to do their jobs and on the facility's ability to conduct business. If an accommodation would cause low morale or disruption due to other employees' fears or prejudices, this will not be considered an undue hardship.[42] The fact that the cost of an accommodation may be high in relation to the employee's wage or salary is not a factor to be considered. What matters are the resources available to the employer.[43]

A prospective employer may require a disabled applicant not to pose a direct threat to the health or safety of the applicant or others in the workplace, if this standard is applied to all applicants for the position.[44] There are very specific, stringent standards which must be followed for an employer to establish that a disabled applicant poses a direct threat to health or safety.

First, there must be a significant risk or high probability of substantial harm. The specific risk must be defined according to the duration of the risk, the nature and severity of the harm, the likelihood the potential harm will occur, and the imminence of the potential harm. Finally, the risk must be current and one that is not speculative or remote.[45]

The assessment cannot be based on speculation that the disability will become worse, that the person will become unable to perform the job in the future, or that the individual may cause increased health insurance or worker's compensation costs or excessive absenteeism for the job site. Employers may not rely on generalized assumptions about risks associated with certain disabilities. The prospective employer must look at each applicant and determine on an objective medical basis whether the disability constitutes a direct threat. If there is a significant risk to health or safety, the employer must consider whether there is any reasonable accommodation which can lower the risk to an acceptable level, or eliminate it.[46]

6. Specific Application of ADA to the Preemployment Process

The ADA is quite specific about the types of inquiries which are impermissible in the preemployment process, whether asked on an application form, in an interview, or as part of a background or reference check. The following questions, or similar questions, may not be asked in the preemployment process:

a. Are you disabled? If so, describe the history of and type of disability.
b. Do you have any limitations on hearing, speech, or vision?
c. Have you been treated for any diseases?
d. Have you been hospitalized? Treated by a psychiatrist?

e. Have you been treated for drug or alcohol abuse?
f. Have you ever filed a worker's compensation claim?
g. How many sick days did you take last year?
h. Please list any conditions or diseases for which you have been treated in the past three years.
i. Are you taking any prescription drugs?
j. If the applicant has an obvious disability or volunteers information, the applicant may NOT be asked questions about the nature, severity or cause of the disability, prognosis, or whether special treatment or leave will be needed.
k. Former employers may not be asked about disabilities, illnesses or workers' compensation history.[47]

By banning such questions in the preemployment process, the ADA attempts to prevent prospective employers from screening out disabled applicants from the selection process before the employer has had an opportunity to actually assess the abilities of the disabled applicant. A prospective employer is not allowed to make assumptions based on written information about a disability. Rather, the prospective employer must now consider each applicant, disabled or not, on the basis of his or her actual capabilities.

There are certain areas which may be inquired into in the pre-offer stage that deal with the applicant's ability to perform the functions of the job for which the applicant is applying. An applicant may be asked to describe or demonstrate how he or she would perform the functions of a particular job with or without an accommodation, if all applicants for that position are asked this question. A written job description is helpful because it identifies the functions of the job, both essential and marginal, which the applicant must perform. [48]If the applicant is not able to perform a job function which is identified as essential, then a reasonable accommodation must be considered, assuming the applicant meets all the other criteria for the job.

The applicant with a known or obvious disability that might interfere with a job function may be asked to describe or demonstrate how he or she would perform job functions with or without an accommodation even if other persons are not asked the same question.[49] For example, if an applicant confined to a wheelchair applies for a warehouse position to load and unload trucks and stock and handle supplies, a prospective employer might reasonably believe that the applicant's disability would interfere with such job functions. Therefore, the applicant could be asked to describe or demonstrate how he or she would perform these functions, even if other applicants are not asked the same question.

If the known or obvious disability of the applicant would not interfere with the performance of job functions, then the applicant may not be asked to describe or demonstrate how he or she would perform the job functions unless all other applicants for the position are asked the same questions.[50] For example, if a person with sight in only one eye applies for the same warehouse position of loading and unloading trucks and stocking and handling supplies, the prospective employer may not believe that the obvious disability would interfere with any job functions. Therefore, this applicant could be asked to describe or demonstrate how he or she would perform the functions of the job only if all applicants for the position are asked this question.

If a disabled applicant states that he or she can perform job functions only with an accommodation, it is permissible for the prospective employer to ask how job functions would be performed and with what accommodations. A prospective employer cannot reject the disabled applicant simply because a reasonable accommodation is needed to perform essential job functions.

Background checks and reference checks may also not inquire into the existence, nature, or severity of a disability. However, former employers may be asked about job functions, tasks performed, quantity and quality of work, how job functions were performed, and compliance with attendance procedures. Former employers should not be questioned about use of sick leave by an applicant. However, former employers may be asked about the applicant's adherence to work rules and attendance policies. If the applicant has a known disability and the applicant has requested an accommodation, a former employer may be asked about accommodations which were provided at that job site.[51]

If employment tests are required as part of the preemployment process, the prospective employer must be sure that the employment tests accurately reflect the skills to be tested. Reasonable accommodations must be made for disabled applicants in the test-taking procedures, including such things as more time to take a test, frequent breaks, an accessible test site, a written instead of oral test or vice versa, a tape recording of test answers, etc. Prospective employers must also assure that tests do not reflect impaired sensory, manual, or speaking skills, unless those skills are the factors the test is designed to measure. If a test screens out, or tends to screen out, an individual with a disability or a class of such individuals on the basis of a disability, it must be job-related and consistent with business necessity.[52]

7. Medical Examinations

A major change made by the ADA in the preemployment process regards medical examinations. An employer may not make medical inquiries or conduct a medical examination until after a job offer has been made.[53] A job offer may be conditioned on the results of a medical examination or inquiry, but only if this is required for all entering employees in similar jobs.

Once a conditional offer of employment has been made, the prospective employer may obtain any information in a medical examination believed to be relevant to the applicant's ability to perform the job in question. If an individual is not hired after a post-offer medical examination, the reasons for not hiring the person must be job-related and consistent with business necessity.[54]

The law is crafted to lay bare a prospective employer's discrimination because of a disability. If a conditional job offer has been made to an applicant, the prospective employer has determined that the applicant meets all other standards and selection criteria for the job. If an offer is withdrawn because of information that is revealed in a medical examination, the employer must be able to prove that the applicant is not able to perform the essential functions of the job, that no reasonable accommodation is available which would enable this individual to perform essential job functions, and that would not impose an undue hardship on the prospective employer. A post-offer medical examination may not disqualify an individual with a disability who is currently able to perform essential job functions because of speculation by the prospective employer that the disability may cause a risk of injury in the future or because of concerns about increased worker's compensation costs, higher insurance costs, higher absenteeism, or the need to provide a reasonable accommodation.[55]

A doctor who conducts a medical examination should not make employment decisions or decide on a reasonable accommodation. The doctor's role in the preemployment process is to advise the employer about the current functional capabilities and limitations of the person in question. The doctor may also advise whether the applicant meets the employer's health and safety standards. The doctor should focus on what the person can and cannot do at the present time. To do so, a doctor must understand what the specific job functions and tasks are which the applicant will be asked to perform.[56]

Medical information obtained through the preemployment process when an applicant has a medical examination after a conditional offer of employment must be kept on separate forms and kept in separate files. Only a limited number of persons should have access to these confidential medical records. These persons include supervisors and managers who may be informed about necessary restrictions and accommodations for the person. First aid and safety personnel may also be informed if the disability might require emergency treatment, or if specific procedures are necessary in case of a fire or an evacuation of a building. Federal officials investigating compliance with the ADA and other federal laws also have access to this information. Finally, relevant information may be provided to worker's compensation offices and insurance companies.[57]

III. Subjective Versus Objective Criteria

In the context of preemployment inquiries, the pieces of information used to make an employment decision are generally categorized as either "subjective" or "objective". Subjective criteria, such as the applicant's attitude, are traits which call for a personal opinion on the part of the employer whereas objective criteria, such as the questions on an application form, are tangible pieces of information. Subjective criteria are more worrisome due to the reliance on individual judgment rather than impersonal standards. The most prevalent use of subjective criteria in preemployment practices arises in interviewing job applicants. Although the value of personal interviews to both the employer and the applicant lies in the subjective nature of the procedure, that same factor is susceptible to bias against females, minorities, the disabled, and older age groups. The question of bias is more likely to arise if a school district relies solely or primarily on the interviewer's evaluation in making an employment decision. In finding personnel evaluations to be discriminatory, the courts typically have described the subjective criteria utilized as vague, elusive, unstructured, undefined, or poorly conceived.[58] The interviewing process is especially suspect where the interviewer does not base his or her evaluation on written guidelines or criteria specific to the job.

To avoid such problems, a school district or college should design its interviewing procedures to guard against interviewer bias and the use of criteria not related to the job. This is done by developing specific guidelines for all interviewers and assuring that such guidelines are consistently followed. In an effort to avoid the most common biases, some school districts utilize screening committees comprised of individuals of both sexes and with varied racial and ethnic backgrounds. Some of these committees function as interviewers while some serve as a final review committee to look at the results of the interview, process to determine who should be offered a job. The interviewer's recommendation must be justifiable, which means that the recommendation must be based on the job requirements and the applicant's qualifications.

It is very beneficial for a school district or college representative to personally meet an applicant and get a better idea of the applicant's qualifications, personality, drive, energy, and enthusiasm, and how he or she will fit into the structure of the school. However, the interviewing process can turn into a very dangerous activity for a school district or college if the interviewer is not well trained. Subjective selection procedures are not discriminatory *per se*, but they must be scrutinized more closely because of their susceptibility to abuse. When the evaluation is subjective, as in the interviewing process, and the interviewer is not a member of the protected group or minority of the rejected applicant, the legitimacy and the non-discriminatory basis for the interviewer's articulated reason for his or her decision will be subject to particularly close scrutiny by the courts. Those involved in the interviewing process must remember that their questions must be job-related. The interview is not the place to ask all of the questions which could not be asked on the application form. Further, it is important that the school district or college secure or develop a set of written guidelines or criteria by which to judge each applicant in the interview situation.

IV. Conclusion

All school districts and colleges desire an application form and an interview process which will lead to the selection of the best person for the job. It is possible for a district in both its application form and interview process to gather a vast amount of information about the applicant so long as the school district keeps in mind the key question: Is the inquiry job-related? It is only human nature to be curious about a job applicant and want to know as much as possible about that person before hiring him or her. However, any employer making inquiries unrelated to the job in question runs the risk of a legal challenge.

ENDNOTES

[1] *See* Andrews v. Drew Mun. Sch. Dist., 507 F.2d 611 (5th Cir. 1975), *cert. dism'd.*, 425 U.S. 559, 96 S. Ct. 1752 (1976).

[2] *See* the Age Discrimination in Employment Act (ADEA), 29 U.S.C. § 631, *et seq.*, and title VII, 42 U.S.C. § 2000e, *et seq.*

[3] *See* regulations implementing the ADEA, 29 C.F.R. § 1625.5.

[4] *See* U.S. v. City of Chicago, 549 F.2d 415 (7th Cir.), *cert. denied*, 434 U.S. 875, 98 S. Ct. 225, *on remand*, 437 F. Supp. 256 (D.C. Ill.), *aff'd.*, 567 F.2d 730 (7th Cir. 1977), *cert. denied*, 436 U.S. 932, 98 S. Ct. 2832 (1978).

[5] 42 U.S.C. § 12101 *et seq.*

[6] 29 C.F.R. § 1630 *et seq.*

[7] The ADA and its effect on the preemployment process is discussed in detail below.

[8] *See* Payne v. Travenol Laboratories, 565 F.2d 895 (5th Cir.), *cert. denied*, 439 U.S. 835, 99 S. Ct. 118 (1978); Crockett v. Green, 388 F. Supp. 912 (D.C. Wis.), *aff'd.*, 534 F.2d 715 (7th Cir. 1975); Griggs v. Duke Power Co., 401 U.S. 424, 91 S. Ct. 849 (1971).

[9] 42 U.S.C. § 12101 *et seq.*; 29 C.F.R. § 1630 *et seq.* In addition, the Equal Employment Opportunity Commission (EEOC) has issued a Technical Assistance Manual to help employers interpret and apply the ADA. This manual (TAM) is highly recommended to readers as a source for guidance in applying the ADA to specific cases. Copies may be obtained by writing to EEOC Office of Communications and Legislative Affairs, 1801 L. Street, N.W., Washington, D.C. 20507.
[10] 29 U.S.C. § 704.
[11] Public school districts and colleges have long been covered by Section 504 of the Rehabilitation Act if they receive federal financial assistance. The requirements imposed by the ADA in the preemployment process are broader and more comprehensive. This chapter will focus on the requirements of the ADA in the preemployment process. Compliance with these requirements will result in compliance with Section 504 requirements regarding the preemployment process.
[12] 42 U.S.C. § 12102(2); 29 C.F.R. 1630.2(g).
[13] 29 C.F.R. § 1630.2(h).
[14] 29 C.F.R. § 1630.2(i).
[15] 29 C.F.R. § 1630.2(j).
[16] 29 C.F.R. § 1630.2(k).
[17] 29 C.F.R. § 1630.2(l).
[18] 29 C.F.R. § 1630.2(m).
[19] 42 U.S.C. § 12114(a).
[20] 42 U.S.C. § 12210(b).
[21] 42 U.S.C. § 12114(c).
[22] 42 U.S.C. § 12211.
[23] 42 U.S.C. § 12112; 29 C.F.R. § 1630.4.
[24] 42 U.S.C. § 12113(a).
[25] 29 C.F.R. §§ 1630.2(n)(1) and (2).
[26] 29 C.F.R. § 1630.2(n)(2).
[27] 29 C.F.R. § 1630.2(n)(3).
[28] *Id.*
[29] EEOC Technical Assistance Manual I - § 3.1 (hereinafter TAM I).
[30] TAM I - § 3.3.
[31] TAM I - § 3.4.
[32] TAM I - § 3.5.
[33] TAM I - § 3.6.
[34] TAM I - § 3.8.
[35] *Id.*
[36] TAM I - § 3.10(1).
[37] TAM I - § 3.10(2).
[38] TAM I - §§ 3.10(3) and (4).
[39] TAM I - § 3.10(5).
[40] TAM I - §§ 3.10(6), (7), (8) and (9).
[41] 29 C.F.R. § 1630.9(a); TAM I - § 3.9.
[42] 42 U.S.C. § 12111(10); TAM I - § 3.9.
[43] TAM I - § 3.9.
[44] 42 U.S.C. § 12113(b); 29 C.F.R. § 1630.2(r).
[45] 29 C.F.R. § 1630.2(r).
[46] TAM I - § 4.5.
[47] TAM I - § 5.5(b).
[48] TAM I - § 5.5(d).
[49] TAM I - § 5.5(f).
[50] *Id.*
[51] TAM I - § 5.5(g).
[52] TAM I - § 5.6.
[53] 29 C.F.R. § 1630.13(a).
[54] TAM I - § 6.4.

[55] *Id.*
[56] *Id.*
[57] TAM I - § 6.5.
[58] *See* U.S. v. City of Chicago, *supra;* EEOC v. Newspaper Production Co., 14 EPD § 7717 (W.D. La. 1977); Rowe v. General Motors Corp., 457 F.2d 348 (5th Cir. 1972).

THE TEXAS PUBLIC INFORMATION ACT

By: Merri Schneider-Vogel

I. Introduction

The Texas Public Information Act[1] (Act) is Texas' freedom of information law. The purpose of the Act is to give the public full information regarding the affairs of government and the official acts of public representatives such as public officials and employees. A school district is a governmental body subject to the Act. As such, public school districts and colleges must make available for examination and copying all information collected, assembled, or maintained by them, unless the information falls within one of the stated exceptions contained in the Act.

Upon receipt of a request for copies of records maintained by a school district, the district must either release the information, assert that the information is protected from disclosure under one of the exceptions of the Act, or request a Texas Attorney General opinion if the information has not already been deemed by the Attorney General to fit within one of the exceptions. The Act includes penalties for willfully destroying, mutilating, or removing public records, for releasing information that is deemed confidential, and for failing to give access to information that is public. This chapter will discuss what information must be disclosed under the Act, what information falls within the stated exceptions, and how your school district can comply with the Act.

II. What Information is Subject to Disclosure?

Information collected, assembled, and maintained by a school district or college is subject to disclosure under the Act unless the information falls within one of the Act's exceptions. A school district is not under an obligation to create documents or to answer questions or interrogatories.[2] However, if the district maintains documents, even if specifically not requested but which contain the information requested, the district is under an obligation to produce those documents.[3] Additionally, a school district or college may not inquire of the requestor why he or she wants the documents, but it may establish proper identification and seek clarification regarding the public records requested.[4]

Information maintained by an independent contractor hired by a school district or college is subject to disclosure. In other words, a school district cannot protect documents from disclosure merely by removing them from their files and asking an independent contractor, such as an attorney, to maintain the documents.[5]

III. What Documents are Protected from Disclosure?

The Act contains many itemized exceptions, not all of which are applicable to school districts or colleges. Those exceptions that are more apt to apply in the school setting are as follows:

A. Section 552.101[6]

Section 552.101 protects information deemed confidential by constitutional, statutory, or common law. For example, the Texas Attorney General has found that an employee's score on an IQ exam and on a personality questionnaire was protected under the constitutional right of privacy.[7] Information maintained by school districts also may be withheld under the common law right of privacy. Information is excepted from mandatory disclosure under Section 552.101 as information deemed confidential by common law right of privacy, if: (1) the information contains highly intimate or embarrassing facts, the publication of which would be highly objectionable to a reasonable person, and (2) the information is not of legitimate concern to the public.[8] If the information meets the first test, it will be presumed that the information is not of legitimate public concern unless the requestor can show that, under the particular circumstances of the case, the public has a legitimate interest in the information notwithstanding its private nature. While the Attorney General has found that a public employee's academic performance, a teacher's performance on the Texas Examination of Current Administrators and Teachers (TECAT), and scores on state licensing exams[9] do not fall within the common law right of privacy and are not exempt from disclosure, certain financial information of employees has been held exempt from disclosure. Payroll information indicating money deducted for an annuity in a private program, background financial information regarding an individual, and payroll information indicating deductions for life insurance if participation is in a private plan not implemented by the school district, are all protected under Section 552.101 and need not be disclosed.[10]

Other information protected under Section 552.101 is information maintained by the district made confidential by federal or state statute. For example, the Internal Revenue Code deems W-4 and W2 forms confidential.[11] Additionally, the Medical Practices Act deems certain medical information of employees maintained by the district confidential.[12] Districts and colleges may also be able to protect information collected during an investigation if the information falls within the informer's privilege which has been found to be incorporated into Section 552.101.[13] Therefore, information containing the identity of a person who reports a violation or possible violation of law to officials charged with the duty to enforce a particular law, which could include a school district, may be protected.

B. Section 552.102[14]

Section 552.102 exempts from disclosure information in personnel files, the disclosure of which would constitute a clearly unwarranted invasion of personal privacy,[15] and transcripts from institutions of higher education maintained in personnel files of professional public school employees. When an employee's educational transcripts are requested, the school district should delete everything except the employee's name, degree, and courses taken.[16]

All information in the personnel file of an individual governmental employee that is public under the Act is available to the individual employee or his or her designated representative. Section 552.102 does not give an employee access to information contained in his or her personnel file if that information is exempt from disclosure under any other exceptions under the Act that are not intended to protect the person's privacy rights.

C. Section 552.111[17]

Section 552.111 excepts from disclosure inter-agency or intra-agency memoranda or letters that would not be available by law to a party in litigation with the agency. Prior to 1993, the Attorney General had interpreted Section 552.111 to exempt from disclosure intra-office or inter-office memoranda that contain advice, opinion, or recommendation.[18] However, relying on an Austin court of appeals decision,[19] the Attorney General has restricted the interpretation of Section 552.111 to exempt only those internal communications consisting of advice, recommendations, opinions, and other material reflecting the policymaking processes of the governmental body at issue.[20] According to the Attorney General, the policymaking functions of an agency do not encompass routine internal administrative and personnel matters. Moreover, Section 552.111 does not protect severable, factual information.[21]

D. Section 552.117[22]

Section 552.117 protects from disclosure the home address, home telephone number, or social security number of each present or former official or employee of a governmental body who has elected confidentiality under Section 552.024.[23] This section also protects information that reveals whether the person has family members. Section 552.024

states that each present or former employee or official must choose whether to allow public access to his or her home address and home telephone number. Such election must be made in writing not later than the fourteenth day after the date on which the employee begins employment with the governmental body, the official is elected or appointed, or the former employee or official ends service with a governmental body. If an election is not made within the fourteen days, the information is subject to public access. However, so long as a request for information is not pending, the person can change his or her election.

E. Other Exceptions

Other exceptions that may be used to protect information from disclosure include information, which, if released would give advantage to competitors or bidders;[24] information pertaining to the location of real or personal property to be used for public purposes prior to public announcement of the project, and information pertaining to appraisals or purchase price of real or personal property to be used for public purposes prior to the formal award of contracts;[25] attorney-client protected information;[26] trade secrets and commercial or financial information obtained from a person and privileged or confidential by statute or judicial decision;[27] student records;[28] and test items.[29]

IV. Requesting an Opinion from the Texas Attorney General

If the Texas Attorney General has not rendered an opinion determining whether the exact type of document requested is subject to disclosure, the district or college must request an Attorney General opinion.

The safest course of action for a school district or college is to request an Attorney General opinion unless there is absolutely no doubt that the information has been previously determined to be protected. For example, if a school district received a request for a copy of a W-4 form, the school district would not have to ask for an Attorney General opinion because the Attorney General has previously found that W-4 forms are deemed confidential by the Internal Revenue Code.[30] Absent an "on point" previous determination, an opinion should always be requested.

Section 552.301 of the Act requires a school district or college to request an Attorney General opinion and state the exceptions that apply within a reasonable time, no later than ten calendar days after receiving a written request. Once the school district requests an Attorney General opinion, no later than the fifteenth calendar day after receiving the written request, it must submit a copy of the request for information, the rationale for asserting the exception, and a copy of the requested information or representative samples of a voluminous amount of information. The information submitted should be labeled to indicate which exceptions apply to which document. If a decision is not requested, the information is deemed to be public information.[31] The Attorney General will not assert any exception not raised by the school district except Section 552.101, the exception pertaining to information deemed confidential by law.

V. A Requestor May Seek a Writ of Mandamus

Sections 552.321-322 state that if a governmental body refuses to request an Attorney General's decision or to supply the public information, the requestor or the Attorney General may seek a writ of mandamus compelling the governmental body to make the information available for public inspection. If an action is brought, the court may award costs of litigation and reasonable attorneys' fees incurred by the party who substantially prevails. In assessing costs and attorneys' fees, the court will consider whether the conduct of the governmental body had a reasonable basis in law and whether litigation was brought in good faith.

VI. Charges for Copies of Requested Documents

Section 552.261 of the Act authorizes a school district or college to charge for copies of public records. The cost shall include costs of copying as well as costs of materials, labor, and overhead unless the request is for fifty pages or fewer of paper records, unless the pages to be copied are located in more than one building or in a remote storage facility. The State Purchasing and General Services Commission adopts rules for governmental bodies to use in determining copying charges. School districts, because they are not state agencies, need not comply with the charges set by the Commission; however, they may not charge more than a 25% variance from the rules set by the Commission.

Section 552.263 of the Act authorizes a school district to require a requestor to pay a deposit or bond for payment of anticipated costs for the preparation of a copy of public information if the charge for the copy is estimated by the governmental body to exceed $100. For example, if a school district received a request for hundreds of pages of information, and the anticipated cost of providing the copies exceeds $100, the district is authorized to require prepayment for those costs in the event the requestor is unable or unwilling to pay after the district expends the resources required to satisfy the request.

School districts may receive requests for inspection of information that exists in an electronic medium. A school district may not charge a fee for access to the information unless complying with the request will require programming or manipulation of data. If manipulation or programming is required, the school district must inform the requestor of the estimated charges necessary to make the information available.

The Act does not state a specific time by which an open records request must be fulfilled. It provides, however, that all governmental bodies should provide suitable copies of public records within a reasonable period of time after the date copies were requested and should make reasonably efficient use of each page of public record so as not to cause excessive cost for the reproduction of public records.

VII. A School District Must Provide Copies and/or Access to Information

Section 552.203 of the Act states that an officer for public records shall promptly produce requested information for inspection and/or duplication in the offices of the governmental body. The officer of public records is defined in the Act as the chief administrative officer of the governmental body and could include superintendents of a school district and the chancellor or president of a public junior college. The Act also provides that if the information is in active use or in storage and not available at a requested time, the officer for public records shall certify this fact in writing to the applicant and set a date and hour within a reasonable time when the record will be available for copying and/or inspection. A district does not have to allow the requestor to remove the original copies of public records from the offices of any governmental body. Section 552.225 states that a person requesting the public information must complete the examination of the information within ten days after the date the custodian of the information makes it available to the person. If the requestor files a written request for an extension, the governmental body may grant two ten-day extensions of time for the requestor to complete the examination.

VIII. Special Right of Access to Confidential Information

Section 552.023 gives a special right of access to records held by a governmental body that contain information relating to the requestor protected from public disclosure by laws intended to protect the requestor's privacy interest. For example, medical records contained in employee's records, although confidential by law under Section 552.101, may not be withheld from the employee. However, if the information is protected under an exception other than one meant to protect the employee's privacy interest, the employee does not have a special right of access to that information.

IX. Specific Information Deemed Public Under the Act

Section 552.022 of the Act states that various types of information are specifically made public information. Those categories applicable to school districts include: (1) reports, audits, evaluations, investigations made of, for, or by governmental bodies upon completion; (2) names, sex, ethnicity, salaries, titles, and dates of employment of all employees and officers of governmental bodies; information in any account, voucher, or contract dealing with the receipt or expenditure of public or other funds by governmental bodies, not otherwise made confidential by law; (3) the names of every official in the final record of voting on all proceedings in governmental bodies; (4) all working papers, research material, and information used to make estimates of the need for, or expenditure of, public funds or taxes by any governmental body, upon completion of such estimates; (5) rules of procedure; (6) descriptions of forms available or the places at which forms may be obtained; (7) instructions as to the scope and contents of all papers, reports or examinations; (8) administrative manuals and instructions to staff that affect members of the public; (9) information that is in a bill for attorneys' fees and that is not privileged under the attorney-client privilege or confidential under other law; (10) information contained in a public court record; and (11) a settlement agreement to which a governmental body is a party unless the agreement is confidential under other law.

X. Penalties for Violating the Law

Sections 552.352 and 552.353 of the Act provide criminal liability for releasing information deemed confidential under the Act and for refusing to give access to, or to permit or provide copying of, public records to any person upon request. A person who violates Sections 552.352 and 552.353 is guilty of a misdemeanor and, upon conviction, may be punished by confinement in the county jail not to exceed six months and/or a fine in an amount not to exceed $1,000.00. A violation under these sections also constitutes official misconduct.

Section 552.351 also provides that any person who willfully destroys, mutilates, removes without permission, or alters public records is guilty of a misdemeanor and upon conviction shall be fined not less than $25.00 nor more than $4,000.00, and/or confined in the county jail not less than three days nor more than three months.

XI. Conclusion

The Act contains specific procedures with which a school district and college must comply. The following is a list of general guidelines to consider in complying with the Act:

1. Always require that the requestor put in writing with specificity the information he or she is requesting.
2. Upon receipt of a written request, the district must determine whether information exists to comply with the request and, if so, whether the information falls within any of the exceptions.
3. If the district believes that the information may fall within an exception, and if the Texas Attorney General has not already decided that the exact information is exempt from disclosure, the school district must request, within ten calendar days from receiving the written request, an Attorney General opinion.
4. If the Attorney General determines that the information is subject to disclosure and the district does not want to disclose the information, the school district must file a lawsuit in Travis County seeking a declaratory judgment that the information is not subject to disclosure and seeking relief from compliance with the decision of the Attorney General.
5. If the district decides to produce documents for copying, and if the anticipated cost of providing copies exceeds $100, the district may ask the requestor for prepayment in cash of the anticipated cost for the preparation of the records, or for a bond.
6. Do not ask the requestor why he or she is requesting the information.
7. Be aware of the costs set by the State Purchasing and General Services Commission for information reproduction and do not exceed them by more than 25%.
8. Be aware that criminal penalties exist for distributing confidential information and for refusing to give access to public information.

9. Notify your employees of their right to determine whether they want the public to have access to their home telephone number, home address, social security numbers and/or information identifying whether they have family members. Have a procedure in place whereby an employee can elect to have this information withheld from disclosure within fourteen days after being hired by the district, and periodically during the term of his or her employment.
10. When in doubt concerning whether requested information is subject to disclosure under the Act, seek the advice of counsel, and/or request a Texas Attorney General Opinion within ten days from receiving the request. Otherwise, the information is deemed to be public.

ENDNOTES

[1] TEX. GOV'T. CODE Ch. 551.
[2] Open Records Decision No. 347 (1982); Op. Att'y Gen. DM-41 (1991); Open Records Decision No. 555 (1990).
[3] TEX. GOV'T. CODE § 552.222; Op. Att'y Gen. MW-307 (1981); Open Records Decision No. 127 (1976); TEX. GOV'T. CODE § 552.021.
[4] The governmental body may not inquire into a requestor's motives for requesting information. *See* § 552.222, Open Records Decision No. 489 (1989).
[5] Open Records Decision Nos. 335 (1982); 192 (1978); 437 (1986). The test for whether the Act applies to information actually held by the outside consultant is whether: (1) the information relates to the governmental body's official duties or business; (2) the consultant acts as an agent of the governmental body in collecting the information; and (3) the governmental body has or is entitled to access to the information. *See* Open Records Decision No. 462 (1987).
[6] TEX. GOV'T. CODE § 552.101.
[7] Open Records Decision No. 600 (1992).
[8] Industrial Found. of the S. v. Texas Indus. Accident Bd., 540 S.W.2d 668 (Tex. 1976), *cert. denied* 430 U.S. 931 (1977); *See also* Ramie v. City of Hedwig Village, 765 F.2d 490 (5th Cir. 1985); Open Records Decision No. 594 (1991).
[9] Klein Indep. Sch. Dist. v. Maddox, 830 F.2d 576 (5th Cir. 1987), *cert. denied*, 485 U.S. 1008 (1988); Open Records Decision No. 467 (1987); Open Records Decision No. 441 (1986); Open Records Decision No. 154 (1977).
[10] Open Records Decision No. 226 (1979); Open Records Decision No. 523 (1989); Open Records Decision No. 545 (1990).
[11] Op. Att'y Gen. H-1274 (1978); Open Records Decision No. 226 (1979).
[12] Open Records Decision No. 370 (1983); Open Records Decision No. 262 (1980). Medical information regarding employees should also be held confidential under the Americans with Disabilities Act (ADA).
[13] Open Records Decision No. 515 (1988).
[14] TEX. GOV'T. CODE § 552.102.
[15] The Attorney General has used the same test announced in *Industrial Foundation of the South, supra* at note 8, in determining if information in personnel files is exempt from disclosure.
[16] Open Records Decision No. 526 (1989).
[17] TEX. GOV'T. CODE § 552.111.

[18] Austin v. City of San Antonio, 630 S.W.2d 391, 394 (Tex. App.–San Antonio 1982, *writ ref'd n.r.e.*); Op. Att'y Gen. H-436 (1974); Open Records Decision Nos. 538 (1990); 470 (1987); 600 (1992).
[19] Texas Dep't of Pub. Safety v. Gilbreath, 842 S.W.2d 408 (Tex. App.–Austin 1992, *no writ*).
[20] Open Records Decision No. 615 (1993).
[21] Open Records Decision Nos. 582; 574; 565 (1990).
[22] Tex. Gov't. Code § 552.117.
[23] Tex. Gov't. Code § 552.024.
[24] Tex. Gov't. Code § 552.104.
[25] Tex. Gov't. Code § 552.105.
[26] Tex. Gov't. Code § 552.107. Information protected by the attorney-client privilege also is exempted from disclosure under § 552.101 as information deemed confidential by law.
[27] Tex. Gov't. Code § 552.110.
[28] Tex. Gov't. Code § 552.114. Section 552.114 of the Act also provides that nothing in the Act shall be construed to require the release of information contained in educational records of any educational agency or institution except in conformity with the provisions of the Family Education Rights and Privacy Act, 20 U.S.C.A. § 1232(g).
[29] Tex. Gov't. Code § 552.122. Open Records Decision No. 511 (1988).
[30] *See* note 11, *supra*.
[31] Tex. Gov't. Code § 552.302.

EMPLOYMENT PRACTICES REGARDING THE DISABLED EMPLOYEE

By: Janet Little Horton

I. Introduction

Title I of the Americans with Disabilities Act (ADA) prohibits discrimination against qualified individuals with disabilities.[1] Title I applies to all public schools and colleges that employ fifteen or more employees, including part-time employees, for twenty or more calendar weeks in a current or preceding calendar year. School districts, regardless of size, are covered by the employment nondiscrimination requirements under Title II of the ADA as well.[2] Title I of the ADA is modeled on Section 504 of the Rehabilitation Act of 1973, 29 U.S.C. § 794. School districts, as recipients of federal funds, have long been subject to the Section 504 requirement that disabled employees not be discriminated against solely on the basis of their disability. The requirements of the ADA are very similar to those of Section 504. The ADA has, however, greatly heightened awareness regarding the obligations of school districts to their disabled employees. This chapter will address the requirements of Title I of the ADA concerning the disabled employee.

II. Who is Disabled?

Title I of the ADA protects a qualified individual with a disability from discrimination on the basis of the disability. A person with a disability is an individual who has a physical or mental impairment that substantially limits one or more major life activities; has a record of such an impairment; or is regarded as having such an impairment.[3] A physical impairment is any physiological disorder or condition, cosmetic disfigurement, or anatomical loss affecting one or more of the bodily systems, such as the neurological, musculoskeletal, special sense organs, respiratory, cardiovascular, reproductive, digestive, genitourinary, hemic and lymphatic, skin, and endocrine systems. A mental impairment is any mental or psychological disorder, such as mental retardation, organic brain syndrome, emotional or mental illness, and specific learning disabilities.

Physical characteristics are not considered disabilities. Physical characteristics include such things as height and weight within normal ranges, eye color, hair color, lefthandedness, etc. Similarly, personality traits are not disabilities. Personality traits include such things as poor judgment, irresponsibility, a quick temper, etc. Environmental, cultural, and economic disadvantages are not considered disabilities.

Major life activities include, but are not limited to, walking, speaking, breathing, performing manual tasks, seeing, hearing, learning, caring for one's self, and working. In other words, these are the activities that the average person can perform with little or no difficulty as part of every day life. A person is substantially limited in performing a major life activity if the individual is unable to perform the activity, or is significantly limited in the ability to perform an activity, as compared to an average person in the general population. In determining whether a person is substantially limited by a physical or mental impairment, one must consider the impairment's nature and severity, how long it will last or is expected to last, and its permanent or long-term impact, or expected impact.

Temporary, non-chronic impairments that do not last a long time and have little or no long-term impact are usually not disabilities. These would include such things as a cold, a sprain, broken bones, allergies, and the flu. These conditions may turn into disabilities in the unusual case. For example, a person with allergies, which would usually be considered a non-chronic impairment, may have allergies to such a severe and extreme degree that the person is not able to perform daily tasks in a work environment. A person may have a broken leg, which is considered a temporary, non-chronic impairment. However, if the bone does not heal, the person may become impaired in his or her ability to walk. In each case, the temporary, non-chronic impairment may have turned into an impairment which substantially limits one or more major life activities and, therefore, may bring the person under the protection of the ADA.

By far the largest category of employees covered by the ADA are those with physical or mental impairments which substantially limit one or more major life activities. Two other categories of persons are also protected by the ADA. The second category of employees protected by the ADA are those persons who have a record or a history of a substantially limiting condition, including those who have been misclassified or misdiagnosed as having a disability. For example, a person may have a history of hospitalization for a drug addiction, but no longer illegally uses drugs. This is a record of a substantially limiting condition. It would be a violation of the ADA to terminate such a person solely on the basis of that record if the person is qualified to perform the essential functions of his or her job.

A third category of persons covered by the ADA are those who are *regarded* as having a substantially limiting condition. For example, an individual may have an impairment which is not substantially limiting but is treated by the school district as substantially limiting. An example of this would be a person who has high blood pressure which is controlled by medication. It would be a violation of the ADA for a school district to terminate this employee simply because the school district believes that the job is too stressful for the employee. If the employee can perform the essential functions of the job with or without reasonable accommodation, then the fact that he or she has high blood pressure is not a basis on which a school district can make a decision to terminate.

This category also includes individuals who have an impairment that is substantially limiting only because of the attitudes of others toward the condition. For example, a school employee who is missing part of an arm because of a birth defect may be perfectly capable of carrying out all the essential functions of the job of a school receptionist. It would be a violation of the ADA to refuse to make the person the receptionist because of fears that the public would not want to deal with the employee because of his or her birth defect.

Those regarded as having a substantially limiting condition may also include individuals with no impairment but who are regarded by a school district as having a substantially limiting impairment. For example, there may be a false rumor in the workplace that a certain employee is positive for the HIV virus. Upon hearing such a rumor, a school district might erroneously take adverse action and terminate the employee. The school district has violated the ADA because, although the person is not actually infected with the HIV virus, the school district has treated the employee as having a substantially limiting condition and has terminated the person based on that condition.

These last two categories of persons protected under the ADA are those who are subject most to society's myths, fears, and stereotypes regarding disabilities. The ADA is meant to protect these employees from discrimination on the basis of a past record or the perception of others. The ADA requires a school district to consider these persons' current capabilities regarding the job in question. It does not allow rejection of these persons from employment because of a past history of an impairment or because of the assumptions or prejudices of others.

The ADA specifically excludes from protection certain categories of persons. The state of drug addiction and alcoholism are protected conditions under the ADA. However, persons who currently illegally use drugs are not protected by the ADA. This includes people who use prescription drugs illegally, as well as those who use illegal drugs. People who have been rehabilitated and do not currently illegally use drugs, or who are in the process of completing a rehabilitation program, are protected by the ADA and may not be terminated from employment because of their past or current participation in a drug rehabilitation program.

The school district may enforce rules against the illegal use of drugs and the use of alcohol in the workplace. The employee who violates these rules, even if he or she is a drug addict or alcoholic, may be disciplined or discharged. The school district is not constrained by the ADA from discharging any person who currently engages in the illegal use of drugs. The school district may discipline or discharge an employee, even if he or she is an alcoholic, whose use of alcohol impairs job performance or conduct to the extent that he or she is not a qualified individual with a disability.

There are other specific exclusions included in the ADA. Those who have sexual behavior disorders, such as transvestitism, transsexualism, pedophilia, exhibitionism, voyeurism, and gender identity disorders not resulting from physical impairments are not protected by the ADA.[4] Individuals who are compulsive gamblers, or subject to kleptomania or pyromania, are not protected by the ADA.[5] Those who have psychoactive substance use disorders resulting from current illegal drug use are not protected by the ADA. Homosexuals and bisexuals are also not protected by the ADA.[6]

III. Application of the ADA

The ADA applies to all employment practices. A covered school district may not discriminate against a qualified individual with a disability solely on the basis of the disability regarding job application procedures, the hiring, advancement, or discharge of employees, employee compensation, job training, or other terms, conditions or privileges of employment. The employment practices covered by the ADA apply to application, testing, hiring, assignments, evaluation, disciplinary acts, training, promotion, medical examinations, layoff/recall, termination, compensation, leave, and benefits. The school district may not discriminate against an employee, whether disabled or not, because the employee has a family, social, or business relationship with an individual with a disability.

IV. Who is a Qualified Individual with a Disability?

An individual with a disability is considered qualified if the person satisfies the required skills, experience, education, and other job-related requirements of the employment position the individual holds, and who, with or without reasonable accommodation, can perform the essential functions of the position. Whether a person is a qualified individual with a disability is a two-part determination. First, the school district must determine whether the individual meets the necessary prerequisites for the job such as education, work experience, training, skills, licenses, certificates, or other job-related requirements. Secondly, the school district must determine if the individual can perform the essential functions of the job with or without reasonable accommodation.

V. Job Functions

An employee may have been disabled at the time of hiring or may have become disabled after being hired for a certain job. In either case, the employee has obviously already met the necessary prerequisites for the job. The school district may be faced with determining whether the employee continues to be able to perform the essential functions of his or her job with or without reasonable accommodation.

An essential job function is a fundamental duty of the position in question. The school district must determine if the function is actually performed as part of the job and whether removing the function would fundamentally change the job. If the job would be fundamentally changed, then the function is essential. Essential functions of a job may change over time as the job is reshaped by the employer and/or the needs of the work environment.

In addition to essential job functions, a job may also have marginal functions. Marginal functions are defined by the ADA as all other job functions which are not essential. A school district may require an employee to perform as many marginal job functions as desired in addition to essential job functions. When a disability prevents an employee from performing a job function, either essential or marginal, then the school district must consider the issue of reasonable accommodation. A school district may be required in some cases to reassign marginal job functions as a reasonable accommodation, but the ADA does not require the reassignment of essential job functions to another employee to accommodate a disabled employee.

A school district may establish job-related qualification standards that apply to all job functions. However, qualification standards that screen out, or tend to screen out, an individual with a disability on the basis of the disability must be both job-related and consistent with business necessity. Job-related means the criteria is a legitimate measure or qualification for a specific job. Job-related criteria may include both essential and marginal functions of the job. A qualification standard is consistent with business necessity only if it relates to an essential function of the job. Even if a qualification standard is job-related and consistent with business necessity, if it screens out an individual with a disability, on the basis of the disability, the school district must consider if that individual could meet the standard with a reasonable accommodation. A school district is not required to lower existing production or evaluation standards regarding quality and/or quantity of work for a given job if these standards are uniformly applied to all employees in that job.

A number of factors are considered in determining whether a job function is essential or not. The school district's judgment is one factor to be considered. Written job descriptions prepared before advertising or interviewing for a job are another factor. The amount of time spent by an employee performing a function is also considered. However, in some cases, a function, although performed infrequently, is essential because there will be serious consequences if the employee is not able to perform it. For example, a bus driver with a disability that would prevent him or her from quickly evacuating children from a bus in case of an emergency may not be able to perform an essential, although infrequent, function of that particular job. The work experience of people who have performed the job is also evidence of the essential functions of the job. A school district may revise a job description and change the essential functions of the job. If a school district is sued for a violation of the ADA, the school district will have the burden to prove that a function is an essential function of the particular job.

VI. Reasonable Accommodation

If an employee becomes disabled during the term of employment and cannot perform one or more essential functions of his or her job, or if a disabled employee's condition changes or the person is transferred to another position and cannot perform one or more essential job functions, then the school district needs to consider whether a reasonable accommodation can be made for the employee. A reasonable accommodation is any modification or adjustment to a job, an employment practice, or the work environment that makes it possible for an individual with a disability to enjoy an equal employment opportunity.[7] Reasonable accommodation is required in three instances. First, reasonable accommodation is required to ensure equal opportunity in the application process. For example, the employment office or the interview site may need to be made accessible to a disabled individual so that he or she may have an equal opportunity to be considered for a position. Second, a reasonable accommodation may be required to enable a qualified individual with a disability to perform the essential functions of a job. Finally, a reasonable accommodation may be required to enable a disabled employee to enjoy equal benefits and privileges of employment. For example, an employee with a disability must be reasonably accommodated to have access to restrooms, lunchrooms, meeting rooms, and other school district services.

The duty to reasonably accommodate is ongoing and may arise as an employee's condition changes, or his or her job changes. An accommodation does not have to be made to a person who is not otherwise qualified for a job. Generally, the individual with the disability is obliged to request a reasonable accommodation. The school district is not required, however, to provide the specific accommodation requested by the disabled individual; a different reasonable accommodation may be offered. The disabled individual may refuse an accommodation offered by the school district, but he or she may then be disqualified from the job if it can only be performed with the accommodation. If the cost of the accommodation would impose an undue hardship on the employer, the individual with the disability should be given the option of providing the accommodation, or paying that portion of the cost which makes it an undue hardship.

There are certain basic principles which govern reasonable accommodation. A reasonable accommodation must be effective, although it does not have to ensure equal results or provide exactly the same benefits or privileges. For example, if the employee lunchroom is on the second floor of a business, and an employee in a wheelchair does not have access to the second floor, it may be an undue hardship on the employer to install an elevator to reach the second floor. However, it may be a reasonable accommodation to establish a comparable lunchroom on the first floor to which the disabled employee would have access. The school district must reasonably accommodate only to reduce barriers to employment, not to fulfill some other reason. A school district would not have to honor a request to transfer a disabled employee to another facility for personal reasons. The accommodation must be work-related.

A reasonable accommodation is just that–reasonable. It does not have to be the best available or the option preferred by the employee, so long as it is effective. A full time reader for a blind employee may be the best accommodation, rather than just a reasonable one, if another employee can perform the reading function as needed. Personal equipment or devices such as hearing aids, glasses, wheelchairs or canes used by the person both on and off the job are not required to be provided by the school district, unless the equipment is needed to meet job-related needs. If an office floor is covered with thick-piled carpeting and manual propulsion of a wheelchair is not possible, then the school district may need to change the carpet, or place a usable surface over the carpet, or provide a motorized wheelchair to be used solely at work. Of course, a school district may always make modifications beyond those which would be considered reasonable under the ADA.

Whether an accommodation is reasonable must be determined on an individual basis. It must take into account the specific abilities and functional limitations of a particular employee with a disability. Not all accommodations are reasonable. If a reasonable accommodation exists, it must be one which would enable the specific individual in question to do the job function. In other words, an accommodation which would meet the needs of one disabled employee might not meet the needs of another employee disabled by the same condition. In determining whether a reasonable accommodation exists, the school district must look at the needs of the specific disabled employee involved. The school district is responsible for notifying applicants and employees of its obligation to provide reasonable accommodation to otherwise qualified disabled persons. This can be done through posters, application forms, vacancy notices, personnel manuals, oral communication and the like.

The term "reasonable accommodation" is not a magic term. An employee merely must request some adjustment or change in the work environment or work situation. The employee is not required to use the specific phrase "reasonable accommodation." If the need for the accommodation claimed by the employee is not obvious, or the school district does not believe it is needed, the school district may request documentation from a doctor or other professional to support the request.

The reasonable accommodation provided by the school district must be effective for the particular individual. In other words, it must give the disabled individual an equally effective opportunity to apply for a job, to perform essential job functions, or to enjoy equal benefits and privileges of the job. In some cases, the accommodation may be obvious and simple. In other cases, the accommodation may not be easy to identify.

The Equal Employment Opportunity Commission (EEOC), which is the governmental agency that investigates complaints made under Title I of the ADA, has suggested a process for identifying a reasonable accommodation. First, the school district must look at the particular job and determine its purpose and essential functions. Next, the school district must consult with the disabled individual to determine his or her specific physical or mental abilities and limitations as they relate to essential job functions. The school district must identify the barriers to job performance and determine ways that those barriers can be overcome. In consultation with the disabled individual, the school district should identify potential accommodations. The school district and the individual should analyze how effective each accommodation would be in overcoming the barriers to performance of essential job functions. The school district also may seek technical assistance from an outside source.

If there are several means of reasonable accommodation, the school district should consider the disabled employee's preference. However, the school district is free to choose among effective accommodations and may choose one less expensive or easier to provide than the one the individual prefers. In some cases, the individual may want to provide his or her own accommodation. However, if the employee later becomes unwilling or unable to provide the accommodation, then the school district may have a duty to take over the provision of the accommodation if it is reasonable.

VII. Undue Hardship

An accommodation does not have to be provided to an employee if it would impose an *undue* hardship on the school district. An undue hardship exists if the accommodation would require significant difficulty or expense in relation to the size of the school district, the resources available, and the nature of the school district's operation. Undue hardship must be determined on a case-by-case basis. Generally, the larger the school district, the greater the expense and effort which will be required under the ADA to accommodate disabled individuals.

An undue hardship exists if the proposed accommodation is unduly costly, extensive, substantial, disruptive, or would fundamentally alter the nature or operation of the school. Numerous factors may be considered in determining whether an accommodation creates an undue hardship. They include such things as the nature and net cost of the accommodation to the school district, the financial resources of the school district, the number of employees at the facility, and the effect of the accommodation on the expenses and resources of the facility.[8] Because a school district has more than one campus, the overall financial resources of the school district, its size, number of employees, and type and location of various facilities will also be considered in determining whether an accommodation is reasonable. Other factors to be considered with multiple campuses and district facilities include the structure and function of the entire workforce, its geographic separateness, and the administrative and fiscal relationship of the specific facility to the larger entity. The impact of the accommodation on the operation of various school district facilities, including the impact on the ability of other employees to perform their jobs and on the facility's ability to conduct its business, must also be considered. However, low morale or disruption of the employee workforce due to other employees' fears or prejudices regarding the individual with the disability will not be considered undue hardship. The fact that the cost of an accommodation may be high in relation to the employee's wage or salary is not a factor to be considered. What matters are the resources available to the school district to accommodate the specific disabled employee. There is no bright line test or specific amount of money above which an accommodation is considered unreasonable.

VIII. Types of Accommodations

There are numerous ways to reasonably accommodate an individual with a disability who is otherwise qualified for a job. The school district, as an employer under Title I, must provide access to a specific individual so that the individual can perform his or her job. However, Title II places an obligation on all school districts, as governmental entities, to ensure that all existing facilities are readily accessible and usable by persons with disabilities, whether or not those persons are employees. There is an exception to this requirement when it would cause a fundamental alteration in the nature of the program or services or would result in an undue financial and administrative burden. Accessibility and usability are determined by viewing the facility in its entirety.

There are numerous ways that an individual's access to the job site and to work-related activities may be accommodated. Reasonable accommodation may include such things as installing an entrance or exit ramp, removing raised thresholds, reserving extra wide parking spaces close to the work site, making restrooms accessible, rearranging office furniture and equipment, making drinking fountains accessible, providing an accessible path of travel to equipment and facilities used by employees, removing potentially hazardous objects from the path of people without vision, and adding flashing lights to alarm bells to alert a hearing impaired employee to an emergency.

Reasonable accommodation may also include such things as job restructuring and modification.[9] This may involve reallocating marginal functions of the job to someone else. The school district is not required to reallocate essential job functions to another employee. Modifying when and how essential job functions are done, however, may be a reasonable modification.

The school district may be required to consider a modified work schedule, such as flexibility in work hours or the work week, or a part-time work week if they do not cause an undue hardship. These accommodations might be applicable to persons who need special medical treatment, people who need rest periods, people whose disabilities are affected by eating and sleeping schedules, people who find it difficult because of a disability to use public transportation during peak hours, and those who must use special transportation to and from work.

A disabled employee may need more flexible leave time for medical treatment, or a temporary condition in the work environment which may be harmful. Such flexible leave time may be considered a reasonable accommodation in certain cases. In addition, an employee who needs leave time for treatment of a serious health condition may be eligible for unpaid leave under the Family and Medical Leave Act (FMLA). The school district is not required to provide additional paid leave to an employee under federal law.

Reassignment to a vacant position may be a reasonable accommodation for an employee when an accommodation is not possible in the employee's present job, or when an accommodation exists, but it would cause an undue hardship to the school district. Reassignment should be to a position equivalent in terms of pay and other job status, if the individual is qualified for the position, it is vacant, or it will be vacant within a reasonable amount of time. If there is no vacant equivalent position for reassignment, and one will not soon become vacant, assignment to a lower graded position may be considered as a reasonable accommodation. The employee's higher salary would not have to be maintained unless other employees reassigned to lower paying positions have had their salaries maintained. Obviously, if an employee is within the terms of a contract, then any reassignment to another position must be at the same salary, regardless of the original salary in the new position. There is no requirement under the ADA to create a new job to reasonably accommodate a disabled employee, to bump an existing employee from a job, or to promote a disabled employee as a form of accommodation.

Reasonable accommodation may include the purchase of equipment or the modification of existing equipment. The individual with the disability may be instrumental in suggesting appropriate equipment changes. Vocational rehabilitation specialists, independent living specialists, or occupational therapists may also be able to suggest appropriate changes.

If the school district gives tests or examinations to its employees, or provides training programs to its employees, these may need to be modified in their administration to provide equal employment opportunities to individuals with disabilities. Examinations should test the person's ability to do the job function, rather than test the limitations caused by the disability. If portions of the examination include manual performance of some type, the employee should be informed in advance so that he or she may request any necessary accommodation to perform the examination. Training programs may need to be modified with regard to the type of material used, or the physical accessibility of the training program.

For the disabled employee with a vision disability, a reasonable accommodation may include providing a reader. Whether this creates an undue hardship will be determined by examining the overall nature of the school district and the resources available to it. A reader could be hired on a part-time, as-needed basis to reasonably accommodate the needs of an employee. In some instances, the reader could be another employee of the district.

A deaf employee might reasonably be accommodated by the provision of an interpreter on an as-needed basis if this does not cause an undue hardship. The nature of the job may only require an interpreter on a periodic basis. The reasonable accommodation should be aimed at providing the deaf employee with the assistance necessary to communicate as required by the duties of the job. Writing notes, signing, or typing may be other methods of communication with the deaf employee.

A reasonable accommodation must fit the specific circumstances of the job, and it must fit the specific circumstances of the disabled employee. In some instances, there may be no accommodation that would allow the disabled employee to perform certain essential job functions. In other instances, an accommodation may exist but it may be unreasonable based on the specific circumstances of the school district. In those two instances, it is permissible to terminate the disabled employee. The disabled employee is no longer a qualified individual with a disability under the ADA.

IX. Medical Examinations

The criteria regarding medical examinations of employees under the ADA are very stringent. A medical examination or medical inquiry of an employee must be job-related and consistent with business necessity.[10] There are numerous circumstances which may lead to a need to obtain medical information about an employee. For example, an employee may have difficulty performing his or her job effectively. If an employee has become unable to perform an essential job function, a medical examination may reveal whether a disability exists which would qualify the person for protection under the ADA. If such a disability exists, then the school district must determine if a reasonable accommodation is available to help the person perform essential functions. However, the medical examination might reveal the absence of any physical or mental impairment which substantially limits a major life activity. In that circumstance, the school district would have no duty to consider a reasonable accommodation for the employee.

The school district may require an employee who has been injured on the job, or who wishes to return to work after an injury or illness, to undergo a medical examination if it is job-related and consistent with business necessity. Such an examination may determine if the individual meets the ADA definition of an individual with a disability if the person has requested an accommodation. The examination may determine whether the person can perform essential job functions of the job held before the injury or illness. The examination may also determine if the employee poses a direct threat to the health or safety of the employee or other persons that cannot be reduced or eliminated by reasonable accommodation. Finally, a medical examination may identify an effective accommodation that would enable the person to perform essential job functions in the person's current position.

A medical examination may be necessary if an employee requests an accommodation on the basis of a disability in the person's existing job, or if the employee is being transferred or promoted to a different job. The medical examination may determine if the person has a disability covered by the ADA and is entitled to an accommodation. The medical examination may also help to identify what an effective accommodation would be.

In certain instances, a medical examination of the employee may not be necessary, but medical inquiries may be appropriate. A medical inquiry may relate to an employee's disability and functional limitations. These inquiries may include consultations with persons who are knowledgeable about various disabilities and accommodations, such as occupational and physical therapists, rehabilitation specialists, and organizations with expertise in adaptations for specific disabilities. All medical inquiries regarding a specific employee must be job-related and consistent with business necessity.

In some instances, federal laws may require periodic examinations or other medical screening and monitoring. The ADA recognizes that a medical examination or inquiry made to comply with a federal law is job-related and consistent with business necessity. In some instances, a state or local law may require that employees in a particular job undergo specific medical examinations or medical inquiries. These are permissible under the ADA only if the inquiries are job-related and consistent with business necessity for the specific individual being examined.

A school district may conduct voluntary medical examinations and medical inquiries as a part of a health program. This is permissible so long as participation in the program is voluntary, the information is confidentially maintained, and it is not used to discriminate against an employee. Tests for the illegal use of drugs are not medical examinations under the ADA. Drug tests are not subject to the restrictions on medical examination.

X. Medical Information

All medical examinations and inquiries yield information to the school district. This information must be treated confidentially. Medical information regarding an employee must be collected and maintained on separate forms, in separate files, and must be treated as confidential medical records. These medical documents should not be placed in an employee's personnel file. The school district must take steps to guarantee the security of an employee's medical information, including keeping the information in a medical file in a separate locked cabinet apart from personnel files, and designating a specific person to have access to the medical file.

Limited exceptions exist to the rule that medical information must be kept confidential. Supervisors and managers may have access to medical information as necessary to determine restrictions on work or duties of an employee and with regard to any necessary accommodations. First aid and safety personnel may be informed, when appropriate, if a disability might require certain specific, or unusual procedures to be used in case of an emergency, or a specific type of emergency treatment for the individual. Relevant information must be provided upon request if government officials are investigating compliance with the ADA, or other federal or state laws which prohibit discrimination on the basis of a disability. Relevant medical information may also be provided to worker's compensation offices in accordance with state law. Finally, relevant information may be provided to insurance companies if the insurance company requires a medical examination to provide health or life insurance for employees of the school district.

XI. Direct Threat to Health or Safety

The school district may require that an individual not pose a direct threat to the health or safety of the individual or others, if this standard is applied to all who hold a particular job. There are very specific and stringent requirements which must be followed for the school district to establish that an employee poses a direct threat. First, there must be a significant risk of substantial harm. In other words, there must be a high probability that substantial harm is likely to occur. Next, the specific risks must be identified by defining the duration of the risk, the nature and severity of the harm, the likelihood the potential harm will occur, and the imminence of the potential harm. The risk must be current and one that is not speculative or remote. This is an assessment that cannot be based on mere speculation by the school district. Rather, the assessment of the risk must be based on objective medical or other factual evidence regarding the specific individual. The school district may not justify an employment action taken on the basis of direct risk simply by speculating that the disability will become worse in the future, that the person will become unable to perform the job in the future, that the individual may cause increased health insurance or worker's compensation costs, or that the person will have excessive absenteeism. If there is a significant risk to health and safety, the employer must consider whether there is any reasonable accommodation which could lower the risk to an acceptable level, or eliminate it.

Instances in which a disabled employee may pose a direct threat to the health or safety of the employee or others will be very rare. These are situations where the school district should act only on reasonable medical judgment that relies on the most current medical knowledge and on the best available objective evidence. A school district may not act based on unfounded assumptions or fears or stereotypes about the nature or effect of the disability. In examining whether a disabled employee poses a direct threat, the district may analyze input from the individual with the disability, the experience of this individual in previous jobs, and documentation from doctors, psychologists, rehabilitation counselors, physical or occupational therapists, or others who have a special expertise regarding the disability involved and/or direct knowledge of the specific individual. In instances where psychological behavior of an employee may suggest a threat to safety, the school district should also examine factual evidence of this behavior to determine if, in fact, evidence of a direct threat exists. A district makes a serious mistake in taking adverse personnel action against a disabled employee by alleging that the employee poses a direct threat if the district is relying on generalized or out-of-date assumptions about the risks associated with certain disabilities. It cannot be overemphasized that the district must act on current reasonable medical knowledge and the other types of evidence previously discussed.

In some instances, the school district may be concerned that the individual poses a direct threat to himself or herself, but not to others. It may act only on valid medical information. There must be evidence of a specific risk to the specific individual and/or other persons. For example, if a disabled employee has narcolepsy and frequently and unexpectedly loses consciousness, a school district could refuse to transfer the employee to the job of bus driver because that person in that position would pose a direct threat to his or her own the health or safety, as well as that of other persons. On the other hand, a school district could not reject a person from employment as a special education director because the person has a past history of mental illness, based on a generalized fear that working in this high stress job might trigger a relapse of the individual's mental illness, if the person is currently capable of performing the essential functions of the job.

Regarding those employees who handle food, the U.S. Department of Health and Human Services is required by the ADA to prepare and update annually a list of contagious diseases that are transmitted through the handling of food and the methods by which these diseases are transmitted. In accordance with established medical opinion, the list issued by the Centers for Disease Control is brief and does not include AIDS or the HIV virus. In any situation where an employee in a food handling job becomes infected with an infectious or communicable disease, the school district may contact the Centers for Disease Control to determine if that disease is on the list for those diseases transmitted through the handling of food. The CDC will also provide information regarding personal hygiene and sanitation in food handling jobs and ways to accommodate someone who may pose a direct threat in a food handling position.

The school district must comply with any federal laws dealing with health and safety requirements. The ADA does not override these obligations. The district does not have to show these requirements are job-related and consistent with business necessity. Consistent with the standards of these other federal laws, however, it still has an obligation under the ADA to consider whether there is a reasonable accommodation in a specific case that will prevent the exclusion of an employee from a job due to health and safety requirements.

Although the ADA does not override state or local laws designed to protect public health and safety, the school district must still consider the ADA in applying both state and local laws to disabled employees. If a state or local law would exclude an individual with a disability from a particular job because of a health or safety risk, the school district must still assess whether a particular individual could pose a direct threat to the health or safety of himself or herself or others under the ADA standard. If a direct threat exists, it must also consider whether it could eliminate or reduce the risk below the level of a direct threat by reasonable accommodation.

XII. Conclusion

The ADA has brought a new awareness and sensitivity to the workplace regarding the disabled employee. School officials who make personnel decisions regarding disabled employees are advised to consult the school district's attorney for guidance on specific issues. Good resources exist to help interpret provisions of the law and regulations. One of the more helpful resources is the Technical Assistance Manual on the Employment Provisions (Title I) of the ADA which is published by the EEOC, and may be obtained by contacting the local EEOC office. With the use of published resources and the advice of counsel when needed, should officials can ascertain that their personnel decisions are in compliance with the broad dictates of the ADA.

ENDNOTES

[1] American with Disabilities Act of 1990, 42 U.S.C.§ 12101-12213.
[2] *Id.* at § 12101.
[3] *Id.* at § 12102(2).
[4] *Id.* at § 12211.
[5] *Id.*
[6] *Id.* at § 12211.
[7] *Id.* at § 12101(9).
[8] *Id.* at § 12101(10).
[9] *Id.* at § 511(b).
[10] *Id.* at ADA § 102(c)(4)(A).

EMPLOYMENT CONTRACTS

By: Jennifer Piskun

I. Introduction

During its 1995 legislative session, the Texas Legislature overhauled the Texas Education Code ("Code"). The entire Code was re-written, including the sections governing teacher contracts. In an attempt to streamline and simplify the rules and regulations that govern teacher contracts, the Legislature combined Chapters 13 and 21 of the former Code and created one probationary period to be utilized for all educators regardless of whether the school district employs its educators pursuant to a "term contract" or "continuing contract." Other changes include the rules and regulations regarding the termination of continuing and term contracts during the term of the contract. Further, the appeals process at the local level and before the Commissioner of Education ("Commissioner") were dramatically changed, with the aim of providing a more efficient and swift appellate process. This chapter will provide a general overview of the new procedures and rules that control teacher contracts. However, it is important to note that the majority of these rules and regulations did not become effective until January 1, 1996. Therefore, for appeals filed prior to that date, the old Code provisions govern the particular teacher contract issue.

II. Types of Contracts

Under the new Code, a school district must employ classroom teachers, principals, librarians, nurses and counselors pursuant to one of three types of contracts: (1) probationary; (2) continuing contract; or (3) term contract.[1] A "classroom teacher" is defined as an "educator who is employed by a school district and who, not less than an average of four hours each day, teaches in an academic instructional setting or a career or technology instructional setting. The term does not include a teacher's aide or full-time administrator."[2] A district is not required to employ anyone else under these types of contracts.[3]

The board of trustees must establish by policy the specific positions or categories of positions to which continuing contracts and term contracts apply. The distinctions should be based on objective considerations such as length of service. A district may now use both term and continuing contracts with teachers.[4]

III. Certification

To be employed as a teacher, teacher intern or teacher trainee, librarian, educational aide, administrator or counselor by a school district, the person must hold an appropriate certificate or permit.[5] Audiologists, occupational therapists, physical therapists, physicians, nurses, school psychologists, associate school psychologists, social workers, and speech language pathologists may not be employed by a school district or perform specific services within those professions for a school district, unless the person is licensed by the state agency that licenses that profession.[6]

A State Board for Educator Certification (SBEC) regulates and oversees all aspects of certification, continuing education, and standards of conduct for public school educators. A fifteen-member board (thirteen appointed by the Governor, one nonvoting member each appointed by the Commissioner of Education and the Commissioner of Higher Education) employs an executive director for day-to-day operations.[7] A comprehensive system of requirements for each class of certificate is to be issued, including certificates for superintendents and principals. Further, the SBEC is to develop rules for an alternative certification program. The rules may not limit the program only to instances when there is a demonstrated shortage of educators in a school district or subject area.[8]

Before a person's contract with a board of trustees is binding, the person must present his or her certificate for filing with the district. One who does not hold a valid certificate may not be paid for teaching or work done before the effective date of issuance of the certificate.[9] However, school districts may issue a school district teaching permit and employ a person as a teacher who does not hold a valid teaching certificate from the SBEC as long as the person holds a baccalaureate degree, or will be teaching only career and technology education.[10] School districts must send the Commissioner a written statement identifying the person, his or her qualifications as a teacher, and the subject to be taught. The person may teach pending action by the Commissioner.[11] The Commissioner has thirty days from the date he or she receives the statement to inform the school district in writing that the Commissioner finds that the person is not qualified to teach.[12] If there is no timely response, the school district may issue a school district teaching permit.[13] The permit remains valid until the school district revokes it for cause. The permit may not be used to teach in another school.[14] A different school district must reinitiate the process.[15]

IV. Probationary Contracts

A "teacher" is defined as a "principal, supervisor, classroom teacher, counselor, or other full-time professional employee required to hold a certificate, or a nurse," for purposes of issuing probationary contracts.[16] The term does *not* include a superintendent. The term does *not* include a person who is not entitled to a probationary, continuing, or term contract under Sec. 21.002, an existing contract, or a district policy.[17]

Probationary contracts shall be issued to all persons who are employed as a teacher by a school district the first time or who have not been employed by the school district for two consecutive school years subsequent to August 28, 1967.[18] Probationary contracts are only issued in one year terms. There can be a maximum of three one-year probationary contracts issued to a person. If, during the third probationary contract year, the board determines it is doubtful that the person should be issued a continuing contract or term contract, the school district may enter into one more one-year probationary contract with the person.[19] After the third year, or the fourth year in specific cases, the school district must terminate the teacher's employment or employ the teacher under a continuing contract or a term contract according to school district policy. If the person hired as a probationary teacher has been employed as a teacher in public education for at least five of the eight years preceding employment with the district, the probationary period can only be for one year.[20] At the end of the first year, the district must terminate the teacher's employment or employ the teacher under a continuing contract or a term contract according to school district policy.[21]

Probationary contracts may be terminated by the board of trustees at the end of any probationary contract period. The following requirements apply: (a) the judgment of the board of trustees is that it is in the best interests of the district to terminate the employment; (b) the board gives notice to the teacher of its intention to terminate the teacher's employment; and (c) this notice is received by the teacher by the 45th day before the last day of instruction required under the current probationary contract.[22] If these requirements are followed, the board's decision is final and may not be *appealed*.[23] If notice of intent to terminate is not received by the teacher not later than the 45th day before the last day of instruction in the contract, the board employs the probationary teacher in the same capacity under: (1) a probationary contract for the next school year, if any of the three-year probationary period is left; or (2) a continuing or term contract, according to district policy, if the teacher has already been employed by the district under a probationary contract for three consecutive school years.[24]

A probationary teacher may be discharged during the probationary contract period for good cause. "Good cause" is defined as the "failure of the teacher to meet the accepted standards of conduct for the profession as generally recognized and applied in similarly situated school districts in the state."[25] In lieu of discharge, the district may suspend the teacher without pay for good cause for a period not to extend beyond the end of the current school year.[26] If a probationary teacher requests a hearing to challenge a discharge during the probationary contract period or a suspension without pay during the probationary contract period, the hearing will be held by a state hearing examiner.[27]

A probationary contract teacher may resign. If a probationary contract is in existence for the next school year and the probationary teacher gives notice of resignation to the board (or its designee) in writing not later than the 45th day before the first day of instruction, the resignation is effective without penalty.[28] The resignation is filed with the board of trustees at the time of mailing if it is mailed by prepaid certified or registered mail to the president of the board or the board's designee at the post office address of the district.[29] The board may consent to the resignation of a probationary teacher at any time.[30] The SBEC may impose sanctions on a probationary teacher who fails to perform on a contract and has not met these criteria.[31]

A teacher may be returned to probationary status in lieu of discharging a teacher employed under a continuing contract, terminating a teacher employed under a term contract, or nonrenewing a term contract.[32] However, the teacher must receive written notice of the proposal of discharge, termination, or nonrenewal and consent in writing to the probationary status.[33] A teacher that is returned to a probationary contract is considered a "first time" employee and must serve a new probationary contract period in accordance with Section 21.102.[34]

V. Continuing Contracts

A "teacher," for purposes of a continuing contract, is a "principal, supervisor, classroom teacher, counselor or other full-time professional employee who is required to hold a certificate, or a nurse."[35] The term does not include a superintendent or a person who is not entitled to a probationary, continuing, or term contract under Sec. 21.002, an existing contract, or district policy.[36]

A continuing contract must be in writing.[37] The teacher must be notified in writing of election to continuing contract status.[38] The teacher has thirty days after the date of notification to file with the superintendent written notification of acceptance of the continuing contract "beginning with the school year following the conclusion of the teacher's probationary period."[39] If the teacher does not file written notification of acceptance during that time, the teacher is considered to have refused the contract. Once employed by a continuing contract, the teacher continues in that position in future school years without annual nomination or reappointment.[40] The continuing contract continues in existence until one of the following occurs: (a) the teacher retires under the Teacher Retirement System; (b) the teacher resigns; (c) the teacher is released from employment at the end of a school year because of a necessary reduction of personnel; (d) the teacher is discharged for good cause by the board at any time; (e) the teacher is discharged for a reason stated in the teacher's contract that existed on or before September 1, 1995; or (f) the teacher is returned to probationary status.[41] The continuing contract may contain other terms consistent with board policy.

A continuing contract teacher has a right to a hearing if the teacher is to be discharged, suspended without pay, or released because of a necessary reduction in force.[42]

The board must notify the teacher in writing of the proposed action and the grounds for it.[43] No later than ten days after the teacher receives the notice, the teacher must notify the board in writing of the desire for a hearing.[44] If the reason for the discharge or suspension without pay relates to the inability or failure of the teacher to perform assigned duties, the teacher has a right to a copy of each evaluation report or any other written memorandum that concerns the fitness or conduct of the teacher. These documents must be requested in writing.[45] The teacher is entitled to a hearing as described before a state hearing examiner.[46] (See Section entitled "Hearings Before Hearing Examiners.") If no hearing is requested after receiving notice, the board of trustees shall take the appropriate action and notify the teacher in writing of the action not later than the 30th day after the date the board sent the notice of the proposed action.[47]

A continuing contract teacher may resign. The teacher may resign without penalty if he or she files a written resignation with the board or its designee not later than the 45th day before the first day of instruction of the following school year.[48] The resignation is considered "filed" with the board on the date it is mailed by prepaid certified or registered mail to the board president or the board's designee at the post office address of the district.[49] The teacher may resign at any time with the consent of the board.[50] The district may ask the SBEC to impose sanctions on a teacher who does not perform on his or her contract and who has not resigned in accordance with these procedures.[51]

VI. Term Contracts

"Teacher" means a "superintendent, principal, supervisor, classroom teacher, counselor, other fulltime professional employee who is required to hold a certificate, or a nurse."[52] The term does not include a person who is not entitled to a probationary, continuing, or term contract under Sec. 21.002, an existing contract, or district policy. [53] A term contract can be issued only after a probationary contract period has been served by the teacher. The term contract must meet certain requirements: (1) the contract must be in writing; (2) the term may not exceed five (5) years; (3) the contract is subject to approval by the board; and (4) a copy of the contract must be provided to the teacher along with a copy of the board's employment policies.[54] The contract should contain certain terms such as: (a) the terms of the employment relationship; (b) the length of the term; (c) the process for renewing or nonrenewing the contract; (d) the process for resigning; (e) the grounds for termination; (f) the teacher's lack of any property interest in the contract beyond its term; and (g) any other terms consistent with board policy.[55]

The term contract must be renewed or nonrenewed before the end of its term. The board has to give notice of renewal or nonrenewal to the teacher not later than the 45th day before the last day of instruction in a school year in which the contract will expire.[56] If notice is not given within this time, then the teacher is reemployed in the same professional capacity for the following school year.[57] These notice requirements do not apply to a superintendent's term contract. The employment policies of the district must include reasons for not renewing a teacher's contract at the end of a school year.[58] The board policies of all school districts must require a written evaluation of each teacher at annual or more frequent intervals. The board must consider a teacher's most recent evaluations before making a decision not to renew a contract if the evaluations are relevant to the reason for the board's action.[59]

If the board notifies the teacher of nonrenewal, the teacher has a right to a hearing before nonrenewal. The teacher has fifteen days after the date notice is received to request a hearing by written notice to the board.[60] If, after proper notice, the teacher does not request a hearing concerning the nonrenewal, the board shall take appropriate action to renew or nonrenew and notify the teacher in writing of the action not later than the 30th day after the date the notice was sent to the teacher.[61]

The board has to provide for a hearing to be held not later than fifteen days after it receives the request for a hearing.[62] The parties can agree in writing to different dates. The hearing is closed unless the teacher requests an open hearing.[63] The board must adopt rules for holding a hearing. At the hearing, the teacher may be represented by counsel, may hear the evidence supporting the reason for nonrenewal, may cross-examine adverse witnesses, and may present evidence.[64] After the hearing, the board shall take appropriate action to renew or nonrenew the contract and notify the teacher in writing of the action not later than the fifteenth day after the date on which the hearing concluded.[65] Instead of holding the hearing itself, the board may choose to use a state appointed hearing examiner.

The nonrenewed teacher may appeal to the Commissioner for a review of the decision of the board. The Commissioner may not substitute his or her judgment for that of the board, unless the board's decision is arbitrary, capricious, unlawful, or not supported by substantial evidence.[66] A teacher may resign from a term contract without penalty by following the same process by which teachers may resign from probationary and continuing contracts.

The term contract may be terminated and the teacher discharged at any time for good cause as determined by the board or a financial exigency that requires a reduction in personnel.[67] The term contract teacher may be suspended without pay for a period not to exceed the end of the school year pending discharge of the teacher or in lieu of terminating the teacher.[68] If the teacher is suspended without pay pending discharge and is not discharged, the teacher is entitled to back pay for the period of suspension.[69]

Superintendents are employed by term contracts. If the board wants to nonrenew the superintendent's contract, it must give him or her written notice not later than the 30th day before the last day of the contract term. The notice must contain reasonable notice of the reason for the proposed nonrenewal.[70] If notice is not timely given, the superintendent is employed in the same professional capacity for the following school year.[71] The superintendent has fifteen days to request a hearing after the date notice is received. The hearing process is the same as for other nonrenewals, either a hearing before the board or before a state hearing examiner.[72] If the superintendent does not request a hearing, the board shall take appropriate action and notify the superintendent in writing not later than the 30th day after the date the board sent the notice to the superintendent.[73] Board policies must establish reasons for nonrenewal. The superintendent can be discharged at any time for good cause.[74] Finally, the superintendent may resign his or her contract in the same way teachers may resign from probationary, continuing and other term contracts.[75]

VII. Hearings Before Hearing Examiners

This process applies only if a teacher requests a hearing after receiving notice of the proposed decision to: (1) terminate a continuing contract at any time (including a reduction in force); (2) terminate a probationary or term contract before the end of the contract period; or (3) suspend the teacher without pay.[76] The process also applies to nonrenewal hearings regarding term contracts if the board has decided to use this process. This hearing process does not apply to a decision to terminate a teacher's employment at the end of a probationary contract period.[77]

Hearing examiners must be lawyers who have been certified by the SBOE as hearing examiners. The Commissioner sets an hourly rate of compensation and sets a maximum amount of compensation a hearing examiner may receive for a hearing.[78] After receiving notice of a proposed action, the parties may select by agreement a person to be the hearing examiner, even if the person is not certified as a hearing examiner, so long as the person is licensed to practice law in Texas.[79] If the agreement is made before a hearing is requested, the request shall include the name of the hearing examiner selected. If the agreement is made after the teacher requests a hearing, the teacher must promptly notify the Commissioner in writing of the person chosen.[80] The teacher and the district may agree in writing that the decision of the hearing examiner will be final and nonappealable on all or some issues.

In all cases where this hearing process applies, the following steps occur: (1) the teacher files a written request for a hearing with the Commissioner not later than the 15th day after the date the teacher received notice of the proposed action, with a copy to the district; (2) the Commissioner uses a randomly ordered list and assigns a hearing examiner who is next in line and who lives in reasonable proximity to the district; (3) the hearing examiner must be assigned not later than the 10th business day after the date the Commissioner receives the request for hearing; (4) the Commissioner immediately notifies the parties; (5) not later than the third day after the date of notification of the assignment of the hearing examiner, either side may object to the hearing examiner for good cause, the objection to be in writing and filed with the Commissioner. If the Commissioner agrees good cause exists, he or she will assign another hearing officer; and (6) if there is no timely rejection, the assignment is final.[81]

Further, the hearings are conducted according to specific rules. The hearing must be held within the geographical boundaries of the school district or at the regional educational service center. The district pays the cost for the hearing examiner, the court reporter, and the production of an original transcript. Each party bears its respective costs, including the cost of discovery and attorneys' fees. The hearing is closed unless the teacher requests it to be open. The hearing examiner may close a hearing if necessary to maintain decorum. A court reporter records the proceedings. The Texas Rules of Civil Evidence apply. The hearing is conducted like a trial without a jury in district court. The hearing examiner may take steps to protect the privacy of a child witness, including closing the hearing. Teacher evaluations and appraisals are presumed to be admissible. The school district has the burden of proof by a preponderance of the evidence.[82]

Hearing examiners have broad powers such as: they may issue subpoenas for witnesses to attend and documents to be produced at the hearing; allow parties to take depositions or use other forms of discovery before the hearing; issue subpoenas for witnesses to attend and documents to be produced at depositions; issue subpoenas for persons who are not employees of the district to attend a deposition or a hearing only upon a showing of good cause; and administer oaths, rule on motions and admissibility of evidence, maintain decorum, schedule and recess the proceeding, and make any other orders according to the Commissioner's rules.[83] It is important to note that all of these procedures can be changed by written agreement of the parties.

At the hearing, the teacher has the right to be represented, hear the evidence on which the charges are based, cross-examine adverse witnesses, and present evidence.[84] Upon conclusion of the hearing, the hearing examiner makes recommendations. The written recommendation consists of findings of fact and conclusions of law. The recommendation may include a proposal for granting relief, such as reinstatement, back pay, or employment benefits, but not attorneys' fees or other costs of the hearing or appeal. A copy is sent to each party, the board president, and the Commissioner. The decision must be timely, or the hearing examiner may not conduct additional hearings for a period not to exceed one (1) year. To be timely, the hearing examiner must complete the hearing and make a written recommendation not later than the 45th day after the date on which the Commissioner receives the teacher's written hearing request.[85] The parties may agree in writing to waive the 45-day deadline.[86]

The board of trustees then considers the recommendation, or may appoint a subcommittee to do so.[87] The board or subcommittee considers both the recommendation and the record of the hearing examiner. The board must do so at the first meeting after issuance of the recommendation for which notice can be properly posted. The meeting must be held not later than the 20th day after the date the board president receives the recommendation and record. The board or subcommittee must allow each side equal time for oral argument, but may limit the amount of time by policy. The board may be advised by an attorney who was not involved in the proceedings.[88]

Not later than the 10th day after the meeting, the board or subcommittee shall announce a decision that includes findings of facts and conclusions of law and may include a grant of relief.[89] The decision may adopt, reject, or change the hearing examiner's conclusions of law or proposal for granting relief. The findings of fact of the hearing examiner may be rejected or changed by the board or subcommittee only after reviewing the record and only if the finding of fact is not supported by substantial evidence.[90] The board or subcommittee shall state in writing the reason, and legal basis for a change or rejection of any kind.[91] A court reporter must record the oral argument and the announcement of the decision, the cost to be borne by the district.[92]

VIII. Appeals to the Commissioner

The teacher has twenty (20) days to file an appeal with the Commissioner after the decision is announced or the board advises the teacher of the decision.[93] The district has twenty (20) days to respond and file the local record for the hearing, including the oral argument before the board.[94] The Commissioner reviews only the local record. The Commissioner must accept written argument, but may grant oral argument. In some instances, the Commissioner may grant an evidentiary hearing solely on the issue of procedural irregularities not reflected in the local record.[95] A decision of the board may not be reversed for a procedural irregularity unless it was likely to have led to an erroneous decision.[96] If the board accepted the hearing examiner's fact finding without modification, the Commissioner may not substitute his or her judgment for that of the board unless the decision was arbitrary, capricious, unlawful, or was not supported by substantial evidence.[97] If the board modified the hearing examiner's fact findings, the Commissioner may not substitute his judgment for the board's unless the decision was arbitrary, capricious or unlawful, or the hearing examiner's original fact findings were not supported by substantial evidence.[98] The written decision of the Commissioner consisting of findings of facts and conclusions of law must be issued not later than the 30th day after the last day on which the district could have responded to the petition for review. Failure to do so means the board's decision is upheld.[99]

IX. Judicial Appeals

Either party may appeal the Commissioner's decision to the local district court in the county in which the school district's central office is located, or, if agreed to by both parties, the district court in Travis County.[100] Any appeal must be filed within thirty (30) days after receiving notice of the Commissioner's decision or after the local board's decision was affirmed by operation of law. A motion for rehearing is not required.[101]

The court reviews the appeal under the substantial evidence rule and may not take additional evidence.[102] The Commissioner's decision may be enforced pending the appeal.[103] The court may not reverse the Commissioner's decision unless it is not supported by substantial evidence or the legal conclusions are erroneous. The court may not reverse a decision because of a procedural error or irregularity, unless it was likely to have led to an erroneous decision by the Commissioner.[104]

X. Conclusion

Chapter 21 of the Texas Education Code offers a school district flexibility in employing its teachers and other professional staff. As with any new law, ambiguities and uncertainties exist. While this writing provides a general overview, Chapter 21 must be read carefully and in its entirety to fully comprehend the intricacies of teacher contracts and related procedural issues.

ENDNOTES

[1] Tex. Educ. Code § 21.002(a) (1995).
[2] Tex. Educ. Code § 5.001(2) (1995).
[3] Tex. Educ. Code § 21.001(b) (1995).
[4] *Id.* at (c).
[5] Tex. Educ. Code § 21.003(a) (1995).
[6] *Id.* at (b).
[7] Tex. Educ. Code §§ 21.031, 21.033 (1995).
[8] Tex. Educ. Code § 21.049 (1995).
[9] Tex. Educ. Code § 21.053 (1995).
[10] Tex. Educ. Code § 21.055(b) (1995).
[11] *Id.* at (c).
[12] *Id.* at (d).
[13] *Id.*
[14] *Id.* at (e).
[15] *Id.*
[16] Tex. Educ. Code § 21.101 (1995).
[17] *Id.*
[18] Tex. Educ. Code § 21.102(a) (1995).
[19] *Id.* at (b).
[20] *Id.*
[21] *Id.*
[22] Tex. Educ. Code § 21.103(a) (1995).
[23] *Id.*
[24] *Id.* at (b).
[25] Tex. Educ. Code § 21.104(a) (1995).
[26] *Id.* at (b).
[27] Tex. Educ. Code § 21.251(a)(2)(3) (1995).
[28] Tex. Educ. Code § 21.105(a) (1995).
[29] *Id.*
[30] *Id.* at (b).
[31] *Id.* at (c).
[32] Tex. Educ. Code § 21.106(a) (1995).
[33] *Id.* at (a) & (b).
[34] *Id.* at (c).
[35] Tex. Educ. Code §§ 21.151, 21.102 (1995).
[36] *Id.*
[37] Tex. Educ. Code § 21.152 (1995).

[38] TEX. EDUC. CODE § 21.153(a) (1995).
[39] *Id.*
[40] TEX. EDUC. CODE § 21.154 (1995).
[41] *Id.*
[42] TEX. EDUC. CODE § 21.159 (1995).
[43] TEX. EDUC. CODE § 21.158(a) (1995).
[44] TEX. EDUC. CODE § 21.159(a) (1995).
[45] TEX. EDUC. CODE § 21.158(b) (1995).
[46] TEX. EDUC. CODE § 21.251(a) (1995).
[47] TEX. EDUC. CODE § 21.159(c)(2) (1995).
[48] TEX. EDUC. CODE § 21.160(a) (1995).
[49] *Id.*
[50] *Id.* at (b).
[51] *Id.* at (c).
[52] TEX. EDUC. CODE § 21.201(1) (1995).
[53] *Id.*
[54] TEX. EDUC. CODE § 21.204(a) (1995).
[55] *Id.*
[56] TEX. EDUC. CODE § 21.206(a) (1995).
[57] *Id.* at (b).
[58] TEX. EDUC. CODE § 21.203(b) (1995).
[59] *Id.* at (a).
[60] TEX. EDUC. CODE § 21.207(a) (1995).
[61] *Id.* at (a)(1) & (2).
[62] *Id.*
[63] *Id.*
[64] *Id.* at (c).
[65] TEX. EDUC. CODE § 21.208(b)(1) & (2) (1995).
[66] TEX. EDUC. CODE § 21.209 (1995).
[67] TEX. EDUC. CODE § 21.211(a)(1) & (2) (1995).
[68] *Id.* at (b)(1) & (2) (1995).
[69] *Id.* at (c).
[70] TEX. EDUC. CODE § 21.212 (1995).
[71] *Id.* at (b).
[72] *Id.* at (c).
[73] *Id.*
[74] *Id.* at (d).
[75] *Id.* at (e).
[76] TEX. EDUC. CODE § 21.251(a)(1), (2), (3) (1995).
[77] *Id.* at (b)(1) & (2).
[78] TEX. EDUC. CODE § 21.252(a) (1995).
[79] TEX. EDUC. CODE § 21.254(e) (1995).
[80] *Id.* at (f).
[81] TEX. EDUC. CODE § 21.254 (1995).
[82] TEX. EDUC. CODE § 21.255 (1995).
[83] *Id.*
[84] TEX. EDUC. CODE § 21.256 (1995).
[85] *Id.*; Tex. Educ. § 21.257 (1995).
[86] TEX. EDUC. CODE § 21.257 (1995).
[87] TEX. EDUC. CODE § 21.258(a) (1995).
[88] *Id.* at (c).
[89] TEX. EDUC. CODE § 21.259(a) (1995).
[90] *Id.* at (c).
[91] *Id.* at (d).
[92] TEX. EDUC. CODE § 21.260 (1995).
[93] TEX. EDUC. CODE § 21.301(a) (1995).

[94] *Id.* at (b).
[95] Tex. Educ. Code § 21.302(a) (1995).
[96] Tex. Educ. Code § 21.303(c) (1995).
[97] *Id.* at (a).
[98] *Id.* at (b)(2).
[99] Tex. Educ. Code § 21.304 (1995).
[100] Tex. Educ. Code § 21.307(a) (1995).
[101] *Id.* at (b).
[102] *Id.* at (e).
[103] *Id.* at (d).
[104] *Id.* at (g).

INVESTIGATING EMPLOYEE WRONGDOING

By: Jeffrey J. Horner

I. Introduction

Public educational entities, whether school districts or colleges, generally are subject to the constraints imposed by the United States Constitution. In addition, various civil rights statutes apply to the functioning of public schools. Dealing with employees in this legal climate must begin with a basic understanding of these legal concerns, particularly when employees are accused of wrongdoing. Public school employees are frequently the targets of investigations for such alleged acts as theft, child abuse, and bribery. Policies and procedures should be developed to ensure compliance with the law in dealing with employees accused of wrongdoing. It is important to make sure not only that policies and procedures are created, but that they are enforced and followed to the greatest extent possible. If these policies and procedures are stringently followed, administrators and school boards stand a significantly better chance that their judgments will be supported in court.

In addition to constitutional law and civil rights considerations, there are various other legal considerations which must be addressed when dealing with alleged employee wrongdoing. Among these considerations are negotiated agreements, employee contracts, handbooks, manuals, possible criminal law constraints, and other influences. This chapter will review the investigation of alleged employee wrongdoing in the school setting, with the hope that the crucial areas of concern will be treated in sufficient detail to provide guidance in most situations.

II. The Legal Setting

The activities of public school districts, colleges, and school officials generally constitute "state action," making federal constitutional guarantees applicable to their employees. In addition, various civil rights statutes such as 42 U.S.C § 1983, 42 U.S.C. § 1981, and 42 U.S.C § 2000e, *et seq.* (Title VII) apply to school districts. These constitutional and civil rights elements must be considered when dealing with employee wrongdoing.

The question frequently arises whether the protections available to a defendant in the criminal law setting apply in the workplace. Courts have traditionally recognized that a public employer has a substantial interest in investigating its employees' alleged wrongful conduct. The law also recognizes that significant administrative barriers or excessive delays in dealing with employee wrongdoing are inappropriate.

For example, the United States Supreme Court addressed the issue of searching an employee's office in *O'Connor v. Ortega.*[1] In *Ortega*, the Court stated: "In the case of searches conducted by a public employer, we must balance the invasion of an employee's legitimate expectations of privacy against the government's need for supervision, control and efficient operation in the workplace."[2] In recognizing this balance, the Court concluded that intrusions on the constitutionally protected privacy interests of government employees for work-related reasons as well as for investigations of work-related misconduct "should be judged by the standard of reasonableness under all circumstances."

Another area of legal concern involves due process. Courts have spoken of due process requirements, once the allegations have narrowed to an employee and there is a proposal to deprive the employee of a contract or other property right in his employment. Due process requirements are triggered by proposed terminations, contract nonrenewals, suspensions without pay, and demotions, but usually not by lateral reassignments or other actions involving no change in salary and benefits. Also, due process requirements only apply to employees with an employment contract or "property right" in their positions, not "at will" employees such as custodians, bus drivers, cafeteria workers, and the like.

In the public employment context, the due process standards articulated by the Supreme Court include: (1) notice of a proposed action, and (2) an opportunity to respond. "The opportunity to present reasons, either in person or in writing, why a proposed action should not be taken is a fundamental due process requirement."[3] In *Loudermill v. Cleveland Board of Education*, the Supreme Court articulated the general requirements for providing due process to public employees with a property right in their positions prior to dismissal or suspension without pay, stating that the employee is entitled simply to: (1) oral or written notice of the charges; (2) an explanation of the employer's evidence; and (3) an opportunity for the accused to present his side of the story.[4] Thus, due process in dealing with employees accused of wrongdoing generally involves independent investigation, followed by notice of the charges and an opportunity for the employee to respond.

III. Report of Alleged Wrongdoing to School Authorities

Reports of wrongdoing can come from a variety of sources. The source of the report and identity of the complainant will affect the process and the extent of the investigation.

A. Anonymous Tips

Only in very limited circumstances can anonymous tips of alleged wrongdoing be relied upon. People who do not identify themselves in making allegations against others will most likely not be of assistance at any point in the investigatory stage. When an anonymous tip is received, an attempt should be made to convince the person to identify him or herself. Absent identification, there is little reason to consider the accusation genuine and credible. However, some accusations may be so serious that some follow-up should be made. For example, the case of *Doe v. Taylor Independent School District*[5] demonstrates that school officials cannot afford to be indifferent to allegations of sexual abuse of a student by a school employee. Allegations involving sexual abuse or other serious matters should receive some investigation, but particularly in cases involving anonymous tips, the rights of the accused employee should be carefully protected. In cases involving less serious allegations of wrongdoing, anonymous tips alone rarely provide enough information to warrant action or further investigation.

B. Verbal Complaints

On receipt of a verbal complaint from a known source, reasonable effort should be made to reduce it to writing as soon as possible. Reducing the complaint to writing will increase the veracity of the complaint and will also help hold the witness to his or her story as time progresses. If the complainant is unwilling to place the allegations in writing, the complaint suffers from many of the same inadequacies as an anonymous tip.

C. Written Complaints

Written complaints or statements generally justify further investigation, unless the complaint is not believable. Placing accusations in writing provides some independent assurance that the claim is genuine or has at least some credibility. Many educational institutions have policies and procedures concerning how complaints should be made by students, employees, and members of the public. School officials should be discouraged from publicizing accusations and complaints about particular individuals, because publicly disseminated accusations can lead to possible defamation problems. For this reason, care must be taken to maintain the confidentiality of any written complaint until acted upon or resolved, subject to any state or federal open records laws.

D. Criminal Complaints

Some complaints against employees may arise from criminal investigation or charges initiated by police authority. If criminal charges are connected with the employment relationship, an independent administrative investigation should be undertaken in almost every case. Of course, the standards applicable to the internal investigation are different than those applicable to investigations conducted by the police. For example, evidence of wrongdoing which is wholly insufficient to sustain a criminal conviction may be more than adequate to justify discipline or discharge in the employment context. The investigation relating to the employment decision can usually proceed independently of the criminal proceedings.

One of the problems encountered in this area is that evidence possessed by the prosecution may not be available for use by an educational institution. Prosecutors generally will not want to expose their witnesses to cross-examination at administrative hearings before the criminal trial. If a prosecutor will not provide evidence or make such evidence available through other sources, employee discipline matters may have to be placed on hold pending the outcome of the criminal case.

E. News Media Reports

The media may be a source of accusations against school employees. When claims surface through the media, they should be independently and properly investigated. Reliance should not be placed upon news accounts for evidence; rather, independent statements arising out of media reports should be obtained when possible.

IV. Common Areas of Complaint

There are many types of complaints which occur with some frequency in the school setting. Although every investigation will be different, in those recurring cases an investigative plan can be developed based upon prior cases. Common areas of complaint include:

(1) misuse or misappropriation of funds, equipment, materials, or personnel;
(2) sexual harassment or sexual misconduct;
(3) drug and alcohol abuse;
(4) mistreatment of children, including child abuse, injury to a child, and misapplication of corporal punishment;
(5) theft;
(6) conflicts of interest;
(7) kickbacks or embezzlement of funds; and
(8) bribery.

V. Conducting the Investigation

Conducting a fair investigation requires adherence to the following practical guidelines: recognition and preservation of the dignity of the individual, treating the accused in a manner in which the investigator would expect to be treated if he or she were the subject of the investigation, and presuming innocence until the investigation is complete. The old adage of "where there's smoke, there's fire" does not apply. False or misleading allegations are not uncommon, and regardless of initial appearances, an accused employee must be presumed innocent until proven otherwise.

In addition to these general guidelines, the investigation should be carefully planned in advance, and should be impartial and confidential to the extent possible and permitted by law. Some educational institutions have structured policies and procedures concerning investigations. Such procedures have the advantage of promoting thoroughness and consistency in investigations, and thus discouraging claims of unfair treatment or discrimination. A disadvantage is that occasionally such procedures can be too rigid for the actions required in different types of investigations. Also, the failure to substantially follow such procedures can potentially give rise to an alleged violation of due process or claim of discrimination. For these reasons, care should be taken and legal advice sought in drafting policies and procedures regarding investigations by your educational institution. The procedures should be drafted in a manner which preserves flexibility to meet the needs of each individual investigation.

A. Receiving the Complaint

The initial complaint should be factually accurate, complete and as timely as possible. The "Jack Webb" theory should be used: "Just the facts, ma'am; just the facts." Avoid making conclusions, subjective opinions, or observations at this point. Be particularly careful not to include opinions or conclusions in the written complaint itself. An inappropriate statement of conclusions may either affect the liberty interests of the accused employee or could constitute defamation.

To the extent possible and permitted by law, the confidentiality of the complaint should be protected. However, make sure that all involved know that simply because a written complaint may be stamped "confidential," it nonetheless is subject to possible disclosure under the law. Careful planning to protect the confidentiality of investigative material promotes cooperation during an investigation. One method of maintaining the confidentiality of this material is involving the school attorney at the early stages of the investigation. Any material collected or generated by the attorney may then be eligible for protection under the attorney/client communication or attorney work product privilege.

It is also important to avoid the "carbon copy" syndrome. Copies of complaints or sensitive investigative material should be distributed only to those individuals who absolutely must know about the complaint. Many lawsuits result simply from making facts about a specific situation known to unnecessary persons.

B. The Progress of the Investigation

After the complaint is received and an investigation appears warranted, it is important to act quickly. Facts will become stale and memories will fade quickly. If the circumstances warrant, consideration should be given to placing accused employees on administrative leave with pay pending the completion of the investigation. Normally, suspension with pay is appropriate in cases that involve possible criminal activity or when it is believed that the accused poses a risk to students, staff, or the school's operation.

An overall plan for the investigation should also be developed. This plan should include identification of witnesses, gathering of documents that need to be reviewed, and pinpointing of places or items to be observed or analyzed. In an effort to resolve disputes at an informal level, the immediate supervisor of the accused person should be responsible for the investigation, if possible. The immediate supervisor should not be involved only in circumstances where the supervisor is involved with filing the complaint, where the supervisor may also be a subject of the investigation, or where the supervisor's involvement would otherwise "taint" the process. Otherwise, the supervisor is the person most likely to know the environment and personalities involved, and should not be allowed to "pass the buck" to an administrative superior. The leadership role of the supervisor should be preserved to the extent possible.

If, for any reason, the immediate supervisor cannot conduct the investigation, it is generally best to have the next level administrator conduct the investigation. In sensitive matters, an attorney may supervise the process. The school attorney should, however, avoid becoming a fact witness which would generally disqualify him or her from prosecuting any subsequent termination and representing the district in any related litigation. Many districts now employ independent counsel to investigate and report to the administration and board in particular situations. This permits the regular school district attorney to perform his or her usual services for the district and represent the district in any subsequent litigation.

C. Witness Interviews and Information Gathering

After identifying the person in charge of the investigation and developing an investigation plan, the first step is normally to interview the complainant. Again, the accused must be presumed innocent until facts prove the misconduct. Get the facts from the complainant–who, what, where, how and why. Several things should be done while interviewing the complainant. The investigator should develop standard questions in advance of interviews. Furthermore, advise the witness of the degree to which the information can be kept confidential. If practicable, obtain a written statement from the witness. In appropriate situations, court reporters or tape recordings can be used. Concentrate on the facts and getting the written statement, and avoid conclusions or opinions. Similar techniques should be used with other fact witnesses.

Special considerations should be used in interviewing minors. Use vocabulary that a child can understand. Generally, one should also obtain parental consent before interviewing children, particularly younger children. The older the child, the less parental involvement is necessary. Consideration should also be given to having the child's parents present at the interview.

D. Interviewing the Accused

After interviewing and collecting information from witnesses, the accused should be interviewed. In most investigations, it is best to interview the accused last. This is particularly true when the accused might exert pressure on others not to testify or when the accused may attempt to destroy evidence. The interview should be planned in advance. Like other interviews, the interviewer should outline or write out the questions and list the topics he or she will cover.

Consider allowing the accused to have a representative present at the interview. The representative can be another employee, a union representative, or even an attorney. However, the representative should not be permitted to argue, cross-examine the investigator, or respond for the accused. The interviewer should control his or her emotions. Be courteous and do not get angry. The tone of the meeting should not be punitive or adversarial; rather, the tone should be investigative. Do not make threats or give ultimatums. In particular, remember that an ultimatum such as "resign or you will be fired" can be construed as the legal equivalent to firing the employee or constructive discharge. Resignations or other agreements obtained through force or coercion are not considered to be voluntary, and can be invalidated.

You should also consider whether an employee should be required to answer written questions or complete an affidavit about the disputed incident. The law allows public employers to require employees to answer questions under oath in investigative situations. Such an investigative technique is supported by the law so long as two conditions are met: first, the questions asked must be narrowly related to the work-related issue being investigated, and second, any statement given by an employee may not be used against that employee in a subsequent criminal prosecution.[6] The refusal by the employee to answer questions under these circumstances can provide independent grounds for termination due to insubordination.

VI. Making the Decision

Once the initial investigation is completed, the appropriate administrator must make a preliminary determination of what action to take before a final meeting with the accused. Even if charges prove groundless, it is imperative that school administrators meet with the accused and review the results of the investigation.

Many factors must be considered before making a decision. These factors include:

1. Is the investigation complete?
2. What are the material facts?
3. Did the misconduct occur when the employee was on or off duty?
4. How serious is the infraction?
5. What are the range of penalties or disciplinary actions available?
6. What is the employee's past record?
7. Are there any mitigating circumstances which should influence the decision?
8. What is the district's practice regarding similar acts in the past?
9. Are the results of the investigation fair and unaffected by any illegal consideration of the employee's race, sex, religion, age, disability, or other protected characteristic?

Once these and other factors have been considered, the administration should be ready to proceed with the final meeting with the accused. The final meeting is an opportunity for the accused to explain, discount, or totally discredit any damaging evidence gathered during the investigation. Once the final meeting has occurred, the administrator should follow up with a written letter or memorandum to bring closure to the investigation. The letter should state the substance of the charges. Furthermore, the letter should briefly describe the evidence obtained, the various conclusions reached as a result of this evidence, and the decision. Finally, the letter should include a section on the proposed actions to be taken by the employer and any recourse that the employee may have from this decision, such as the opportunity for a hearing before the school's governing body in appropriate cases. Furthermore, it is important that the administration document receipt of the letter by the employee. This can be accomplished through hand delivery or certified mail.

VII. Conclusion

The standard of conduct applicable to schools reflects the unique position of public school districts in our society as government agencies charged with the mission of educating young people. So long as the investigation of alleged wrongdoing by employees is school-related, the school has significant discretion over how to conduct the investigation. The investigation should, however, be conducted in a manner that allows wrongdoing to be detected but protects the dignity of the accused. You should treat any employee accused of wrongdoing in a way that you would hope to be treated in a similar situation. The dignity and character of the accused employee should be preserved at all times.

Successful investigations begin with planning and end with a result. In between these two points, considerable leadership and skill must be applied. Although a high level administrator, lawyer, or central office person may actually coordinate the investigation, the participation of the employee's immediate supervisor, when appropriate, is important to a successful investigation. Without the immediate supervisor providing leadership, the task then falls on others who are less familiar with the players and do not have responsibility for their daily supervision. Above all, care must be exercised to avoid trampling on the rights of any individual. These guidelines, along with the advice of counsel when needed, should help standardize and improve a school district's internal investigation process. By doing so, the objective of investigations should be more easily obtainable and the legal rights of both the school district and the accused will be better preserved.

ENDNOTES

[1] 107 S. Ct. 1492 (1987).
[2] 107 S. Ct. 1492, 1499.
[3] Loudermill v. Cleveland Bd. of Educ., 470 U.S. 532, 546 (1985).
[4] *Id.*
[5] Doe v. Taylor ISD, 15 F.3d 443 (5th Cir. 1994).
[6] *See* Lefkowitz v. Turley, 414 U.S. 70, 94 S.Ct. 316 (1973); Gulden v. McCorkle, 680 F.2d 1070 (5th Cir. 1982).

DOCUMENTATION FOR TEACHER IMPROVEMENT OR TERMINATION

By: Kelly Frels

I. INTRODUCTION

The primary objective of a school district's teacher evaluation system is to improve teachers' performance so they can become more successful and contribute to the objectives of the district. If the evaluation does not produce this positive result, the teacher must be replaced, either by resignation or termination. The district's evaluation system thus serves a secondary function–the removal of the unsatisfactory teacher.

Depending upon the nature of the teacher's contract with a school district, various degrees of procedural due process must be observed in relieving a person of the position if he or she does not resign. In many situations, this process culminates with a hearing before the board of trustees to determine whether there is cause to terminate the teacher. In teacher termination hearings, principals often are met with the claim that there is too little documentation or evidence of help being given to the teacher; therefore, the principal has not done his or her job in working with the teacher. In other cases, the claim is made that the principal has developed so much documentation that the teacher has been harassed. At other teacher termination hearings, complaints are made that the process is unfair and that the teacher did not know of these "attacks." As a result, some principals have been unwilling to bring a recommendation for termination to the board of trustees.

In an effort to provide support for the principal and to help ensure the fair treatment of teachers who are evaluated, the author recommends a system of documentation similar to that described below, which can be used in conjunction with virtually any school district's evaluation system. This documentation system can be used in districts which utilize the various contractual schemes authorized by Texas statutes. This documentation system is founded on the concept of communication, and its goal is to humanize the evaluation and documentation process with the ultimate objective of improving a teacher's performance to an acceptable level. If a teacher's performance does not improve, the system is designed to provide an incentive for voluntary resignation or, if voluntary resignation is not received, to provide the necessary documentation for the principal to recommend the teacher's termination.

II. Documentation System

This documentation system becomes an essential ingredient in preparing the district for a hearing before the school board; and if necessary, in preparing for appeals and lawsuits filed with the Texas Commissioner of Education, an arbitrator, or a court. This system can also provide the necessary documentation to sustain the termination if the teacher files a discrimination complaint with the Equal Employment Opportunity Commission, the Texas Commission on Human Rights, or the United States Department of Education. Furthermore, adherence to a system of this nature can help prevent constitutional questions from becoming significant issues. If there is systematic documentation of poor performance before a teacher engages in a protected speech-related activity, the performance deficiency may continue to be addressed as needed and termination can be recommended. In contrast, the absence of such documentation prior to a teacher's engaging in protected speech-related activity may render the termination of the teacher extremely difficult. The First Amendment issues raised by this example are discussed in more detail in another chapter.

The documentation contemplated in a teacher evaluation system involves the use of several types of written memoranda which commonly follow some informal verbal communication. First, specific incident memoranda should be used to record conferences with a teacher concerning more significant events. Second, summary memoranda should be used to record conferences with a teacher in which several incidents, problems, or deficiencies are discussed. Third, visitation memoranda should record observations made of a teacher's on-the-job performance. Fourth, an assessment instrument should be used to evaluate the teacher's overall performance.

The documentation concerning a teacher should be used for several purposes. It enables the principal to follow a teacher's actions and performance, thus enabling the principal to pinpoint weaknesses and problem areas. It also enables the teacher to understand his or her problems and take corrective steps if necessary. Finally, if a teacher's performance does not improve, it serves as concrete evidence to support a recommendation for termination. Care should be taken to ensure that this process conforms with state law and school board policies.

A. Memoranda to the File

Whenever a principal observes an incident or behavior which is not of a significantly serious nature to require an immediate conference with the teacher but which should be considered in the teacher's evaluation or at a general conference with the teacher, it is appropriate for the principal to prepare a short file memorandum. If possible, the principal should first mention the concern to the teacher informally. These file memoranda may be in various forms, such as notations on a calendar or in a notebook with separate pages designated for specific individuals. These file memoranda should include the name of the teacher, the name of the principal, the date of the occurrence, and the facts of the event observed. These file memoranda can be used for conferring with the teacher concerning the incident or incidents, assessing the teacher's performance, and refreshing the memory of the principal for testimony at any proceeding or hearing relative to the teacher's performance. These file memoranda should be used sparingly and only for minor matters.

Most administrators who use the file memoranda find it helpful if the employees are aware that these memoranda are being kept and encourage the teachers to review any file memoranda concerning their performance. It is always helpful to effective communication when the principal makes informal mention of the concern as it occurs. Under the Texas Public Information Act,[1] copies of these file memoranda normally need not be given to the teacher unless the teacher requests them. However, if the copies are not given to the teacher, they should not be used in a subsequent hearing in an attempt to establish facts. Actually, the best practice is to incorporate the contents of these file memoranda into a summary memorandum or evaluation which is given to the teacher after a conference.

Even though it may not be the intention of the principal to use these documents as future evidence or to share the file memoranda with the teacher, the memoranda should be written with the knowledge that they may be used in a future proceeding or made available to the teacher through a request under the Public Information Act. For example, if file memoranda are being used to refresh a principal's memory at a hearing, in Texas and most other states the attorney for the teacher is entitled to see copies of the documents. Thus, care should be taken with file memoranda, as with any other memoranda, not to write or record anything in a manner that could cause future embarrassment. A good practice is to record facts rather than personal opinions and conclusions in file memoranda. Evidence of a principal's frustration or hostility can backfire in later proceedings, so memoranda should be kept as neutral and objective as possible.

B. Specific Incidents Memoranda

If the principal observes an incident or behavior, or has a complaint from a third party, it may be appropriate to send the teacher a memorandum concerning the incident. This memorandum should be sent only after the principal conducts any needed investigation and holds a conference with the teacher at which time the incident is discussed and the teacher's viewpoint considered. The memo should summarize the third party's complaint, any response, the principal's determination, and any directives and reprimands to the teacher. If the incident is serious enough that termination is to be recommended immediately, such recommendation should be stated.

Incidents should be faced head-on, as they occur. The failure to confront problems, infractions, and deficiencies at the time they occur can weaken a later case for termination. For example, suppose several incidents occur in the fall of a school year, but they are not mentioned to the teacher by the principal. An attempt to use those incidents to support a proposed termination in the spring of that school year may prove difficult. The teacher will claim that he or she is being treated unfairly because the reasons for termination were not disclosed to the teacher during the school year. Not dealing with the problems as they occur makes the principal appear to be arbitrary or devious and weakens the termination proposal.

It is wise to have the teacher acknowledge receipt of the specific incident memorandum by signing a copy. If the teacher does not agree with the facts stated in the memorandum or the action taken, the teacher should be given the opportunity to respond in writing either on the memorandum itself or through a separate document. This action can be accomplished by inviting the teacher to make a written statement concerning any differences of fact or opinion expressed by the principal in the memorandum by a certain date or within a given number of days. For example, the final paragraph of a memorandum might state, "If you disagree with the facts or conclusions stated in this memorandum, please advise me in writing no later than (date) so we can meet and discuss these differences." By so doing, any disagreement can be noted, and the differences hopefully resolved immediately. In serious situations where the employee has proven to be recalcitrant or of questionable veracity, one might consider a final sentence such as, "If you do not respond, I will assume you agree with the facts stated in this memorandum." Statements such as the latter example should be used sparingly.

If the specific incident concerning the teacher comes from a third party such as a parent or student, care must be taken to fully examine the facts and to determine whether the third party's information is correct. It is improper and potentially disastrous to base a decision to terminate on information from a third party when the truthfulness and reliability of the allegation has not been established. Upon receiving a third party complaint, the principal should make an investigation by conducting whatever discussions are necessary to determine the accuracy of the complaint. If possible, get the complaint in writing. The third party should be advised that if adverse action is taken against the teacher based on this incident, the third party must be available to testify before the board, an arbitrator, or a court. If the third party will not agree to appear as a witness, other independent evidence must be available to establish the relevant facts at a hearing. Otherwise, action adverse to the teacher should not be taken. The principal must be certain to obtain the teacher's side of the story; this usually occurs in a conference with the teacher. If there is a discrepancy in the third party's story and the teacher's story, the principal should make further attempts to determine the truth. It may be necessary to have the teacher confront the complainant in an informal conference to determine what actually occurred.

It may not be possible for the principal to have agreement concerning what happened, so the principal must determine whose story he or she believes. If the principal has enough facts to make an accurate determination, a specific incident memorandum can be prepared. Such a memorandum should explain the findings made by the principal and the reasons for those findings. Specific directives or suggestions to the teacher might also be included.

C. Visitation and Summary Memoranda

In some school districts, it is a common practice for principals to summarize visits to a teacher's classroom. If visitation forms or checklists are used or if visitation memoranda are prepared, the content should be reviewed with the teacher, and the teacher should be given a copy. Suggestions for improvement should be made in a conference and noted in the memorandum. A visitation memorandum may be used in a termination process, but usually the results of a visitation are reviewed in a summary memorandum or in the assessment document.

Summary memoranda are ideal ways to outline the results of conferences concerning several incidents, classroom visitations, or conferences regarding general teacher performance. Through such memoranda, the matters referred to in the file memoranda can be incorporated. Matters not reflected in other memoranda can be reduced to writing, directives can be given to the teacher, and standards can be established. Also, evidence that a conference was held and certain subjects discussed can be established. A copy of each summary memorandum should be given to the teacher, and the teacher should be given an opportunity to offer in writing any differences with the facts and conclusions stated in the memorandum. If a teacher disagrees and files a response, a subsequent conference should be held to try to resolve any differences which may exist.

The same comments applicable to the specific incident memoranda are applicable to summary memoranda, with the major differences being that summary memoranda are designed to cover general conferences with the teacher on several matters rather than on a specific incident.

D. Evaluation Document and Close-Out Memorandum

The assessment or evaluation or performance document should be completed as prescribed by the policies and procedures of the district. A summary narrative or memorandum should be considered for each negative assessment noted in the document. If the assessment is such that the teacher might be terminated if no improvement is shown, the teacher should be advised that failure to improve could result in a recommendation for termination. Furthermore, it is wise to include instructions or specific directions for improvement. Such a practice not only is helpful to the teacher, but also strengthens the argument that the teacher has been treated fairly if the principal's actions are later questioned. Through the use of such evaluation documents, the teacher will be fully informed of his or her deficiencies which could result in a proposal to terminate should those deficiencies not be remedied according to the instructions given for improvement. All identified deficiencies of the teacher and any problems which have been encountered during the assessment period should be included in the assessment document. If a deficiency from previous years has not been remedied by the teacher, it should also be noted in the assessment. In order to avoid difficulties with ratings on the evaluation, a straightforward and truthful assessment should be made. A fair system of evaluation must require the setting of standards and expectations at the beginning of the school year, with the principal following through with the implementation of those standards through the evaluation process.

If the communication in the conference is effective, and is properly reflected in the memorandum, a teacher will rarely have the occasion to respond again. However, a further response from the teacher sometimes does result, and another conference may be necessary. At some point the memorandum writing must be brought to a close, and in informal circumstances, the sending of the close-out memorandum to this conference may be appropriate. In the close-out memorandum, the language inviting a response from the teacher is deleted, and the teacher is advised that the matter should be considered closed.

III. Recommendations for Practice

- The memorandum should be sent only after a conference with the teacher.
- In preparing any memorandum, reliance should be made on the facts. Concluding statements and opinions not supported by the facts should

be avoided. For example, in a classroom visitation memorandum, the observation that the teacher's classroom was disorderly, without any explanation, is not very specific or effective. Rather, the principal should note that he or she saw three children in the classroom talking during class and saw one child playing in back of the room. The principal should note that these acts were unnoted by the teacher or were not corrected by the teacher.

- In preparing a memorandum, inflammatory words should be avoided. For example, rather than to characterize an action as insubordination, the action might be factually described, and the teacher's action should be referred to as a failure to comply with specific official directives or school board policy.
- Directives given in a memorandum should be positive and specific, and educational jargon should be avoided. When directing a sometimes tardy teacher to arrive at school on time, state: "You are required to be at school by 7:30 a.m., and you will be expected to have signed in by that time," rather than, "You are required to be at school on time." Precise directives like these tend to avoid real or imagined confusion about what is expected.
- The specific incident memorandum, the summary memorandum, the visitation memorandum, and the assessment document should be personalized as much as possible. The key to the success of this documentation system is to provide an opportunity for the principal and the teacher to sit down and mutually resolve problems and determine the future actions of the teacher.
- Care should be taken to treat all teachers alike, especially when dealing with absences and tardiness. It is destructive and embarrassing to have a teacher's attorney present a school's sign-in sheet at a hearing to show that other teachers have more tardies and more absences than the teacher who is being proposed for termination.
- One should never write a memorandum to a teacher when one is angry. It is much better to reflect for a day or so or to call in a third party to review a memorandum prior to sending it. By doing so, the principal can avoid statements which might be regretted later.
- To be effective, any memorandum must be prepared and sent to the teacher soon after the incident and the subsequent conference occur. Under no circumstances should a memorandum be prepared after a decision to terminate has been made and backdated to reflect the incident upon which the proposed termination will be based.
- The evaluator should be careful to ensure that the teacher believes he or she has been fairly treated. One should remember that if the teacher's performance does not improve and a recommendation for termination

is made, the fairness of the process will be judged by the members of the board and, possibly, by the state's commissioner of education, an arbitrator, or a judge.

- Normally the only documents which would be used as documentary evidence at a termination hearing would be the summary memoranda and the evaluation or assessment instruments. Specific incident and visitation memoranda should be used only when necessary to refresh the principal's memory while testifying concerning the specific facts of an event.

IV. Non-teacher Employees

This chapter focuses upon the documentation of teachers, as they constitute the majority of school employees, and are much scrutinized because of their influence upon young people. Nonetheless, there are many school district employees who are not teachers, and their job performance should also be documented whenever appropriate. The documentation system described above can be applied to non-teacher employees, and provides the same benefits of either improving communication and performance, or assembling support for disciplinary action or termination. Careful documentation can be particularly critical for non-teacher employees who are not subject to regular assessments, and thus may have no indication of their job performance in their personnel files.

V. Conclusion

Documentation of job performance can improve employees' performance and help open lines of communication about potential problems. To achieve these benefits, however, documentation must be performed fairly and consistently with regard to all employees. Consistency helps safeguard against claims of discrimination and unfair treatment, and helps provide a reliable record in those instances where proposing an employee's termination is necessary.

ENDNOTES

[1] Tex. Gov't Code § 551.000, *et.seq.*

IMPLEMENTING A MEANINGFUL GRIEVANCE PROCESS

By: Kelly Frels

I. Introduction

The grievance process has been viewed by many school administrators as a vehicle for employees and their labor organizations to achieve individual and organizational objectives. In many instances, this has been the result because administrators have not been prepared to process grievances in a meaningful and effective fashion. The grievance process can be a constructive tool in resolving problems between supervisors and employees. The effective resolution of employee concerns is, of course, central to the operation of a successful school system. This chapter is designed to aid school administrators in understanding the legal requirements for grievances under Texas law and provide suggestions on how to effectively process them.

II. Legal Standards for the Presentation of Grievances

The right of citizens to present grievances to governmental bodies is recognized in the Texas Constitution:[1]

"The citizens shall have a right, in a peaceable manner, to assemble together for their common good; and apply to those invested with the powers of government for redress of grievances or other purposes, by petition, address, or remonstrance."

School district and college employees are citizens, so they are entitled to petition and present grievances to boards of trustees.[2] There is no constitutional requirement that a board of trustees negotiate or even respond to the complaint filed by employees. The board must, however, ". . . stop, look and listen . . ," as it is required by law to consider the petition, address or remonstrance.[3] This consideration by the board can be achieved through a variety of procedures from an informal presentation under the "hearing of citizens" portion of the agenda to a complete hearing with witnesses and cross-examination. If the employees do not like or agree with the board's response, the remedy then lies in the ballot box unless, of course, the employee otherwise has a cause of action sustainable in a court or before the Texas Education Agency under Section 7.057 of the Texas Education Code.

Chapter 617 of the Texas Government Code[4] (Chapter 617) prohibits strikes by and collective bargaining with public employees. Chapter 617 does, however, recognize the right of public employees to present grievances:

"This chapter does not impair the right of public employees to present grievances concerning their wages, hours of employment, or conditions of work either individually or through a representative that does not claim the right to strike.[5]

The presentation of a grievance is a unilateral procedure initiated by the employee. A collective bargaining agreement, on the other hand, is a result of a bilateral procedure culminating in a meeting of the minds involved and binding the parties to the agreement.[6] Texas law prohibits school districts from entering into collective bargaining agreements with labor organizations representing public employees.[7]

Districts are required to have someone in a position of authority hear grievances presented by employees. There is, however, no requirement that districts have a specific policy or process for employees to present grievances. Chapter 617 itself does not require that a board of trustees ultimately hear the presentation of an employee grievance. The requirement that the board consider the grievance arises instead under Article 1, Section 27 of the Texas Constitution.[8] Most districts have found that having a specific policy for the presentation of grievances is helpful in achieving order in the resolution of disputes.

Some grievance policies are simple and straightforward, while others are more complex. The differences are the results of employee organization activity and influence, the adoption of various grievance models offered by various organizations, differences in local politics, and many other factors. The most important factor that contributed to the adoption of complex policies was the long-standing State Board of Education rule requiring local hearings. This State Board rule prescribed a "due process" type hearing before the board for grievances and other local disputes. This hearing process required boards to spend endless hours listening to witnesses and argument. It also provided a forum for lawyers' theatrics and trial by exhaustion. To avoid the log jam of hearings before the board, some districts had the superintendent or hearing committees hear the grievances under the State Board requirements and make a recommendation to the board. The hearing before the board was based on the record developed before the hearing body, and permitted only argument of the parties or their representatives, without further live testimony.

In *Professional Association of College Educators v. El Paso County Community District* and *Corpus Christi Independent School District v.*

Padilla,[9] it was recognized that a "due process" grievance hearing before the board of trustees was not required by Texas law. Furthermore, the State Board of Education repealed its local hearing rule several years ago, so school districts are currently free to provide a less complex system for the resolution of grievances.

School districts should be certain to enumerate their employee grievance procedures with specificity in their policies. Each district must develop a policy that will serve its unique needs. The possible variations of these policies are virtually endless, so long as the resulting policies comply with the applicable legal standards. Districts should review their grievance policies periodically to ascertain that they cover all relevant situations and that they are operating in an effective and meaningful manner. Districts wishing to revise their policies should consult their school attorneys for assistance in developing new policies in compliance with the Texas Constitution, statutes, and case law.

III. Common Questions Concerning Grievances

Grievance policies provide the basic structure for processing grievances. When these policies are applied to real-life situations, conflicts invariably arise about their implementation. Most of these conflicts have legal implications. Set out below are some common questions asked by administrators concerning the implementation of the grievance process:

Who may present an employee's grievance? An employee is clearly entitled to present his or her own grievance. The grievance may also be presented by a "representative." Representative is not further defined in Chapter 617, so representative may include a friend, spouse, or fellow employee, as well as a lawyer or a union official. If a representative presents the grievance, the school district may require that the designation as representative be made verbally or in writing.[10] The only statutory restriction is that the representative must not claim the right to strike.[11] No public employee unions or labor organizations currently active in Texas appear to claim the right to strike. If a school district disagrees with a labor organization's disclaimer of the right to strike, the school district bears the burden of proving that the no strike disclaimer was invalid.[12] As a practical matter, the no strike issue is not of current concern in Texas.

Must the designated representative of the employee be allowed to present the grievance even at the "informal" stage? Once a representative has been designated by the employee, that representative must be permitted to present the grievance at all steps, including any informal step when the employee is required by policy to discuss the grievance with his or her supervisor. Once an employee designates a representative, that representative may present the grievance, and the district may not even require the employee to personally hand the grievance to the designated administrator. A logical extension of this holding is that an employee need not personally be present at any grievance proceeding, and that the district's representative need deal only with the employee's representative.[13]

Must a district consider grievances filed on behalf of a group of employees? Most grievance policies provide that grievances filed by individual employees may be consolidated when the subject matter and relief requested are similar. At least one court has held that public employees may present individual grievances collectively, and a governmental body cannot deny them that right.[14] To ensure that each employee is indeed a participant in a group grievance, it is reasonable to require that each grievant be identified by name and either sign the grievance or sign a designation of a representative to present the grievance.

After a representative is designated, may the district's representative conduct a hearing or otherwise discuss the merits of the grievance with the employee without the representative being present? Clearly, the school officials cannot conduct a grievance meeting or hearing without the representative having the opportunity to be present. Likewise, it would probably be a violation of Chapter 617 to directly discuss the merits of a grievance with the employee without the representative having the opportunity to be present. The more difficult issue is whether the representative is entitled to be present on other occasions such as assessment sessions, where the merits of a pending grievance are intertwined with the assessment process. If the grievance and the assessment can be kept separate, that should be done. If the two cannot, one approach would be to permit the teacher's representative to be present as an observer at the assessment conference. This should allow the normal process of the school to proceed, yet prevent the employee from being prejudiced and possibly raising a subsequent challenge to the grievance process.

Is an employee's representative entitled to be present at conferences and meetings initiated by a supervisor? An employee is not generally entitled to have a representative present at a meeting initiated by the supervisor. These meetings are generally to discuss performance and matters of school business. In fact, an employee who refuses to attend supervisor-initiated meetings because his or her representative is not available could face termination for insubordination and/or failure to comply with official directives. Termination should, of course, be undertaken with a degree of care and should be reserved for serious violations. An occasion when an employee might be entitled to a designated representative is when the conference is called for a stated purpose, but the discussion in actuality deals with the subject matter of a grievance pending before the administrator.

Many feel that an employee should be allowed to have a representative present when an administrator discusses dismissal with the employee. If the employee requests that a representative be present at such a meeting, it seems reasonable to grant the request if the delay in having the representative present will not unreasonably compromise the dismissal process or any related matters such as an investigation. Some have found that the presence of a third party is more often a help than a hindrance in these sensitive situations.

Many administrators do not object to the presence of a third party at supervisor-initiated sessions, but choose to clearly define the representative's role at the outset. For example, when an employee is involved in an occurrence where the facts of the situation are disputed, an investigating administrator may prefer to hear the employee's side of the story directly from the source. If so, the administrator may request the employee's representative to refrain from commenting until after the employee has given his or her version of the facts. However, the administrator has no specific means of enforcing the request.

Many administrators feel that the third party can observe how reasonably the employee was treated and provide input to the employee on his or her position relative to the administrator. There are instances, of course, where the presence of a third party can be used to foster conflict or dissension within the organization, and care needs to be taken to identify these situations in advance and strive to defuse them. Most administrators will invite another administrator or representative into the session once the employee shows up with a third party who the administrator allows to remain. This person can provide independent testimony about the session should a conflict over what occurred develop.

What matters are included in "wages, hours of work and conditions of work" under Chapter 617? In collective bargaining states, wages, hours, and conditions of work are words of art and are defined terms. This is not so in Texas. The Attorney General has opined that wages, hours of work, and conditions of work should be broadly construed to include virtually any topic that is work-related.[15] One court has observed that the Texas Supreme Court seems to agree with the Attorney General's view.[16]

Opinions of the Commissioner of Education concerning employee evaluations seemingly support the broad definition of wages, hours of work and conditions of work. Employees are entitled to present grievances concerning the evaluation process through the board level as provided for other grievances. It is permissible for a district to provide for an informal grievance process concerning the content of an evaluation before the evaluator or the superintendent, so long as a "stop, look and listen" process such as speaking at the hearing of citizens before the board is provided. The Commissioner has held, however, that the board should not substitute its judgment on particular ratings for the professional judgment of a trained evaluator.[17]

Who must hear a grievance? Although there is no requirement for a district to have a grievance procedure, someone in authority must hear a grievance. There is no legal requirement for the person in authority to take any action, however.[18] Most grievance policies are set up where the grievance is first heard by the immediate supervisor, because that is typically the most effective place for grievances to be resolved. If the immediate supervisor cannot resolve the grievance, it generally can be appealed to higher levels within the administration.

Chapter 617 does not require that the board hear a grievance that has already been presented to someone in a position of authority. The board is required only to "stop, look and listen" to an employee under Article 1, Section 27 of the Texas Constitution, and that may be accomplished at the hearing of citizens part of the agenda.

What type of hearing must be held by the person in a position of authority to hear the grievance? There is no particular format required for hearings before the person hearing the grievance. There is no requirement for sworn testimony or cross-examination. There is also no requirement that the time for the presentation of the grievance be unlimited. A reasonable time limit for the presentation may be imposed. From a practical standpoint, the meeting should provide a meaningful opportunity to hear the employee or his or her representative and attempt to resolve the dispute. If the district's policies or procedures prescribe a specific hearing process, that process must be followed. It is a good practice to record the proceedings, either by tape recorder or stenographically.

Does a representative get to talk for the employee to the extent that the person conducting the grievance hearing cannot talk with the employee? Because a primary purpose of the grievance hearing should be an opportunity to resolve differences, the person conducting the hearing should attempt to involve the employee in the discussion to the extent possible. It does appear, however, that once a representative has been designated by the employee, the representative may do the talking for the employee. Although it does not make much sense, the employee probably does not even need to be present for a hearing.

May the policies provide that the hearing before the school board be presented in writing only? A district's policies may provide that the presentation of a grievance to the board be made in writing without the presentation of evidence or a oral presentation. Whether to disallow an oral presentation is a policy decision that will vary by the district.[19]

IV. Open Meetings Questions

Are grievance hearings conducted by administrators or committees before they get to the board level subject to the Texas Open Meetings Act ("Act")? Meetings or hearings on grievances before administrators are not subject to the Open Meetings Act. This is also true when hearings are held before a committee, or a hearing officer, that does not have power to make binding, enforceable decisions, but to make recommendations to the board. No public notice must be given of these meetings and access to the meetings may be restricted.[20]

When a grievance reaches a school board, may the school board hold a grievance hearing in executive session? Chapter 551 of the Texas Government Code contains the provisions of the Act.[21] Section 551.074 provides that a school board does not have to hold an open meeting "to deliberate the appointment, employment, evaluation, reassignment, duties, discipline or dismissal of a public officer or employee; or to hear a complaint or charge against an officer or employee." Section 551.074 specifies, however, that it does not apply "if the officer or employee who is the subject of the deliberation or hearing requests a public hearing." Therefore, unless a grievant requests that his or her grievance hearing be held in open session, the board may conduct the hearing in closed session. Any board action concerning the grievance must, of course, be made in open session. If an employee requests that the hearing be held in open session, the board must conduct the grievance hearing in open session, and the board may not deliberate on the grievance in closed session unless the employee allows the board to deliberate in executive session. If a board wants to deliberate in closed session when an employee has requested an open hearing, the board must ask the employee's permission to deliberate in executive session and then comply with the employee's decision.[22]

Who controls whether an executive session is held when the grievance is a complaint against another employee and not just a complaint about what a policy is or how it has been applied? A related question is whether a board may go into executive session to conduct a grievance hearing when the grievant requests an open hearing but the grievance involves a complaint against another employee. This question is governed by Section 551.082 of the Act. Section 551.082 provides that the school board does not have to hold an open meeting to deliberate a case "in which a complaint or charge is brought against an employee of the school district by another employee and the complaint or charge directly results in a need for a hearing."[23] The same section specifies, however, that it does not apply "if an open hearing is requested in writing . . . by the employee against whom the complaint or charge is brought."[24]

This language has been interpreted to mean that a board may retire into executive session to hear a complaint against another employee even when the person bringing the complaint requests an open hearing, if (1) the complaint or charge against the other employee is a substantial portion of the complaint and (2) the employee complained of does not want an open hearing. If the complaint against another employee is only tangentially related to the grievant's grievance, and if the grievant wants the hearing to be in open session, the board must conduct the grievance hearing in open session.

At the beginning of a grievance hearing, the board president can advise the grievant that the board will go into executive session if the focus of the grievance is going to be a complaint against another employee. The board president can then monitor the substance of the grievant's grievance to determine whether the complaint against another employee is incidental to the employee's complaint or whether it forms the major basis of the complaint. Boards must exercise care not to conduct grievance hearings in executive session when the focus of the grievance is not a complaint against another employee. The board or superintendent should determine whether the employee wants an open meeting. If the employee against whom the complaint is made requests an open hearing in writing, the board must conduct the hearing in open session, regardless of the wishes of the grieving employee.

How do school districts properly give notice of an employee grievance hearing when it is unknown whether the hearing will be open or closed? The meeting notice for a grievance hearing should be posted so the hearing can be in open or closed session. A notice that should accomplish this is set out below:

Hear the grievance of Unhappy Employee.

This grievance hearing may be conducted in open or executive session under Section (2)(g) or (h)(2) of the Open Meetings Act.

The grievance hearing will thereby be noticed for either a closed or open session with the decision to be made as late as the time of the hearing.

V. Conclusion

A school district should strive to have an employee grievance process that permits disgruntled employees to air their complaints and work with school authorities to fashion a resolution. A district's grievance policy should be specifically set out by policy, and should be applied as fairly and consistently as possible. In cases where a resolution is possible, the grievance process should allow for a quick resolution of complaints that minimizes personality conflicts and disruption of work. In cases where no resolution is possible, the grievance process should provide a record of fair treatment of the aggrieved employee and meaningful attention to the employee's concerns. In either case, an effective grievance process can help minimize the negative impact of inevitable employee disputes.

ENDNOTES

[1] Tex. Const. Article 1, § 27.
[2] Professional Ass'n of College Educators v. El Paso County Community Dist., 678 S.W.2d 94 (Tex. App.–El Paso 1984, *writ ref'd n.r.e.*).
[3] *Id.* at 96.
[4] TEX. GOV'T CODE §§ 617.001 - 617.005.
[5] TEX. GOV'T CODE § 617.005.
[6] Beverly v. City of Dallas, 292 S.W.2d 172 (Tex. Civ. App.–El Paso 1956, *writ ref'd n.r.e.*).
[7] TEX. GOV'T CODE § 617.002.
[8] Corpus Christi Indep. Sch. Dist. v. Padilla, 709 S.W.2d 700 (Tex. App.–Corpus Christi, 1986, *no writ*).
[9] 678 S.W.2d 94 and 709 S.W.2d 700. *See* endnotes 2 and 8, *supra*.
[10] Sayre v. Mullins, 681 S.W.2d 25 (Tex. 1984); Corpus Christi Am. Fed'n of Teachers v. Corpus Christi Indep. Sch. Dist., 572 S.W.2d 663 (Tex. 1978); Lubbock Professional Firefighters v. City of Lubbock, 742 S.W.2d 413 (Tex. Civ. App.–Amarillo 1987, *writ ref'd n.r.e.*).
[11] TEX. GOV'T CODE § 617.005.
[12] Dallas Indep. Sch. Dist. v. American Fed'n of State, County and Mun. Employees, Local Union No. 1442, 330 S.W.2d 702 (Tex. Civ. App.–Dallas 1959, *writ ref'd n.r.e.*).
[13] Lubbock Professional Firefighters v. City of Lubbock, *supra* at 417.
[14] *Id.* at 417-418.
[15] Op. Atty. Gen. No. JM-177 (1984).
[16] Corpus Christi Indep. Sch. Dist. v. Padilla, *supra* at 706.
[17] Etzel v. Galveston Indep. Sch. Dist., 231-R-9-885 (Comm. Educ. 1986) and Falvey v. Alief Indep. Sch. Dist., 113-R3-1185 (Comm. Educ. 1987).
[18] Op. Atty. Gen. No. H-422 (1974); Corpus Christi Indep. Sch. Dist. v. Padilla, *supra*.
[19] Eller v. Beaumont Indep. Sch. Dist., 194-R10-393 (Comm. Educ. 1993) and Eller v. Beaumont Indep. Sch. Dist., 009-R10-992 (Comm. Educ. 1993).
[20] City of Austin v. Evans, 794 S.W.2d 78 (Tex. Civ. App.–Austin 1990 *writ history*); Op. Atty. Gen. No. JM-340 (1985).
[21] TEX. GOV'T CODE §§ 551-002 - 551.146.
[22] Corpus Christi Classroom Teachers Ass'n v. Corpus Christi Indep. Sch. Dist., 535 S.W.2d 429 (Tex. Civ. App.–Corpus Christi 1976, *no writ*); James v. Hitchcock Indep. Sch. Dist., 742 S.W.2d 701 (Tex. App.–Houston [1st Dist.] 1987, *writ denied*).
[23] TEX. GOV'T CODE § 551-082.
[24] *Id.*

SECTION 3

Students

TORT LIABILITY AND GOVERNMENTAL IMMUNITY

By: Jeffrey J. Horner

I. Introduction

On frequent occasions, schools are involved in circumstances which could give rise to tort liability–on athletic fields, on school buses, in shop classes, in teacher terminations, and even on student field trips. These situations always raise the question of the legal liability of school districts and colleges and their individual employees. Injured parties will sue school districts and colleges and their employees, claiming that school-related negligence caused the injury. This chapter will outline both state and federal law regarding school district liability for personal injuries, known as torts.

II. Legal Authority

A. State Law

1. School Districts and Junior Colleges

Generally, Texas school districts are immune from tort claims brought by injured students and other individuals. Texas courts have repeatedly declared that independent school districts are agencies of the state and, while exercising governmental functions, are immune from suits against them grounded in negligence. Numerous cases have asserted and re-asserted this doctrine of governmental immunity. For instance, in *Braun v. Trustees of Victoria Independent School District*,[1] the plaintiff claimed that the negligence of school officials concerning the location and pruning of a tree caused her injuries. The court first considered whether an independent school district could be held liable for negligence. It stated: "There can be no question but that an independent school district is an agency of the state and, while exercising governmental functions, is not answerable for its negligence in a suit sounding in tort."[2] Similarly, the Texas Supreme Court held in *Barr v. Bernhard*[3]: "The law is well settled in this state that an independent school district is an agency of the state and, while exercising governmental functions, is not answerable for its negligence for a suit sounding in tort."[4] Other courts have arrived at a similar conclusion.[5]

The Texas Legislature, however, has carved out one very limited exception to this general blanket of governmental immunity. The Texas Tort Claims Act ("Act"), Tex. Civ. Prac. & Rem. Code § 101.001, *et seq.*, exposes school districts to liability for damages when the negligence of an officer or employee of a school district arising from the operation or use of a motor vehicle causes injury or death to an individual. The Act states, in relevant part:

> § 101.021. A governmental unit in the state is liable for: (1) property damage, personal injury, and death proximately caused by a wrongful act or omission or negligence of an employee acting within his scope of employment if: (a) the property damage, personal injury, or death arises from the operation or use of a motor-driven vehicle or motor-driven equipment . . . [6]

Section 101.051 of the Act further states: "Except as to motor vehicles, the provisions of the Act shall not apply to a school district or a junior college district." In addition, even if injury or death arises from the negligent use of a motor vehicle, the liability of school districts and junior colleges is limited by the Act. The liability of a district is limited to money damages in a maximum amount of $100,000 for each injured person and $300,000 for each single occurrence for bodily injury or death, and $100,000 for each single occurrence for injury to or destruction of property.[7] Thus, the Act exposes school districts and junior colleges to limited liability for negligence only in situations involving the operation or use of motor vehicles.

The Texas Supreme Court has also interpreted the Act. In *Barr v. Bernhard, supra*, the court, after recognizing the general doctrine of governmental immunity for school districts, discussed the effect of the Act upon that immunity. It stated:

> The Texas Tort Claims Act was enacted in 1970. Section 3 of that Act provided for a waiver of governmental immunity for the use of publicly owned motor vehicles, premises defects, and injury arising out of the conditions or use of property. With respect to the liability of the school district, however, the Legislature provided for more limited waiver of immunity. Section 19A of the Act states that a school district's liability is limited to causes of action arising from the use of motor vehicles.[8]

Thus, the immunity accorded school districts under common law remains intact aside from this limited exception provided for in the Act.

Courts have also applied this immunity to a variety of other common law tort claims, including defamation, intentional infliction of emotional distress, tortious interference with contractual relations, wrongful discharge, and invasion of privacy.[9] These cases render school districts nearly totally immune from liability under state tort law.

The only lingering question regarding school district immunity is that a district must be acting in a governmental capacity to retain its immunity. The courts have uniformly considered the provision of educational services to be governmental in nature.[10] An independent school district is an agency of the state and the activities of the district are in furtherance of the state's obligation to provide for the general welfare of the public. No court has recognized that independent school districts can act in any capacity other than a governmental one. The court stated in *Braun*, "There is quite a distinction between a school district and a city or town–cities and towns exercise a dual function, to wit, governmental and proprietary, while a school district is purely a governmental agency and exercises only such powers as are delegated to it by the state. It performs no proprietary functions which are separate and independent of its governmental powers."[11] Other courts have uniformly held that school districts can only act in a governmental capacity.[12]

If the aforementioned requirements are met, then school districts will not be held liable for the negligent acts of their employees except in situations involving the negligent use of motor vehicles, and even then subject to monetary limitations under the Act.

2. Individual Employees

Tex. Educ. Code § 22.051 (formerly § 21.912) provides, in part, as follows:

> (a) A professional employee of a school district is not personally liable for any act that is incident to or within the scope of the duties of his position of employment, and that involves the exercise of judgment or discretion on the part of the employee, except in circumstances where a professional employee uses excessive force in the discipline of students or negligence resulting in bodily injury to students.
>
> (b) This section is not applicable to the operation, use or maintenance of any motor vehicle.

The Supreme Court of Texas has declared that "a professional school employee is not personally liable for the acts done within the scope of employment and which involve the exercise of judgment and discretion except in circumstances where in disciplining a student, the employee uses excessive force or his negligence results in bodily injury to a student."[13] In

Barr, a student was working at a school district-owned farm. A calf he was weighing at the farm inadvertently struck a support pole of a building, causing the building's roof to collapse upon him. The student sustained serious and permanent injuries. He brought suit against both the school district and numerous district employees, alleging negligence in several respects.

Concerning the individual defendants, the court addressed the interpretation of Section 22.051's predecessor. The court expressly interpreted the last clause of subsection (b) of the statute, the terms of which qualify the immunity for professional employees, by stating that there will be no personal liability "except in circumstances where professional employees use excessive force in the discipline of students or negligence resulting in bodily harm to students." The court noted that at first glance, a reading of the last clause would seem to sanction personal liability for professional school employees who use excessive force in the discipline of students or who "use negligence" that results in bodily injury to students.[14] The court continued:

> Such a reading would be incorrect, however, because it is inaccurate to say that a person "uses negligence"; negligence occurs as a result of an act or omission by an individual. Because of this ambiguity, the meaning of the last clause is rendered uncertain and is susceptible to conflicting interpretations. Therefore, we are required to interpret the language of the statute involved in order to ascertain the intent of the Legislature.[15]

On the basis of this interpretation, the court concluded that the Legislature intended the last clause of subdivision (b) to limit the liability of professional school employees to acts incident to the discipline of students.[16] It examined the entire statute and considered this interpretation to be the only reasonable meaning that the statute could be given. According to the court, to hold otherwise would be to give subdivision (b) a meaning out of harmony or inconsistent with the other provisions of the statute.[17]

As a result, the Supreme Court of Texas held:

> We hold § 21.912(b) of the Texas Education Code to mean that a professional school employee is not personally liable for acts done within the scope of employment, and which involve the exercise of judgment or discretion, except in circumstances where disciplining a student, the employee uses excessive force or his negligence results in bodily injury to the student.[18]

The Supreme Court's decision in *Barr* has been upheld and cited favorably by other Texas courts.[19] Indeed, the Texas Supreme Court expressly reaffirmed its interpretation of Section 21.912 in *Hopkins v. Spring Independent School District*.[20] The primary issue before the Supreme Court in *Hopkins* was a re-evaluation of its interpretation of Section 21.912 as outlined in *Barr*. In *Hopkins*, the Court upheld its interpretation of Section 21.912 rendered in *Barr*. The Supreme Court reaffirmed the doctrine that individual employees of school districts cannot be held personally liable for acts incident to or within the scope of employment which involve the exercise of judgment or discretion, except when in the course of disciplining a student the employee uses excessive force which results in injury to the student. As the Supreme Court stated: "We remain committed to our original interpretation of Section 21.912 of the Education Code. The judgment of the court of appeals is affirmed."[21] Courts have applied the protections of Section 21.912 to many types of tort claims, including defamation, invasion of privacy and the intentional infliction of emotional distress.[22]

Cases interpreting Section 21.912 will likely be applied by the courts to interpret Section 22.051, because the statutes are nearly identical.[23] Therefore, under Section 22.051, individual employees are entitled to the same type of immunity enjoyed by school districts.

B. Federal Law

1. School Districts and Junior Colleges

Injured parties also allege that conduct by school officials violates their rights secured under the Due Process Clause of the Fourteenth Amendment to the United States Constitution. Suits of this nature are generally filed in federal court under 42 U.S.C. § 1983 (Section 1983). Section 1983 affords a plaintiff a cause of action when two elements are present: (1) the conduct complained of is committed by a person acting under color of state law; and (2) that conduct deprives an individual of a statutory or constitutional right.[24] Local governmental units, such as school districts and junior colleges, are considered "persons" to which Section 1983 applies.[25] School districts cannot be held liable under Section 1983, however, unless an individual is deprived of a constitutional or statutory right.

Injured students and other individuals often allege that the negligence and/or gross negligence of school officials deprived them of their constitutional rights and caused their injuries. However, merely negligent conduct is not actionable under the Constitution. In two cases, the Supreme Court held that a person's constitutional rights protected under Section 1983 are not implicated by the negligent acts of a state official causing an unintended loss of or injury to life, liberty or property.[26]

In *Daniels v. Williams*, the petitioner was a prisoner in a Virginia penitentiary. He sought damages for injuries allegedly sustained when he fell in a prison stairway. He claimed that a pillow was negligently left in the stairwell by the respondent, a deputy who was stationed at the jail. The petitioner claimed that the respondent's negligence deprived him of his liberty interest in freedom from bodily injury. The petitioner also claimed he was without an adequate state remedy because the defense of sovereign immunity was available to the respondent under Virginia law. The district court granted the respondent's motion for summary judgment, and the Fourth Circuit Court of Appeals affirmed.

The United States Supreme Court affirmed the decision of the Fourth Circuit. Justice Rehnquist delivered the Court's opinion. The Court noted that the guarantee of due process is normally applied only to deliberate decisions of governmental officials to deprive a person of life, liberty or property.[27] The court considered the action by the prison custodians of leaving a pillow on prison stairs to be quite remote from the deliberate action always necessary to constitute a deprivation of one's constitutional rights.

The court concluded its analysis by stating:

> Petitioner alleges that he was injured by the negligence of respondent, a custodial official at the city jail. Whatever other provisions of state law or general jurisprudence he may rightly invoke, the Fourteenth Amendment to the United States Constitution does not afford him a remedy.[28]

Thus, *Daniels* stands for the proposition that mere negligence and/or gross negligence is insufficient to trigger the protections of Section 1983. As the Supreme Court has indicated in the past, the Fourteenth Amendment should not be applied as "a font of tort law to be superimposed upon whatever systems may already be administered by the States."[29] Only in the face of outrageous or "egregious" actions by state officials should Section 1983 provide redress for plaintiffs.[30]

The Fifth Circuit Court of Appeals enunciated a standard of "callous" or "deliberate" indifference to hold school districts or individual employees liable under the United States Constitution in *Lopez v. Houston Independent School District*.[31] In *Lopez*, the plaintiff alleged that both the school district and numerous individual employees wrongfully deprived him of a safe environment when he was beaten on a school bus by other students. Specifically, he alleged that: 1) the bus driver failed to come to his assistance when the fight occurred, and 2) the bus driver failed to provide him with first aid and assistance and failed to take him to a hospital after the fight had been stopped. Lopez sued not only the Houston Independent School District, but also individual employees of the district, including the bus driver. The case against all defendants was dismissed at the trial level, and the case was appealed to the Fifth Circuit.

At the Fifth Circuit, the summary judgment entered on behalf of all defendants except the bus driver was affirmed. Summary judgment in favor of the bus driver was reversed, and the case was remanded back to the district court for a trial on the merits against him. The Fifth Circuit reversed and remanded because it determined that there was a material fact issue on whether the bus driver acted with "callous indifference" to the rights of the plaintiff.[32] Thus, the Fifth Circuit established the standard that a plaintiff must prove "callous indifference" in the conduct of a school employee to recover against the school district.

Even assuming that a student has stated a legitimate cause of action, Section 1983 is implicated against a school district only if a plaintiff, through the execution of a policy or toleration of a custom by a governmental unit, is deprived of his or her constitutional rights.[33] School districts are not strictly liable under Section 1983 for the unconstitutional acts of school personnel; a plaintiff must show a wrongful school district policy or custom to recover against the district.

The Fifth Circuit has addressed the policy or custom issue on numerous occasions in the past. It has followed the standards established by the U.S. Supreme Court in *Monell v. Department of Social Services*, by determining that isolated incidents of negligence do not constitute the kind of systematic abuse that is actionable under Section 1983.[34]

2. Individual Employees

Individual school employees are often sued in their official capacities. Actions for damages against a party in his or her official capacity are, in essence, actions against the governmental entity of which the officer is an agent.[35] Thus, the same standard must be applied to Section 1983 liability for officials sued in their official capacities as is applied to the governmental entity itself.[36] That is, a governmental officer must participate in the implementation of a policy or toleration of a custom which causes the deprivation of a plaintiff's constitutional rights.

Liability in one's individual capacity involves a different analysis, however. The United States Supreme Court has addressed the issue of individual liability under Section 1983 on numerous occasions. In *Harlow v. Fitzgerald*,[37] the plaintiff brought suit for damages against both the U.S. Government and numerous individual defendants under Section 1983 for his allegedly unlawful discharge from the United States Air Force. In *Harlow*, the court held that in actions brought under the United States Constitution against federal officials, the immunity of these officers could only be defeated by a showing of their lack of objective good faith.[38] While the case did not address the immunity of state officials sued under Section 1983, the Court stated:

It would be untenable to draw a distinction for purposes of immunity law between suits brought against state officials under § 1983 and suits brought directly under the Constitution against federal officials.[39]

Harlow was applied to Section 1983 actions in *Davis v. Scherer*.[40] In *Davis*, the U.S. Supreme Court applied the holding of *Harlow* directly to Section 1983 cases against state governmental agencies when it held:

Officials are shielded from liability for civil damages insofar as their conduct does not violate clearly established statutory or constitutional rights of which a reasonable person would have known.[41]

As a result of *Davis*, school officials are not liable under Section 1983 in their individual capacities unless, while acting within the scope of their employment, they violate the clearly-established constitutional rights of a person at the time of the disputed incident.

The requirements for establishing individual liability under Section 1983 were made even more stringent by the United States Supreme Court in *Mitchell v. Forsyth*.[42] The Court in *Mitchell* stated that unless a plaintiff's allegation establishes a clear violation of an established constitutional right, a defendant is entitled to summary judgment on that issue prior to even the commencement of discovery.[43] Furthermore, a denial of summary judgment based on the doctrine of qualified immunity is an interlocutory decision which is immediately appealable, notwithstanding the absence of a final judgment.[44]

III. Conclusion

State and federal law invoke similar standards of recovery for plaintiffs. Under state law, the doctrine of governmental immunity applies, except in situations involving the use or operation of motor vehicles or the administration of punishment. Generally, both employees and school districts will be shielded from liability in all other situations involving alleged negligent actions. Likewise, federal law requires that employees act with "callous" or "deliberate" indifference to the rights of individuals before they will be subject to liability, and shields governmental entities from liability, absent proof of a policy or custom of deliberate indifference to constitutional rights. Thus, in general, school districts, junior colleges, and school officials in Texas are shielded from tort liability in the vast majority of cases involving personal injuries.

ENDNOTES

[1] 114 S.W.2d 947 (Tex. Civ. App.–San Antonio 1938, *writ ref'd n.r.e.*).
[2] 114 S.W.2d at 949.
[3] 562 S.W.2d 844 (Tex. 1978).
[4] 562 S.W.2d at 846.

[5] *See, e.g.,* Garza v. Edinburg Consol. Indep. Sch. Dist., 576 S.W.2d 1916 (Tex. Civ. App.–Corpus Christi 1979, *no writ*); Coleman v. Beaumont Indep. Sch. Dist., 496 S.W.2d 245 (Tex. Civ. App.–Beaumont 1973, *writ ref'd. n.r.e.*); Pierson v. Houston Indep. Sch. Dist., 698 S.W.2d 733 (Tex. App. [14th Dist.]–Houston 1985, *writ ref'd n.r.e.*).
[6] TEX. CIV. PRAC & REM. CODE § 101.021.
[7] TEX. CIV. PRAC. & REM. CODE § 101.023.
[8] 562 S.W.2d at 846.
[9] *See, e.g.,* Williams v. Conroe Indep. Sch. Dist., 809 S.W.2d 954 (Tex. App.–Beaumont 1991, *no writ*); Brown v. Houston Indep. Sch. Dist., 763 F. Supp. 905 (S.D. Tex. 1991).
[10] Garza v. Edinburg Consol. Indep. Sch. Dist., *supra* at e.n. 5; Braun v. Trustees of Victoria Indep. Sch. Dist., *supra* at e.n. 1.
[11] 114 S.W.2d at 950.
[12] *See, e.g.,* McManus v. Anahuac Indep. Sch. Dist., 667 S.W.2d 245 (Tex. App. Houston [1st Dist.] 1984, *no writ*); Treadaway v. Whitney Indep. Sch. Dist., 205 S.W.2d 97 (Tex. Civ. App.–Waco 1947, *no writ*); Duson v. Midland County Indep. Sch. Dist., 627 S.W.2d 428 (Tex. Civ. App.–El Paso 1981, *no writ*); Dillard v. Austin Indep. Sch. Dist., 806 S.W.2d 589 (Tex. App.–Austin 1991 *writ denied).*
[13] 562 S.W.2d 844 at 849.
[14] *Id.* at 848.
[15] *Id.*
[16] *Id.* at 849.
[17] *Id.*
[18] *Id.*
[19] *See, e.g.,* Wagner v. Alvarado Indep. Sch. Dist., 598 S.W.2d 51 (Tex. Civ. App.–Waco 1980, *writ ref'd n.r.e.*).
[20] 736 S.W.2d 617 (Tex. 1987).
[21] 736 S.W.2d at 622.
[22] *See* Williams v. Conroe Indep. Sch. Dist., *supra* at e.n. 9.
[23] Gallegos v. Escalon, 918 S.W.2d 62 (Tex. App.–Corpus Christi 1996, n.w.h.) (Sections 21.912 and 22.051 remain identical in substance).
[24] *See generally* Baker v. McCollan, 443 U.S. 137 (1979); Parratt v. Taylor, 541 U.S. 527 (1981).
[25] Monell v. Department of Social Serv., 436 U.S. 658 (1978).
[26] Daniels v. Williams, 474 U.S. 327 (1986); Davidson v. Cannon, 474 U.S. 344 (1986).
[27] 106 S. Ct. at 665.
[28] *Id.* at 667.
[29] Paul v. Davis, 424 U.S. 693, 701 (1976).
[30] On the same day, the Court decided the *Daniels* case using the same analysis.
[31] 817 F.2d 351 (5th Cir. 1987).
[32] 817 F.2d at 355.
[33] Monell v. Department of Social Serv., *supra.* at e.n. 24.
[34] 626 F.2d 1316 (5th Cir. 1980).
[35] Universal Amusement Co., Inc. v. Hofheinz, 646 F.2d 996, 997 (5th Cir. 1981).
[36] Monell v. Department of Social Serv. of New York, *supra.*
[37] 102 S. Ct. 2727 (1982).
[38] 102 S. Ct. at 2738.
[39] *Id.*
[40] 104 S. Ct. 3012 (1984).
[41] *Id.* at 3020.
[42] 105 S. Ct. 2306 (1985).
[43] 105 S. Ct. at 2316.
[44] *Id., See also* Johnson v. Jones, 115 S. Ct. 2151 (1995) (limiting interlocutory appeals solely to questions of law).

THE FIRST AMENDMENT RIGHTS OF STUDENTS

By: Christopher B. Gilbert

I. Introduction

Each morning, around 8:00 a.m., millions of bells ring across this country, admitting the nation's children into our public schools. But as they walk through that door, what rights do they bring with them into the schools? The extent that students are protected by the First Amendment while in school is a complex and controversial question that has been the subject of much litigation. In its seminal student free speech case, *Tinker v. Des Moines Independent Community District*, the U.S. Supreme Court declared that students do not "shed their constitutional rights to freedom of speech or expression at the schoolhouse gate."[1] But it is equally clear that they do not bring in all their rights. The courts have repeatedly stated that school children do not have the same First Amendment rights that adults do.[2] This chapter will chart the twisted path taken by the courts in deciding the balance to strike between a student's right to free speech and a school's need to maintain discipline and order in the school environment.

II. The Supreme Court Speaks: *Tinker*, *Fraser*, and *Kuhlmeier*

The first of the U.S. Supreme Court's modern trilogy[3] of cases addressing free speech in the public schools was *Tinker v. Des Moines Independent Community School District*,[4] decided during the height of the Vietnam War. *Tinker* involved a group of students who were disciplined for wearing black armbands to school to protest the war. After losing in both the district court and the court of appeals, the students' right to wear the armbands, and hence their right to symbolic speech, was upheld by the Supreme Court through its famous, and oft-repeated, schoolhouse gate quote. Although the Court noted the need for school officials to maintain order and discipline, it was concerned that there was no evidence that the armbands had actually caused any disorder or disruption of the educational process. Undifferentiated fear or apprehension of disturbance is not enough, warned the Court, to justify stifling free speech. Indeed, such a hazardous freedom was seen as a strength of American society.

Despite its deference to the rights of students, the Court recognized that there would be situations in which a school could constitutionally regulate the speech of its students. Specifically, a school could regulate speech where the speech would "materially and substantially interfere with the requirements of appropriate discipline in the operation of the school."[5] In addition, the Court noted the importance of the specific facts of each case in applying the above standard. Because there had been no showing of disruption in *Tinker*, and thus no showing that the speech had adversely affected other students, the Court held that the school policy violated the First Amendment.[6]

The broad deference given to student free speech rights by *Tinker* remained the law until the mid-1980s. In 1985, the Supreme Court decided *New Jersey v. T.L.O.*,[7] which held that school officials generally needed only a "reasonable suspicion" to search students at school, and not the probable cause usually required in the adult world. Although *T.L.O.* dealt with the Fourth Amendment, its warning that the *Tinker*-bestowed rights of students were being circumscribed was confirmed the following year in *Bethel School District No. 403 v. Fraser*.[8] *Fraser* involved a student who had made a nominating speech during a school assembly that the Court described as an "elaborate, graphic, and explicit sexual metaphor." The speech apparently shocked the school–which suspended Matthew for three days and removed his name from the list of potential graduation speakers–and the Supreme Court, which overturned the appellate court's opinion that *Tinker* mandated a decision in favor of Matthew.

In distinguishing *Tinker*, the Court focused on what it considered to be important factual differences between the two situations. It first noted what it called a "marked distinction" between the "political" nature of the armbands in *Tinker* and the "sexual" nature of Matthew's nominating speech. Stressing the importance of teaching students "the boundaries of socially appropriate behavior,"[9] the Court declared that even the most heated of political arguments requires a consideration "for the personal sensibilities of the other participants and audiences."[10] The Court reiterated that student/children rights are not necessarily coextensive with adult rights. Referring to *Cohen v. California*, an older case that had upheld the right of an adult to wear a leather jacket that said "Fuck the Draft,"[11] the Court summed up the difference by stating that "the First Amendment gives a high school student the classroom right to wear Tinker's armband, but not Cohen's jacket."[12]

Second, although the Court did not actually state that under *Tinker* it found the student's speech to be "materially and substantially" disruptive, it was clearly influenced by the fact that he had apparently caused quite a stir. The evidence showed that students at the assembly hooted and yelled, and that some "by gestures graphically simulated the sexual activities pointedly alluded to in respondent's speech."[13] Other students appeared to be "bewildered and embarrassed." One teacher reported that she had to skip part of her lesson the following day to discuss the speech. The combination of the sexual nature of the speech and its response apparently was enough in the Court's eyes to distinguish it from the speech in *Tinker*. The Court concluded by repeating a famous quote from the *dissent* in *Tinker*, which stated that the Constitution does not compel school officials "to surrender control of the American public school system to public school students."[14]

Two years after the Supreme Court was shocked by the nominating speech, it decided *Hazelwood School District v. Kuhlmeier*.[15] *Kuhlmeier* involved the extent to which school officials could censor a school newspaper written by students as part of their Journalism II course. The school's practice was for the principal to review each article before it was published. After reviewing the May 1983 edition, the principal objected to two articles: one on student pregnancy and the other on divorce. The principal was concerned that even though false names had been used, the identities of the pregnant students might still be discernable. He was also concerned that the parents in the divorce article were not given a chance to respond to the claims of their children. Because the publication deadline was imminent, the principal directed the journalism teacher to pull the articles, rather than have them rewritten. Suit was brought by students on the newspaper's staff.

Although recognizing its decision in *Tinker*, the Court stressed the importance of leaving the decision of what speech is proper in the classroom to the discretion of local school boards.[16] The Court then turned to a method of analysis different than that used in either *Tinker* or *Fraser*: the forum analysis, employed in such educational cases as *Perry Education Association v. Perry Local Educators' Association*[17] and *Widmar v. Vincent*.[18] Under the forum analysis, public property can be one of three different types of forums: a public forum, which allows the greatest amount of unrestricted speech; a closed or nonpublic forum, where reasonable restrictions on speech are permissible; or the hybrid "limited public forum." Limited public forums involve property that is generally not considered to be a traditional public forum, but that has nonetheless been opened by the government for expressive activity. They are subject to the same standards as traditional public forums.[19]

The *Kuhlmeier* Court began by noting that the public schools are not traditional public forums. It then went on to state the following rule:

> [S]chool facilities may be deemed to be public forums only if school authorities have by policy or by practice opened those facilities for indiscriminate use by the

> general public, or by some segment of the public, such as student organizations. If the facilities have instead been reserved for other intended purposes, communicative or otherwise, then no public forum has been created, and school officials may impose reasonable restrictions on the speech of students, teachers, and other members of the school community.[20]

The Court warned that there must be "clear intent" to create a public forum,[21] and that inaction or permitting limited discourse would not suffice. To find the intent, the Court looked to district policy. The Court found that the limited rights given to the students involved in developing the newspaper did not overcome the fact that the policy granted the journalism teacher and the principal final authority over what was printed. Because the evidence showed that the principal had a reasonable basis for removing the articles from a non-public forum, the students' free speech rights had not been violated.

III. Evaluating the Trilogy: Can *Tinker* be Reconciled with *Fraser* and *Kuhlmeier*?

Where *Tinker* undoubtedly marked a high point in pro-student decisions, *Kuhlmeier* just as clearly showed a shift toward giving local school officials more discretion over what speech would be allowed on their campuses. There has been much debate on the proper relationship between these three cases. Student groups stress the importance of *Tinker* and attempt to paint *Fraser* and *Kuhlmeier* as narrow exceptions to the "schoolhouse gate" rule, limited to obscene speech and publications, respectively. School administrators prefer the much more recent *Kuhlmeier* and the nebulous standards of *Fraser*, dismissing *Tinker* due to its age and the vague and passive nature of the speech it involved. There is no language in either *Fraser* or *Kuhlmeier*, however, that suggests that they were only intended as exceptions to a more general *Tinker*. There is also no suggestion that they were meant to limit *Tinker*. Both positions are based on the simplistic notion that there need only be one rule to cover all sorts of speech. They ignore the possibility that *Tinker* and *Kuhlmeier*, at least,[22] were intended to deal with two distinct types of speech by establishing two different rules.

This bifurcated approach to student speech on campus is supported by the language of *Kuhlmeier* itself. The newspaper staff had argued that under *Tinker*, the articles had not materially disrupted classwork or resulted in substantial disorder in the school, and that therefore the school could not censor the speech. This argument was adopted by the Eighth Circuit, which held for the students. In reversing the Eighth Circuit, the Supreme Court set forth the bifurcated system:

> The question whether the First Amendment requires a school to tolerate particular student speech–the question that we addressed in *Tinker*–is different from the question whether the First Amendment requires a school affirmatively to promote particular student speech. The former question addresses educators' ability to silence a student's personal expression that happens to occur on the school premises. The later question concerns educators' authority over school-sponsored publications, theatrical productions, and other expressive activities that students, parents, and members of the public might reasonably perceive to bear the imprimatur of the school. . . . Educators are entitled to exercise control over this second form of student expression. . . .[23]

Therefore, the key question in student speech situations is how the speech is being delivered: is it being delivered through the use of school property or as part of an official school activity–a *Kuhlmeier* situation–or is it merely coincidental that it occurred at school–a *Tinker* situation? By recognizing that the two cases were meant to deal with different situations, an educator can better predict how a court would likely rule on new situations as they develop.

IV. The Developing Caselaw: Student Speech in a Post-*Kuhlmeier* World

Recent cases have tended to follow the bifurcated model of dealing with student speech. One current hot issue dealing with student free speech rights is the extent to which dress codes are permissible. That the clothes a student wears constitute expression protected by the First Amendment is beyond doubt; *Tinker* itself, after all, dealt with armbands. School administrators are frequently concerned, however, not only with overt messages printed on t-shirts but with the more subtle messages conveyed by the type of clothing worn by students. Dress codes are also seen by some as a means for dealing with gangs on campus, because gangs frequently announce their presence by wearing certain types of clothing or certain colors.

Without looking at the case law, speech on student clothing would appear to fall under the *Tinker* standard. Any message conveyed by what a student wears is really just speech that "happens to occur on the school premises"[24]; it could just as easily occur on the streets or in the malls. With the possible exception of costumes in school plays or school uniforms, it is hard to argue that the messages on student clothing are conveyed through some school property or activity or bear the "imprimatur of the school."[25] In general, the few cases dealing with dress codes appear to validate this analysis. In *Jeglin v. San Jacinto Unified School District*,[26] a federal district court examined the constitutionality of a school policy that prohibited the wearing of all clothing bearing sports insignia. The policy had been implemented as a measure to counter what the district felt was a growing gang presence. In analyzing the policy, the court relied *solely* on *Tinker*; *Kuhlmeier* and *Fraser* were not even cited. Likewise, in *McIntire v. Bethel School, Independent School District No. 3*,[27] which dealt with a t-shirt that read "[t]he best of the night's adventures are reserved for people with nothing planned,"[28] the court relied primarily on *Tinker*. It found both *Kuhlmeier* and *Fraser* to be inapplicable, because such shirts could not reasonably be viewed as bearing the imprimatur of the school.[29]

Simply because *Tinker* supplied the applicable standard for deciding the above dress code cases rather than *Kuhlmeier*, however, did not mean that the students automatically won. *Tinker* does allow a school to censor student speech if facts exist that would reasonably lead school officials to forecast substantial disruption of or material interference with school activities.[30] After finding *Tinker* to be the applicable standard, both the *McIntire* and the *Jeglin* courts searched the records for such facts. In *McIntire*, the court found none; it simply could not see how a t-shirt with such a vague message could cause much disruption. The only testimony actually suggested otherwise: Jana Corso, the shirt's designer, testified that she had worn it to school as many as ten times, and it had never caused a problem.[31]

The *Jeglin* court, however, showed more deference to school officials and the gang-related purpose of the dress code. Because there was no evidence of gang presence at the elementary school level, and only a negligible presence at the middle school level, the court invalidated the policy as abridging the free speech rights of elementary and middle school students. It upheld the policy, however, at the high school, where evidence demonstrated some sort of gang problem. What was interesting about the *Jeglin* decision, and what showed the court's deference to the judgment of the school officials, was that the policy was upheld even though most of the testimony was that gang members did not wear the prohibited sports clothing. Several witnesses testified that gang members wore "dickies" and white shirts, not sports clothing. According to the student body president, the policy had not affected the gang members at all, and only showed that school officials were not in touch with what was going on on campus. Even though the court found the witnesses credible, and warned school officials to review and revise its policies from time to time, it found the dress code to be a reasonable response where the facts showed the gang presence might lead to material and substantial disruption.

Dress code litigation is still in its infancy. About the only thing that is certain is that nothing is yet certain. In June 1994, the Seventh Circuit Court of Appeals decided *Baxter v. Vigo County School Corporation*,[32] which dealt with t-shirts worn by an elementary school student, that read "Unfair Grades," "Racism," and "I Hate Lost Creek."[33] The principal of the school moved for summary judgment on the grounds of qualified immunity. School officials are shielded from liability for civil damages "insofar as their conduct does not violate clearly established statutory or constitutional rights of which a reasonable person would have known."[34] The question was therefore whether the student had a clearly established right to wear her t-shirts. The Seventh Circuit said she did not. Although it recognized that *Tinker* was the dominant authority, it felt that *Kuhlmeier* and *Fraser* had "cast some doubt" on the extent to which students retain their *Tinker*-bestowed rights. In particular, the court pointed to statements in *Fraser* that a student's age should be considered. Because the student was significantly younger than the students in *Tinker*, *Kuhlmeier*, and even *Fraser*, the court could not conclude that her right to wear her shirts was clearly established.

As one could reasonably predict that dress codes would be analyzed under *Tinker*, it seems just as likely that school publications, such as newspapers and yearbooks, would be analyzed under the factually-similar *Kuhlmeier*. In *Planned Parenthood v. Clark County School District*,[35] Planned Parenthood sued the district after several high school principals refused to accept Planned Parenthood advertisements for their schools' newspapers and yearbooks. The district's policy, which was remarkably similar to that in *Kuhlmeier*, gave principals the right to accept or refuse specific advertisements, and expressly reserved the right to deny advertising space to any business or person that did not serve the best interests of the particular school. After noting in its opening sentence that the case was controlled by the Supreme Court's decision in *Kuhlmeier*, the court found the district's policy to be constitutional. In light of the policy restrictions, and the fact that the district's purpose in allowing advertisement at all in its publications was merely to defray expenses, the court could not find the "clear intent to create a public forum" required by *Kuhlmeier*.[36]

That the court found *Kuhlmeier* controlling or that it found that the district had not created an open forum was not that surprising, considering the many factual similarities to *Kuhlmeier*. What was interesting was the way the court dealt with the factual differences and the reasonableness of the decision to exclude Planned Parenthood from the schools' publications. Planned Parenthood had argued strenuously that *Kuhlmeier* was not applicable, because *Kuhlmeier* had dealt with student speech and Planned Parenthood was an outside organization. Although the court recognized the difference, it refused to limit the applicability of *Kuhlmeier*: "The publication is the same and the audience is the same, whether the source for the speech is from inside the school or outside, or is paid or free."[37] The court also found that the district's desire to avoid being forced to open itself to views counter to those of Planned Parenthood was reasonable. Several schools claimed that if Planned Parenthood was allowed to advertise, pro-life organizations would demand equal space, and that the school publications would thereby eventually become forums for debate on the controversial issue of family planning. The desire to prevent this, agreed the court, was a reasonable goal.[38]

In *Poling v. Murphy*,[39] a student used language that was found to be "discourteous" and "rude." He admitted that he had taken a gamble and attempted to gain a few extra votes by making fun of an assistant principal's stutter. The Sixth Circuit Court of Appeals found that the school's desire to promote civility and the art "of stating one's views without indulging in personalities" were legitimate pedagogical concerns under *Fraser* and *Kuhlmeier*, and that therefore the speech did not deserve First Amendment protection.

The Fourth Circuit Court of Appeals has ruled that school mascots or symbols are the type of school-sponsored or promoted speech regulated by *Kuhlmeier*. In *Crosby v. Holsinger*,[40] the court found that a principal's decision to change his high school's "Johnny Reb" mascot after he received complaints from black students and parents did not violate the First Amendment. A group of students had sued the principal, alleging a collective constitutional right in their school's symbol.[41] After deciding that a school mascot "bears the stamp of approval of the school itself," the court found that the principal's concern regarding the complaints was reasonable. Although the principal had opened the selection of a new mascot to outside suggestions, this did not create an open forum because it permitted only limited discourse, as opposed to indiscriminate use.[42]

Although several courts have now looked at the First Amendment rights attaching to speeches made during school elections, at least one court has examined a different aspect of the election process: the distribution of campaign literature and timing of debates. In *Alabama Student Party v. Student Government Association of the University of Alabama*,[43] a group of students interested in running for school office challenged regulations that (1) restricted the distribution of campaign literature to three days prior the election, (2) only allowed such distribution at residences or outside campus buildings, (3) prohibited any distribution on election day, and (4) limited debates to the week of the election. The regulation was passed to minimize the disruptive effect of the election on the campus. Although the court noted that the regulations were "rather narrow and limiting," it found that they were not unreasonable and were therefore constitutional. Although by holding the elections the university had allowed some speech, a public forum had not been created because the university had limited the forum to a specific intended purpose: *i.e.*, "a supervised learning experience for students interested in politics and government."[44] Therefore, the time, place, and manner restrictions placed on the election did not violate the students' First Amendment rights.

V. Religious Speech

Perhaps the most difficult speech situation facing school officials today is when students speak about religious matters. When a student speaks about political or social matters, a school official need only worry about maintaining school discipline and decorum. But when the speech is religious, a new concern is injected: the possibility that the school might violate the Establishment Clause if the speech is allowed. Although the religious aspect of the speech implicates the various First Amendment religion clauses, private religious speech is as fully protected under the Free Speech Clause as non-religious speech.[45] Courts will treat each case under *Tinker* and *Kuhlmeier*, according to how the speech is delivered.

Pure religious speech usually involves student speeches, presentations, or oral reports. These cases are analyzed under the forum analysis of *Kuhlmeier* because speeches are usually seen as "school sponsored." In *Settle v. Dickson County School Board*,[46] a student sued her teacher for violating her free speech rights under the First Amendment after the teacher gave the student a "zero" on her research paper on the life of Jesus Christ. The teacher gave the "zero" for the following reasons: (1) the student failed to obtain prior permission for the topic; (2) it would be difficult for the student to write and the teacher to grade such a paper, where the student had strong personal beliefs in the subject; (3) the teacher "knew" that personal religious beliefs were just not appropriate for the public schools; (4) the fact that the student already knew a lot about the life of Jesus defeated the purpose of the research project; (5) "the law says we are not to deal with religious issues in the classroom"; and (6) the assignment required the use of four sources, and all the information on Jesus derives from one source: the Bible. The court focused on a teacher's "broad authority" over grades and class assignments, and ruled that the proffered reasons for the "zero" were all reasonable, even if some of them were wrong. Referring to *Kuhlmeier*, the court held that "where learning is the focus, as in the classroom, student speech may be even more circumscribed than in the school newspaper or other open forum."

In both *DeNooyer v. Livonia Public Schools* and *Duran v. Nitsche*, elementary school students attempted to discuss their personal religious beliefs as part of oral reports delivered in class.[47] Both cases determined that under *Kuhlmeier*, the teachers had not created open forums in their classrooms because they retained some control over the students' choice of topics and the manner in which the presentation was to be made. Because the forums were closed, the restrictions only needed to be "reasonably related to legitimate pedagogical concerns."[48] The "legitimate pedagogical concern" approved by both courts was a concern that elementary school students would believe that the religious speech was endorsed by their teachers. A child psychologist in *DeNooyer* testified that not only would the children believe that their teacher approved of the speech and its views, but that children that age, when confronted by diverse views, tend to become confused and believe that the views opposing their own are "dumb."[49] Whether this was true was deemed irrelevant; both courts felt that it was still a legitimate concern. The importance attributed to the impressionable age of the children, however, makes it unclear whether either case would be applicable to similar speech in a high school setting, where the students are more mature.[50]

A recent line of United States Supreme Court cases has made it clear that in general religious speech is not an area that must always be avoided; in fact, where a school creates a broad, neutral forum, banning religious speech from that forum is unconstitutional viewpoint discrimination. In *Lamb's Chapel v. Center Moriches Union Free School District*,[51] the Court held that it was unconstitutional viewpoint discrimination to prohibit a church from showing a film series on child raising on school property solely because of the religious perspective of the church and the film series. Although *Lamb's Chapel* involved an actual church, student groups wishing to meet for religious purposes have been permitted to do so for similar reasons.[52] Student noncurriculum groups wishing to use school property are governed by the Federal Equal Access Act, 20 U.S.C. § 4071, which prohibits public secondary schools which have established limited open forums from discriminating against student groups on the content, religious or otherwise, of the groups' speech.

In addition, a school may not deny funding to certain religious groups where similar funding is generally available to other groups. In *Rosenberger v. Rector & Visitors of the University of Virginia*[53], the court ruled that it was unconstitutional to deny funding to "Wide Awake," a magazine with a Christian orientation, where funding was made widely available to publications with a non-religious perspective. The Court made it clear that it was not ruling that the school had to directly fund the religious organization that published Wide Awake; analogizing to its decisions allowing religious groups to use public facilities on a neutral, first-come basis,[54] the court held that where the University provided publishing services (through reimbursement) on a neutral basis, it could not deny Wide Awake those services because of the magazine's religious perspective.

To what extent school officials may or must allow the distribution of religious literature on school grounds is another issue related to the free speech rights of students. Although analytically these cases appear to fall somewhere in between *Kuhlmeier* and *Tinker*, *Tinker* has generally provided the applicable standard: a school may not completely forbid the distribution of religious literature unless the facts demonstrate or reasonably forecast a material and substantial disruption of school activities.[55] Not all courts agree, however, that the "material and substantial disruption" test is the only test to use in distribution cases. In *Slotterback v. Interboro School District*, the court applied both *Tinker* and a forum analysis similar to that of *Kuhlmeier*. The court concluded that regarding private, personal communication between students, the government had intended to create a limited public forum in the public schools because such speech was part of the educational experience. Therefore, the school needed to show a compelling interest in regulating the distribution of religious literature, and that the means it had adopted were narrowly tailored to meet its goal.[56]

What complicates literature distribution cases is that schools usually raise the Establishment Clause as a defense: that they *must* prohibit such distribution or risk promoting religion. The Establishment Clause defense has not been very successful. In *Hedges v. Wauconda Community Unit School District No. 118*,[57] the only court of appeals to have so far addressed the issue held that a school may not forbid the distribution of religious material on school grounds on the basis that persons might perceive the school to be endorsing the distributed material and its religious message. The *Slotterback* court agreed that a reasonable observer (*i.e.*, student), at least at the high school level, would not perceive that by allowing distribution, the school was endorsing the message of the material.[58]

Although a school may not completely forbid the distribution of literature, it may reasonably regulate the time, place, and manner of such distribution.[59] The *Hedges* court upheld a policy that limited distribution to a half hour before and after school, from a table near the main entrance to the school.[60] Likewise, the *Slotterback* court felt that it was reasonable to prohibit the distribution of literature in a school's hallways and classrooms.[61] Such restrictions must be reasonable, however. The *Slotterback* court held unconstitutional a restriction that prohibited distribution before school at school doors but allowed it after school, because the court could not see a difference between the two. It also struck down a restriction that forbid distribution at tables near the cafeteria at lunch, because the evidence showed other groups had distributed there peacefully in the past.[62]

A more interesting restriction was upheld by the Seventh Circuit in *Hedges*. There, the school district had a policy that prohibited the distribution of more than ten pamphlets not written by students themselves. The policy was designed to encourage students to write their own material, and the court agreed that if students were not allowed to turn in the written material of others, they should not be allowed to distribute it, either. The "under 10" provision was seen as a reasonable accommodation for students who just wished to share some professional material with their friends.[63]

VI. The First Amendment and the School Library

Of all the rooms in a public school, the library is accorded a special place under the First Amendment. The Supreme Court has described libraries as places of "free and unfettered learning," and emphasized that the voluntary nature of choosing books in a library removes many of the concerns that parents frequently have that their children are being coerced to read certain books. Because of this special status, school boards "may not remove books from school library shelves simply because they dislike the ideas contained in those books and seek by their removal to proscribe what shall be orthodox in politics, nationalism, religion, or other matters of opinion."[64] In *Board of Education, Island Trees v. Pico*, the Supreme Court held unconstitutional the removal of a list of books the school board had found to be "anti-American, anti-Christian, anti-Semitic, and just plain filthy." Likewise, the removal of *The Learning Tree* for advancing the religion of "secular humanism" was also unconstitutional.[65] Removing an anthology of poetry because of objectionable, offensive language was unconstitutional, because students have a right to read and be exposed to controversial thoughts and language.[66] The most recent book removal case found that removing the book *Annie on My Mind*, which dealt with a fictional romantic relationship between two teenage girls, was unconstitutional where it was clear that the school board members who voted to remove the book did so because they disapproved of the book's homosexual content. [67]

A school district, however, does not abdicate total control of its library to the First Amendment. First, a school board may clearly remove books from a library that are found to be pervasively vulgar or educationally unsuitable.[68] In addition, although school boards are limited in what they may remove from a library, they actually have a substantial legitimate role in deciding what should go in the library in the first place.[69] At least one court has found that the school board "[c]learly . . . can determine what books will go into a library and, indeed, if there will be a library at all."[70] Religious books may be shelved in the library, as long as no specific sect is favored and provided that they do not show a preference for religious works in general.[71] In addition, the Fifth Circuit Court of Appeals, which has jurisdiction over Texas, has recently reversed a district court decision that the removal of a book on voodoo from a school library was unconstitutional.[72] The district court had found that the majority of the school board voted to remove the book because it was offensive, inappropriate, dangerous, or because it advanced the religion of voodoo. The Fifth Circuit commented that while this would indeed be unconstitutional, the deposition testimony of eight of the twelve school board members who voted to remove the book was simply not enough, for summary judgment purposes, to establish "the single decisive motivation behind the board's removal decision."[73] Therefore, the court remanded the case for a trial on the merits.

ENDNOTES

[1] Tinker v. Des Moines Indep. Comm. Dist., 393 U.S. 503, 506, 89 S. Ct. 733, 736 (1969).

[2] *See, e.g.,* Sable Communications of Cal. v. Federal Communications Comm'n, 492 U.S. 115 (1989) (holding that "dial-a-porn" that is accessible to minors may be regulated, even where the material is not obscene by adult standards); Action for Children's Television v. Federal Communications Comm'n, 852 F.2d 1332 (D.C. Cir. 1988) (Ginsburg, J.) (holding that the FCC may limit children's access to indecent material on television, even where the material is not constitutionally obscene).

[3] The first major student free speech case to reach the Supreme Court was West Virginia Bd. of Educ. v. Barnette, 319 U.S. 624 (1943), which struck down as unconstitutional a school resolution that required all students to salute the American flag. Although for years *Barnette* was *the* pro-student First Amendment decision, it has been eclipsed by *Tinker* and later decisions.

[4] *Tinker, supra.*

[5] *Id.* at 738 (quoting Burnside v. Byars, 363 F.2d 744, 749 (5th Cir. 1966)).

[6] It also did not help the school's position that school officials admitted at trial that fear of disruption had not been the prime motivator behind prohibiting the armbands; rather, the school policy had been aimed at "the principle of the demonstration" itself. The officials had apparently felt that schools were not the proper place for demonstrations of any sort. *Id.* at 738 n.3.

[7] New Jersey v. T.L.O., 469 U.S. 325 (1985).
[8] Bethel Sch. Dist. No. 403 v. Fraser, 475 U.S. 675 (1986).
[9] *Id.* at 3163.
[10] *Id.*
[11] Cohen v. California, 403 U.S. 15, 91 S. Ct. 1780 (1971).
[12] *Fraser,* 106 S. Ct. at 3164 (quoting Thomas v. Board of Educ., Granville Cent. Sch. Dist., 607 F.2d 1043, 1057 (2d Cir. 1979) (Newman, J., concurring)).
[13] *Id.* at 3162.
[14] *Id.* at 3166 (citing Tinker, 89 S. Ct. at 746 (Black, J., dissenting)).
[15] Hazelwood Sch. Dist. v. Kuhlmeier, 484 U.S. 260, 108 S. Ct. 562 (1988).
[16] *Id.* at 567-68.
[17] Perry Educ. Ass'n v. Perry Local Educators' Ass'n, 460 U.S. 37, 103 S. Ct. 948 (1983).
[18] Widmar v. Vincent, 454 U.S. 263, 102 S. Ct. 269 (1981).
[19] For a fuller description of the forum analysis, *see Kuhlmeier*, 484 U.S. at 267, 108 S. Ct. at 567; Cornelius v. NAACP Legal Defense & Educ. Fund, 473 U.S. 788, 797, 105 S. Ct. 3439, 3446 (1985); *Perry Educ. Ass'n*, 460 U.S. at 47, 103 S. Ct. at 956.
[20] *Kuhlmeier*, 108 S. Ct. at 568 (internal citations and quotations omitted).
[21] *Id.* at 569.
[22] *Fraser* is in some ways a more difficult case to fit into a category, in large part because the Court did not provide much analysis. However, in the bifurcated system discussed below, because the speech was delivered as part of a school assembly, *Fraser* would be decided under *Kuhlmeier* and the decision would likely be the same.
[23] *Kuhlmeier*, 108 S. Ct. at 569-70.
[24] *Id.* at 570 (describing *Tinker*).
[25] *Id.*
[26] Jeglin v. San Jacinto Unified Sch. Dist., 827 F. Supp. 1459 (C.D. Cal. 1993).
[27] McIntire v. Bethel Sch., Indep. Sch. Dist. No. 3, 804 F. Supp. 1415 (W.D. Okla. 1992).
[28] Apparently this phrase was a take-off on a popular alcohol advertisement.
[29] *Id.* at 1426.
[30] *Tinker*, 89 S. Ct. at 738.
[31] *McIntire*, 804 F. Supp. at 1422.
[32] Baxter v. Vigo County Sch. Corp., 26 F.3d 728 (7th Cir. 1994).
[33] "Lost Creek" was the name of the student's school.
[34] Harlow v. Fitzgerald, 457 U.S. 800, 818, 102 S. Ct. 2727, 2738 (1982).
[35] Planned Parenthood v. Clark County Sch. Dist., 941 F.2d 817 (9th Cir. 1991).
[36] *Id.* at 823 (citing *Kuhlmeier*, 108 S. Ct. at 569).
[37] *Id.* at 827.
[38] *Id.* at 830.
[39] Poling v. Murphy, 872 F.2d 757 (6th Cir. 1989).
[40] Crosby v. Holsinger, 852 F.2d 801 (4th Cir. 1988).
[41] *Id.* at 802 n.1. The court declined to decide whether such a right actually existed, in light of its holding under *Kuhlmeier* and *Fraser*.
[42] *Id.* at 802-03 n.2.
[43] Alabama Student Party v. Student Gov't Ass'n of the Univ. of Ala., 867 F.2d 1344 (11th Cir. 1989).
[44] *Id.* at 1347.
[45] Capitol Square Review & Advisory Bd. v. Pinette, 115 S. Ct. 2440, 2446 (1995).
[46] 53 F.3d 152 (6th Cir. 1995).
[47] DeNooyer v. Livonia Pub. Sch., 799 F. Supp. 744 (E.D. Mich. 1992), *aff'd.*, 1 F.3d 1240 (6th Cir. 1993) (second grader attempted to show a videotape of herself singing proselytizing religious song); Duran v. Nitsche, 780 F. Supp. 1048 (E.D. Pa. 1991), *vacated on unknown grounds*, 972 F.2d 1331 (3d Cir. 1992) (fifth grader attempted to distribute a survey on God and present an oral report on the power of God).
[48] *Duran*, 780 F. Supp. at 1052; *DeNooyer,* 799 F. Supp. at 748 (both citing *Kuhlmeier*, 108 S. Ct. at 571).
[49] *DeNooyer*, 799 F. Supp. at 747 n.4.

[50] The Supreme Court appears to believe that secondary students are capable of making such a distinction, because "[t]he proposition that schools do not endorse everything they fail to censor is not complicated." Mergens v. Board of Educ., 496 U.S. 226, 259-60, 110 S. Ct. 2356, 2372 (1990).
[51] Lamb's Chapel v. Center Moriches Union Free Sch. Dist., 113 S. Ct. 2141 (1993).
[52] *See* Good News/Good Sports Club v. School Dist. of the City of Ladue, 28 F.3d 1501 (8th Cir. 1994).
[53] 115 S. Ct. 2510 (1995).
[54] *See, e.g., Lamb's Chapel* at note 55; *Mergens* at note 54.
[55] *See e.g.,* Clark v. Dallas Indep. Sch. Dist., 806 F. Supp. 116, 120 (N.D. Tex. 1992); Slotterback v. Interboro Sch. Dist., 766 F. Supp. 280, 297 (E.D. Pa. 1991).
[56] *Slotterback*, 766 F. Supp. at 293.
[57] Hedges v. Wauconda Community Unit Sch. Dist. No. 118, 9 F.3d 1295 (7th Cir. 1993).
[58] *Slotterback*, 766 F. Supp. at 296.
[59] *Hedges*, 9 F.3d at 1301; *Slotterback*, 766 F. Supp. at 299.
[60] *Hedges*, 9 F.3d at 1301.
[61] *Slotterback*, 766 F. Supp. at 299.
[62] *Id.*
[63] *Hedges*, 9 F.3d at 1301-02.
[64] Board of Educ., Island Trees v. Pico, 457 U.S. 853, 872, 102 S. Ct. 2799, 2810 (1982).
[65] Grove v. Mead Sch. Dist., 753 F.2d 1528 (9th Cir. 1985).
[66] Right to Read Defense Comm. v. School Comm. of the City of Chelsea, 454 F. Supp. 703, 712 (D. Mass. 1978).
[67] Case v. Unified Sch. Dist. No. 233, 908 F. Supp. 864 (D. Kan. 1995).
[68] *Pico*, 457 U.S. at 872, 102 S. Ct. at 2810; Campbell v. St. Tammany Parish Sch. Bd., 64 F.3d 184, 189 (5th Cir. 1995).
[69] *Pico*, 457 U.S. at 870, 102 S. Ct. at 2810.
[70] *Right to Read Defense Comm.*, 454 F. Supp. at 711.
[71] Roberts v. Madigan, 702 F. Supp. 1505, 1513 (D. Colo. 1989), *aff'd*, 921 F.2d 1047, 1055-56 (10th Cir. 1990).
[72] *See* Delcarpio v. St. Tammany Parish Sch. Bd., 865 F. Supp. 350, 361 (E.D. La. 1994), *rev'd sub. nom.,* Campbell v. St. Tammany Parish Sch. Bd., 64 F.3d 184 (5th Cir. 1995).
[73] *Campbell*, 64 F.3d at 191.

STUDENT DISCIPLINE LAW

By: Jeffrey J. Horner

I. Introduction

Often, school administrators and school attorneys have struggled with the appropriate procedures to be followed in the discipline of public school children. In part, this is due to the seemingly endless changes in student discipline law over the last ten years. The student discipline laws were again changed significantly with the enactment of Senate Bill 1 during the 1995 legislative session. Specifically, Senate Bill 1 created Chapter 37 of the Texas Education Code, which contain significant changes in student discipline law. This chapter will outline Senate Bill 1 and provide an overview of current Texas student discipline law. Further, it will provide practical tips on how to handle discipline cases.

II. General Overview of Senate Bill 1

A. General Provisions

Senate Bill 1 makes significant revisions to what was formerly Section 21.031, *et seq*. of the Texas Education Code. Most of the provisions relating to the administration of discipline now appear under Chapter 37 of the new Texas Education Code, effective September 1, 1995. This new law details numerous changes in the law; an array of disciplinary options is available.

First, under Texas Education Code § 37.001, each school district must adopt a code of student conduct by September 1, 1996. It must establish standards of student conduct and specify the circumstances under which a student may be removed from the classroom, campus, or an alternative education program (AEP). It also must outline the conditions under which a student may be suspended or expelled.

Under § 37.001(b), a teacher with knowledge that a student has violated the student conduct code shall file with the principal or other appropriate administrator a written report documenting the violation. A copy of the written report must also be sent to the student's parents. Under § 37.007(g), the school district must inform each teacher of the conduct of a student who has engaged in an expellable offense. Under § 37.018, each school district must provide a copy of the new Texas Education Code sections and local policy relating to student discipline to each teacher and administrator.

B. Suspensions

Under § 37.005, a principal or other administrator may suspend a student who engages in conduct for which the student may be placed in an AEP. School districts may create their own lists of conduct for which alternative education placement or suspension is appropriate. A suspension may not exceed three (3) school days. However, under the new law there is no limitation on the number of suspensions an individual may receive; presumably, a student can be suspended an unlimited number of times.

Further, § 37.005 does not provide specific rights of appeal or review of a suspension. However, pursuant to the dictates of *Goss v. Lopez,*[1] a landmark student discipline case decided by the United States Supreme Court, minimal due process should be afforded a student prior to the imposition of a suspension, including oral or written notice of the reasons for suspension and an informal opportunity for the student to give his or her side of the story. There is no requirement to consider alternative discipline techniques before suspending a student. Furthermore, under the new law suspensions are limited to three (3) days, as opposed to six (6) days per semester under the prior law.

C. Removal by Teachers

Section 37.002(a) allows teachers to send students to the principal's office to maintain effective discipline in the classroom. The principal must respond by employing discipline management techniques consistent with the student code of conduct. Further, if a teacher documents that a student repeatedly interferes with the teacher's ability to communicate effectively with the other students or determines that the student's behavior is so unruly, disruptive, or abusive that it seriously impairs the teacher's ability to communicate with students, the teacher then may remove the student to the principal for placement in another classroom, inhouse suspension, or an AEP. In addition, the principal may not return the student to the teacher's class without the teacher's consent unless it is determined that return to the teacher's class is the best or only alternative available. This section thus gives teachers increased rights in removing students from classes, and makes it less likely that an unruly student will return to the original teacher's class.

D. Placement Review Committee

The recent changes to the Education Code also require the establishment of a placement review committee at each school. Under § 37.003, the purpose of the committee is to determine the placement of a student when a teacher refuses to return the student to his or her class, and to make recommendations to the school district regarding the readmission of expelled students. § 37.009(a) requires that not later than the third class day after the day a student is removed from the class by the teacher, the principal must schedule a hearing with the principal or his or her designee, the student, the parent or guardian, and the removing teacher. Following this hearing, the principal must order placement of a student for a period consistent with the student conduct code. The Education Code does not specify the type of hearing required.

E. Alternative Education Programs

The new law also allows removal of students to AEPs. With the exception of behavior where removal to an AEP is required, the new legislation is silent as to when a school district may place a student in an AEP. School districts most likely have the discretion to remove students to AEPs for any type of misconduct identified in the student conduct code. The code should delineate in writing that removal to an AEP may be a consequence for a particular act of misconduct. Certain types of misbehavior require mandatory removal to an AEP. These types of misconduct include:

1. Engaging in any conduct punishable as a felony;
2. Assault;
3. Terroristic threats;
4. Selling, giving or delivering to another person, possessing or being under the influence of marijuana, a controlled substance, or other dangerous drug;
5. Selling, giving, delivering, possessing, or being under the influence of an alcoholic beverage;
6. Engaging in conduct that contains the elements of an offense relating to abusable glue or aerosol paint;
7. Public lewdness;
8. Indecent exposure; or
9. Engaging in conduct that contains the elements of retaliation against a school employee.

Furthermore, this section prohibits a student placed in an AEP from attending or participating in school-sponsored or school-related activities.

Senate Bill 1 is silent regarding the maximum or minimum length of removal to an AEP. However, before a school district can place a student in an AEP for a period that extends beyond the current school year, it must determine that: (1) the student's presence in the regular classroom program or at the student's regular campus presents a danger of physical harm to the student or another individual, or (2) the student has engaged in serious or persistent misbehavior that violates the school district's student code of conduct.

Students possess appeal rights for placements into AEPs. Specifically, if a student's placement in an AEP, whether mandatory or permissive, extends beyond the next grading period, a student's parent or guardian is entitled to notice and an opportunity to participate in the proceeding before the school board or its designee regarding the placement. The decision of the board or its designee is final and non-appealable. To lessen the workload of school boards, the author suggests delegating the hearing to a designee.

Further, a student placed in an AEP for 120 days or more shall be provided with a review of his or her status at intervals not to exceed 120 days. At the review, the student or the parent or guardian must be given the opportunity to present arguments supporting the student's return to the regular classroom program.

Section 37.019 of the Code relates to emergency placement. The principal or his/her designee may order the immediate placement of a student in an AEP if the principal or his designee reasonably believes that the student's behavior is so unruly, disruptive, or abusive that it seriously interferes with the teacher's ability to effectively communicate with the students in a class, the ability of the student's classmates to learn, or with the operation of school or a school-sponsored activity.

Specific requirements exist for AEPs. Specifically, AEPs must be provided in a setting other than the student's regular classroom on or off the regular school campus. The curriculum in an AEP must focus on English language arts, mathematics, science, history, and self-discipline. Schools must also provide supervision and counseling, and may provide for a student's transfer to a different educational setting. The school district must allocate to an AEP the same expenditure per student that would be allocated to the student's school if the student were attending his or her regular campus.

F. Expulsions

The new law also allows for expulsion from school under specified circumstances. Under § 37.007, a student shall be expelled from school if the student, on school property or while attending a school-sponsored or school-related activity on or off school property, engages in the following conduct:

1. Uses, exhibits, or possesses a firearm, illegal knife, club, or prohibited weapon;
2. Commits the offense of aggravated assault, sexual assault, or aggravated sexual assault;
3. Commits the offense of arson;

4. Commits the offense of murder, capital murder, or criminal attempt to commit murder or capital murder;
5. Commits the offense of indecency with a child;
6. Commits the offense of aggravated kidnaping; or
7. Brings a firearm to school.

A student may also be expelled if the student, after being placed in an AEP, continues to engage in serious and persistent misbehavior that violates the district's student conduct code. Further, a student may be expelled if he or she engages in conduct which contains the elements of felony criminal mischief under the Texas Penal Code.

If a student is expelled for bringing a firearm to school, the student must be expelled from his or her regular school setting for a period of at least one (1) year. There are no other direct limitations on the length of expulsions. Theoretically, a school district could indefinitely expel a student for these mandatory offenses.

Before a student can be expelled, the school board or its designee must provide a student with a hearing which affords him/her appropriate due process as required by the United States Constitution. At the hearing, the student must be represented by the student's parent or guardian or another adult who can provide guidance to the student. If the decision to expel a student is made by the board's designee, the decision may be appealed to the board. Thus, a full evidentiary hearing need not be held before the school board. Rather, the evidentiary hearing can be held before the designee, with any appeal to the board being based on the record developed before the designee. The decision of the board may be appealed by trial *de novo* to a district court in the county in which the school district's central administrative office is located. Under State Board of Education rules[2], which are still in effect, the process which must be provided a student prior to expulsion includes:

1. Prior notice of the charges;
2. The right to a full and fair hearing;
3. The right to adult representation or legal counsel;
4. The opportunity to testify and present evidence and witnesses;
5. The opportunity to examine the evidence presented by the school administration and to question the administration's witnesses; and
6. Notice before the hearing of the administration's witnesses and any documents that the district intends to use at the hearing, in sufficient time before the hearing to allow preparation of a defense.

Under Section 37.010(g), if an expelled student enrolls in another school district, the board of trustees of the district that expelled the student must provide to the district in which the student enrolls a copy of the expulsion order. The statute also allows an emergency expulsion if the principal or his/her designee reasonably believes the action is necessary to protect persons or property from imminent harm.

G. County Juvenile Courts and Juvenile Boards

The Education Code also provides for the establishment of county juvenile courts and juvenile boards. Each student conduct code must outline the responsibility of each county juvenile board concerning the establishment and operation of a county juvenile AEP.

Section 37.01 requires that not later than the second business day after the date a student discipline hearing is held under § 37.009, the school board or its designee must deliver a copy of the order expelling or placing a student in an AEP to the authorized officer of the juvenile court in the county in which the student resides. The court officer may determine that a petition should be filed, alleging that the student is in need of supervision or engaged in delinquent conduct, or that the student should be referred to an appropriate state agency.

Furthermore, a court may not order a student expelled under § 37.007 to attend a regular classroom, regular campus, or an AEP as a condition of probation, unless the juvenile board has entered into a memorandum of understanding with the school district concerning the juvenile probation department's role in supervising and providing other support services. If a student is expelled under § 37.007, upon recommendation of the placement review committee or on the school district's own initiative, the district may readmit the student while the student is completing any court disposition requirements. After the student has successfully completed any court disposition requirements, the school district may not refuse to admit the student, but the district may place the student in its AEP.

Section 37.001 creates a new type of AEP. Counties with populations of 125,000 or more must develop a juvenile justice AEP, subject to the approval of the Texas Juvenile Probation Commission. For these counties, juvenile justice AEP's must be established no later than September 1, 1996. Under § 37.11(b), if a student is found to engage in conduct relating to a mandatory expellable offense, and a student is found by a juvenile court to have engaged in delinquent conduct under Title 3 of the Family Code, the juvenile court must require the juvenile justice AEP in the county in which the conduct occurred to provide educational services to the student and order the student to attend the program from the date of his or her adjudication. The requirements for juvenile justice AEPs are similar to the requirements for AEPs under § 37.008. A juvenile justice AEP must operate at least seven (7) hours per day for one hundred eighty (180) days per year. A student transferred to the juvenile justice AEP by a juvenile court must participate in the program for the full period ordered by the juvenile court, unless the student's school district agrees to accept the student before the date ordered by the court. The juvenile court may not order a period of transfer to a county juvenile justice AEP for a period that exceeds the term of the probation ordered by the juvenile court.

Under § 37.012, a school district in which a student is enrolled on the date the juvenile court orders the student to attend a juvenile justice AEP must transfer to the county juvenile board funds equal to the district's average per student expenditure in AEPs provided under § 37.008. Further, counties must expend funds received under § 37.012 on juvenile justice AEPs.

III. Practical Tips for Discipline Cases

A. Investigation

Generally, the first step in a student discipline case is the investigation of the alleged misconduct. Often, a complaint of student misconduct comes to an assistant principal. For example, a teacher may report that students have been fighting on the playground. After receiving such a report from the teacher, it is standard procedure for the administrator to talk to an accused student and ask whether he or she committed the act in question and to give their sides of the story. If the student agrees with the teacher's report, the confession ends the matter, and the appropriate punishment may be imposed. However, if the student disagrees with the facts, the administrator should make further inquiry if there are other witnesses who have facts concerning the event. If there are simply two views of what happened, the school official may believe whomever he or she feels is the most credible. This process is the "hearing" contemplated by *Goss v. Lopez* for suspensions.

B. The Hearing Process

School districts have considerable flexibility in determining the procedures used for student discipline hearings. More formal procedures are necessary in expulsion cases, as outlined in the aforementioned State Board of Education rules. Some school districts require such hearings be held initially before the school board. However, most districts provide that board designees, usually administrators such as principals, hear expulsion cases first. In Texas, the option is left to the school district, although expulsions can be appealed by students to the school boards as a matter of right.

The author suggests leaving the initial expulsion hearing to the board designee, who is usually the school principal. Several benefits may be attained by using this method. Having the designee hold the hearing helps assure that the student receives appropriate due process at the earliest time and at the lowest administrative level. Also, communication at this level is generally easier than if the hearing is held at the board level, and there is less likelihood of attorney involvement at lower-level hearings. The absence of attorneys may assist in the resolution of cases without the need for long and protracted hearings or other proceedings. Perhaps the most important reason to hold the initial hearing before the designee is that the designee is usually the person in charge of the school building. By having the designee make decisions regarding discipline, his or her authority and leadership role are enhanced.

Because a student is entitled to a fair hearing, the designee should avoid becoming overly involved in investigating the case prior to the hearing. In those few cases in which the designee may become intimately involved in the investigation, he or she should request that the superintendent appoint another administrator to hear that particular case. In the expulsion hearing, the board president, if the hearing is before the board, or the board's designee, if the hearing is at a lower level, will preside and present the ground rules. The Texas Open Meetings Act does not apply to hearings before the board's designee, so a hearing at this level is not open to the public.

At a hearing before the board's designee, he or she may read a standard outline with any appropriate additions to cover the specific case at hand. This outline should be handed out to all in attendance so everyone will be apprised of the ground rules. The administration has the burden of going forward and proving by a preponderance of the evidence that the student violated a rule and should be expelled. Because it is not a criminal proceeding, the reasonable doubt standard does not apply. If the student has an attorney at the hearing, the district may wish to have the school district's attorney in attendance to represent the administration or simply to keep the other attorney from controlling the hearing.

The proceeding should be tape recorded or recorded by a court reporter. This recording can later be used for appeals to the board, and eventually to prepare a transcript if the case is appealed to the courts. Court reporters' transcripts are considerably more expensive than tape recordings, and in most instances a good tape system will suffice for recording the proceedings. However, if a case appears to be a particularly difficult or complex one, or one which will likely be appealed, use of a court reporter may be advisable.

The administration should begin the proceedings by presenting its case. After the administration has presented its witnesses and evidence, the student should then present his or her witnesses. Again, time limits should generally not be placed on the presentations; however, the designee may impose reasonable restrictions on the presentation of evidence. If the designee is in doubt about the admission of any evidence, it is usually safer to admit it to ensure that all relevant evidence is considered.

After the evidence has been presented, the designee should allow rebuttal evidence and closing arguments. The designee may then deliberate and render a decision. The decision should have two parts. The first finding is whether the student violated the rule, and the second finding is the appropriate punishment. The designee may also render a decision at a later date. However, unless there are unusual circumstances, it should be rendered within a few days after the hearing. Any oral decision made at the time of the hearing should be confirmed in writing with an explanation of the basis for the decision. The designee should make specific findings of fact, and should also delineate the appropriate punishment for any offense.

C. Appeals to the School Board

If the designee determines that the student committed the acts in question and that expulsion is the appropriate punishment, under Texas law the student is entitled to appeal to the school board. The appeal to the board can be based upon the record made by the designee. That is, the board can listen to the tape recording or read the transcript of the proceeding before the designee and review any documents presented to the designee. If the appeal before the board is based on the record developed before the designee, the student and his or her parents should be so advised in the original notice letter relating to the designee's hearing.

Prior to the hearing before the board, the student and his or her parents should receive written notice of the date of the hearing and the procedure to be followed. The procedure for the hearing should be similar to that followed in an appellate argument. That is, the two sides each have an opportunity to present their cases based upon the evidence presented at the earlier hearing. No new evidence should be submitted to the board, although some districts permit new evidence to be introduced at the board hearing on the record if the student or his or her parents can demonstrate good cause why the evidence was not submitted at the hearing before the designee. Once it has considered the record and heard arguments from both sides, the board can deliberate and make its decision. The board should also adopt findings of fact and conclusions of law in support of its finding, and should send a letter to inform the parents and student of its decision. Once again, it is appropriate for the board to make its decision either at the time of the hearing or at a later date. Generally, the sooner the decision is made, the better.

If the student makes an appeal to the board based on a completely new hearing of the evidence, a letter similar to that sent by the board designee should be sent to the parents concerning the ground rules for the hearing. In this instance, the hearing before the board will be completely redone. That is, the witnesses will have to testify again. The outline used by the designee can be adapted for use by the board. Again, this outline should be provided to all parties so everybody knows what the procedures will be. It is appropriate that the school district use an attorney at the board hearing if the student has an attorney. The procedures for a full hearing before the board are generally the same as the initial hearing before a designee.

The administration and the student or his or her parents should be permitted to present proposed findings of fact and conclusions to the board. These findings can be simple and can track those made by the designee if the evidence supports them. If the designee's decision is well written, the board can sustain the administration's actions and adopt the designee's findings as those of the board.

Once a vote is taken concerning the discipline of a student, the board should write a letter to the parents and student, formally notifying them of the board's decision. If the board finds that the student did commit the acts and should be punished, the board should state the outcome of its vote. The student and parent or guardian will then have the right to take any appeal allowed under law. If the punishment is expulsion, the proper appeal is to state district court in the county in which the school district's administrative offices are located. The board should also send notice of the expulsion to all appropriate administrative agencies as outlined in the Education Code.

IV. Conclusion

The passage of Senate Bill 1 has greatly complicated student discipline matters for Texas school districts. Other than in cases of severe misbehavior which constitute expellable offenses, school districts are responsible for the ongoing supervision and education of students who engage in misconduct, primarily through the establishment of required AEPs. Further, the new law establishes county juvenile AEPs, which afford educational services to students outside of the regular school environment. Many public officials at both the school district and county levels are now directly involved in student discipline. Only time will tell whether this interactive effort will provide positive results for Texas school districts in dealing with student misbehavior.

ENDNOTES

[1] 419 U.S. 565 (1975).
[2] *See* 19 Tex. Admin. Code § 133.23.

APPLICATION OF FOURTH AMENDMENT TO SEARCHES AND SEIZURES CONDUCTED BY SCHOOL OFFICIALS

By: Jeffrey J. Horner
and
Richard A. Peebles

I. Introduction

This chapter concerns the applicability and scope of the Fourth Amendment to the United States Constitution to searches and seizures conducted by school officials. The purpose of the Fourth Amendment is to safeguard the privacy and security of individuals against unreasonable searches and seizures by government officials. Therefore, the determination of the reasonableness standard governing any specific class of searches involves balancing the government's need to search against the invasion of individual privacy and security. The Supreme Court has decided that, although the Fourth Amendment applies to searches conducted by school officials, the need to maintain an orderly environment in school requires an easing of the restrictions to which searches by public authorities are ordinarily subject. More specifically, in *New Jersey v. T.L.O.* the Court held that the legality of a search of a student does not require that it be based on probable cause that the student has violated or is violating the law, but rather that, under all the circumstances, the search conducted was reasonable and based on reasonable suspicion.[1]

II. What Circumstances Justify a Search

The first inquiry in determining the reasonableness of any search is whether there are circumstances justifying the search at its inception. For the search of a student to be justified at its inception, there must be reasonable suspicion that the search will uncover evidence that the student has violated or is violating either the law or the rules of the school.

To illustrate what constitutes "reasonable suspicion," we should contrast that phrase with the standard usually employed in searches and seizures–probable cause. The probable cause standard requires that the authority conducting a search have facts within his personal knowledge, or communicated to him by others, which are sufficient in themselves to warrant a person to believe that the search will uncover evidence of a crime.[2] The Supreme Court has diluted the strength of the probable cause standard in recent years, noting that it involves a probability, not a certainty, that criminal evidence will be uncovered, and that it involves practical considerations of everyday life on which reasonable and prudent people, not legal technicians, act. Nonetheless, the probable cause standard is often used in situations involving the police to invalidate searches conducted on the basis of tips by informants where a court finds that the reliability of the information is questionable. In contrast, the reasonable suspicion standard involves more of a common sense standard adjusted to the school setting. Under this standard, a school official must have specific and articulable facts, along with rational inferences taken from those facts, which warrant the belief that a search will uncover evidence of an infraction.[3]

The impact of the reasonable suspicion standard is two-fold. First, in cases where an official conducting the search personally observes facts which lead him or her to believe, based on experience with students as a school official, that a search of a student will produce evidence of a violation of state law or a school rule, then the official has reasonable grounds to conduct the search. That is, to a limited extent, the official may rely upon his or her experience as a school official to infer from a student's behavior that the student has violated the law. The official must still have specific facts which warrant this inference, but such information should be subject to less scrutiny than a search conducted outside the school setting.

Second, when a school official conducts a search based upon information supplied by a third party, a court is less likely to examine the reliability of the information under the more exacting requirements of probable cause. Instead, an official's reliance on such information should be reasonable based on the circumstances of the case. For example, reliance upon a report from another teacher or school official that the student has violated school rules or the law should, in most cases, be sufficient to warrant a search for evidence of the violation. Reliance on the report of another student is more questionable, and if the official could personally observe facts corroborating the student's report, it would be best to do so. Reliance on anonymous tips or information from students unknown to the official is not advised without further corroboration of the infraction from informed sources.

III. How to Conduct the Search

A school official is not required to obtain a warrant before searching a student who is under his authority. However, for the search of a student to be reasonable the search must be reasonable in relation to the objectives of the search and not excessively intrusive in light of the student's age, sex, and the nature of the suspected infraction.[4] Generally, a higher showing of cause is required as the intrusiveness of the search increases. Moreover, the intrusiveness of the search should correspond to the seriousness of the infraction to some degree. Although the court in *T.L.O.* refused to establish different standards based on evaluating the relative importance of rules governing student conduct, common sense dictates that minor infractions do not warrant intrusive searches. For example, conducting a strip search to find a cigarette or missing dollar bill is never justified.

The search should be aimed solely toward finding evidence of the infraction. If, during the search, the official finds evidence of further infractions, an additional search may be justified. For example, suppose while examining a student's purse for evidence of alcohol possession on campus, an official notices rolling papers, commonly associated with the use of marijuana. Under these circumstances, further exploration of the purse is justified for the purpose of producing evidence of drug-related infractions. Although this was not the objective of the initial search, the discovery of the rolling papers would probably be reasonable cause for the suspicion of a further infraction justifying an additional search.

The Fourth Amendment normally requires that for a search to be reasonable, the suspicion of an infraction must be particularized with respect to each individual searched–*i.e.*, individualized suspicion.[5] The Supreme Court has not decided whether individualized suspicion is an essential element of a reasonable search in the school setting; indeed, in *T.L.O.*, the Court suggested that there may be extraordinary circumstances justifying a mass search without particularized suspicion as to each individual searched. However, the majority rule, including Texas, is that individualized suspicion must exist for the search to be reasonable.[6]

For example, suppose an athletic team travels on a bus to play a game at another school. To prevent the use of alcohol or drugs on the trip, school officials require that each student have his or her luggage searched as a condition to going on the trip. Such a general search is not based on individualized suspicion, and therefore, would probably run afoul of the Fourth Amendment.

IV. What Can be Searched

The nature of the object to be searched may affect the determination of whether a search is reasonable. A search of a student's person triggers the "reasonable under all the circumstances" test of *T.L.O.* Obviously, searches of items such as purses and other personal effects implicate similar concerns.

However, courts generally agree that a student has a diminished expectation of privacy in items such as school lockers and desks. This is because schools retain ownership and joint control of such property. Consequently, most courts uphold inspections of desks and lockers by school officials for the purpose of uncovering contraband.[7] If the official conducting the search has reasonable suspicion to believe a locker contains evidence of an infraction, the search should be upheld. Moreover, in cases where reasonable grounds might not be as clear, advance notice to students that lockers and desks are subject to search by school officials should be sufficient to outweigh the student's privacy interest and justify the search. Advance notice affords the student the opportunity to limit the effect of the intrusion by not keeping highly sensitive materials in the locker, thus mitigating the intrusiveness issue. Notice can easily be provided by including the school's policy on locker searches in the student handbook and on school bulletin boards.

Student automobiles are not subject to joint control by school officials, regardless of whether they are parked on school property. Therefore, the search of a student's car is only justified when an official has reasonable suspicion that evidence of contraband is inside the car. However, courts have held that officials may patrol the parking lots and look into the cars without being subject to any Fourth Amendment constraints, generally on the theory that such actions do not constitute a search and seizure. Moreover, if evidence of a violation is discovered upon such a patrol, this alone can form the reasonable suspicion justifying a further search of the automobile. If the student is in the car when the illicit object is discovered, the official can subject the car to a reasonable search at that time. If not, it would be best to contact the student first and, if possible, obtain consent before searching.

Searches of objects such as lockers and cars are often conducted through the use of sniff dogs. The sniffing of school lockers and cars on school property does not constitute a search.[8] Therefore, in the conducting of the sniff search alone, the Fourth Amendment does not apply. However, a sniff search is only useful to the extent it is followed by a further search of the objects upon which the dog alerts. The search of the car or locker is a search within the Fourth Amendment and requires reasonable grounds for suspecting the existence of an infraction. If the dog can be shown to be reasonably reliable, *i.e.*, reasonably certain to detect the current presence of contraband, the dog's alert will generally constitute reasonable suspicion. The sniff of a student's person, however, is a search and requires reasonable grounds, independent of the dog's alert, that the student possesses contraband.

Highly intrusive searches such as strip searches should be undertaken only when absolutely necessary and when supported by specific reasonable suspicion requiring such a search. Intrusive searches are closely scrutinized by the courts, and if found to violate the Fourth Amendment, can lead to an award of substantial damages to the affected student. Therefore, as a general rule school districts should avoid strip searches.

School officials should be prepared to justify any intrusive search, including strip searches, by demonstrating that the search was supported by reasonable suspicion of a serious offense, that the search was no more intrusive than necessary to look for the suspected contraband, and that the search was reasonable in light of the student's age and sex. If absolutely necessary, a strip search of any kind should be performed by an adult of the same sex as the student. To protect both parties, schools may choose to require the presence of an adult witness, also of the same sex. To give proper notice to students and parents, school policies regarding personal searches should be publicized in student handbooks or in material that is similarly distributed.

V. Impact of an Illegal Search

An illegal search of a student may result in a civil suit based on a claim of damages for invasion of privacy. Apart from civil damage claims, however, the usual remedy for an illegal search is to prevent evidence thereby obtained from being used at a subsequent trial or hearing. This "exclusionary rule" may also apply to searches conducted by school officials. Because the Supreme Court found the search in *T.L.O.* to be valid under the Fourth Amendment, it did not decide whether the "exclusionary rule" would apply in the context of a search conducted by a school official. Although the state courts are split on this issue, the current rule in Texas is that a school may not use evidence obtained in violation of the Fourth Amendment to impose punishment on students.[9] Other states follow a similar rule.[10] Likewise, use of such evidence in a criminal proceeding would be prohibited. This underscores the fact that the Fourth Amendment exists to deter unlawful invasions by governmental officials. The "exclusionary rule" is seen as a method of deterring such invasions, and thereby upholding the values behind the amendment. Because the Supreme Court failed to rule on the issue in *T.L.O.*, school officials in Texas must realize that the exclusionary rule can be applied to both criminal and school disciplinary proceedings.

VI. Outside Police Involvement

Although the Supreme Court did not to rule on the issue in *T.L.O.*, in most cases where the municipal or county police are involved in a search, the higher probable cause standard will be required. Especially when the fruits of the search are to be used in a criminal prosecution, courts require a greater degree of certainty before a search can be conducted. Moreover, courts are attuned to the possibility that the police might allow school officials to conduct a search, being held to the lesser reasonableness standard, and then use the evidence found by the school officials in a later prosecution. Such an attempted subterfuge of the probable cause requirement will likely be scrutinized heavily by the courts. On the other hand, when the police are involved, but the purpose of the search is to enforce a school rule, courts will probably allow a search under the reasonableness standard.[11]

VII. Consent

A search is always permissible if consent is voluntarily given by the individual subject to the search.[12] Moreover, in cases involving school property such as lockers, some courts hold that the consent of school officials will suffice. Consent obtained by the parent or guardian of a student subject to a search should similarly be upheld. Therefore, before conducting any search, a serious effort should be undertaken to obtain voluntary consent from the student or others in a position to consent for him. Consent which is coerced or otherwise given involuntarily is inappropriate and will not justify a search.

VIII. Urinalysis

A few early student urinalysis cases frowned upon this practice without the existence of individualized suspicion. For example, in *Brooks v. East Chambers I.S.D.*[13], on Fourth Amendment grounds a federal district court enjoined the school district from implementing a drug testing program for all students who desired to participate in extracurricular activities. However, in *Vernonia School District v. Acton*, the U.S. Supreme Court held that a school district's policy that authorized random urinalysis testing of student athletes did not violate a student's right to be free from unreasonable searches.[14] Thus, the *Acton* case permits school districts to enact random urinalysis of students, at least with respect to athletes, where the school district can articulate a reasonable basis for the policy. The school district in *Acton* presented evidence of drug use by students as the basis for its policy; it is unclear whether a school district with no indication of student drug use could legally implement random urinalysis testing. Further, this issue has not been decided in other contexts, such as the student body at large. For the time being, the *Acton* decision applies only to student athletes.

IX. Policies and Handbooks

It is crucial for school districts to have specific policies governing searches of students and their personal effects. The policies should reflect the legal standards described above, and should refer to the reasonable suspicion standard for beginning a search. To ensure consistent application, search policies should be included as a part of periodic in-service training for school administrators.

In addition to being included in a school district's policy manual, search policies should be publicized in student handbooks or in some other material that is routinely given to students and their parents. In this way, students and parents are put on notice that searches may be performed when warranted by reasonable suspicion. As noted earlier, student handbooks may be used to notify students that school property such as lockers and desks may be searched for contraband. Student handbooks can also be used to explain school policies regarding the search of automobiles and other student property, and to explain any specific policies governing personal searches. Providing notice of search policies to students and parents can help prevent disputes about the validity of searches by school officials. However, the policies can also be used as ammunition if school officials fail to follow them. School administrators responsible for student discipline must be familiar with search policies, and must strive to apply them fairly and consistently.

X. Conclusion

School children have legitimate expectations of privacy that are protected by the Fourth Amendment. However, school officials, in fulfilling their duty to maintain a proper environment in which learning can take place, have the power to conduct reasonable searches of students under their authority. To ensure that a search does not violate the Fourth Amendment, the following procedures are recommended. Initially, before conducting a search, an official should have within his or her knowledge, from facts either observed personally or communicated by others whom the official knows to be reliable, reasonable suspicion that a search of a student or his property will uncover evidence of an infraction of a law or school rule. The student should always be asked to voluntarily consent to the search; if that consent is not forthcoming, then the student's parent or guardian should be contacted. The search should be aimed at uncovering evidence of the specific infraction the student is suspected of having committed; however, if other contraband is observed during the search, a further search is justified if the contraband constitutes reasonable grounds for believing another infraction has been committed. School officials should be sensitive to the intrusiveness of the search. The student's age and sex as well as the nature of the suspected infraction should be considered.

The Supreme Court noted in *T.L.O.* that the need to properly regulate the school environment demands an easing of Fourth Amendment restrictions so that school officials can supervise student conduct according to reason and common sense. As long as officials conduct searches according to this maxim, their supervision in the schools should be supported by the courts.

ENDNOTES

[1] New Jersey v. T.L.O., 105 S. Ct. 733 (1985).
[2] Beringer v. United States, 338 U.S. 160, 175 (1949).
[3] 105 S. Ct. at 740.
[4] *Id.*
[5] *See, e.g.*, Horton v. Goose Creek I.S.D., 690 F.2d 471 (5th Cir. 1982), *cert. denied*, 103 S. Ct. 3536 (1983); Jones v. Latexo I.S.D., 499 F. Supp. 223 (E.D. Tex. 1980).
[6] Horton v. Goose Creek I.S.D., *supra*; *see also* Bellvier v. Lund, 438 F. Supp. 47 (N.D.N.Y. 1977).
[7] *See* Horton v. Goose Creek I.S.D., *supra*, at e.n. 5.
[8] *Id.*
[9] Jones v. Latexo I.S.D., 499 F. Supp. at 237.
[10] *See, e.g.*, Morale v. Grigel, 422 F. Supp. 988 (D.N.H. 1976); Smyth v. Lubbers, 938 F. Supp. 777 (W.D. Mich. 1975).
[11] *See* Salazar v. Luty, 761 F. Supp. 45 (S.D. Tex. 1991). With regard to school-employed police, *see* Coronado v. State, 806 S.W.2d 302 (Tex. App.–Texarkana 1991) (this case imposes the reasonable suspicion standard on school, as opposed to outside, police officers.).
[12] Jones v. Latexo I.S.D., 499 F. Supp. at 239.
[13] 730 F. Supp. 759 (S.D. Tex. 1989).
[14] Vernonia Sch. Dist. v. Acton, 115 S. Ct. 2386 (1995).

EDUCATION OF CHILDREN WITH DISABILITIES

By: Christopher P. Borreca

I. Introduction

No other area of law related to the public education of students has expanded more rapidly and with more controversy and emotion than the education of children with disabilities. Since 1975, virtually every federal court in the United States has been faced with the responsibility of interpreting complex federal and state laws concerning school-age individuals with disabilities, the rights of those students, and the obligations owed to them by a public school system. This area of special education law has even developed into a specialty of its own, with many attorneys concentrating time in this field of practice to the exclusion of any other area of law. This fact has grown to be both a source of comfort as well as apprehension for parents and school administrators alike.

This is a complex and changing area of law. The purpose of this chapter will be to provide the reader with a basic overview of special education law, both federal and state, along with a review of several important case law milestones which have further defined the rights of children with disabilities. When faced with a situation which requires a detailed analysis of a school district's legal rights and responsibilities under the law, the prudent administrator is encouraged to consult his or her school attorney for further guidance. In fact, at press time, the Individuals With Disabilities Education Act (IDEA) and the Texas regulations pertaining to special education were being proposed for extensive revision. The reader is cautioned that subtle differences between the subject matter detailed in this chapter and current law may exist, due to the proposed changes. The current version of the IDEA (20 U.S.C. § 1401, *et seq.*), its implementing regulations (34 CFR Parts 300 and 301), and Texas State Board of Education Rules and Commissioner's Regulations, (19 TAC Chapter 89), should be consulted for further clarification.

II. The Individuals with Disabilities Education Act

A. Background

The Education for All Handicapped Children Act ("EAHCA") was passed by Congress and signed into law in 1975. The EAHCA has been amended several times and is now known as the Individuals with Disabilities Education Act ("IDEA"). The IDEA represents the most comprehensive statement by the federal government in the history of the United States concerning the rights of disabled children as related to public education. Prior to the IDEA's passage, however, several federal court decisions established a disabled child's right of access to a free appropriate public education, using an equal protection analysis similar to the reasoning used by the United States Supreme Court in *Brown v. Board of Education.*[1] In the first of these cases, *Pennsylvania Association for Retarded Children (PARC) v. Pennsylvania,*[2] a state association and a group of parents of children with mental retardation sought a declaratory judgment that several state statutes which excluded children with mental disabilities from programs of education and training in the public schools were unconstitutional. The court's decision was the first time a federal court recognized the right of children with mental disabilities to a *free appropriate public education* in the *least restrictive setting* possible. The court held that students with such disabilities must have equal access to the same education provided to other students, and that such education must be provided in a fashion most appropriate to the student's learning capacities. The court also recognized a procedural right to an impartial hearing which allowed parents to contest a school's classification or placement decision for their disabled child.

In the second major case which served as a precursor to the IDEA's enactment, *Mills v. Board of Education,*[3] another federal district court ordered the public schools of the District of Columbia to provide to each child of school age a free and suitable publicly-supported education, regardless of the degree of the child's mental, physical, or emotional disability or impairment. The *Mills* court also held that if no public school facilities could meet the needs of a student with disabilities, the school district must provide adequate alternative educational services. The judicial concepts of a right to a free appropriate public education for all disabled children, along with the guarantee of procedural due process, found their way into the main structure of the Act.

In direct response to the *PARC* and *Mills* decisions, and the string of litigation which they initiated across the country, Congress enacted the IDEA in 1975. It sets forth the federal requirement that all children with disabilities have access to a free appropriate public education. Congress intended to provide a nationwide, statute-based right for children with disabilities to be provided with equal access to the same educational opportunities as non-disabled children. Today, millions of children with disabilities who would not have had this opportunity without this legislation receive educational services.

Not all of Congress's original intentions for implementing the IDEA have developed into reality, however. It was originally intended that Congress would appropriate approximately 40% of the total costs necessary to implement the IDEA's provisions. In reality, the federal share of funding is currently approximately 8% of total costs, with state and local sources funding the remainder of the costs. Congress also intended that with the passage of the IDEA, parents would not have to resort to litigation to remedy their child's educational deprivation.[4] Ironically, the IDEA itself has spawned extensive litigation since its inception, as its language is clarified in the courts and the rights of children with disabilities evolve over time.

B. Specific Provisions of the IDEA

Under the IDEA, all children with disabilities between the ages of 3 to 21 are entitled to special education and related services necessary for them to benefit from educational programs. Some children are eligible for services from the time of birth. The IDEA specifically defines children eligible for services as those who have been identified with mental retardation, hearing impairments including deafness, speech or language impairments, visual impairments including blindness, serious emotional disturbance, orthopedic impairments, autism, traumatic brain injury, other health impairments, and specific learning disabilities. The IDEA's primary components include the requirements that individualized educational programs (IEPs) be designed for all children with disabilities and that such children be educated in the least restrictive environment *(i.e.*, with nondisabled children where possible) appropriate for the disabled child. For students aged 16 or above, the school district must include an individual transition plan to assist the child with entry into vocational skill development. Each school district is responsible for initiating and conducting meetings for purposes of developing, reviewing, and revising the IEP of a child with disabilities. In Texas, these meetings are known as Admission, Review, and Dismissal (ARD) meetings and the group of persons meeting is known as the ARD Committee.

If appropriate public education programs are not available for specific children, those children must be placed in private programs at public expense. The IDEA also guarantees extensive procedural rights in the evaluation and placement of children with disabilities. Parents who object to the school district's proposed IEP are guaranteed an impartial due process hearing. In Texas, either party can appeal the hearing officer's decision to state or federal court, where a civil suit can be filed.

Also embodied in the Act itself, and further defined by judicial opinions, are the concepts of "zero reject," "free appropriate public education," "extended year services," "related services," "least restrictive environment," and "due process procedural requirements." These concepts, and some of the judicial opinions which have refined them, are discussed below.

1. Zero Reject Concept

Intrinsic to the basic objectives of the IDEA is the obligation on the part of the public school district to identify and serve handicapped children who are not receiving an education, with priority being placed upon identifying the most severely handicapped children not being served.

Prior to the IDEA's passage, a school district could effectively deny services to a severely disabled student, on the basis that the child was not likely to derive any educational benefit from instructional services. Even after the Act's passage, educators grappled with the obligations presumably owed to profoundly handicapped individuals by public school districts. Judicial opinions have clarified this obligation. In the case of *Timothy W. v. Rochester School District,*[5] the IDEA's concept of "zero-reject" was firmly established. The student suffered from severe spasticity, cerebral palsy, brain damage, joint constractures, dislocated hips, scoliosis, cortical blindness, and quadriplegia. The lower court held that if a child is incapable of cognitive learning, he is not entitled to an individualized educational program under the IDEA. The First Circuit Court of Appeals disagreed and overturned the lower court's decision. The court wrote that the IDEA contains no requirement that a disabled child demonstrate that he could benefit from special education to be eligible to receive services. School districts cannot, therefore, impose an eligibility requirement of "educability" for disabled children seeking educational services.

A school district may provide a child with less than a regular school day, however, when the individual circumstances call for a reduction in the amount of instruction due to the child's unique needs. The Fifth Circuit Court of Appeals in *Christopher M. v. Corpus Christi Independent School District*[6] recently held that a four-hour school day for a severely disabled child was appropriate under the IDEA. The court held that it was appropriate to balance the disabled child's limited ability to benefit from more than a one-half day of instruction against the apparent pain and suffering he experienced from prolonged sensory stimulation in determining the appropriate program. The child suffered hyperextension, sweating, facial discoloration, breathing distress and fatigue when subjected to a full day of instruction. The shortened school day, therefore, was appropriate educationally for that particular child.

2. Free Appropriate Public Education

The primary requirement of the IDEA is to provide each disabled child with a free appropriate public education (FAPE) and the basic means for translating this requirement into reality is the child's IEP. The IEP is developed by the ARD Committee, which consists of the child's teacher, along with a representative of the school administration, the child's parents or guardians, and other persons depending on the specific needs of the child. The plan addresses the child's present abilities and special needs. It specifies objectives to be achieved and the support services and instruction necessary to reach those objectives. The IEP objectives are used as a means to plan and periodically re-evaluate the child's progress.

Courts have been swift, however, to dismiss any notion that a school district must *guarantee* the achievement of such objectives or that the failure to achieve such objectives translates into a breach of contract. In *McDowell v. Fort Bend Independent School District*,[7] the court held that proposed goals in an IEP did not mean substantive guarantees. The student's parents brought suit, alleging that, because the student had not reached a certain level of learning, the IEP failed, resulting in a violation of the IDEA and state law. The court disagreed, stating that the "failure or success of an educational program is not something that can be judged on a *res ipsa loquitur* theory of law; *i.e.* when a child does not succeed, the school must have failed to do its job." The court concluded that while there may be a state constitutional mandate of *equal educational opportunity*, such a mandate does not exist to guarantee *equal results*.

The U.S. Supreme Court, in *Hendrick Hudson District Board of Education v. Rowley*,[8] held that the FAPE requirement under the IDEA was intended "more to open the door of public education to handicapped children on appropriate terms than to guarantee any particular level of education once inside." The IDEA is meant to provide disabled children with a basic floor of educational opportunity. Finding that equal access was the IDEA's goal, the Supreme Court stated that the role of the judiciary is to first, determine whether the state has complied with the IDEA's procedural safeguards and second, determine whether the IEP is reasonably calculated to enable the child to receive educational benefits. The Supreme Court dodged the establishment of any one test for determining when a FAPE had been provided, but did enunciate a standard for regulating the content of education programs:

> Insofar as a State is required to provide a handicapped child with a "free appropriate public education," we hold that it satisfies this requirement by providing personalized instruction with sufficient support services to permit the child to benefit educationally from that instruction. Such instruction and services must be provided at public expense, must meet the State's educational stan-

> dards, must approximate the grade levels used in the state's regular education, and must comport with the child's IEP. In addition, the IEP, and therefore the personalized instruction, should be formulated in accordance with the requirements of the Act and, if the child is being educated in the regular classrooms of the public education system, should be reasonably calculated to enable the child to achieve passing marks and advance from grade to grade.

Unfortunately, the IDEA itself and the *Rowley* decision left open the question of how to measure educational benefit and how much benefit is required to provide a disabled child with a FAPE. Most courts presently evaluate the *Rowley* standard by assessing whether special education has produced *satisfactory* or *meaningful* progress toward achievement of a disabled child's unique educational needs. *See Board of Education v. Diamond*,[9] ("any benefit at all" test expressly rejected); *Hall ex rel. Hall v. Vance County Bd. of Educ.*,[10] (district can't discharge its duty by providing a program that produces only some trivial and minimal academic advancement); *In re Conklin*,[11] (where a child's progress is "de minimis," and where there is evidence that the potential exists for *more* than "de minimis" progress without undue burden to the school district, it is fair to infer that, due to deficiencies in the program offered, the school district failed to provide an "appropriate" education). The provision of a free appropriate public education remains at the center of the school district's obligations to a child with disabilities. Judicial opinions will continue to define this fairly nebulous provision under the IDEA.

3. Extended School Year Programs

Federal appellate courts have held that states cannot place artificial limitations on the number of days of instruction that can be provided for children with disabilities. In analyzing the need for summer services, courts have held that a child is entitled to an extended school year if it would be a *necessary*, not merely beneficial component of an appropriate education for the child. *See Rettig v. Kent City School District.*[12] Extended school year services should be provided if they would prevent severe and substantial regression of skills or knowledge retained by the child so as to seriously affect his progress toward self-sufficiency.

In the case of *Cordrey v. Euckert*,[13] the court held that the need for extended school year services should be demonstrated empirically, based on evidence of prior regression and slow recoupment of skills without summer programming. While citing the obvious advantages of "hard empirical proof," the court stated that only in the absence of such proof may the need for extended school year services be proven by expert opinion, based upon a professional individual assessment. The *Cordrey* court noted that this student's regression occurred throughout the entire regular school year and only minimal recoupment took place during that time period. The court was unpersuaded that lengthening the school year during the summer months would provide any substantially additional benefit.

The Fifth Circuit Court of Appeals, in *Alamo Heights Independent School District v. State Board of Education*,[14] provided a test for Texas school districts to use in considering the need for extended year services. The court framed the issue to be whether the child will experience severe or substantial regression during the summer months in the absence of a summer program. The court held that if the child benefits meaningfully within his potential from instruction under a proper IEP over a school year, extended school year services may not be required under the law, unless the benefits accrued during the regular school year will be significantly jeopardized if the child is not provided with such an extension.

4. Least Restrictive Environment

A cornerstone of the IDEA has been its strong imperative to provide instruction to students with disabilities in the least restrictive environment (LRE) with non-disabled children to the maximum extent appropriate for the disabled student. This requirement, of course, has generated a significant amount of controversy, as educators and courts have attempted to define what constitutes the LRE that is appropriate for a specific child. As the Fifth Circuit Court of Appeals noted in the case of *Daniel R.R. v. State Board of Education*,[15] the IDEA's mandate to provide *appropriate* programs for children with disabilities also qualifies and limits the school district's obligation to place children in regular classrooms. The *Daniel R.R.* decision basically established a two-part test to determine whether a child is being educated in the least restrictive environment. First, the court will inquire if the child can be provided a satisfactory education in the regular classroom with the help of supplemental aids and services. The Fifth Circuit held that while the school must make more than a token effort to supply supplementary aids and services, it need not try in every way imaginable to enable the child to continue in the regular education setting. If the child cannot be provided a satisfactory education in the regular classroom, the court will then ask if the child will be mainstreamed to the maximum extent appropriate at other non-academic times of the school day such as lunch and recess.

Courts called upon to evaluate a school district's compliance with the LRE requirement will make an individualized, fact-specific inquiry that requires them to examine carefully the nature and severity of the child's handicapping condition, his or her needs and abilities, and the school's response to the child's needs. If the court believes that the district has not made the effort to provide the child with supplementary aids and services and to modify the regular education program as necessary, the court's inquiry ends and the district will be found in non-compliance with the IDEA.

An examination of the facts of the *Daniel R.R.* case may help the reader understand the court's analysis. When this case arose, Daniel was a six year old boy with Down's Syndrome and a speech impediment. Daniel attended El Paso ISD in a half-day pre-kindergarten class with regular education students. In the school district's opinion, this placement was not successful. The teacher spent most of her time with Daniel and was unable to teach the other students. The teacher modified 90%-100% of the curriculum for Daniel. The district proposed placing Daniel in an early childhood class with other disabled children. Daniel would have lunch three days a week with non-disabled children if his mother were present. Daniel would also have contact with non-handicapped children during recess. The court found that mainstreaming into a regular education class was not appropriate in this case because it was inappropriate to modify the curriculum beyond recognition, the regular class did not offer Daniel educational benefit, and Daniel's presence in the regular pre-kindergarten class was unfair to other students because of the amount of extra time the teacher spent with Daniel. The court found that the school district's proposal offered an appropriate amount of mainstreaming for Daniel's individual needs.

In 1991, the Ninth Circuit Court of Appeals, in *Sacramento City Unified Sch. Dist. v. Holland*,[16] found that a child's placement in the segregated special education class, however, did not satisfy the Act's LRE requirement. That court held that the school district had not given sufficient consideration to placing the child in the regular classroom with supplemental aids and services, a concept also known as "inclusion." The court listed four factors to decide if a student has been educated in the least restrictive environment to the maximum extent appropriate: (1) the educational benefits available to the child in the regular classroom, supplemented with appropriate aids and services, as compared to the educational benefits of the special education classroom; (2) the non-academic benefits to the disabled child of interaction with non-disabled children; (3) the impact that educating the child with disabilities on the education of other students in the regular classroom; and (4) the cost of the supplemental aids and services necessary for the child to receive an appropriate education in the regular classroom. The court noted, however, that a school district must balance the needs of each disabled child against the needs of other children in the district. If the cost of educating a disabled child in a regular classroom is so great that it would significantly impact upon the education of other children in the district, then education in a regular classroom is not appropriate.

The Third Circuit Court of Appeals, in *Oberti v. Board of Education*,[17] also recently provided additional support for the concept of inclusion and for providing special education services to the disabled child in the regular classroom. The court required the New Jersey school district to make every possible accommodation to instruct a child with Down's Syndrome in the regular classroom. The court held that under the IDEA, segregated placement is not appropriate if the child can be educated satisfactorily with supplemental services and aids in his or her regularly assigned class. The court held that inclusion, while not specifically mentioned in the statute, is nonetheless a right under the IDEA's concept of least restrictive environment. The burden is on the school district to justify any segregated placement by a preponderance of the evidence.

This is an evolving area of the law. Educators, administrators, and attorneys are cautioned to pay close attention to the guidelines provided under the IDEA, as well as the interpretation of these guidelines by courts in various jurisdictions. The issue of what establishes a school district's compliance with providing an appropriate education in the least restrictive environment remains to be clearly defined.

5. Related Services

Related services are defined under the IDEA as transportation and such developmental, corrective, and other supportive services (including speech pathology and audiology, psychological services, physical and occupational therapy, and recreation) as may be required to assist a child with a disability to benefit from special education, and includes the early identification and assessment of disabling conditions in children. The above list is not all-inclusive, and Texas regulations further include art therapy, corrective therapy, interpreting services, music therapy, orientation and mobility instruction, and psychological services.

The disabled student's IEP must detail the related services to be used to meet the goals outlined in the plan. It is significant to note that the IDEA and the court cases construing the related services provisions hold that school districts are obligated to provide only those related services necessary or required for children with disabilities to benefit from education programs. For instance, in the case of *McNair v. Oak Hills Local School District*,[18] the court held that a school district was not required under the IDEA to provide special transportation for a hearing impaired child. While special transportation might be a related service in some circumstances, in this case the child exhibited no problems using the regular school transportation system and thus, had no educational need for transportation services.

Of particular concern to school districts are those services demanded by a parent which appear to be medical in nature and would traditionally be provided by a doctor or nurse. The case of *Irving Independent School District v. Tatro*,[19] is an example of such a situation. In that case, an eight year old student was unable to voluntarily empty her bladder and had to be catheterized every three to four hours. The catheterization required the assistance of a school nurse. The U.S. Supreme Court held that without such assistance, the student would be unable to attend school and would therefore be denied access to a free and appropriate public education.

Because the IDEA prohibits expenditure of public funds to pay for medical services, with the exception of those necessary for diagnostic or evaluative purposes, the nature of the services is examined before a court will require that any specific related service be provided. The two-part test as enunciated in *Tatro* is: (1) is the service a "supportive service required to assist a handicapped child to benefit from special education; and (2) is the service a medical service that goes beyond diagnosis or evaluation?" Medical services which must be performed by a physician are generally excluded. Medical services which can be performed by a layman or school nurse are generally acceptable under the related services provision, as long as they meet the two-part *Tatro* test. These services are more in the nature of school health services than medical services.

Because of the undefined nature of what constitutes "educational benefit" and the difficulty in proving that a particular related service is "necessary" to achieve such benefit, the area of related services has resulted in extensive litigation. In addition, the test for determining whether a service is medical, but not for diagnosis and evaluation, or whether it is a school health service remains unclear. These areas will likely remain the subject of continued litigation until there is further statutory definition of what constitutes a necessary related service.

6. Due Process Procedures

One of the most notable features of the IDEA is the extensive array of procedural "safety nets" provided to parents of students with disabilities. It is through these due process procedures that differences between school districts and parents are resolved. The U.S. Supreme Court, in *Rowley*, cautioned that the first step a court must take in evaluating whether a free appropriate public education has been offered is to examine a district's compliance with the procedural requirements of the IDEA. The procedural requirements, unfortunately, weave a veritable web of potential problems for the unwary district which may have the best intentions of providing an appropriate program but has overlooked a critical procedural step.

The primary procedural safeguards provided to parents under the IDEA consist of specific notice requirements, the opportunity to examine educational records, parental participation in the ARD process, consent prior to initial evaluation or initial placement in special education, and review procedures to enable a parent to appeal a decision of the child's ARD Committee. The prudent administrator will carefully evaluate the district's compliance with these procedural requirements before proceeding to a due process hearing upon the perceived strength of the substantive program to the child. Any violation of the procedural requirements of the IDEA may result in a finding that the school district failed to provide a child with a free appropriate public education. Some of the most notable features of the procedural requirements are discussed below.

The IDEA states that a school district must notify parents after an initial determination that their child needs special education and related services. Notice alone is not sufficient to satisfy the procedural safeguards; parental consent must be given prior to any initial action being taken. The IDEA states that consent is required whenever the educational agency wants to conduct a preplacement evaluation or make an initial placement in a special education program. The notice given to parents must be in writing and in a form which can be comprehended by an average citizen. If the parents do not speak English, the notice must be in their native language. If the parents refuse to consent to initial evaluation or the initial provision of special education services, the school district may ask for a hearing to override this lack of consent.

Each handicapped child's education must be tailored to the child's needs through an IEP. The IEP is to be prepared by the ARD Committee with parental involvement and approval, and must be reviewed annually. In conjunction with the requirements of parental involvement in the development and review of the IEP, the IDEA contains procedural safeguards to guarantee the rights of disabled children and their parents.

Notice must be given to parents prior to any proposed change or a refusal to initiate change of any service required by the IDEA. Additional notice provisions require that parents be fully informed of procedures under the IDEA as they affect their child.

Whenever a disagreement occurs, either the parents or the school district may request an impartial due process hearing conducted by an impartial due process hearing officer of the Texas Education Agency (TEA), who makes an independent decision. When a hearing is requested, it must be held and a written decision issued within forty-five (45) days of the initial request, unless the timeline is waived by the parties.

Once the hearing process is initiated, the parents must be informed of available services to aid them during the hearing process. At the hearing, the parents have the right to be accompanied by counsel. All hearing costs are paid by the educational agency, with the exception of attorneys' fees. The parties pay their own attorneys' fees and costs unless the parents prevail, in which case the school district must pay all or a portion of the parents' reasonable attorneys' fees and costs.

The IDEA requires that both parties have the right to present evidence and to cross-examine any witnesses of the opposite party. In Texas, regular evidentiary rules apply to the administrative proceedings. Under the IDEA, any evidence to be presented at the hearing must be disclosed to the opposing party at least five days prior to the hearing or be subject to exclusion.

A due process hearing officer appointed by the TEA will conduct the hearing. The express statutory requirement for hearing officers is that they must be impartial. In Texas, all special education hearing officers are attorneys. After the hearing, the hearing officer must prepare written findings of fact and a decision. Any party aggrieved by the findings and decision has a right to file a civil suit with respect to the complaint in state or federal court. This applies to school districts and parents alike.

Under the "stay-put" provision of the IDEA, the child is to remain in his or her current educational placement during the administrative and judicial proceedings. If the child is applying for admission to a public school, then he or she must be so placed until the administrative and/or judicial proceedings are final. Parental agreement is required for this, as previously discussed. If both the parents and the school district agree, the child can be placed in an alternative program pending resolution of the disputed issue.

The extensive due process procedures required under the IDEA serve a noble purpose, namely to provide a means to ensure that both the school district and parents alike can settle disputes fairly and that unfair advantage is not taken because of the relative amount of resources available to either party. To the unwary or the uninitiated, however, the requirements can be quite foreboding and potentially harmful. It is always wise for the district and its attorney to assess compliance with the procedural requirements before deciding whether to take a case to litigation.

7. Discipline of Children with Disabilities

The use of disciplinary techniques with children with disabilities requires an understanding of the due process procedures described above, the intricacies of the evaluation process and careful attention to the particularities of Texas regulations in this area. The Supreme Court, in *Honig v. Doe*,[20] eliminated all possibility that dangerous disabled students could be removed from school premises simply by using due process procedures applicable to non-disabled students. The Court held that a proposed removal of more than ten days (an expulsion) constitutes a change of placement and, thus, triggers the requirement that an ARD Committee convene and conduct an assessment of whether the disabled student's misconduct was caused by his or her disability, or was the result of an inappropriate placement. If the answer to either inquiry is yes, expulsion is not possible, and the district is obligated to provide an appropriate public education, taking the misbehavior into account in the IEP.

If the misbehavior is not caused by the disability, or an inappropriate placement, an expulsion may occur, however, educational programming must not cease during the course of the expulsion. This requirement had its origin in the case of *S-1 v. Turlington*.[21] It has now been applied to all school districts in the United States by the Office of Special Education Programs (OSEP) of the Department of Education.

The ARD Committee must act on current assessment data in making disciplinary determinations. If such data is not current, a court or hearing officer will likely rule that any disciplinary action taken violates the IDEA. It is not sufficient for the ARD Committee to merely determine that the student knows the difference between right and wrong or that the student is not seriously emotionally disturbed. Judgments cannot be based on label alone. There must be an individualized determination in each case of whether the student's particular disability caused the misbehavior in question. For the student with multiple disabilities, the district must conduct a linkage analysis for each of the student's disabling conditions.

The ARD Committee which convenes to determine the misbehavior-disability link must follow all procedural requirements of the IDEA. The parent must be involved in the decision-making. The parent may disagree with any decision made by the ARD committee, including a decision that the behavior was not caused by the disability, and request an appeal.

During the pendency of the appeal, the student must remain in his or her then current placement, unless the parties agree otherwise. This "stay put" provision applies even if the student is dangerous to himself or others. An exception now exists in the IDEA for the disabled student who brings a firearm to school. Such a student may be placed in an interim alternative setting for not more than forty-five (45) days by the ARD Committee.

The district is not, however, without recourse when faced with a disabled student who, although dangerous, has not brought a firearm to school. There is potential relief for the district from the "stay put" provision during the pendency of a due process hearing or appeal. Appropriate instructional methods such as detention or time-out can continue to be used if they do not constitute a change of placement. Disciplinary sanctions in the student's IEP may be imposed. A suspension of up to or less than ten days may be imposed, although in Texas, by state law, a suspension of only three consecutive days may be imposed. As a matter of last resort, the school district may attempt to obtain an injunction to change a dangerous student's placement during the appeal. Factors the court will consider include:

(1) Will the school district be irreparably harmed absent an injunction?
(2) Will the prospective injury to the school district outweigh injury the student will sustain as a result of the injunction?
(3) Will the school district succeed on the merits of the case on appeal?
(4) Will an injunction disserve the public interest?

This last resort is rarely used and should be attempted only after the parties have failed to agree to an alternative temporary placement, and a dangerous condition actually exists.

Finally, the Texas regulations pertaining to disciplinary procedures for children with disabilities are quite complex and should be reviewed in detail before attempting any discipline of a disabled student which might result in a change of placement. As of press time, these regulations were found at 19 TAC §§ 133.21-133.28a.

III. Section 504 of the Rehabilitation Act

Section 504 of the Rehabilitation Act of 1973 states,

No otherwise qualified individual with a disability . . . shall, solely by reason of her or his disability, be excluded from the participation in, be denied the benefits of, or be subjected to discrimination under any program or activity receiving Federal financial assistance . . . ."

Under this statute, no school district that provides public education to its children can discriminate against any child with disabilities who resides within its jurisdiction. Section 504 provides an independent source of rights for children with disabilities in addition to the IDEA. Unlike the IDEA, which promises funds to school districts that comply with its regulations for educating disabled children, Section 504 is a civil rights, nondiscrimination statute. It provides no funding. Section 504 is enforced by the United States Department of Education's Office of Civil Rights (OCR), as well as state and federal courts.

Section 504 provides many of the same procedural safeguards and guarantees as are provided under the IDEA. School districts must undertake to identify and locate every qualified disabled person in the district's jurisdiction who is not receiving a public education. Districts shall provide a FAPE to each qualified disabled person within the jurisdiction, regardless of the nature and severity of the disabling condition. Appropriate education is defined as the provision of regular or special education and related services that are designed to meet individual educational needs as adequately as the needs of non-handicapped persons are met. Section 504 also provides for evaluation and placement procedures which shall (1) draw upon information from a variety of sources, including aptitude and achievement tests, teacher recommendations, physical condition, social or cultural background, and adaptive behavior; (2) establish procedures to ensure that information obtained from all such sources is documented and carefully considered; (3) ensure that the placement decision is made by a group of persons, including persons knowledgeable about the child, the meaning of the evaluation and the placement options; and (4) ensure that the placement decision is made in the least restrictive environment. Discrimination is also prohibited in nonacademic and extracurricular services and activities, including counseling services and athletics.

School districts are cautioned that the reach of Section 504 extends not only to students who possess the thirteen handicapping conditions listed under the IDEA, but may also include students with conditions such as Attention Deficit Disorder ("ADD") or Tourette's Syndrome *if* such students meet the definition of "disabled person," namely a person who:

(1) Has a mental or physical impairment that substantially limits one or more major life activities; or
(2) has a record of such an impairment; or
(3) is regarded as having such an impairment.

Despite the fact that Section 504 was enacted in 1973, the effects of the statute are evolving constantly, and school districts must be constantly aware of their obligations under this statute. Careful attention to Office of Civil Rights decisions and letter memoranda is essential. District officials are especially cautioned to consider Section 504 eligibility when implementing any disciplinary technique for a student who might be considered disabled under Section 504 but who is not served under the IDEA.

IV. Conclusion

Statutes mandating the provision of educational services to children with disabilities have been one of the greatest achievements of state and federal legislation. All children have benefited greatly from the inclusion of disabled students in the regular classrooms. Students who cannot be served in the regular classroom may receive appropriate programming in alternative settings. School districts have worked admirably alongside parents and advocacy organizations to ensure that legal rights are upheld and public responsibilities are fulfilled.

The gains of disabled students, however, have not come without some costs, both monetary and otherwise. The federal government has yet to fulfill its original intent of assuming a much greater share of the funding of the IDEA's mandates. The due process procedures mandated under the Act have too often turned districts and parents into adversaries, when joint cooperation might have resulted in more positive results. With the advent of the Handicapped Children's Protection Act of 1990, parents may now receive all or a portion of their attorneys' fees if they prevail in their legal disputes with school districts concerning their disabled children. This change in the law has created greater access to the due process procedures for many parents who were otherwise excluded from asserting their rights. The possibility of attorneys' fee awards, unfortunately, has also spawned a new generation of "disability rights advocates," sometimes more motivated by the possibility of personal financial gain than by obtaining rights for their clients under the IDEA.

For many of these reasons, changes to the IDEA are currently being proposed in Congress, including mandatory mediation and sanctions imposed upon parties who unnecessarily resist reasonable settlement of disputes or protract litigation. The reauthorization of the IDEA in upcoming years will no doubt bring additional changes to the educational rights of children with disabilities and the responsibilities of public school districts. Despite the fine-tuning which may be necessary, however, what is "good" about the IDEA far outweighs what is "bad." School districts can take pride in implementing what is historically the most comprehensive, responsible, and civilized public system of educating children with disabilities.

ENDNOTES

[1] 347 U.S. 483 (1954).
[2] 343 F. Supp. 279 (E.D. Pa. 1972).
[3] 348 F. Supp. 866 (D.D.C. 1972).
[4] S. Rep. No. 168, 94th Cong., 1st Sess. 7-9 (1975), *reprinted in* 1975 U.S.C.C.A.N. 1425, 1431-33.
[5] 875 F.2d 954 (1st Cir.), *cert. denied*, 493 U.S. 983 (1989).
[6] 933 F.2d 1285 (5th Cir. 1991).
[7] 737 F. Supp. 386 (S.D. Tex. 1990).
[8] 458 U.S. 176 (1982).

[9] 808 F.2d 987 (3d Cir. 1986).
[10] 774 F.2d 629 (4th Cir. 1985).
[11] 946 F.2d 306 (4th Cir. 1991).
[12] 539 F. Supp. 768, 778 (N.D. Ohio 1981), *aff'd in part and vacated in part on other grounds* 720 F.2d 463 (6th Cir. 1983).
[13] 917 F.2d 1460 (6th Cir. 1990), *cert. denied*, 111 S. Ct. 1391 (1991).
[14] 790 F.2d 1153 (5th Cir. 1986).
[15] 874 F.2d 1036 (5th Cir. 1989).
[16] 14 F.3d 1398 (9th Cir. 1994).
[17] 995 F.2d 1204 (3rd Cir. 1993).
[18] 872 F.2d 153 (6th Cir. 1989).
[19] 468 U.S. 883 (1984).
[20] 108 S. Ct. 592 (1988).
[21] 635 F.2d 342 (5th Cir.), *cert. denied*, 454 U.S. 1030 (1981).

ATTENDANCE, RESIDENCY, AND ABSENCES

By: Jennifer W. Jacobs

I. Introduction

This chapter will address issues faced by public school districts regarding students' attendance. In particular, this chapter reviews when the child must attend school (see Section II–Attendance), where the child may attend tuition-free (see Section III–Residency), and what consequences can be imposed for absences (see Section IV–Absences).

II. Attendance

The Texas Education Code and the Texas Administrative Code contain numerous specific laws about attendance in Texas public schools. Eligibility to attend Texas public schools is governed by Texas Education Code § 25.001. Students who are five years of age or older and under twenty-one years of age on the first day of September of any school are eligible to attend.[1]

Compulsory student attendance is addressed by Texas Education Code § 25.085, *et seq*. The age guidelines for compulsory attendance are defined differently than the age parameters for free attendance. Children who are at least six years of age, or less than six and have previously been enrolled in the first grade, and who have not completed the academic year in which the seventeenth birthday has occurred, are required to attend school. Exemptions from the mandatory attendance requirement are found in § 25.086 of the Texas Education Code and include: (1) children attending a private or parochial school; (2) certain handicapped children; (3) children with a temporary physical or mental condition requiring absence; (4) children expelled from school; and (5) seventeen year olds who have graduated or who are enrolled in a class for a high school equivalency examination.

The school attendance officer enforces the compulsory attendance laws. Texas Education Code § 25.088 governs the selection of an attendance officer, and Section 25.091 enumerates the powers and duties of the attendance officer.

Criminal sanctions exist for the violation of the mandatory attendance law. Section 25.093 of the Education Code provides that a parent is guilty of a class C misdemeanor for failing to require a child to attend school. Under Section 25.094, a child may also be found guilty of a class C misdemeanor for failing to attend school.

In addition to statutory law governing attendance, school district officials should be aware of the United States Supreme Court decision in *Plyler v. Doe*.[2] *Plyler* involved the decision of the Tyler Independent School District to charge tuition for the education for all children who were unable to document the legality of their residence in the United States. The Supreme Court found that this requirement, based on former Texas Education Code § 21.031, violated the equal protection clause of the United States Constitution. Accordingly, illegal aliens must be provided a tuition-free education if they can document their residence in the school district.

III. Residency

A child who resides within the boundaries of a district with his or her parent or legal guardian may attend the district's schools tuition-free.[3] Problems arise for districts when children reside in a district with someone who is not the child's natural parent or legal guardian. This situation frequently arises under several different circumstances: (1) where the child's parents are missing, in jail, or not able to care for the child, and the child lives with a relative or friend without the benefit of a legal custody proceeding; (2) when a high school student lives with a host family when his or her parents move out of the district; (3) when a student lives independently before age eighteen; or (4) when a student claims to live in the district Monday through Friday, but elsewhere on the weekends. Deciding whether to allow these children to attend schools tuition-free presents two questions for the district: (1) can these children attend the schools tuition-free; and (2) if so, what are the consequences for the district?

For years, Texas courts held that public schools may require a child to live with a parent or legal guardian to attend school without paying tuition. As a result of recent legislative changes and court decisions, this policy has changed. At publication time for this book, a student can live separate from a parent or guardian and attend tuition-free, so long as the student does not live apart from his or her parents for the purpose of participating in extracurricular activities. This section will review the relevant section of the Texas Education Code, recent legislative changes, and various state courts' interpretations of the Education Code requirements for residency.

Section 25.001 of the Texas Education Code establishes the admission and residency requirements of the Texas public schools. Section 25.001(a) and (b) provides that the board of trustees of any free public school shall admit into school free of tuition all persons between the ages of five and twenty-one, if such person or his parent, guardian, or person having lawful control resides within the school district boundaries. The United States Supreme Court has approved such residency requirements in the field of public education, so long as the requirements are appropriately defined and uniformly applied.[4]

The United States Supreme Court has not considered the question of whether a school district may require the child's guardian in the district to acquire permanent legal guardianship or managing conservatorship as a condition of the child's enrollment. This practice had been approved for years by the Texas state courts,[5] but was recently disapproved by a federal court in the Eastern District of Texas.[6] The changes in the law in 1992 now restrict a district's ability to exclude students who live apart from a parent or guardian.

According to Texas Education Code § 25.001(d), a child who lives apart from parents or guardians has the right to attend school where the child resides, so long as the child does not live in the district for the primary purpose of participating in extracurricular activities. School districts can no longer require a student to live with a parent or legal guardian to attend school in the district where the student resides.

In 1995, the Texas Legislature amended the residency statute to provide specified circumstances when a district can deny admission to a student who lives apart from his or her parent or guardian. Under Texas Education Code § 25.001(d)(1), if the student has engaged in conduct or misbehavior within the preceding year that has resulted in a removal to an alternative education program or an expulsion, the district is not compelled to enroll that student. As of the date of publication, this exception applies only to students who live separate and apart from their parents or guardians.

For any student not living with his or her parent or legal guardian, the district should investigate the circumstances of why the child resides in your district. The district should gather information to establish whether the child lives in the district for purposes other than participating in extracurricular activities. If the student's answers reveal that the child is in the district for the primary purpose of participating in extracurricular activities, admission can be denied, subject to appeal to the school board. The school district can also inquire about whether the student lives in the district full-time, if the student drives into the district, and where he or she really resides fulltime. If the student truly resides elsewhere, the student may be denied the right to attend school in your district.

Once the district has determined that the child can attend schools in the district on a tuition-free basis, some practical problems may arise for the district if the child does not live with his or her parent or legal guardian. Examples of these practical problems include:

1. Who can sign a field trip permission slip?
2. Who can consent to medical care?

3. Who is responsible for the child's expenses (student fees, destruction of books, etc.)?
4. Who is responsible for the child's attendance?
5. Who is the "parent" for special education proceedings?

As a general matter, the author suggests that the district try to contact the legal guardian or parent of a child when an issue arises regarding the child. Letters should be sent by certified mail, return receipt requested, and copies of these letters and notes of attempts to contact the parent should be retained in the student's file. In the event that the district cannot locate the parent or the parent does not respond to letters, then the district has no choice but to work with the responsible adult with whom the child resides. The district may ask this adult to sign for field trips, and to be responsible for the child for attendance, discipline, and grade reporting.

Section 32.001 of the Texas Family Code governs who may consent to medical care of a minor. Any of the following persons may consent to medical treatment when the person with power to consent cannot be contacted and that person has not given actual notice to the contrary:

1. a grandparent,
2. an adult sibling,
3. an adult aunt and uncle,
4. an educational institution with a valid authorization form from the person having the power to consent, or
5. any adult who has care and control of the child and has valid authorization from the person having the power to consent.

Unless there is a court order to the contrary, school administrators should always first try to reach a parent regarding medical care. If the parents are divorced, the district should attempt to contact the managing conservator (*i.e.*, the parent who has custody of the child) unless there is a court order to the contrary. If a parent cannot be reached, then the school can contact a grandparent, adult sibling, or adult aunt or uncle. These persons may consent to medical care and do not need any written authorization from the person having the power to consent. For an adult with care and control of the minor or an educational institution to consent to medical care, the person or school must have a valid authorization. A valid authorization is a written consent signed by someone with power to consent. The district should not consent to medical care unless the authorization to consent is signed by a legal guardian or authorized parent.

There are certain circumstances under which a minor can consent to medical care. These circumstances are outlined in Section 32.003 of the Family Code, and they generally relate to treatment for sexually transmitted diseases or chemical dependency. This provision is of greater concern to the treating physician than to the school district.

IV. Absences

Texas Education Code § 25.087 governs student absences. A child may be excused from the compulsory attendance law for "temporary absence resulting from any cause acceptable to the teacher, principal or superintendent."[7] Districts are required to excuse students from school for religious holy days.[8] Schools shall also excuse a student for a temporary absence resulting from appointments with health care professionals if that student commences or returns to school on the same day of the appointment.[9] Students whose absences are excused shall be allowed a reasonable time to make up work.

A student may not be given credit for a class if the student attends school less than ninety percent (90%) of the days the class is offered, unless there are extenuating circumstances.[10] Each district is required to have attendance committees to determine what constitutes extenuating circumstances. Classroom teachers should comprise a majority of the membership of the attendance committee. The district's school board shall establish guidelines to determine what constitutes extenuating circumstances. A student who is denied credit may appeal the attendance committee's decision to the school board. The decision of the board may be appealed by trial *de novo* to the district court.

V. Conclusion

Student attendance and residency statutes have changed significantly in recent years. The old preconception that a student can be denied admission if he or she does not live with his or her parents or guardians is no longer applicable. Careful consideration should be given to the new laws before making a decision on the admission of a student. Further, absences must be reviewed more scrupulously to determine whether a student can be given course credit. In extreme cases, attendance committees must decide this issue. If an individual case falls within the gray areas of these new laws, the author suggests seeking the counsel of your school attorney.

ENDNOTES

[1] Tex. Educ. Code § 25.001(a).
[2] 457 U.S. 202 (1982).
[3] Tex. Educ. Code § 25.001(b)(1).
[4] Vlandis v. Kline, 412 U.S. 441 (1973); Martinez v. Bynum, 461 U.S. 321 (1983).

[5] Rodriguez v. Ysleta Indep. Sch. Dist., 663 S.W.2d 547 (Tex. App.–El Paso 1983, *no writ*) and Jackson v. Waco Indep. Sch. Dist., 629 S.W.2d 201 (Tex. App.–Waco 1982, *writ ref'd n.r.e.*).
[6] Byrd v. Livingston Indep. Sch. Dist., 674 F. Supp. 225 (E.D. Tex. 1987).
[7] Tex. Educ. Code § 25.087(a).
[8] Tex. Educ. Code § 25.087(b).
[9] Tex. Educ. Code § 25.087(b).
[10] Tex. Educ. Code § 25.092.

SEXUAL ABUSE OR HARASSMENT OF STUDENTS

By: Raymond L. Gregory

I. INTRODUCTION

Unquestionably, our schools have become increasingly dangerous. Schools were formerly safe havens for students, where a student's greatest fears were crossing the school bully and not having a date to the prom. Those times are long gone. In present times, students fear for their physical well-being as gangs and weapons become commonplace. Even more distressing are acts of sexual abuse or harassment perpetrated on unwitting students by school employees or fellow students. This change in the school environment has created an increase in litigation filed by students who have been victimized by sexual abuse or harassment in the school environment.

Litigation in this area typically arises under facts similar to the following scenarios. A female student is befriended by a school teacher. The teacher's interest becomes more than simply a desire to assist the student in her school work. At the urging of the employee, an amorous relationship commences. After the breakup of the relationship several months later, the student and her family bring suit against the school district, district supervisory officials, and the teacher, alleging the violation of federal law. Or, a student regularly rides the school bus to campus. Over the course of the school year, a student of the opposite sex begins to taunt the student with sexually suggestive comments. Offended by the comments, the student reports the abuse to the bus driver, who fails to control discipline on the bus. Eventually, the taunting rises to a level such that the student is ostracized by his or her peers and is forced to stop riding the bus. The student and his or her family bring suit against the school district and supervisory officials for violation of federal law.

Litigation in this area raises several interesting questions, as courts attempt to balance the rights of students against the supervisory demands placed on school officials. Can school districts be held liable for the actions of their students, over whom school officials exercise only minimal control? Furthermore, can school districts and supervisory officials be held liable for the actions of their employees, particularly when employees step over the line and commit acts of sexual abuse toward students? This chapter will review the recent litigation in this area, with an emphasis on cases which speak specifically to sexual abuse or harassment perpetrated by employees and students in the school environment.

II. Employee-to-Student Abuse or Harassment

A. Claims Under Section 1983

1. Background of Litigation Under Section 1983

Most of the reported cases involving the sexual abuse or harassment of students by employees arise under 42 U.S.C. § 1983 ("Section 1983"). Section 1983 is the federal statute that provides recourse for an individual who has suffered a deprivation of his or her constitutional or statutory rights at the hands of persons acting under color of state law.[1] To recover under Section 1983, the plaintiff must prove two elements:

(a) the conduct complained of was committed by a person acting under color of state law; and,

(b) the conduct deprived the plaintiff of rights, privileges, and immunities secured by the Constitution and laws of the United States.[2]

Section 1983 is used in a variety of suits brought against governmental entities and officials, including school districts and school employees. A school employee who engages in unwelcome sexual relations with a student is subject to Section 1983 liability, because that type of conduct violates the student's right to bodily integrity recognized under the Due Process Clause of the Fourteenth Amendment to the United States Constitution.[3] In addition to targeting the employee/perpetrator, however, the resulting lawsuits generally target school districts, high-level school administrators, and other potential "deep-pocket" defendants. The relevant question, thus, is whether these entities and officials can be held liable for their subordinates' deprivation of a student's constitutional rights.[4]

2. A School District's Liability Under Section 1983 For The Acts Of Its Employees

In a line of cases beginning with *Monell v. Department of Social Services.*,[5] courts have refused to impose strict liability against governmental entities for the wrongful acts of their employees.[6] This line of reasoning was affirmed by the United States Supreme Court in *Jett v. Dallas Indep. Sch. Dist.*[7] Thus, a local governing body cannot be held liable for constitutional violations merely because one of its employees committed an illegal act. To be held liable under Section 1983, a school district must have somehow permitted or furthered the illegal act through its own policies or practices.[8]

As mentioned above, a Section 1983 plaintiff must prove that he or she was injured by a person acting under color of state law and that the injury constituted a deprivation of a constitutional right. To prevail against a governmental entity, such as a school district, the plaintiff bears the burden of establishing that the violation was caused by an unconstitutional *policy* or *custom* sanctioned by governmental officials who have final policy-making authority.[9] This requirement means that a plaintiff must establish that the school district's governing board actually adopted an unconstitutional policy, or that the school board otherwise knew about or acquiesced in a deeply imbedded custom or practice that resulted in a constitutional violation.[10]

a. Liability In Cases Involving Sexual Abuse Or Harassment

The leading case regarding school district liability in situations involving sexual abuse or harassment of students by employees is *Gonzalez v. Ysleta Indep. Sch. Dist.*[11] In that case, a student complained of sexual abuse by her teacher, and the complaints were specifically considered by the local school board. As a result of the complaints, the school district conducted an investigation, transferred the teacher to a new campus, and directed the teacher to seek counseling. About two years after the transfer, the teacher sexually assaulted another student. Thereafter, the teacher was convicted on charges of indecency with a child and ultimately was fired from his job.

The second student later filed a civil suit against the school district. At trial, the jury found in favor of the student and awarded her damages of $500,000.00. The school district argued in a post-verdict motion, which ultimately was denied, that it was liable for the student's injuries only if the decision made by the school board (*i.e.*, to order the teacher to seek counseling and to transfer the teacher) manifested *deliberate indifference* to the constitutional rights of the child.

On appeal, the United States Court of Appeals for the Fifth Circuit held that under *Jett v. Dallas Indep. Sch. Dist.* and other prevailing authorities, the school district's board of trustees was responsible for determining school policy.[12] The Fifth Circuit also held that the school board's conscious decision to transfer the teacher, as opposed to employing other disciplinary techniques, was a *policy* decision attributable to the school district. The school district argued that, nevertheless, the plaintiff had the burdensome requirement of proving that the school board *deliberately* chose measures that would prove inadequate. Thus, under the school district's reasoning, Section 1983 would provide a remedy only if the school board's decision was made with *deliberate indifference* to the student's constitutional rights.

The Fifth Circuit agreed with the school district and held that Gonzalez' claim required a showing of deliberate indifference prior to holding the district liable for any allegedly mistaken personnel decision:

> We do hold, however, that YISD may be held liable in this case *only* if the Board of Trustees' decision to transfer [the teacher] to [the student's] elementary school manifested a *deliberate indifference* to the welfare of school children.[13]

The court went on to conclude that the trial evidence was insufficient to sustain the jury's verdict under this standard.

The bottom-line result of *Gonzalez* and other cases dealing with sexual abuse of students by employees is that a plaintiff must demonstrate *deliberate indifference* by the local school board as a basis for recovery under Section 1983.[14] To avoid liability under Section 1983, school districts should be able to demonstrate that they are not deliberately indifferent to the rights of their students. The safest and easiest way to accomplish this goal is to take every report of sexual abuse or harassment seriously and conduct a thorough investigation of each reported incident.

b. Liability For Failure To Properly Train

Many plaintiffs in cases involving sexual abuse or harassment also assert a *failure to train* cause of action under Section 1983. Typically, plaintiffs will allege that the school district failed to train its students, teachers, and administrators in the reporting and investigation of sexual abuse or harassment, knowing that this failure to train would lead to a violation of students' constitutional rights.

Courts have recognized *failure to train* claims under Section 1983 since the United States Supreme Court's decision in *City of Canton v. Harris*.[15] In that case, the Supreme Court held that a municipality may be held liable under Section 1983 based on failure to train its employees. The Court further held, however, that such liability will be imposed only where the failure to train amounts to deliberate indifference to the rights of the citizens affected. Two cases involving failure to train claims brought against school districts are *Thelma D. v. Board of Educ.* and *Jane Doe A. v. Special Sch. Dist.*

In *Thelma D.*,[16] the plaintiffs contended that the local school board had a custom of failing to afford training for the detection and investigation of alleged incidents of child abuse. The United States Court of Appeals for the Eighth Circuit, relying on *City of Canton v. Harris*, held that the plaintiffs had the burden of establishing that the school board knew its procedures were inadequate and would likely result in a violation of students' constitutional rights. In rejecting the plaintiffs' claims, the Eighth Circuit recognized that the school district had developed and implemented policies and procedures for handling complaints of sexual abuse. Furthermore, the school district had implemented various programs to instruct principals on laws and reporting procedures, and to train school employees in detecting and investigating incidents of child abuse. Also, the school district employed social workers trained in the detection and prevention of child abuse. Based on this evidence, the court concluded that the plaintiffs had not sufficiently established deliberate indifference on the part of the school board to impose liability based on a failure to train theory.[17]

In *Jane Doe A.*,[18] the plaintiff argued that the school district was guilty of deliberate indifference to the rights of handicapped children due to an inadequate training program for bus drivers, teachers, supervisors, and bus aides with respect to child abuse. The Eighth Circuit held that the plaintiffs failed to raise a material fact issue of deliberate indifference, and absolved the district on the failure to train claim.

To avoid Section 1983 liability based on failure to train, school districts should enact policies for reporting and investigating incidents of alleged sexual abuse or harassment; design and enact programs to train their students in the reporting of sexual abuse and harassment; and, design and enact programs to train their teachers and administrators in the reporting and investigation of sexual abuse and harassment. All school personnel should be periodically reminded of their obligation to report any suspected child abuse to the authorities in accordance with the requirements of the Texas Family Code.

3. Supervisory Officials' Liability Under Section 1983

In addition to suing school districts for violation of Section 1983, plaintiffs typically join high-level school administrators, such as superintendents and principals, as defendants. The leading case in this area is *Doe v. Taylor Indep. Sch. Dist.*,[19] wherein the United States Court of Appeals for the Fifth Circuit established the legal standard for finding a supervisor liable under Section 1983 for the wrongful conduct of a subordinate.

To recover from supervisory officials, a plaintiff must establish that:

(a) The defendant learned of facts or a pattern of inappropriate sexual behavior by a subordinate pointing plainly toward the conclusion that the subordinate was sexually abusing a student;

(b) The defendant demonstrated deliberate indifference toward the constitutional rights of the student by failing to take action that was necessary to prevent or stop the abuse; and

(c) The defendant's failure to take action caused a constitutional injury to the student.[20]

To avoid individual liability under Section 1983, supervisory school officials should take every report of sexual abuse or harassment seriously and conduct a thorough investigation of each reported incident. Both the report and the investigation should be documented in writing. Following each investigation, supervisory officials should take whatever action is necessary to prevent or stop the abuse. Possible actions can range from an official directive to cease the offensive conduct to the initiation of termination proceedings.

B. Claims Under Title IX

1. Evolution Of Title IX Claims

In addition to claims under Section 1983, most of the reported decisions involving sexual abuse or harassment of students, particularly the more recent cases, involve claims under Title IX of the Education Amendments of 1972.[21] Title IX claims stem from the United States Supreme Court's decision in *Franklin v. Gwinnett County Pub. Schs.*,[22] wherein the Court held that Title IX provides a damages remedy, in limited cases, for sexual harassment and abuse of students. The Court in *Franklin* held that a student's ability to recover monetary damages in Title IX cases is limited to those cases where the student can show intentional, gender-based discrimination by the local school board.

2. History of Title IX

The United States Congress enacted Title IX[23] pursuant to the Spending Clause in the United States Constitution[24] to proscribe gender-based discrimination in educational programs and activities receiving federal financial assistance. Legislation enacted under the Spending Clause is in the nature of a contract: in return for federal funds, the various states agree to comply with federally imposed conditions.[25] Because the receipt of federal funds is consensual, not mandatory, the United States Supreme Court has held that the *recipient* of federal funds should not be held liable for damages absent notice that it is committing some act in violation of the federal requirements.[26] In reaching this conclusion, Justice White noted that courts must recognize and respect the privilege of a recipient to withdraw from a program and terminate its receipt of funds rather than assume the further obligations and duties imposed by the courts.[27]

The legislative history and text of Title IX demonstrate that its purpose is to prohibit *institutional* practices of gender-based discrimination.[28] During floor debates, representatives spoke of discriminatory *policies*.[29] The Supreme Court explained that Congress "wanted to avoid the use of federal resources to support discriminatory *practices*."[30] Similarly, in *Floyd v. Waiters*,[31] the court held that the language of Title IX is aimed at discrimination in a "program or activity," not random assaults.

As can be seen from the text and history of Title IX and its regulations,[32] Title IX does not unambiguously create a damages remedy for employee-to-student harassment. There is no authority or legislative history demonstrating that Congress intended to expose school districts to unlimited liability based on the unauthorized acts of an unlimited pool of potential tort-feasors (*i.e.*, all district employees and students). Nevertheless, the *Franklin* decision indicates that students may sue school districts for damages under Title IX for acts of sexual abuse or harassment.

3. School District Liability Under Title IX For Sexual Abuse Or Harassment

To remain true to the history and intent of Title IX, a Title IX plaintiff must demonstrate intentional, gender-based discrimination by the school board to recover.[33] As the court explained in *Howard v. Board of Educ.*, the "threshold" issue in a Title IX lawsuit is whether the entity receiving the federal aid actually participated in the discriminatory act:

> Absent knowledge or direct involvement by the school or educational agency, it is difficult to characterize any form of sexual discrimination as an authorized program or activity of the school. Moreover, it is difficult to imagine that Congress intended to open schools and educational agencies to virtually unlimited liability based on the conduct of their employees.[34]

To meet the intentional discrimination standard, a Title IX plaintiff must show that the school district or institution actually intended to discriminate against the student; it is insufficient for the plaintiff merely to show that the institution knew or should have known of the sexual harassment and failed to take appropriate corrective action.[35] In addition, the plaintiff must attribute the intentional gender-based discrimination to the institution's decision-maker (*i.e.*, the school board) to recover under Title IX. [36]

In the few reported post-*Franklin* decisions addressing whether sexual abuse or harassment of students by employees violates Title IX, courts have refused to impose liability without a showing of *intentional discrimination* by the local school board. For example, in *R.L.R. v. Prague Public Sch. Dist.*, the court held that the plaintiff, an eighth grade student who was sexually involved with her coach, could not prevail under Title IX because she did not present any evidence showing a pattern of discrimination, much less intentional discrimination.[37] Likewise, in *Floyd v. Waiters*, the court refused to impose liability against the school district because even if the actions of two security guards in assaulting students constituted sexual discrimination, the local school board was not involved in the discrimination. Therefore, the court could not find intentional discrimination by the district's decision-maker.[38] Finally, in *Doe v. Petaluma City Sch. Dist.*, the court rejected the plaintiff's argument that she need only show that the district knew or should have known of discrimination against her. The court dismissed the plaintiff's complaint pursuant to Federal Rule of Civil Procedure 12 because there were no allegations of intentional discrimination by the school board. Thus, the plaintiff had failed to plead a cause of action.[39] It is clear, therefore, that to recover under Title IX, a plaintiff must meet the burdensome task of showing intentional, gender-based discrimination by the local school board.

4. Common Law Agency Principles Do Not Apply

Many plaintiffs claim that courts should, in determining whether school districts are liable for the sexual abuse or harassment of students by employees, follow the procedures and standards of Title VII of the Civil Rights Act of 1964.[40] Under Title VII, common law agency principles govern when an employer is liable for sexual abuse or harassment committed by its employees. However, logic and prevailing law dictate that Title VII principles do not apply to Title IX cases.[41]

While isolated decisions have applied Title VII principles in Title IX cases, differences in the statutes preclude wholesale adoption of Title VII standards in a Title IX case. First, Title VII defines "employer" to include the employer's "agents."[42] Conversely, Title IX prohibits discrimination on the basis of sex under an education "program or activity" receiving federal financial assistance.[43] The statutory definition of "program or activity" relates to operations, not personnel.[44]

Second, Title VII places a statutory ceiling on damages.[45] In contrast, Title IX contains no statutory limitation. If the typical plaintiff's analysis of Title IX liability were adopted, financially strapped school districts could face greater exposure under Title IX than large corporations face under Title VII.

Third, a Title VII plaintiff in Texas must bring an administrative claim within three hundred (300) days of the discriminatory act. This protects employers from having to defend against stale claims. In contrast, Title IX contains no statute of limitations; rather, students are subject to the personal injury limitations period created by state law. In Texas, the two-year limitations period is tolled for minors until they reached the age of majority.[46] Thus, for example, a high school girl who alleges harassment by a classmate would be able to file a Title IX claim against her school district up until her 20th birthday, long after the 300 day limitation under Title VII expired.

Fourth, Title VII has a series of regulations that relate to sexual harassment in the work-place.[47] Title IX does not have similar regulations relating to the classroom. Comparing the regulations, it is apparent that Title VII principles are not intended to be transferred into Title IX litigation.

In short, the generous Title VII liability standard is tempered by numerous provisions that protect the employer from stale claims and unlimited liability. In contrast, while Title IX lacks features such as a cap on damages, the standard for obtaining damages is higher.

5. Individual Liability Under Title IX

While many plaintiffs in cases involving sexual abuse and harassment assert claims against individual defendants, a majority of the cases addressing the issue have concluded that Title IX does not authorize a cause of action against individuals.[48] The court's reasoning in *Doe v. Petaluma City Sch. Dist.* is particularly instructive.

In *Doe,* a junior high student brought an action against the school district, a school counselor, and the principal, alleging the defendants failed to stop sexual harassment of the student by her peers. The court held that there is no cause of action against individuals under Title IX and, therefore, dismissed the plaintiff's Title IX claims as to the school counselor and principal. The court reasoned that because Title IX "prohibits discrimination against beneficiaries in programs and activities that receive federal financial assistance, . . . it is the educational institution that must be sued for violations of Title IX."[49] The court further asserted that the "fact that administrative enforcement is directed at the institution that receives federal funds suggests that the private right of action is similarly confined to actions against the institution."[50]

The *Petaluma* decision is the only decision in which a court addressing individual liability under Title IX undertook a lengthy analysis of the issue. Nonetheless, the majority of cases presented with a Title IX cause of action against an individual have found no such liability.

III. Student-to-Student Harassment

A. Claims Under Section 1983

1. School District's Liability Under Section 1983 For The Acts Of Its Students

As in cases of employee-to-student harassment or abuse, a plaintiff alleging student-to-student harassment in violation of Section 1983 must prove that he or she was injured by a person acting under the color of state law and that the injury constitutes a deprivation of rights, privileges, or immunities secured by the U.S. Constitution or federal law.[51] To prevail against the school district, the plaintiff must show that the violation was caused by an unconstitutional policy or custom sanctioned by governmental officials who have final policy-making authority.[52] As noted earlier, this requirement means that a plaintiff must establish that the school district's governing board actually adopted an unconstitutional policy, or that the school board otherwise knew about or acquiesced in a custom or practice that led to a constitutional violation.[53]

a. Generally, There Is No State Action In Cases of Student-To-Student Harassment

Section 1983 imposes liability upon defendants who intentionally deprive a plaintiff of his or her constitutional rights while the defendant is acting under color of state law. The "under color of state law" requirement is jurisdictional and limits the reach of federal judicial power.[54] The lack of state action dooms most plaintiffs' claims in cases of student-to-student harassment or abuse.[55] Numerous courts have held, in fact, that school officials are not constitutionally responsible for violence against students by non-state actors.[56]

b. Courts Do Not Impose A Legal Duty On School Districts To Protect Students From Other Students

Despite many plaintiffs' arguments to the contrary, school districts do not have a constitutional duty to protect students from harm inflicted by third parties.[57] In *DeShaney v. Winnebago County Dep't of Social Servs.*, the plaintiffs alleged that a state social worker negligently placed a boy with his abusive father, who battered the child nearly to the point of death. On final disposition of the case, the United States Supreme Court held that the state defendants could not be held liable for failing to protect an individual from private violence, even though the social workers allegedly facilitated the violence. The Court reasoned that due process means a restraint on governmental power, not a guarantee of safety or an affirmative duty to protect citizens from each other. The only exception to this rule arises when the state takes a person into its custody against his or her will and actually restrains his or her personal liberty (*e.g.*, imprisonment or involuntary commitment to a mental hospital).

In cases of student-to-student harassment or abuse, the alleged perpetrators are private actors akin to the abusive father in *DeShaney*; it is they, not school officials, who allegedly harmed the plaintiffs.[58] Two post-*Deshaney* decisions from the United States Court of Appeals for the Fifth

Circuit address this issue. In *Johnson v. Dallas Indep. Sch. Dist.*,[59] the court held that the school district could not be held liable for the shooting death of a student at a school dance by another student. In *Walton v. Alexander*,[60] the court held that a school superintendent could not be held liable under Section 1983 to a student who resided in a residential school for the deaf and who was allegedly raped twice by a classmate.

Some plaintiffs have attempted to circumvent *DeShaney* and its progeny by arguing that public school students are akin to incarcerated prisoners, *i.e.* compelled to attend school, and that schools, like prisons, should have an affirmative duty to protect students based on the custodial relationship doctrine. This analogy has not been embraced by the courts. As stated in *DeShaney*, a state's affirmative duty to protect individuals who are incarcerated arises from the actual physical limitations that the state has imposed on their freedom to act.[61] The public schools of Texas have not so restrained the personal liberty of their students that the students can be compared to prisoners. Students (and their parents) have choices about where to live, where to go to school, and how to travel to school. In fact, in *Walton v. Alexander*, the Fifth Circuit Court of Appeals rejected a "special relationship" argument, even though the student attended a residential school for the deaf and lived in the school's dormitory:

> Although Walton's freedom was curtailed, it was he who voluntarily subjected himself to the rules and supervision of the school officials. Walton's willful relinquishment of a small fraction of liberty simply is not comparable to that measure of almost total deprivation experienced by a prisoner or involuntarily committed mental patient . . . [E]xtending the Due Process Clause to impose on the state the obligation to defend and to pay for the acts of non-state third parties is a burden not supported by the text or history of the Clause, nor by general principles of constitutional jurisprudence.[62]

Consistent with the Fifth Circuit's analysis in *Walton*, numerous courts have rejected the argument that public schools have a special relationship toward their pupils giving rise to an affirmative constitutional duty to protect.[63]

In short, there is no constitutional right to be protected from peer violence. *DeShaney* and its progeny make it clear that the state's knowledge that a person may be in danger does not create a duty to intervene. This reasoning was used in *Graham v. Independent Sch. Dist. No. I-89*,[64] where the plaintiffs alleged that their son was murdered at school by another student with a gun and that school officials knew that the other student was dangerous and possessed a gun. Applying *DeShaney*, the court held that "foreseeability cannot create an affirmative duty to protect when plaintiff remains unable to allege a custodial relationship."[65]

2. Supervisory Officials Liability Under Section 1983

As in cases of employee-to-student abuse or harassment, plaintiffs alleging student-to-student harassment typically join high-level school administrators as defendants. The prevailing law in this area is *Doe v. Taylor Indep. Sch. Dist.*[66] While *Doe* is not directly on point in cases of student-to-student harassment, the Fifth Circuit reason that to recover a plaintiff must establish that:

(a) The defendant learned of facts or a pattern of inappropriate sexual harassment pointing plainly toward the conclusion that the student was sexually harassing another student; and,

(b) The defendant demonstrated deliberate indifference toward the constitutional rights of the student by failing to take action that was necessary to prevent or stop the harassment; and

(c) The defendant's failure to take action caused a constitutional injury to the student.[67]

As in Section 1983 cases involving allegations of employee-to-student abuse or harassment, supervisory officials can avoid Section 1983 liability for student-to-student harassment by taking every report of student-to-student sexual harassment seriously and conducting a thorough investigation of each reported incident. Following each investigation, supervisory officials should take whatever action is necessary to prevent or stop the abuse. Possible actions can range from separating the students to expulsion of the offending student.

B. Claims Under Title IX

In addition to claims under Section 1983, most of the reported decisions involving sexual harassment of students by other students assert claims under Title IX. As in cases brought by students alleging abuse or harassment by district employees, plaintiffs alleging violations of Title IX resulting from student-to-student harassment base their claims on the recent United States Supreme Court decision in *Franklin v. Gwinnett County Pub. Schs.*[68] However, in contrast to the cases involving employee-to-student abuse or harassment, the law in cases involving student-to-student harassment is clearer and more favorable to school districts.

In April 1996, the United States Court of Appeals for the Fifth Circuit, in *Rowinsky v. Bryan Indep. Sch. Dist.*,[69] held that students may not recover money damages from school districts under Title IX for sexual harassment caused by other students. The Fifth Circuit opinion conflicts with a February 1996 decision from the United States Court of Appeals for the Eleventh Circuit, which held that students may sue under Title IX for peer harassment.[70] The decision from the Eleventh Circuit was subsequently vacated pending rehearing by the Eleventh Circuit *en banc*.[71] At the time of publication, the *en banc* decision was not available. Because of the possible conflict between the Fifth and Eleventh Circuits, the plaintiffs in *Rowinsky* have asked the United States Supreme Court to hear the case.

In *Rowinsky*, two female junior high school students alleged that boys on the school bus physically and verbally harassed them. The girls alleged that they reported their complaints to school officials and that the officials allegedly took no effective action. The school district's summary judgment evidence demonstrated that the boys at issue were punished. The girls subsequently brought suit under Title IX. The students argued that Title IX protects them from abuse inflicted by fellow students. The district court rejected the students' claim, and the Fifth Circuit, in a two-to-one decision, affirmed.

The Fifth Circuit acknowledged that Title IX provides a monetary remedy to students who are subjected to intentional sexual discrimination. The court, however, distinguished discrimination caused by *school officials* from discrimination caused by *fellow students.* Focusing on the history and wording of the statute, the court held that Title IX does not encompass discrimination by third parties. The court examined Title IX's legislative history, including debates on the Senate floor, which showed that the sponsors of the bill were concerned about institutional practices and policies, such as discriminatory admissions policies. "The drafters of Title IX recognized that it was not a panacea for all types of sex discrimination," the court wrote. The court implied that Congress could amend Title IX in the future if Congress desires to broaden its scope.

The court concluded by holding that a student could pursue a Title IX action only if he or she could establish that the school district responded to sexual harassment claims differently based on sex: "Thus, a school district might violate Title IX if it treated sexual harassment of boys more seriously than sexual harassment of girls, or even if it turned a blind eye toward sexual harassment of girls while addressing assaults that harmed boys." The court indicated that such evidence was lacking in the *Rowinsky* case.

To prove intentional, gender-based discrimination by the school board, as contemplated by the *Rowinsky* court, plaintiffs in student-to-student misconduct cases must prove more than just a failure by school officials to respond to the misconduct. Intentional discrimination means that the plaintiff must establish objective facts tending to demonstrate that, but for his or her gender, school officials would have responded differently. Several cases demonstrate what plaintiffs must show.

For example, in *Pfeiffer v. School Bd. for Marion Center Area*,[72] the Title IX plaintiff alleged that her dismissal from the National Honor Society for premarital sexual activity was discriminatory because a similarly situated boy was not dismissed. The court held that evidence concerning the boy was relevant to the claim of disparate treatment.

In contrast, in *Seamons v. Snow*,[73] the student was unable to show that his gender made a difference. In *Seamons*, a student named Brian was subjected to a hazing incident while he was naked in a locker room. The incident was videotaped. Brian allegedly was told that "boys will be boys." Football season was canceled for the remainder of the year, which allegedly increased student hostility toward Brian. The football coach publicly showed hostility toward Brian. The student brought a Title IX claim, alleging a "hostile environment." The district court concluded that Brian's allegations–failure to adopt a grievance procedure and failure to discipline the football coach–did not support the claim that the defendants were motivated by an intent "to treat Brian negatively because he is a boy." The district court also rejected Brian's "hostile environment" theory and concluded that it was "inappropriate" to apply Title VII law:

> Title IX does not expressly create a cause of action based on negligence for hostile environment. It would be inappropriate for this Court to import the hostile environment sexual harassment from Title VII into this Title IX action.[74]

In *Yusuf v. Vassar College*,[75] the male plaintiff, a college student, alleged that he received a stiffer penalty for sexual harassment than his roommate received for assault. The court held that discipline is discriminatory if (a) the student is innocent but is found guilty because of his gender, or (b) if the student is the victim of selective enforcement. The student must allege, however, specific facts raising an inference that gender bias was a motivating factor. "Such allegations might include . . . statements by members of the disciplinary tribunal, statements by pertinent university officials, or patterns of decision-making that also tend to show the influence of gender."[76] The court emphasized that it "did not believe that Congress meant Title IX to impair the independence" of schools in disciplining students. The court ultimately concluded that the plaintiff had stated a claim under the first theory (*i.e.*, that gender had affected the outcome of the hearing).

In *Ruh v. Samerjan*,[77] an affair between a male college professor and a female student ended badly, and the student filed several complaints that were not resolved to her satisfaction. In rejecting the student's claim of intentional gender discrimination, the court stated:

> There is no support . . . to justify a finding that the university defendants would have acted differently if a female, rather than a male, were charged with misconduct . . . A careful examination of the plaintiff's pleadings fails to disclose any suggestion that her complaints . . . were intentionally mishandled because of either party's gender. Indeed, she acknowledges that she received a response from the university defendants as to every one of her complaints. While she did not get the responses she desired, and in some cases, the responses were delayed, there is nothing to support a claim of intentional discrimination . . .[78]

Although the *Rowinsky* decision limits school districts' exposure to actions for money damages, schools and colleges must continue to respond to all claims of student-to-student harassment in a fair and even-handed manner, consistent with the student code of conduct and local board policy. All claims should be investigated and documented, and appropriate discipline should be assigned when necessary.

IV. Conclusion

Given the ever-increasing sexual and litigious nature of our society, one would not expect litigation involving sexual abuse and harassment to wane. Most plaintiffs will probably continue to proceed under Section 1983 and Title IX, as tort immunity laws in many states preclude recovery against school districts and their employees under state law.[79] However, absent a finding of "deliberate indifference" by school district officials, the chances of recovery by a student against anyone other than the offending employee or student are remote, especially for student-to-student sexual harassment.

A student is somewhat more likely to be successful on a claim of alleged sexual abuse or harassment by school employees, because the courts recognize a limited constitutional duty for school districts to protect students from known sexual abuse perpetrated by its employees. However, even in that situation a student must prove that school district officials had knowledge of the inappropriate activities and demonstrated deliberate indifference to the violation of the student's rights. Proof of mere negligence or inadequate remedial action is insufficient for students to recover under Section 1983 or Title IX.

In cases of student-to-student sexual harassment, recent cases have held that no constitutional duty of protection exists under which a public school student can assert a claim under Section 1983. Only in very limited circumstances, such as the residential school setting, could such claims be successful under Section 1983. Student-to-student harassment is also unlikely to be actionable under Title IX, which requires a showing of intentional gender-based discrimination.

Despite the low likelihood of ultimate liability, however, school districts and school officials should actively work to avoid these difficult claims. Any allegations of sexual harassment or sexual abuse of a student in the school environment should be promptly investigated. If remedial action is warranted, school officials should take appropriate action in accordance with district policies and procedures, and should produce and retain written documentation regarding the situation. Prompt and sensitive handling of sexual harassment or sexual abuse allegations can help prevent costly and disruptive litigation.

ENDNOTES

[1] The definition of the phrase *color of state law* has been the subject of much litigation. *See e.g.,* Doe v. Taylor Indep. Sch. Dist., 15 F.3d 443 (5th Cir. 1994) (*en banc*). The relevant issue is whether an official is acting pursuant to his or her duties as an employee of a state agency or political subdivision. *See also* Becerra v. Asher, 921 F. Supp 1538 (S.D. Tex. 1996).

[2] Baker v. McCollan, 443 U.S. 137, 140-41 (1979); Doe v. Rains County Indep. Sch. Dist., 66 F.3d 1402, 1406 (5th Cir. 1995).

[3] Doe v. Rains County Indep. Sch. Dist., 66 F.3d at 1406-07.

[4] *Id.*

[5] 436 U.S. 658 (1978).

[6] *See, e.g.,* Pembaur v. City of Cincinnati, 475 U.S. 469, 477-78 (1986); Lopez v. Houston Indep. Sch. Dist., 817 F.2d 351, 353 (5th Cir. 1987).

[7] 491 U.S. 701, 735-37 (1989), *on remand*, 7 F.3d 1241 (5th Cir. 1993).

[8] Monell v. Department of Social Serv., 436 U.S. at 691-92; *see also* Spann v. Tyler Indep. Sch. Dist., 876 F.2d 437, 438-39 (5th Cir. 1989).

[9] *See generally* Collins v. City of Harker Heights, Tex., 503 U.S. 115, 120-21 (1992); Jett v. Dallas Indep. Sch. Dist., 7 F.3d 1241, 1245 (5th Cir. 1993).

[10] *See* Gonzalez v. Ysleta Indep. Sch. Dist., 996 F.2d 745, 749 (5th Cir. 1993).

[11] 996 F.2d 745.

[12] 996 F.2d at 752; *see also* Kinsey v. Salado Indep. Sch. Dist., 950 F.2d 988, 995 (5th Cir. 1992) (*en banc*).

[13] *Id.* at 760 (emphasis added).

[14] *Id.* at 757; *accord* Gates v. Unified Sch. Dist. No. 449, 996 F.2d 1035 (10th Cir. 1993) (holding that to prove a case against a school district, a plaintiff has to prove: (a) the existence of a continuing, persistent, and widespread practice of unconstitutional misconduct

by the school district's employees; (b) deliberate indifference to, or tacit approval of, such misconduct by the school district's policy-making authorities (the school board) after notice to the officials of that particular misconduct; and, (c) injury by virtue of the unconstitutional acts pursuant to the board's custom, and that the custom was the moving force behind the unconstitutional acts). *See also,* Black v. Indiana Area Sch. Dist. 985 F.2d 707 (3d Cir. 1993); Thelma D. v. Board of Educ., 934 F.2d 929 (8th Cir. 1991); Jane Doe A. v. Special Sch. Dist., 901 F.2d 642 (8th Cir. 1990).

[15] 489 U.S. 378 (1989).

[16] 934 F.2d 929.

[17] *Id.* at 935.

[18] 901 F.2d 642.

[19] 15 F.3d 443 (5th Cir.) (*en banc*), *cert. denied*, 115 S. Ct. 70 (1994).

[20] 15 F.3d at 452.

[21] 20 U.S.C. § 1681, *et seq.*

[22] 503 U.S. 60 (1992).

[23] Title IX provides in pertinent part: "No person in the United States shall, on the basis of sex, be excluded from participation in, be denied the benefits of, or be subjected to discrimination under any education program or activities receiving Federal financial assistance . . . ." 20 U.S.C. § 1681(a).

[24] U.S. Const. Art. I, § 8, cl. 1.

[25] South Dakota v. Dole, 483 U.S. 203, 206-07 (1987); Pennhurst State Sch. & Hosp. v. Halderman, 451 U.S. 1, 17-18 (1981).

[26] Guardians Ass'n v. Civil Serv. Comm'n of New York, 463 U.S. 582, 596-98 (1983) (Title VI case).

[27] *Id.* at 597 (*citing* Pennhurst State Sch. & Hosp. v. Halderman, 451 U.S. at 29-30).

[28] *See, e.g.*, Legislative Report, U.S. Code Cong. & Admin. News p. 2426 (1972) (showing Congress was concerned about unequal admissions policies for women); *see also* Cohen v. Brown Univ., 991 F.2d 888, 894 (1st Cir. 1993) ("the statute's heart is a broad prohibition of gender-based discrimination in all *programmatic* aspects of an educational institution").

[29] *See* Cannon v. University of Chicago, 441 U.S. 677, 704 n.36 (1979) ("[a]ny college or university which has [a] *policy* which discriminates . . . is free to do so . . . but such institutions should not be asking the taxpayers of this country" to pay for it).

[30] *Id.* (emphasis added).

[31] 831 F. Supp. 867 (M.D. Ga. 1994).

[32] The federal regulations under title IX are void of language that provides guidance in analyzing sexual harassment as sexual discrimination. The regulations instead concern institutional policies and practices affecting equality in athletics, admissions, and other activities. 34 C.F.R. § 106. The regulations require schools to adopt and publicize "grievance procedures providing for prompt and equitable resolution of student and employee complaints." 34 C.F.R. § 106.8. Rather than discuss harassment, the regulations contain minute details on how to operate an athletic program. *See* 34 C.F.R. § 106.41(c), *et seq.*

[33] *E.g.*, Howard v. Board of Educ., 876 F. Supp. 959, 974 n.10 (N.D. Ill. 1995); Seamons v. Snow, 864 F. Supp. 1111, 1117-18 (D. Utah 1994), *aff'd in part, rev'd in part*, 34 F.3d 226 (10th Cir. 1996); Floyd v. Waiters, 831 F. Supp. at 876; *see also* Canutillo Indep. Sch. Dist. v. National Union Fire Ins. Co., 900 F. Supp. 844, 847 (W.D. Tex. 1995); *but see* Leija v. Canutillo Indep. Sch. Dist. 887, F. Supp. 947 (W.D. Tex.), *appeal docketed*, No. 95-50791 (5th Cir. 1995).

[34] 876 F. Supp. at 974; *accord* Seamons, 864 F. Supp. at 1117-18 (noting that title IX does not create a hostile environment claim based on negligence of the school district); *see also* Cannon, 441 U.S. at 704 n.36 (discussing legislative history showing that the statute is aimed at discriminatory "policies" and observing that Congress "wanted to avoid the use of federal resources to support discriminatory practices").

[35] Doe v. Petaluma City Sch. Dist., 830 F. Supp. 1560, 1757 (N.D. Cal. 1993).

[36] R.L.R. v. Prague Pub. Sch. Dist., 838 F. Supp. 1526, 1531 (W.D. Okla. 1993).

[37] *Id.*

[38] 831 F. Supp. at 876.

[39] 830 F. Supp. at 1576.
[40] 42 U.S.C. § 2000e, *et seq.*
[41] The Supreme Court has acknowledged that title IX is patterned after title VI of the Civil Rights Act of 1964 (42 U.S.C. § 2000d) and must be construed in a similar fashion. *Cannon*, 441 U.S. at 694-96. In accordance with this reasoning, courts have refused to employ title VII principles. *See, e.g.*, Howard v. Board of Educ., 876 F. Supp. at 974 n.10; Seamons v. Snow, 864 F. Supp. at 1118; R.L.R. v. Prague Pub. Sch. Dist., 838 F. Supp. at 1534; *see also* Mennone v. Gordon, 889 F. Supp. 53, 57 (D. Conn. 1995) (concluding that there are "major differences" between title VII and title IX); Rosa H. v. San Elizario Indep. Sch. Dist., 887 F. Supp. 140, 142 (W.D. Tex. 1995) ("no doubt . . . that in the Fifth Circuit, title IX is to be analyzed under principles from Title VI"); Bougher v. University of Pittsburgh, 713 F. Supp. 139, 145 (W.D. Pa.) (refusing to "transfer wholesale" EEOC guidelines into an area for which they were not drafted), *aff'd on other grounds*, 882 F.2d 74 (3d Cir. 1989).
[42] 42 U.S.C. § 2000e(b); Meritor Sav. Bank v. Vinson, 477 U.S. 57, 72 (1986).
[43] 20 U.S.C. § 1681(a).
[44] Comparing the two statutes, and noting the absence of agency provisions in the definitions in title IX, the courts in both *Howard* and *Floyd* held common law agency principles do not apply to claims under title IX. Howard v. Board of Educ., 876 F. Supp. at 974; Floyd v. Waiters, 831 F. Supp. at 876; *accord* Slaughter v. Waubonsee Comm. College, 1995 WL 579296 (N.D. Ill. Sept. 29, 1995) (not reported); R.L.R. v. Prague Pub. Sch. Dist., 838 F. Supp. at 1534; Alexander v. Yale Univ., 459 F. Supp. 1, 4 (D. Conn. 1977) ("the concept of mere *respondeat superior* appears ill-adapted to the question of title IX sex discrimination based on harassment incidents"), *aff'd*, 631 F.2d 178 (2d Cir. 1980).
[45] 42 U.S.C. § 1981a(b)(3).
[46] Tex. Civ. Prac. & Rem. Code §§ 16.001(a)(1), 16.003.
[47] 29 C.F.R. §§ 1600.735-101 through 1608.12.
[48] *See* Lipsett v. University of P.R., 864 F.2d. 881, 901 (1st Cir. 1988) ("in implying a cause of action under title IX, the Supreme Court has considered only actions against educational institutions . . . accordingly, the separate liability of the supervisory officials must be established, if at all, under § 1983, rather than under title IX"); Clay v. Board of Trustees of Neosho County Comm. College, 905 F. Supp. 1488, 1495-96 (D. Kan. 1995); (not reported); Bowers v. Baylor Univ., 862 F. Supp. 142, 1455-46 (W.D. Tex. 1994); Seamons v. Snow, 864 F. Supp. at 1116; Doe v. Petaluma City Sch. Dist., 830 F. Supp. at 1576; Bougher v. University of Pittsburgh, 713 F. Supp. 139, 143 (W.D. Pa.), *aff'd on other grounds*, 882 F.2d 274 (3d Cir. 1989); Garza v. Galena Park ISD, 914 F. Supp. 1437 (S.D. Tex. 1994).
[49] 830 F. Supp. at 1576-77.
[50] *Id.* at 1577.
[51] Monell v. Department of Social Serv., 436 U.S. at 691; 42 U.S.C. § 1983.
[52] *See generally* Collins v. City of Harker Heights, Tex., 503 U.S. at 120-21.
[53] *See* Gonzalez v. Ysleta Indep. Sch. Dist., 996 F.2d at 749.
[54] Jojola v. Chavez, 55 F.3d 488, 492 (10th Cir. 1995).
[55] *See, e.g.*, Woodward v. City of Worland, 977 F.2d 1392, 1397-1401 (10th Cir. 1992), *cert. denied*, 113 S. Ct. 3038 (1993) (rejecting an equal protection claim premised on sexual harassment among co-workers because the wrongdoers did not use stateconferred authority to harm the complainants).
[56] *See, e.g.*, Dorothy J. v. Little Rock Sch. Dist., 7 F.3d 729, 732 (8th Cir. 1993); D.R. v. Middlebucks Area Vocational Sch., 972 F.2d 1364, 1369 (3d Cir.) (*en banc*), *cert. denied*, 506 U.S. 1079 (1993); Hunter v. Carbondale Area Sch. Dist., 829 F. Supp. 714, 717-18 (M.D. Pa.), *aff'd*, 5 F.3d 1489 (3d Cir. 1993), *cert. denied*, 114 S. Ct. 903 (1994); Russell v. Fannin County Sch. Dist., 784 F. Supp. 1576, 1580 (N.D. Ga. 1992), *aff'd*, 981 F.2d 1263 (11th Cir. 1992); Elliott v. New Miami Bd. of Educ., 799 F. Supp. 818, 820 (S.D. Ohio 1992).
[57] DeShaney v. Winnebago County Dep't of Social Serv., 489 U.S. 189 (1988).
[58] *See also* Davidson v. Cannon, 474 U.S. 344 (1986) (dismissing lawsuit against prison officials for allegedly failing to protect inmate from violent attack by fellow prisoner despite receiving warning about possible attack).
[59] 38 F.3d 198, 201-02 (5th Cir. 1994), *cert. denied*, 115 S. Ct. 1361 (1995).

[60] 44 F.3d 1297, 1305 (5th Cir. 1995) (*en banc*).
[61] 489 U.S. at 199. The fact that children are less able than adults to protect themselves also is irrelevant: "Neither the state compulsory attendance law nor any other state rule required their attendance on the Claypoole school bus. Their parents, their primary caretakers, were free to arrange any other form of alternate transportation or escort them to school personally . . . *we acknowledge, as plaintiffs stress, that school children may be reluctant to seek help in situations of this kind . . . but these concerns are products of the age and circumstances of children; they do not emanate from any state imposed restraint.*" Black v. Indiana Area Sch. Dist., 985 F.2d at 714 (emphasis added); *see also* Dorothy J. v. Little Rock Sch. Dist., 7 F.3d at 732 (student's mental retardation did not constitute a *state*-imposed restraint on freedom to act).
[62] 44 F.3d at 1305.
[63] *See, e.g.*, Jojola v. Chavez, 55 F.3d at 491-92; D.R. v. Middlebucks Area Vocational Technical Sch., 972 F.2d at 1369; J.O. v. Alton Community Unit Sch. Dist., 909 F.2d 267, 271-72 (7th Cir. 1990); Maldonado v. Josey, 975 F.2d 727, 729-30 (10th Cir. 1992), *cert. denied*, 507 U.S. 914 (1993); Dorothy J. v. Little Rock Sch. Dist., 7 F.3d at 732; *cf.* Tucker v. Callahan, 867 F.2d 909, 913 (6th Cir. 1989) (finding no § 1983 liability where on-duty police officer watched as the plaintiff was severely beaten by third party in a parking lot); McKee v. City of Rockwall, 877 F.2d 409, 415-16 (5th Cir. 1989) (refusing to hold city liable for injuries sustained by the plaintiff after the police refused to arrest her boyfriend in response to her call for help), *cert. denied*, 493 U.S. 1023 (1990).
[64] 22 F.3d 991 (10th Cir. 1994).
[65] *Id.* at 994.
[66] 15 F.3d 443 (5th Cir.) (*en banc*), *cert. denied*, 115 S. Ct. 70 (1994).
[67] 15 F.3d at 452.
[68] 503 U.S. 60 (1992).
[69] 80 F.3d 1006 (5th Cir. 1996).
[70] *See* Davis v. Monroe County Bd. of Educ., 74 F.3d 1186 (11th Cir.), *reh'g en banc granted, opinion vacated*, ___ F.3d ___ (11th Cir. 1996).
[71] ___ F. 3d ___, 1996 WL 438188.
[72] 917 F.2d 779, 785 (3d Cir. 1990).
[73] 864 F. Supp. 1111, 1118, *aff'd in part, rev'd in part*, 84 F.3d 1226 (10th Cir. 1996).
[74] *Id.*
[75] 35 F.3d 709 (2d Cir. 1994).
[76] *Id.* at 715.
[77] 816 F. Supp. 1326 (E.D. Wisc. 1993), *aff'd*, 32 F.3d 570 (7th Cir. 1994).
[78] *Id.* at 1331.
[79] Many states are governed by the doctrine of governmental or sovereign immunity, which protects public entities and their employees from liability in negligence suits. A good example of a system of sovereign or governmental immunity exists in Texas. The doctrine of sovereign immunity has been a part of Texas jurisprudence for approximately 160 years. *See, e.g.*, Braun v. Trustees of Victoria Indep. Sch. Dist., 114 S.W.2d 947 (Tex. Civ. App.–San Antonio 1938, *writ ref'd*); Hopkins v. Spring Indep. Sch. Dist., 736 S.W.2d 617 (Tex. 1987). This doctrine has been abrogated only slightly through the passage of the Texas Tort Claims Act, TEX. CIV. PRAC. & REM. CODE § 101.001, *et. seq.* Under the Texas Tort Claims Act, school districts and junior colleges generally retain their common law immunity, with the only exceptions relating to the negligent use or operation of motor vehicles by their employees. In addition, school employees are entitled to official immunity under Texas common law and section 22.051(a) of the Texas Education Code. *See, e.g.*, Barr v. Bernhard, 562 S.W.2d 844 (Tex. 1978); Hopkins v. Spring Indep. Sch. Dist., *supra*.